ENVIRONMENTAL LAW INSTITUTE

ENVIRONMENTAL CRIMES DESKBOOK

AN ELI DESKBOOK

Published with support from the Andrew W. Mellon Foundation

ELR
ENVIRONMENTAL LAW REPORTER
Environmental Law Institute
Washington, D.C.

1616 P Street NW, Washington, DC 20036

Published 1996.

Printed in the United States of America
ISBN 0-911937-63-3

ENVIRONMENTAL CRIMES DESKBOOK

The Environmental Law Institute®

Table of Contents

About the Authors . . .

John F. Cooney is a partner in the Washington, D.C., office of Venable, Baetjer, Howard & Civiletti. Mr. Cooney maintains an active practice covering a broad range of environmental, regulatory, and administrative law issues, including internal Executive Branch policymaking and litigation under the Clean Air Act, the Clean Water Act, and RCRA. Mr. Cooney served for five years as Deputy General Counsel of the Office of Management and Budget, where he was responsible for addressing legal issues presented in rules submitted for White House policy review, including rules issued under all major environmental statutes. Previously, Mr. Cooney served as an Assistant to the Solicitor General. Mr. Cooney graduated magna cum laude from Brown University in 1970 with a degree in Economics, and from the University of Chicago Law School in 1973.

Judson W. Starr is a partner in the Washington, D.C., office of Venable, Baetjer, Howard & Civiletti. Mr. Starr is involved in defending individuals and entities charged with environmental crimes, white-collar defense, and the structuring and management of auditing and preventive programs for corporate clients. He served on the staff of the Administrator of the U.S. Environmental Protection Agency and was the first Chief of the Environmental Crimes Section of the U.S. Department of Justice from 1982 until 1988. He is Co-Chairman of the Committees on Environmental Crimes of the Business Law and Criminal Law Sections of the American Bar Association and is a member of the Environmental Crimes Advisory Group, U.S. Sentencing Commission. Mr. Starr is a graduate of Washington & Jefferson College and the Georgetown University Law Center.

Joseph G. Block has been a partner in the Washington, D.C., office of Venable, Baetjer, Howard & Civiletti since October 1991. From 1985 to 1991, he was in the Environmental Crimes Section of the U.S. Department of Justice, and was Chief of the Section from September 1988 to May 1991. He then served for several months as Special Assistant for Criminal Enforcement at the U.S. Environmental Protection Agency before entering private practice. He is experienced in both environmental enforcement litigation and white-collar criminal defense. He is a graduate of the University of Michigan and Harvard Law School.

Thomas J. Kelly Jr. is a partner in the Washington, D.C., office of Venable, Baetjer, Howard & Civiletti. Mr. Kelly concentrates in the area of defense of environmental and white-collar crimes, and has represented numerous large companies under investigation for allegedly violating environmental laws. He is a former Assistant U.S. Attorney for the District of Columbia and was a 1991 recipient of the Young Lawyer of the Year Award of the Bar Association of the District of Columbia. Mr. Kelly is a graduate of LaSalle College and The Catholic University of America Law School.

Andrew R. Herrup is an environmental associate in the Washington, D.C., office of Venable, Baetjer, Howard & Civiletti. His practice focuses on criminal and civil litigation, Native American law, and international environmental issues. Mr. Herrup has authored several articles on trade and the environment and is a staff member of the Trade and Environment Policy Advisory Committee for the Office of the U.S. Trade Representative. Mr. Herrup is a 1991 graduate from the University of California at Los Angeles School of Law and holds an undergraduate degree, with high honors, from the University of Michigan.

Valerie K. Mann is an associate in the Washington, D.C., office of Venable, Baetjer, Howard & Civiletti. Her practice emphasizes environmental law and concentrates on federal and state environmental criminal defense matters. She also has extensive experience in civil enforcement and Superfund litigation. Ms. Mann graduated from Rutgers College, magna cum laude, in 1988 and from the University of Virginia Law School in 1991. She also served as a law clerk to Judge Robert G. Doumar of the U.S. District Court for the Eastern District of Virginia in 1991-1992.

Gregory S. Braker is an environmental attorney in the Washington, D.C., office of Venable, Baetjer, Howard & Civiletti. His practice spans criminal, civil, and regulatory proceedings concerning the Clean Air Act, the Clean Water Act, RCRA, CERCLA, TSCA, and Native American law. He also represents companies and trade groups in rulemaking and legislative proceedings concerning these areas of law. Mr. Braker is a 1992 graduate of the Georgetown University Law Center. He also holds a graduate degree in Composition and Rhetoric, with high honors, from the University of Maryland, and an undergraduate degree, magna cum laude, from Evangel College.

Foreword

The environmental movement's efforts since Earth Day 1970 have resulted in a massive legal response aimed at curbing pollution and conserving resources. With the hindsight of 25 years of legal activism, American environmentalists can point to many significant successes, but they are keenly aware of how far they have fallen short in achieving their objectives. This shortfall in environmental protection mirrors defects in the development of environmental law and administration.

These defects are caused primarily by a distorted emphasis on command-and-control regulation and administrative agency law, with a corresponding failure to develop the environmental dimensions of criminal and private law, e.g., torts and business law. This is rapidly changing, however. The environmental law of the last decade has seen an explosion of liability cases under Superfund and the creation of a new field—criminal environmental law.

Although Congress passed the first criminal environmental statute in 1899, prosecutions were infrequent and involved only misdemeanors. Until the 1980s, no federal environmental statute provided felony sanctions. With the addition of harsher penalties for violations and increased prosecutions, criminal environmental law has in recent years become a major concern for environmental managers and has been one of the fastest growing areas of the law. Since the Department of Justice formed its Environmental Crimes Division in 1982, federal prosecutors have obtained 1,074 pleas and convictions from 1,481 indictments, resulting in $296,582,000 in penalties and 561 years in prison terms.

Criminal environmental law combines two of the most complex and arcane fields in law: History-driven criminal law and technically complex environmental law. The innovations of criminal environmental law veer far from the basics familiar to criminal practitioners. Traditional concepts of knowledge and intent and restraints on implying employer responsibility have evolved rapidly, stretching conventional notions of fairness to shock corporate managers. Above all, the sheer size and difficulty of the task of bridging the two fields dismays the novice.

Enter the *Environmental Crimes Deskbook*. It begins with an analysis of the major issues, offering the insight and expertise of John F. Cooney, Judson W. Starr, Joseph G. Block, and Thomas J. Kelly Jr.—partners in the Washington, D.C. law firm of Venable, Baetjer, Howard & Civiletti—and Andrew R. Herrup, Valerie K. Mann, and Gregory Braker, who are associates at the firm.

In plain English, the authors lay out for you the basic concepts of criminal environmental law and how they fit into the larger context of environmental regulation. The authors specialize in criminal environmental law and are familiar with how these complex matters play out both from the viewpoint of private practitioners and as former enforcement officials. They illuminate complex matters by placing policy decisions in the context of the historical development of the field—developments that they helped shape.

The authors begin by describing how an effective enforcement program emerged in the Justice Department and EPA despite various obstacles, including disagreements between and within the agencies about prosecutorial decisions. They then discuss the knowledge element as it is particularly applied in environmental criminal law. The authors provide a detailed "how-to" guide for responding to an environmental criminal investigation, describing several basic—but essential—procedures that the target of a governmental investigation should follow. Finally, they discuss the ramifications of an environmental criminal conviction.

In addition to the analysis, the *Environmental Crimes Deskbook* includes the text of the criminal provisions of the major federal environmental statutes, and agency guidance on such issues as general enforcement policy, specific EPA and Justice Department investigative and prosecutorial procedures, parallel proceedings, and environmental self-audits. It also includes sample forms and pleadings, such as search warrants, indictments, and plea agreements.

As with all ELI Deskbooks, the *Environmental Crimes Deskbook* is your ready reference. Keep it by your desk. Carry it to meetings. Our editors have carefully screened materials to include only the information that environmental lawyers need most.

The *Environmental Crimes Deskbook*, as part of ELI's books program, benefits from a revolving fund provided by the Andrew W. Mellon Foundation. It also benefits from the expertise of our publications division, as talented a group as you are likely to find anywhere. In this case, Jacqueline McNamara edited the analysis and compiled the materials for the book, and Linda Johnson produced the book, with assistance from Bill Straub, Carolyn Fischer, and Scott Custin.

The *Environmental Crimes Deskbook* serves as shelf-mate to other ELI Deskbooks: *Superfund Deskbook, Clean Water Deskbook, NEPA Deskbook, Environmental Law Deskbook, RCRA Deskbook, Oil Pollution Deskbook, Wetlands Deskbook,* and *Clean Air Deskbook*. Like *ELR—The Environmental Law Reporter* from which they grow, you can look to our deskbooks for the best in environmental law.

—J. William Futrell, President
Environmental Law Institute

Acknowledgements

The authors gratefully acknowledge the contributions to this project of Brigid Kenney, Thomas M. Lingan, and Richard H. Mays of Venable, Baetjer, Howard & Civiletti, and Joshua I. Barrett of DiTrapano & Jackson in Charleston, West Virginia. Special thanks are due to JaneAnn Heilman, who tracked EPA policy papers, indictments returned, and pleas entered in all federal environmental criminal cases during the preparation of this book, while supporting the authors' practices and enduring the first year of law school.

Criminal Enforcement of Environmental Laws

Criminal Enforcement of Environmental Laws

Table of Contents

Criminal Enforcement of Environmental Laws

by John F. Cooney, Judson W. Starr, Joseph G. Block, and Thomas J. Kelly Jr.
Andrew R. Herrup, Valerie K. Mann, and Gregory Braker

Introduction

Environmental prosecutions involve a unique mixture of civil and criminal elements. The defense lawyer is constantly torn between two basic and contradictory instincts: The desire to cooperate with the regulator and the adversarial instinct to give the prosecutor information only when it will support a decision not to indict. Civil litigators and white-collar criminal defense lawyers will approach this problem from different angles. But both types of lawyers will encounter the same immutable conflict, and will find that there are aspects of the problem that do not respond well to their normal operating style.

The civil litigator is used to dealing with the regulator and appealing for exercise of its discretion. Environmental lawyers are more forthcoming with information and hope to explain away the violation, or at worst negotiate a sanction that minimizes compliance costs and preserves the company's operational flexibility. The civil lawyer may be taken aback when a criminal prosecutor enters the scene, because the prosecutor has different powers, plays by more stringent rules, and has different goals from regulatory enforcers.

The criminal lawyer is used to dealing with prosecutors, and is trained to disclose information grudgingly and only when it may deflect the matter to a civil resolution or reduce the charges. Criminal counsel is frustrated by the constant disclosures about its operations that its client, the regulated entity, must continue to provide the regulatory agency, and thus the prosecutor, during the investigation. The criminal lawyer may be frustrated that the client has to be forthcoming because the regulator has leverage over its business fortunes through the ability to withhold discretion under existing permits or to impose stringent new requirements long after the criminal matter has been resolved.

Criminal enforcement is an indispensable feature of effective environmental regulation. Its significance will increase in the future, as long as augmented appropriations and favorable judicial decisions facilitate the initiation of more prosecutions. The critical aspect of any criminal investigation is the government's exercise of discretion whether to pursue an environmental violation civilly or criminally. Therefore, it is important to examine the policy factors that enter into this decision and how these considerations developed as the federal environmental crimes program matured.

History of the Federal Environmental Crimes Program

The federal environmental crimes program developed as an outgrowth of the civil enforcement effort. The program was developed in piecemeal stages, with Congress giving little systematic consideration to the policy goals, the institutional structure, or the elements of the offenses. Some argue that the original congressional objective for the effort was to promote regulatory compliance; others, prevention of pollution; and still others, imposing punishment on violators and leveling the playing field between honest and dishonest competitors. Despite the confusion about its goals, between 1980 and 1990, dedicated prosecutors at the U.S. Department of Justice (Justice) and criminal investigators at the U.S. Environmental Protection Agency (EPA) demonstrated the crucial need for an environmental crimes program. They devised sensible enforcement priorities and won a series of court victories that established the foundation for a successful effort. The program has enjoyed broad public support, and its development has been replicated at the state and local levels.

At the same time, the criminal enforcement program has suffered from the lack of comprehensive thought paid to its organizing principles, and the ad hoc nature of succeeding congressional reactions. Enforcement policies and techniques have evolved only after protracted wrangling by competing bureaucracies over issues that appear incapable of permanent resolution. Nevertheless, an effective criminal enforcement program emerged despite the obstacles, and the program's history continues to influence decisions about what conduct will be prosecuted criminally and under what circumstances.

Spontaneous Origin of the Program

Congress first made environmental pollution a federal crime in the Refuse Act of 1899, which made it a misdemeanor to "throw, discharge, or deposit" any refuse matter into navigable waters without a permit.[1] Violation of the Refuse Act is a public welfare offense, for which violators are held strictly liable.[2] This provision, although enforced infrequently, survived to serve as the model for criminal provisions when the new era of environmental consciousness dawned in 1970.[3] It established the vital precedent that environmental crimes could be treated as public welfare offenses.

The first modern attempt to devise an environmental crimes provision was §113(c) of the Clean Air Act (CAA) Amendments of 1970,[4] which punished violations of the Act as a misdemeanor. The statute proved substantially unenforceable, however.[5] Enforcement was not based on a permitting system, so there was no clear delineation of the

1. 33 U.S.C. §§407, 411 (sections 13 and 16 of the Rivers and Harbors Appropriation Act of 1899).
2. *See, e.g.*, United States v. White Fuel Corp., 498 F.2d 619, 4 ELR 20531 (1st Cir. 1974). The public welfare offense doctrine is discussed more fully *infra*.
3. Importantly, in *United States v. Standard Oil Co.*, 384 U.S. 224 (1966), which was handed down just before the effort to draft new environmental laws began, the U.S. Supreme Court held that the Refuse Act could be used to combat pollution as well as to remove obstacles to navigation.
4. Pub. L. No. 91-604, 84 Stat. 1676, §113(c) (1970).
5. *See* James Miskiewicz and John S. Rudd, *Civil and Criminal Enforcement of the Clean Air Act After the 1990 Amendments*, 9 PACE ENVTL. L. REV. 281 (1992). Most successful prosecutions under this provision were for violations of the work rules under the asbestos national emission standard for hazardous air pollutants, rather than for core air pollution violations. *See, e.g.*, United States v. Buckley, 934 F.2d 84, 21 ELR 21113 (6th Cir. 1991).

particular legal obligations applicable to a source. In addition, because there were few reporting and recordkeeping obligations, enforcement authorities could not routinely and cost effectively review whether an individual source had violated its obligations.

Congress learned quickly from its mistakes. In 1972, substantial improvements were incorporated in the criminal enforcement provision of the Federal Water Pollution Control Act (FWPCA).[6] Section 309(c) provided misdemeanor penalties for any "negligent or willful" discharge of pollutants into navigable waters without a permit or in violation of a permit issued under the Act.[7] The crucial breakthrough was tying enforcement to the permit system. This allowed systematic and cost-effective detection and punishment of violations, either by environmental groups, which could bring suits for damages,[8] or by federal or state governments, which could prosecute violations criminally, civilly, or administratively. The threat of criminal punishment added an additional compliance incentive for sources that already were within the permit system. The most common targets of criminal prosecutions in the early years, however, were "midnight dumpers"—individuals or entities operating outside the system without the required permits.[9]

The FWPCA proved enforceable and produced some of the first precedents that demonstrated the feasibility of a large-scale environmental crimes effort.[10] Further, investigation of potential crimes under the Act gave prosecutors firsthand experience discovering traditional Title 18 crimes while in pursuit of novel environmental cases. In fact, environmental crimes are frequently charged in conjunction with conspiracy, aiding and abetting, submission of false statements, mail fraud, perjury, and obstruction of justice.[11]

The environmental crimes program accelerated with passage of the Solid Waste Disposal Act Amendments of 1980, which provided, for the first time, felony penalties for the treatment, storage, or disposal of hazardous wastes without a permit.[12] The amendments coincided with the effective date of the provisions delegating permit writing authority to states with EPA-approved programs.[13] These events led to the issuance of large numbers of enforceable limits in a relatively short period of time. The statute proved to be an effective way of prosecuting both midnight dumpers and permitted firms that tried to reduce waste treatment costs through unauthorized disposal.[14]

Especially in the program's early years, the vast majority of environmental prosecutions involved violations of the Resource Conservation and Recovery Act (RCRA) or the FWPCA.[15] RCRA prosecutions in particular were popular at the local level because they gave U.S. Attorneys the means to respond to public outcries about the dumping of hazardous wastes. In the 1970s and early 1980s, however, EPA and Justice concentrated their enforcement efforts on civil cases and did not specifically dedicate resources to a criminal effort.

Development of a Formal Enforcement Program

Systematic efforts to think through the application of criminal provisions to environmental violations can be traced to a series of speeches given in the late 1970s by then-Assistant Attorney General James Moorman. In 1978, Moorman announced that Justice would prosecute "willful, substantive violations of the pollution control laws," and that grand jury investigations had been convened against both corporations and individuals.[16] In 1979, Moorman announced in congressional testimony that he was reallocating resources from the original enforcement strategy of seeking to compel compliance with the regulatory deadlines of the CAA and the FWPCA to a more ambitious strategy of seeking to punish actual instances of regulated sources' noncompliance.[17]

At the outset of the criminal enforcement effort, Moorman clearly articulated two issues that have proved controversial throughout the life of the program. First, he directly challenged EPA to upgrade its inspection resources to accommodate the special investigative demands of criminal cases.

> We must move, particularly in the field of toxics and hazardous waste, to a different type of case. These cases will require a substantial improvement in EPA's investigative capability. EPA must improve its ability to audit the pollution control operations of plants; the ability to obtain and analyze samples of many toxic pollutants; and the ability to track down and identify surreptitious discharges.[18]

Second, he identified the importance of clearly defined standards to delineate the kinds of cases that should be prosecuted criminally.

6. Pub. L. No. 92-516, 86 Stat. 816 (1972).
7. 33 U.S.C. §1319(c).
8. *See* Michael S. Greve, *Private Enforcement, Private Rewards: How Environmental Citizen Suits Became an Entitlement Program*, *in* MICHAEL S. GREVE AND FRED L. SMITH JR., ENVIRONMENTAL POLITICS (1992).
9. *See* United States v. Ward, 676 F.2d 94, 12 ELR 20285 (4th Cir.), *cert. denied*, 459 U.S. 835 (1982) (defendants unlawfully disposed of oil laced with polychlorinated biphenyls (PCBs), in violation of the Toxic Substances Control Act (TSCA), by spraying it along a highway from a truck).
10. *See, e.g.*, United States v. Phelps Dodge Corp., 391 F. Supp. 1181, 5 ELR 20308 (D. Ariz. 1975); United States v. Frezzo Bros., 602 F.2d 1123, 9 ELR 20556 (3d Cir. 1979), *cert. denied*, 444 U.S. 1074 (1980); United States v. Distler, 671 F.2d 954, 11 ELR 20340 (6th Cir.), *cert. denied*, 454 U.S. 827 (1981).
11. *See, e.g.*, United States v. Brittain, 931 F.2d 1413, 21 ELR 21092 (10th Cir. 1991), where the utilities director of a small city was convicted of 18 felony counts of submitting false data on monitored effluent data, in violation of 18 U.S.C. §1001, and two misdemeanor counts under FWPCA §309(c)(1), for directing his staff not to report discharges that were required by permit.
12. Resource Conservation and Recovery Act (RCRA), 42 U.S.C. §6928(d), ELR STAT. RCRA §3008(d), as amended by Pub. L. No. 96-482, 94 Stat. 2334 (1980).
13. Pub. L. No. 94-580, 90 Stat. 2809, §2 (1976) (codified as amended at 42 U.S.C. §6926).
14. *E.g.*, United States v. Greer, 850 F.2d 1447, 18 ELR 21387 (11th Cir. 1988); United States v. Protex Indus., Inc., 874 F.2d 740, 19 ELR 21061 (10th Cir. 1989).
15. Between fiscal years 1983 and 1992, 317 defendants were charged under RCRA, 205 under the FWPCA, and only 68 under the CAA. Miskiewicz and Rudd, *supra* note 5, at 374.
16. James W. Moorman, Assistant Attorney General, Land and Natural Resources Division, U.S. DOJ, Address at the A.L.I.-A.B.A. Course of Study on Environmental Law, Washington, D.C. (Feb. 10, 1978) (transcript available from the A.L.I.-A.B.A. Course Department, 4025 Chestnut St., Philadelphia, PA 19104).
17. *Enforcement of Environmental Regulations, 1979: Hearings Before the Subcomm. on Environmental Pollution of Senate Comm. on Environment and Public Works*, 96th Cong., 1st Sess. 339 (1979) (statement of James W. Moorman, Assistant Att'y Gen., Lands and Natural Resources Division, DOJ).
18. *Id.* at 348-49.

> This investigatory capability should be directed toward situations where there exists the greatest likelihood of abating significant environmental harm or damage to the public health, or where there appears to be a serious offender involved, either in terms of repeated and continuing violations or violations of a serious magnitude.[19]

In 1980, Attorney General Benjamin Civiletti reinforced this enforcement initiative by serving notice that Justice would target individuals as well as corporate offenders.

> We will also emphasize personal responsibility. I do not view violations of pollution laws as simply the acts of corporations. It is self-evident that the work of corporations is carried out by individuals. . . . Thus, we shall attempt to identify the corporate acts so that the law may be truly enforced and its real deterrent effect mobilized.[20]

But despite these intellectual breakthroughs, Justice had no criminal enforcement structure or formal environmental program in place as the Carter Administration left office. In January 1981, the environmental crimes program had few resources, limited statutory authority, no enforcement principles or priorities, and little track record in court. Development of the institutional mechanisms and enforcement policy was left to the Reagan Administration. Despite the controversy surrounding EPA throughout the 1980s, the Reagan years witnessed the successful launch and consolidation of an effective criminal enforcement program.

Institutional Structures

Before large-scale efforts could succeed, Justice and EPA had to evolve internal organizational arrangements to prosecute environmental crimes. In these initial efforts, fault lines clearly emerged, both within Justice and between EPA and Justice, that continue to mark the program.

Justice initially sidestepped the question whether to locate the criminal enforcement program in the Lands and Natural Resources Division[21] or the Criminal Division. Instead, it created an informal coordination mechanism between the two divisions. The Criminal Division assumed responsibility for cases involving Title 18 crimes, such as false statements, obstruction of justice, and mail fraud; the Lands Division prosecuted violations of environmental regulations. This institutional arrangement proved unwieldy, however, and failed to provide programmatic leadership. Further, the client agency—EPA—had a marked preference toward working with the Lands Division, whose environmental lawyers already represented the Agency in civil cases. EPA perceived the Lands Division to be more receptive to its concerns and maintained regular communications with its attorneys, to the exclusion of the Criminal Division.

Eventually, the ever-increasing number of criminal cases forced Justice to establish a permanent institutional arrangement. In November 1982, a three-lawyer Environmental Crimes Unit was established in the civil Environmental Enforcement Section of the Lands Division to focus exclusively on criminal cases. Part of the impetus for creating this specialized unit was the difficulty Justice had encountered in dealing with EPA. During the Carter Administration, EPA enforcement personnel had referred many cases for prosecution that Justice rejected for poor investigatory work. Nearly 60 percent of EPA's criminal referrals were declined.[22]

In response to these problems, EPA created a separate Office of Criminal Enforcement in January 1981.[23] As part of this initiative, each EPA Region was authorized to hire its own criminal investigators. Criminal enforcement languished, however, under Anne Gorsuch's regime as EPA Administrator. The program suffered from slow hiring practices and the first outbreak of what has been a cyclical argument within EPA over the proper organization of its enforcement effort.[24] Finally, in October 1982, the first cohort of experienced criminal investigators reported to work at EPA. They gradually introduced a more practical law enforcement perspective to EPA's investigative efforts. For a long time, however, the criminal program remained something of a poor relation in contrast to EPA's core civil enforcement program.[25]

Thus, by November 1982, both Justice and EPA had developed appropriate institutional structures within which to pursue environmental violators. Each agency began a long-term educational program to persuade Congress to expand its resources to amplify the program's reach. For example, in May 1987, Justice upgraded its criminal enforcement efforts by creating a freestanding Environmental Crimes Section (ECS) within the Lands Division. By 1992, the ECS had grown to 28 attorneys. Its work was complemented by the Federal Bureau of Investigation (FBI), which had 100 special agents working on environmental criminal cases. Between 1982 and 1992, EPA's staff grew from 6 to 62 criminal investigators.[26] The Pollution Prevention Act of 1990 further established as a goal that EPA would employ a total of 200 criminal investigators by October 1995.[27]

Expansion of Statutory Authority

The environmental crimes initiative benefitted from improved institutional structures, but suffered from limited resources and inadequate statutory authority. In particular, many U.S. Attorneys displayed little interest in pursuing

19. *Id.* at 349.
20. Benjamin R. Civiletti, U.S. Attorney General, Address at the University of Michigan Law School Senior Day Ceremony, 14-15 (May 17, 1980) (transcript on file with the authors).
21. In 1990, the division was renamed the Environment and Natural Resources Division.
22. *EPA's Law Enforcement Authority, 1983: Hearings Before the Subcomm. on Oversight and Investigations of the House Comm. on Energy and Commerce*, 98th Cong., 1st Sess. 92 (1983) (testimony of F. Henry Habicht II).
23. Memorandum from Barbara Blum, Deputy Administrator, U.S. EPA, to EPA's Regional Administrators, the Director of the National Enforcement Investigation Center (NEIC), and the Acting Assistant Administrator for Enforcement (Jan. 5, 1981) (discussing creation of the Office of Criminal Enforcement).
24. *See* Carol M. Browner, *Environmental Protection Agency, in* A.B.A., Section on Natural Resources, Energy, and Environmental Law, 1993: The Year in Review 142 n.2.
25. During the early and mid-1980s, both EPA and Justice concentrated their resources on the use of administrative and civil sanctions to bring polluters into compliance with RCRA.
26. Joseph G. Block, *Environmental Criminal Enforcement in the 1990's*, 3 Vill. Envtl. L.J. 33, 34-35 (1992).
27. Pub. L. No. 101-593, 104 Stat. 2962, Title II, §202 (1990). The authorizing language simply establishes a goal; whether it is reached depends on whether different committees approve, and the full Congress enacts, sufficient appropriations.

expensive and difficult environmental cases when the crimes could be punished only as misdemeanors and there was little prospect that individual defendants actually would be incarcerated on conviction. Despite an agreement with EPA to become more active, the FBI also was reluctant to commit its investigative resources to support misdemeanor prosecutions.

Throughout the 1980s, Congress gradually clarified the scope of the environmental criminal provisions, upgraded the crimes from misdemeanors to felonies, and provided for greater fines and longer terms of imprisonment. Major benchmarks included the Hazardous and Solid Waste Amendments (HSWA) of 1984,[28] the Superfund Amendments and Reauthorization Act of 1986,[29] and the Water Quality Act of 1987.[30] In particular, favorable public response to RCRA felony charges was largely responsible for turning local federal prosecutors into champions of the environmental crimes program. Finally, in the CAA Amendments of 1990, Congress upgraded its penalty provisions to felonies[31] and converted air enforcement to a permit program.[32] This initiative will result in more effective civil and criminal enforcement against a large universe of regulated entities.

Success of the Program

From the crucial events of October 1982 until April 7, 1995, Justice obtained indictments against 443 corporations and 1,068 individuals. During that time, 334 organizations and 740 individuals were convicted by plea or verdict.[33] Justice recovered $297 million in criminal penalties, $125 million of which was obtained from the *Exxon Valdez* oil spill alone. Sentences totaling 561 years of imprisonment (not counting actual time served) were imposed against those convicted.

Development of Formal Enforcement Standards

Justice and EPA have enormous latitude in deciding which cases to prosecute criminally. This discretion has sparked complaints both from the regulated community, which contends that there is little predictability about which violations will be prosecuted criminally as opposed to civilly, and from congressional critics, who argue that more criminal cases should be filed.

The agencies' formal policy guidance about the decision to prosecute simply identifies criteria that may be considered. For example, in October 1982 EPA issued a memorandum identifying five factors to determine when criminal prosecution is appropriate: (1) the degree of scienter, or intent to violate the law; (2) the nature and seriousness of the offense; (3) the need for deterrence; (4) the violator's compliance history; and (5) the need for simultaneous civil or administrative enforcement actions.[34] Like most multifactor analyses, the memorandum provides few concrete tests for determining whether a particular case will be handled criminally or civilly. In many respects, it simply establishes the terminology within which the arguments for and against prosecution should be framed.

Justice's policy has concentrated on persons operating outside the regulatory or permit system, such as midnight dumpers, and persons operating inside the system who seek to avoid detection of regulatory violations by submitting false or incomplete information.[35] In 1987, Assistant Attorney General Henry Habicht stated that Justice brings environmental cases against individuals who are fully knowledgeable of the regulatory requirements: "These cases do not involve technical breaches of rules that require a Ph.D. to fathom; rather they mainly involve blatant failures to obtain any of the required permits for toxic pollutant disposal or deliberate falsification of required discharge-monitoring reports. . . ."[36]

In January 1994, EPA publicly responded to criticism of its criminal referrals by reiterating that criminal prosecution was inappropriate when there was no evidence of evil intent and when there was no actual or threatened harm to the environment or human health.[37] Justice has never publicly adopted or disavowed this position. But these public statements are not legally binding on the agencies. The actual policy is established by the pattern of charging decisions. There remains substantial controversy over whether the cases that are prosecuted do, in fact, exhibit actual mens rea and harm.

Despite the experience gained in hundreds of cases over the years, EPA and Justice have not better defined the standards for prosecution. Early in the program, a balancing factor compensated for the lack of external guidance: Justice was concerned that it had to make some showing of mens rea in court. Recent judicial decisions have effectively eliminated this requirement, however. Now, once a decision is made to prosecute a case criminally, the government can make out a prima facie case simply by proving that a violation occurred and that the defendant was aware of its

28. Pub. L. No. 98-616, 98 Stat. 3221 (codified as amended at 42 U.S.C. §§6901-6992).

29. Pub. L. No. 99-499, §109, 100 Stat. 1613, 1632-33 (codified as amended at 42 U.S.C. §9603(b)(d)).

30. Pub. L. No. 100-4, §312, 101 Stat. 7, 42-44 (codified at 33 U.S.C. §1319(c)). This law also eliminated the prior "negligent or willful" mental element and replaced it with a hierarchy of offenses, under which negligent violations could be punished as misdemeanors and knowing acts as felonies. 33 U.S.C. §1319(c), ELR STAT. FWPCA §309(c).

31. Pub. L. No. 101-549, §701, 104 Stat. 2399, 2672 (codified as amended at 42 U.S.C. §7413(c)).

32. The need for an air permit program modeled on the FWPCA system was foreseen as early as 1981. *See* William F. Pedersen Jr., *Why the Clear Air Act Works Badly*, 129 U. PA. L. REV. 1059 (1981).

33. Memorandum from Peggy Hutchins, Paralegal, to Ronald A. Sarachan, Chief, Environmental Crimes Section, Environmental Criminal Statistics FY83 Through FY94 (Apr. 7, 1995) (reproduced in Appendix A of this book).

34. Memorandum from Robert M. Perry, Associate Administrator, to Regional Counsels, Regions I-X, Criminal Enforcement Priorities for the Environmental Protection Agency (Oct. 12, 1982) (reproduced in Appendix A of this book) [hereinafter Perry Memorandum].

35. Interview with Judson Starr, *Corporation Crime Reporter* 5, 7 (May 4, 1987) [hereinafter Starr Interview]; F. Henry Habicht II, *The Federal Perspective on Environmental Criminal Enforcement: How to Remain on the Civil Side*, 17 ELR 10478, 10481 (Dec. 1987).

36. Memorandum from F. Henry Habicht II, Assistant Attorney General, Land and Natural Resources Division, to Arnold I. Burns, Deputy Attorney General, Appropriateness of Incarceration in Environmental Criminal Cases (Sept. 5, 1986) (reproduced in Appendix A of this book) [hereinafter Habicht Memorandum].

37. Memorandum from Earl E. Devaney, Director, Criminal Enforcement, U.S. EPA, to All EPA Employees Working in or in Support of the Criminal Enforcement Program, The Exercise of Investigative Discretion (Jan. 12, 1994) (reproduced in Appendix A of this book) [hereinafter Devaney Memorandum].

actions. Thus, the most important aspect of a case is the government's wholly discretionary determination whether to proceed criminally or civilly, and if the decision is to proceed criminally, then whether to charge only the corporation or include individuals as well.

As a result of this development, virtually every violation of the principal environmental statutes, however technical, may now be prosecuted criminally. Regulatory requirements range from the simple to the enormously complex. Few entities can be expected to attain 100 percent compliance, especially at large facilities. Criminal prosecution is a possibility in all such cases. Thus, it is important that the government carefully weigh the decision to impose the ultimate sanction of criminal prosecution.

Defining prosecutorial guidelines is difficult, and law enforcers instinctively shy away from any statement or action that might signal what violators can get away with. Nonetheless, there are compelling public policy reasons why Justice and EPA should undertake the effort to identify clearly for the regulated community what conduct the government will not tolerate and will prosecute criminally.

The reality is that enforcement agencies cannot police the field alone; they must rely on corporations to regulate themselves. From an environmental protection standpoint, it is vital that companies understand what the government considers to be the most important problems, so that the regulated entity can determine how to formulate its corporate policy, prioritize its compliance efforts, and allocate its internal resources. This is especially important when prosecutorial decisions may be based, in part, on a company's compliance attitude. If the government is going to punish companies for failing to assign the right priority to particular environmental problems, then it is critical—both from a pollution avoidance and a fair notice perspective—that the government set forth in advance what it deems important, and not force regulated entities to read its mind.

There is a second significant reason for having clear prosecutorial guidance: The absence of more sharply defined principles has contributed significantly to the political problems the environmental crimes program has experienced in recent years.[38]

Just as nature abhors a vacuum, bureaucracies despise subjective standards and the exercise of judgment. In many instances, there has been little difference between the cases that Justice has prosecuted criminally and those that have proceeded civilly—other than the decisionmaker's intuition as to whether a case warranted indictment. On close issues, reasonable people will disagree. For every decision not to indict, proponents of prosecution can accurately point to the cases in which similar facts led to criminal charges. In such subjective decisions, it is difficult for the official to provide a concrete explanation that will satisfy all critics. And there is no way to resolve policy disputes by recourse to neutral principles.

This problem is especially acute when the mental component—ordinarily, the principal determinant of criminal cases—is no longer an element of the offense. Any effort to differentiate among violations based on the guilty intent of the offender is subject to the retort that the reviewer is attempting to stifle a potential prosecution by introducing nonstatutory factors. Critics can rationally ask "Why should the prosecutor hold back?" when the law does not impose such a constraint.

In the final analysis, the indeterminate nature of environmental crimes has contributed heavily to the politicization of the program. In their efforts to avoid giving violators arguments against indictment, prosecutors have rendered themselves defenseless against critics.

Problems in Managing the Program

The success of the environmental crimes program is, to a substantial degree, the product of Justice's original policy decision to maintain a degree of centralization in the administration of the program. By placing formal responsibility for approval of significant criminal prosecutions in the ECS, and ultimately the Assistant Attorney General in Washington, D.C., Justice tried to ensure that cases would be selected in a manner that minimized risk to crucial EPA regulatory interpretations; that similar cases would be treated alike, even though they arose in different parts of the country; and that potentially precedent-setting cases would be carefully presented and would have the attention of Justice's high-level management. As a result, Justice's case selection decisions have been highly effective in producing good precedents in court.

As the program grew successful, however, the policy of centralization increasingly generated friction, both between Justice and its client EPA and between Washington and the U.S. Attorneys. EPA believed that Justice was not sufficiently aggressive in bringing criminal cases. The U.S. Attorneys also responded negatively to efforts by Washington to assert more actual control over case selection and management. They chafed at clearing potentially popular cases through Washington and argued strenuously for a more distributed system in which they would regain their discretion and responsibility.

Disagreements With EPA About Prosecutorial Decisions

At the beginning of the criminal enforcement program, Justice adopted a conservative position about the kinds of cases it would bring and the level of evidentiary support necessary to approve an indictment. Prosecutors understood that case selection was critical in the early stages of developing legal doctrine, and that a precedent-setting loss could be fatal to the entire effort. Further, Justice reviewers concluded that the quality of the cases referred from EPA was often poor and failed to reflect an understanding of the evidentiary demands necessary to prove guilt beyond a reasonable doubt. This lack of confidence in the quality of EPA's investigations strained working relations between the agencies.

From EPA's viewpoint, Justice appeared to be interested in bringing only cases that were certain victories. Justice declined to pursue many cases that EPA referred for prosecution, and did not adequately explain why. Many EPA staffers—who were not the ones having to stand up in court—did not receive Justice's response as an implicit criticism of EPA's investigatory work. Instead, they came to believe that Justice was more interested in not losing cases than in winning major victories, and that Justice would pursue only those cases for which it ran no risk at trial—after EPA had handed Justice all the evidence necessary to con-

38. The struggle between Justice headquarters in Washington, D.C., and local U.S. Attorneys is discussed more fully *infra*.

vict. EPA was concerned that this bureaucratic attitude slowed down the development and referral of cases, inefficiently concentrated investigative resources on a small number of cases, and generally created significant but unnecessary obstacles to bringing environmental violators before juries.

EPA's critique is a variant of familiar complaint within government: Justice's litigating divisions tend to treat other agencies in a bureaucratic fashion rather than as clients with whom maintaining a dialogue is important. The solution is simply stated but hard to implement under the daily pressures of litigation. Justice staff need to do a better job of explaining their reasoning to EPA, so that the Agency understands the decision in the instant case and can fine tune its investigative efforts to anticipate Justice's concerns in the next case.

The Struggle for Primacy Within Justice

The environmental crimes program originally featured a greater degree of energy in Washington and a lesser degree of initiative by U.S. Attorneys. Local prosecutors had limited familiarity with environmental law, and some offices faced resource constraints that made it difficult to pursue misdemeanor cases. At the same time, there were compelling reasons for centralizing these cases in a national office. First, environmental regulations are complex, and special expertise is needed to understand what constitutes a crime under the regime. Second, many environmental rules were not written with criminal enforcement in mind, and delicate judgment is required in order to determine whether a technical violation can or should be prosecuted criminally. Third, centralized case selection and case preparation by environmental experts helped ensure success in the initial generation of cases that established the crucial precedents for the program's development. Finally, given the difficulty in defining whether cases should be prosecuted criminally, civilly, or administratively, centralized policy control furthered the goal of consistency in charging decisions.

During the program's early years, there was little friction. The ECS prosecuted many of the most sensitive cases itself. For cases in which U.S. Attorneys had the lead role, procedures adopted in 1984 provided that all proposed RCRA indictments had to be submitted to the Assistant Attorney General, and that the charges could not be filed until Washington had completed its review.[39] But Washington exercised its formal authority with a light hand, and local prosecutors had few complaints about limits on their discretion.

In the late 1980s, however, the situation began to change. By then, a series of disasters (Love Canal, Times Beach, Chernobyl, Bhopal, and the *Exxon Valdez*) had persuaded the public that the threat of environmental degradation was real and that criminal prosecutions were warranted in many instances.[40] Environmental cases also became more attractive due to the enhancement of the crimes to felonies and the U.S. Sentencing Commission's 1987 issuance of sentencing guidelines for individual offenders, virtually assuring incarceration for persons convicted of environmental felonies.[41] Local prosecutors also had developed considerable expertise and believed that they could better evaluate the wisdom of a potential case because it had to compete for their attention with possible prosecutions under dozens of other statutes. At the same time, the rationale for centralized control began to diminish somewhat, ironically because of the precedents that the ECS had established through successful prosecutions.

The issue was squarely joined in 1990, when Washington began to exercise more aggressively the authority formally reserved to it by Justice policies. A group of U.S. Attorneys used internal Justice processes to challenge the Assistant Attorney General's authority to approve the filing of indictments and the acceptance of plea bargains in many kinds of environmental prosecutions. The battle coalesced around one of the most common issues in bureaucracies: Whether the U.S. Attorney's obligation to provide Washington with prior notice of its intent to file charges in a case in which it had the lead role carried with it the requirement to obtain advance approval, or whether Washington's role was merely consultative and advisory.

In January 1993, the departing Bush Administration attempted to establish a new line of demarcation between Washington and the U.S. Attorneys. This policy reserved to the Assistant Attorney General the right to veto proposed indictments in 10 priority areas that experience showed to be the most sensitive types of environmental prosecutions:

> (1) RCRA violations, where a defense has been raised, or is reasonably likely to be raised, that an alleged hazardous waste is not a "solid waste";
> (2) wetlands violations;
> (3) charges under provisions of the 1990 CAA Amer 'ments;
> (4) knowing endangerment cases;
> (5) charges based on negligence (except as part of a plea bargain);
> (6) violations based on a strict liability theory (except as part of a plea bargain);
> (7) charges based on the "responsible corporate officer" doctrine;
> (8) charges involving federal facilities;
> (9) cases in which evidence to be presented was derived from self-auditing by regulated entities, or otherwise implicated the Department's policy on audits and voluntary disclosure;[42] and
> (10) any matter of national interest, including the first prosecution under a particular statute or rule, or a prosecution involving application of a rule whose validity is significantly in doubt.[43]

39. DEPARTMENT OF JUSTICE MANUAL §5-3.724 (1984).

40. A 1991 public opinion survey by Opinion Research Corporation on behalf of Arthur D. Little found that 84 percent of adults surveyed rated pollution and environmental damages as more serious business crimes than price-fixing or insider trading. Seventy-four percent of the respondents also stated that business executives should be held personally liable for environmental injuries caused by their companies. Jack Doyle, *Audits Are Their Own Reward*, ENVTL. F., Jan./Feb. 1992, at 38.

41. *See* U.S. SENTENCING COMMISSION, GUIDELINES MANUAL (Nov. 1994) [hereinafter SENTENCING GUIDELINES].

42. U.S. DOJ, FACTORS IN DECISIONS ON CRIMINAL PROSECUTIONS FOR ENVIRONMENTAL VIOLATIONS IN THE CONTEXT OF SIGNIFICANT VOLUNTARY COMPLIANCE OR DISCLOSURE EFFORTS BY THE VIOLATOR (July 1, 1991) (reproduced in Appendix A of this book) [hereinafter FACTORS IN DECISIONS ON CRIMINAL PROSECUTIONS].

43. OFFICE OF THE ATTORNEY GENERAL, BLUESHEET REVISION TO THE U.S. ATTORNEYS' MANUAL ON ENVIRONMENTAL CRIMES (Jan. 12, 1993) (amending DEPARTMENT OF JUSTICE MANUAL §5-11.110E) [hereinafter 1993 BLUESHEET REVISION].

U.S. Attorneys maintained their opposition to this document, and the issue was introduced into oversight hearings that the House Energy and Commerce Committee was conducting on the environmental crimes program. The effort to promote more decentralization gained support from EPA's Director of Criminal Enforcement. To increase the pressure on the Justice Department, Congress also deferred confirmation of the Assistant Attorney General-designate.

In order to put this inherited issue behind her, Attorney General Janet Reno issued a new policy directive on August 23, 1994, that will result in returning to U.S. Attorneys some of the authority Washington attempted to claim in 1990.[44] The 1994 policy divides prosecutions into "national interest cases" and lower priority cases.[45] The ECS and U.S. Attorneys will jointly handle national interest matters. These include cases that present novel issues of law (including the first case under a statute or rule); simultaneous investigations in multiple federal judicial districts; cases with foreign policy implications; and urgent or sensitive issues, including those of major interest to Congress or the President.[46] Through this mechanism, Washington is assured of policy primacy in cases of national significance, if only by its greater ability to raise disputed issues to a policy level within Justice. In lower priority cases, the 1994 policy makes clear that Washington has no formal veto authority over indictments or pleas.[47] Although the Assistant Attorney General still must be notified in such cases, the clear thrust of the policy change is to grant far greater autonomy to local prosecutors in the types of environmental prosecutions that have become routine as the program has matured.[48]

Recent Changes in the Environmental Crimes Program

The environmental crimes program has shown significant changes over the last few years. Understanding the thrust of these developments is critical for any practitioner asked to advise a client whether a civil investigation may take a sudden turn toward criminal enforcement.

The most important change is that Justice and EPA have become more aggressive in their charging decisions and are now prosecuting different and more complicated kinds of cases. In earlier years, criminal prosecutions were largely restricted to entities operating without a required permit, persons who falsified or fabricated reporting data, and egregious violations of easily understood regulatory provisions. Now, Justice is willing to bring criminal charges against both companies and individuals for a broader variety of regulatory violations.

Second, because courts have defined the mens rea requirement as rather minimal, there is noticeably less emphasis on the scienter criterion in charging decisions, regardless of what the formal guidance documents may state. Instead, the amount of environmental harm that occurred is the primary influence in the exercise of prosecutorial discretion. Simply stated, the more serious the harm, the greater the likelihood of criminal prosecution.[49] The factor of prior compliance history also has taken on increased significance. Violations that once might have been handled civilly are now being prosecuted in order to impose individual deterrence on an entity that has repeatedly broken the law.[50]

Third, U.S. Attorneys are making prosecutorial decisions more frequently. Local prosecutors are more sensitive to community sentiment, and may be attracted to different cases than are Washington staff, who are better attuned to more abstract policy impulses. Who prosecutes the case makes a definite difference in the priority attached to a violation.

Fourth, questions have arisen repeatedly about the need for a qualified privilege or other safe harbor for companies that conduct effective internal audit programs, through which they report environmental violations that the government is not aware of and otherwise might never detect.

From a regulatory policy perspective, the best method of protecting the environment is for facilities themselves to detect and remediate environmental problems as early as possible, so that harmful discharges never occur. And from an engineering and management perspective, the best approach is to conduct periodic self-audits and systematically document for corporate policymakers all violations or potential problems, so that responsibility can be assigned and compliance monitored. The paper records that allow for management coherence could be a two-edged sword, however. The same documents could give a prosecutor an ironclad criminal case, especially in a universe where mens rea is irrelevant. This risk could make companies reluctant to institute formal self-audit programs, to the detriment of the environment.[51]

From an enforcement perspective, however, prosecutors naturally oppose any evidentiary restrictions that might create impediments to successful litigation. Enforcement personnel thus have reacted negatively to recognition of a privilege that might hinder their ability to rely on internal corporate audit documents, which might well provide a road map for successful prosecution of a violation. EPA and Justice have adopted guidance to attempt to ease concerns.[52] But many in the regulated community object that the documents have had the opposite effect, because they clearly show that the enforcers intend to preserve their options to use these reports in prosecutions.

The regulated community continues to express concern

44. Office of the Attorney General, Bluesheet Revision to the U.S. Attorneys' Manual on Environmental Crimes (Aug. 23, 1994) (reproduced in Appendix A of this book) [hereinafter 1994 Bluesheet Revision].

45. *Id.* at 3 (amending Department of Justice Manual §5-11.105).

46. *Id.*

47. *Id.* (amending Department of Justice Manual §5-11.104).

48. *Id.* at 4 (amending Department of Justice Manual §5-11.107).

49. Remarks of Richard B. Stewart, Assistant Attorney General, A Day With Justice, to the National Law Center for the Public Interest, at 11 (May 30, 1990) (transcript on file with the authors). The criminal prosecutions following the *Exxon Valdez* disaster and the Ashland Oil tank collapse are the most visible examples of this factor's influence.

50. James M. Strock, *Protecting the Environment: EPA After 20 Years*, Trial, Aug. 1990, at 1, 2.

51. For example, in a 1993 survey of corporate legal officers, 70 percent responded that they did not believe that full compliance with the matrix of federal and state environmental requirements was possible. Marianne Lavelle, *Environment Vise: Law, Compliance*, Nat'l L.J., Aug. 30, 1993, at S1, S2.

52. *See* Factors in Decisions on Criminal Prosecutions, *supra* note 42; U.S. EPA, Voluntary Environmental Self-Policing and Self-Disclosure Interim Policy Statement, 60 Fed. Reg. 16875 (Apr. 3, 1995) (reproduced in Appendix A of this book).

that the narrow focus on facilitating those few prosecutions that do occur would adversely affect or deter a great deal of unambiguously pro-environmental conduct by the large number of companies that are sincerely interested in complying with their environmental obligations. Several states have already adopted statutory audit privileges, and the issue continues to gain visibility.[53]

Major Outstanding Issues for the Program

As the environmental crimes program enters its mature years, there are five outstanding policy questions around which the debate over the future of the effort will revolve:

(1) Should environmental crimes be strict liability offenses, or should some showing of intent to violate the law or a discharge permit be required?

(2) Should an internal audit privilege be recognized?

(3) How should policy disagreements be resolved between Justice and EPA about case selection and the sufficiency of the evidence necessary to justify proceeding with a criminal prosecution?

(4) Should Justice's program be run in a centralized manner by policy officials in Washington? Should leadership rest with the U.S. Attorneys? Or should the answer be different depending on whether cutting-edge cases or garden-variety prosecutions are involved? If authority is distributed to U.S. Attorneys and EPA Regions, should more precise policy guidance be issued to define the circumstances in which criminal prosecution is appropriate?

(5) What is the appropriate period of incarceration for a criminal conviction? Are the current federal sentencing guidelines too severe in this respect?

Lawyers defending environmental investigations that may have criminal implications must remain aware of these questions at all times. Their resolution will significantly affect the ultimate policy decision whether to pursue a particular environmental violation civilly or with the full weight of the criminal law.

How the Environmental Crimes Program Operates

The environmental crimes program works from the baseline created by EPA's civil reporting and enforcement mechanisms. The unique features of this system are that (1) some instances of noncompliance are expected from even the best managed facilities and (2) virtually every act of noncompliance may be prosecuted criminally.

Criminalization of All Civil Rules

Criminal enforcement can be divided, in conceptual terms, into charges against three classes of defendants: (1) those who operate without a required permit; (2) those who violate the terms of a permit; and (3) those who violate a self-enforcing EPA rule, or an administrative or judicial order. Essentially every violation of a civil rule or permit is technically subject to criminal prosecution. There is no minimum quantitative requirement to differentiate which illegal discharges should be prosecuted civilly or criminally. And with infrequent exceptions such as "knowing endangerment" prosecutions,[54] there is no meaningful knowledge requirement to serve as a filter.

Environmental requirements are drafted in such minute detail that rule and permit violations occur frequently. As former Associate Attorney General Webster Hubbell stated "[t]he complex and ever-expanding array of environmental statutes and regulations [and] *the inevitability of some degree of non-compliance* . . . creates an understandably daunting climate for corporate management."[55] Studies have shown that even the environmental managers of companies with the most aggressive compliance programs have concluded that 100 percent compliance is not possible, given the detailed nature of the requirements and the trip wires intentionally built into rules and permits.[56]

There is little, if any, difference among the essential elements of administrative, civil, and criminal charges. For example, FWPCA §309(c)[57] establishes a six-tier hierarchy of enforcement provisions, including:

- two levels of administrative penalties;
- civil penalties enforceable in court;
- misdemeanor offenses;
- ordinary felonies; and
- aggravated felonies (knowing endangerment).

Under this carefully calibrated scheme, all essential elements of the first five levels of offense are the same except for the mental element. And courts have interpreted the knowledge provision to require only the most general showing of the defendant's awareness of his or her own actions in order to obtain a felony conviction.[58]

In sum, virtually every civil case represents a potential criminal case. The government has enormous discretion whether to proceed civilly or criminally, or to decline to act altogether. Thus, agency policy guidelines on case selection and prosecution are critically important.

EPA Case Selection Guidelines

EPA Investigation and Referral Policy

An October 1982 memorandum from EPA's then-Associate Administrator for Enforcement stated that criminal referrals will be confined to "the most serious cases of environmental misconduct."[59] While recognizing that EPA "is free to pursue criminal sanctions in every situation presenting evidence supporting the requisite elements of proof," the

53. The audit issue is discussed in greater detail *infra*.

54. The crime of knowing endangerment is discussed more fully *infra*.

55. Webster L. Hubbell, *Department of Justice—A Tough but Fair Approach to Environmental Crimes*, *in* A.B.A., Section on Natural Resources, Energy, and Environmental Law, 1993: The Year in Review 145 (emphasis added).

56. *See* Judson W. Starr et al., *Prosecuting Pollution*, Legal Times, May 31, 1993, at 6 (Special Report).

57. 33 U.S.C. §1319(c), ELR Stat. FWPCA §309(c).

58. United States v. Weitzenhoff, 1 F.3d 1523, 23 ELR 21322 (1993), *amended*, 35 F.3d 1365, 24 ELR 21504 (9th Cir. 1994), *cert. denied*, 115 S. Ct. 939 (1995); United States v. Hopkins, 53 F.3d 533, 25 ELR 21178 (2d Cir. 1995).

59. Perry Memorandum, *supra* note 34, at IV-5.

memorandum concludes that as a matter of both enforcement policy and resource allocation, such "unrestrained use of criminal sanctions is neither warranted nor practical."[60] The memorandum identifies five criteria that should be addressed in determining whether a criminal referral is appropriate:

- *the scienter requirement*—criminal prosecution is normally limited to cases in which the prospective defendant has "guilty knowledge" or intent to violate the law;
- *the nature and seriousness of the offense*—this factor focuses on the "extent of environmental contamination or human health hazard" resulting from the prohibited conduct. It considers the duration of the conduct, toxicity of the pollutants, proximity to humans, quality of the receiving media, and "public sentiment supporting strong enforcement action." It also considers the impact of the conduct on EPA's regulatory functions, such as falsification of reports and tampering with monitors;
- *the need for deterrence*—this factor primarily targets particularly deliberate offenses or those that result in serious environmental contamination or human health hazard;
- *compliance history*—repeated environmental violations may trigger criminal enforcement to achieve effective individual deterrence; and
- *the need for simultaneous civil or administrative enforcement actions*—this factor addresses cases of noncompliance that pose ongoing risks to the environment or human health that must be addressed in a separate civil action for an injunction. However, because of differing civil and criminal standards of proof and constraints on criminal discovery, initiation of parallel proceedings "should be avoided except where clearly justified."[61]

The memorandum also sets forth EPA's investigative priorities under various statutes. The highest priority is reserved for cases in which the violation caused or threatened significant environmental contamination or risk to human health. Other priority areas involve willful violations of regulatory requirements including destruction, falsification, or concealment of records or tampering with monitoring devices.[62]

The factors and priorities EPA identified in 1982 have not been refined significantly since. Consequently, they continue to serve as the best guide to when EPA will initiate a criminal investigation or refer a case to Justice for possible prosecution. For example, the next significant EPA enforcement policy memorandum, circulated broadly within the Agency in September 1987, largely reiterated the 1982 list of factors, including: knowing or willful behavior; careful attention to the elements of the offense (including scienter); the adverse impact on EPA's regulatory functions if reporting information is falsified or concealed; harm to human health or the environment; "patterns or practices" (i.e., the subject's compliance history); and deterrence of others within the regulated industry.[63]

In 1990, EPA restated its enforcement priorities in the course of attempting to enhance coordination and case selection by the regional offices.[64] The guidance attempts to focus resources better on programmatic goals, rather than on simply responding to events. Reflecting the case law, it also deemphasizes the role of guilty knowledge in the institution of criminal cases. The guidance provides that review for possible criminal prosecution is appropriate when there has been misconduct that threatened EPA program goals or priorities, and one or more factors indicating aggravated environmental misconduct, including: a history of repeated violations; deliberate, knowing, or willful misconduct; concealment of misconduct or falsification of required records; tampering with monitoring or control equipment; operation of pollution-related activities without a permit; and actual illegal discharges that created a threat of harm to the environment or human health.[65]

In 1994, the head of EPA's Office of Criminal Enforcement attempted to differentiate the most significant and egregious cases, for which criminal investigation is appropriate, from those in which civil or administrative action should be pursued. The two principal criteria are significant environmental harm and culpable conduct.[66]

"Significant environmental harm" may consist of actual or threatened harm to human health or the environment. The source's failure to report an actual discharge serves as an additional factor favoring criminal investigation.[67] Further, such an investigation may be appropriate if the illegal conduct represents a trend or common attitude in the regulated community, and a single criminal case could have substantial deterrent effect on many firms.

"Culpable conduct" may be inferred from several factors, including a history of repeated violations, deliberate misconduct, concealment of misconduct or falsification of required records, tampering with monitoring or control equipment, and operating a business without required permits. With respect to the mental element, the memorandum simply notes that although federal environmental statutes do not require proof of specific intent, evidence "that a violation was deliberate will be a major factor indicating that criminal investigation is warranted."[68]

EPA Policy on Enforcement Based on Ambiguous Rules

EPA issued a second policy document in 1990 that responded to perceived enforcement problems stemming from

60. *Id.*

61. *Id.* at IV-7 to IV-10. Issues involved in parallel proceedings are discussed *infra*.

62. *Id.* at IV-10 to IV-18.

63. Memorandum from Thomas L. Adams Jr., Assistant Administrator, to Assistant Administrators et al., Environmental Criminal Conduct Coming to the Attention of Agency Officials and Employees (Sept. 21, 1987) (reproduced in Appendix A of this book).

64. Memorandum from James M. Strock, Assistant Administrator, to Regional Administrators and Assistant Administrators, Regional Enforcement Management: Enhanced Regional Case Screening (Dec. 3, 1990) (reproduced in Appendix A of this book).

65. *Id.* at 16-18.

66. Devaney Memorandum, *supra* note 37, at 3. EPA also acknowledges the role of legislative intent concerning case selection, and criticism that "EPA's criminal program is imposing its powerful sanctions indiscriminately." *Id.* at 2, 7.

67. EPA's "investigative resources should generally be targeted toward those cases in which the failure to report is coupled with actual or threatened environmental harm." *Id.* at 4.

68. *Id.* at 5.

the ambiguity in certain substantive Agency rules defining impermissible conduct.[69] The document promulgated additional procedures to be followed before initiating a criminal investigation, if the case presents either a factual or legal issue of first impression. The memorandum notes that such cases may have national repercussions and deserve careful attention because of the need in criminal cases for clear and unambiguous legal standards and facts that prove guilt beyond a reasonable doubt.[70] For this reason, the policy—which coincided with passage of the 1990 CAA Amendments—establishes procedures for greater internal coordination in potentially precedent-setting cases.

Justice Prosecution Policy

Justice bases its decisions whether to bring environmental criminal cases on the *Federal Principles of Prosecution*, which follows a conservative charging philosophy and provides that the government will decline to prosecute if the evidence does not support a reasonable probability of conviction.[71] Even if there is evidence sufficient to convict, a prosecutor may decide not to bring a case if no substantial federal interest would be served, or if civil or administrative remedies would provide an adequate noncriminal alternative to prosecution.[72]

As previously noted, Justice's environmental criminal prosecutions have concentrated on persons operating outside the regulatory or permit system, e.g., midnight dumpers, and persons operating inside the system who seek to avoid detection of violations of regulatory requirements by submitting false or incomplete information. From the outset, Justice has been aware that criminal prosecutions against corporations alone are insufficient to create proper incentives for deterrence, because artificial entities can shrug off a fine as a cost of doing business. Thus, Justice has long prosecuted both companies and the individuals within them, in the expectation that a realistic threat of imprisonment would change behavior. On the basis of its experience, Justice defined in 1987 the situations in which it would prosecute individuals, as well as corporations, for environmental offenses. Justice's policy emphasizes the factor of "willful, deliberate, rational, and pre-meditated" violations in prosecuting individuals.[73] Justice has formally stated that it brings environmental cases against individuals who are fully knowledgeable of the regulatory requirements.[74]

Prosecution of Individuals

Justice has long had a policy—not committed to formal guidance documents—of prosecuting the highest ranking individual in a company responsible for a violation. In 1984, a Justice official stated:

> [I]f fines alone were all the Government sought in prosecuting environmental crimes, the responsible decision-makers and actors would not be exposed and would go substantially unpunished—only the shareholders would suffer. Therefore, to achieve the desired level of deterrence and respect for environmental laws, those individuals who are themselves responsible for any wrongdoing must face the risk of imprisonment.[75]

In a 1987 interview, the official further noted that the most effective use of the environmental criminal investigation is to ferret out the individual corporate officer who is responsible; experience shows that this is the best means of galvanizing corporate action.[76]

Until the mid-1980s, courts were generally disinclined to sentence environmental offenders to serve actual terms of imprisonment. Justice waged a long policy battle to persuade federal judges of the appropriateness of incarceration in environmental cases.[77] The sentencing guidelines issued on November 1, 1987, reinforced these arguments by officially confirming the appropriateness of incarceration of individuals for crimes involving hazardous wastes.[78]

Justice Policy on Prosecutions Based on Ambiguous Rules

The cases Justice is asked to prosecute increasingly involve allegations of departures from complicated regulatory provisions, which were not written with an eye toward criminal enforcement.[79] These provisions can be difficult even for experts to interpret because EPA rule writers frequently employ open-ended and flexible terms in order to sweep within the civil regulatory system as much of the targeted conduct as possible.

Justice recognizes the sensitivity of the question whether to apply a complex rule for the first time in the context of a criminal prosecution. In part, this concern reflects the prosecutor's desire to win whichever of the many potential cases competing for attention that he or she decides to bring. In part, it recognizes the fairness problem involved in announcing an interpretation for the first time in an indictment[80] or seeking to incarcerate a person for not following

69. Memorandum from James M. Strock, Assistant Administrator, to Director, National Enforcement Investigations Center et al., Initiation of Criminal Investigations in Cases Presenting an Issue of First Impression (Oct. 22, 1990) (reproduced in Appendix A of this book).

70. *Id.* at 1.

71. U.S. DOJ, FEDERAL PRINCIPLES OF PROSECUTION 8-10 (1980).

72. Hubbell, *supra* note 55, at 144.

73. Judson W. Starr, Chief, Environmental Crimes Section, U.S. DOJ, Countering Environmental Crimes in the United States, Remarks Before the Environmental Law Committee of the International Bar Association 6-7 (Sept. 5, 1984) (transcript on file with the authors) [hereinafter Starr Remarks].

74. *See supra* note 36 and accompanying text.

75. Starr Remarks, *supra* note 73, at 6-7.

76. Starr Interview, *supra* note 35.

77. As late as September 1986, then-Assistant Attorney General Habicht sought to counteract this history by making a case for seeking incarceration in environmental criminal cases. He argued that incarceration is appropriate in certain cases, such as those of midnight dumpers, who willfully evade the law for profit. Habicht Memorandum, *supra* note 36.

78. SENTENCING GUIDELINES, *supra* note 41, §§2Q1.2-.3. The method by which individuals are sentenced under the guidelines is discussed in detail *infra*.

79. *See* John F. Cooney, *Defenses to the Second Generation of Environmental Criminal Prosecutions*, *in* A.L.I.-A.B.A., CRIMINAL ENFORCEMENT OF ENVIRONMENTAL LAWS 41-44 (1994).

80. In *General Electric Co. v. U.S. Environmental Protection Agency*, the D.C. Circuit summarized the law as follows:

> In the absence of notice—for example, where the regulation is not sufficiently clear to warn a party about what is expected of it—an agency may not deprive a party of property by imposing civil or criminal responsibility. Of course, it is in the context of criminal liability that this "no punishment without notice" rule is most commonly applied. . . .

a construction of a rule or permit term that was previously implicit.[81] Finally, the policy tacitly recognizes the operation of the rule of lenity, which requires the court in a criminal case to resolve any ambiguity in a statute or rule in favor of the accused.[82] For these reasons, the 1993 Justice bluesheet revision[83] made cases of first impression a priority for Washington involvement.

Justice currently follows a relatively aggressive charging philosophy with respect to ambiguous environmental rules. In 1993, Associate Attorney General Hubbell stated "[b]ecause environmental law is complex and rapidly evolving, it is *sometimes* appropriate to use civil enforcement to clarify the law, explain regulations, and create legal standards before seeking to apply the law in a criminal context."[84]

By contrast, other divisions within Justice traditionally follow a more conservative philosophy. For example, the Antitrust Division would refuse to prosecute criminally when any of four special factors were present: (1) confusion of the law; (2) truly novel issues of law or fact; (3) confusion caused by past prosecutorial decisions;[85] or (4) clear evidence that the defendants did not appreciate the consequences of their actions.[86]

Of these factors, the first two appear to be of particular concern for the new generation of environmental crimes cases. EPA is now referring, and Justice is under considerable political pressure to consider for criminal prosecution, cases in which the agency rules are susceptible to multiple readings or where the theory of liability has not previously been invoked in a civil or criminal case. Experience in other litigation divisions indicates that "[c]riminal indictments, particularly felony indictments, in such cases raise important issues of fairness which in turn may affect the likelihood of obtaining a conviction."[87]

Thus, as Justice considers initiating a criminal case based on a potentially ambiguous construction of a rule or permit term, prosecutors face an unavoidable question: Whether their zeal to pursue the violator rigorously should be tempered by equitable considerations or the possibility that a judge's or jury's sympathy for a defendant who appears unfairly charged may check the development of a promising line of cases.

Civil Rules and Reporting Obligations

Periodic reporting obligations incorporated within permits serve as built-in triggers for enforcement actions. Permits issued under federal environmental statutes traditionally have specific, extensive data-collection and paperwork generation obligations. Indeed, the breadth, cost, and burden of the monitoring obligations necessary to meet EPA information demands are collectively one of the most frequent policy criticisms of environmental regulation.[88]

EPA vigilantly polices industry compliance with monitoring and reporting obligations. Justice frequently brings cases for tampering with detectors or falsifying reporting data.[89] Regulated companies often complain about criminal prosecution for what are essentially "paperwork" violations, and which may not involve any actual discharge of pollutants into the environment.

But the literature on the appropriateness of criminal sanctions squarely supports the government's decision to make the integrity of the reporting system a high priority. Absent honest reporting, the cost to society of detecting excessive discharges would be high. An accurate reporting system, on the other hand, significantly reduces the amount of pollution discharged into the environment because a company or municipality that complies faithfully with permit conditions will detect and self-report most actionable exceedances of its permit. This self-reporting reduces search and detection costs, and allows regulators to enforce the law cheaply and efficiently. Indeed, for statutes having a civil monetary enforcement program that "private attorneys general" may invoke, environmental groups may also be active enforcers, thus further reducing the budgetary costs for government agencies.[90]

The Relationship Between the Source and the Regulator

A company that is under investigation for environmental violations cannot maintain the same formal, adversarial posture toward the government as is typically followed in other white-collar criminal fields. The regulatory agency has the authority to demand continuing information disclosures while the criminal case proceeds, and often has the power to impose significant controls over operations at the company's facilities. These two factors—the source's self-interest and the ability of the government to compel continuing disclosure—force the company, like it or not, to maintain a working relationship with the government even while the company is under criminal investigation or indictment.

☐ *Self-Interest.* The permit writer has enormous power over the regulated source, through its discretion to impose onerous substantive obligations, tight deadlines for compliance, or implicit requirements to purchase expensive pollution-control equipment. On the other hand, if the relation-

---

> Although the agency must always provide "fair notice" of its regulatory interpretations to the regulated public, in many cases the agency's pre-enforcement efforts to bring about compliance will provide adequate notice.

53 F.3d 1324, 1328-29, 25 ELR 20982, 20983-84 (D.C. Cir. May 12, 1995, *as corrected* June 19, 1995).

81. *See* United States v. Heuer, 4 F.3d 723, 23 ELR 21357 (9th Cir. 1993), *cert. denied*, 114 S. Ct. 1190 (1994).
82. *See, e.g.*, United States v. Bass, 404 U.S. 336 (1971).
83. 1993 Bluesheet Revision, *supra* note 43. This revision was superseded in 1994 by Attorney General Reno. *See supra* note 44 and accompanying text.
84. Hubbell, *supra* note 55, at 144 (emphasis added).
85. *See* United States v. Pennsylvania Indus. Chem. Corp., 411 U.S. 655, 670, 3 ELR 20401, 20407 (1973) (defendant entitled to present evidence to establish defense that it was "affirmatively misled" by the long-standing official interpretation of the Refuse Act into believing its conduct did not violate that law).
86. Donald J. Baker, *To Indict or Not to Indict: Prosecutorial Discretion in Sherman Act Enforcement*, 63 Cornell L. Rev. 405 (1978).
87. *Id.* at 415.
88. *See, e.g., Clinton, Gore Slam House Attempts to Break Up Environmental Alliance*, 25 Env't Rep. (BNA) 2538 (Apr. 28, 1995) (remarks of President Clinton on EPA project to cut paperwork burden by 25 percent or 20 million hours).
89. *See, e.g.*, United States v. Hopkins, 53 F.3d 533, 25 ELR 21178 (2d Cir. 1995) (corporate vice president convicted of ordering employees to tamper with water discharge monitoring samples).
90. Greve, *supra* note 8, at 109.

ship between the regulator and the company is good, the permit authority can exercise its discretion in a manner that reduces compliance costs substantially.

This point is dramatically illustrated by the following civil regulatory matter. EPA originally proposed that the owners of the Navajo Generating Station—a large electric power plant in Arizona that was built to pump water from the Grand Canyon—reduce its sulfur dioxide emissions by 70 percent, measured on a 30-day average basis, in order to protect wintertime visibility in the Grand Canyon. The plant operator estimated that this would require installation of two scrubber modules per unit, at a total cost of $4.4 billion over the life of the plant. The owners countered with a proposal that EPA adopt an annual averaging time, which would permit the plant to achieve 90 percent reduction while requiring only one module per unit. This approach would produce better environmental protection and reduce compliance costs to $2 billion. Because of the trust developed through a regulatory negotiation, EPA eventually agreed to annual averaging, apparently for the only time in the history of CAA implementation.[91]

The reverse of the Navajo power plant situation is also possible—the permitting authority can impose regulatory terms that can drive up costs and put a company it distrusts at a significant competitive disadvantage. Intransigent behavior can make a bad relationship worse. Further, most environmental criminal cases end in settlements or litigated orders that require the company to take significant remedial actions. Accordingly, even when it is under investigation or indictment, a regulated entity has strong incentives to preserve working relations with the permit writer who largely will dictate these future compliance terms.

☐ *Compulsory Disclosure*. The government has many ways besides grand jury process to obtain information from a source during a criminal investigation.[92] First, all permitting and reporting obligations continue during the investigation and prosecution of a crime at an operating facility. The regulator's data demands are both unilateral and unremitting. Second, the defendant corporation may not invoke the Fifth Amendment privilege against self-incrimination to prevent disclosure of these reporting documents.[93] And any withholding or misleading modification of these documents is likely to be punished severely as obstruction of justice. Third, regulatory authorities have administrative authority to visit the facility under investigation, and as long as the administrative entry is not a sham to facilitate a warrantless search for purely criminal purposes, evidence discovered during the visit likely will not be stricken under the entrapment by estoppel doctrine.[94]

In sum, the regulator has multiple ways to harm or shut down a company aside from obtaining an environmental criminal conviction. Although the situation may be somewhat different for individuals who are targets of such an investigation, it is usually essential to the company's long-term business interest to preserve a relationship with the civil authorities even as the prosecution against it proceeds.

The FWPCA Permit Program

Most major EPA enforcement programs are based on the original FWPCA permit program.[95] Under this approach, each source is required to obtain a permit that collects in one place—either in specific terms or by reference—all the pollution-control obligations to which the source is subject at each discharge point. Permits often go into enormous detail, specifying such factors as what pollutants the source may discharge and in what quantities, the averaging times that will be used in measuring compliance, the monitoring techniques that the source must use, and what information the source must disclose to the regulator and how frequently. In cases in which the permit is defective and does not accurately reflect all of the legal obligations to which the source is subject, the source has the benefit of the so-called permit shield, under which proof that a facility has complied with all permit terms is a complete defense to allegations that it violated the law.[96]

The CAA Permit Scheme

Under the CAA Amendments of 1990,[97] EPA is implementing an operating permit system that represents the first significant improvement to the FWPCA approach. Within the next few years, every source of significant air emissions in the country (an estimated 34,000 facilities) will be required to obtain a comprehensive permit from EPA or an authorized state. The permit will set forth all air emission requirements to which the source is subject; a schedule of compliance with new requirements; and monitoring, recordkeeping, and reporting requirements.

In creating the operating permit system, Congress expressly intended to facilitate more aggressive enforcement of the CAA. Few criminal cases have ever been brought under this law because of the difficulty prosecutors have faced in proving that an emissions violation at one plant caused an entire area to exceed levels established by the governing state implementation plan. The new permitting system will allow more effective enforcement by defining precisely the individual emissions requirements applicable

91. *See* Central Ariz. Water Conservation Dist. v. U.S. Environmental Protection Agency, 990 F.2d 1531, 23 ELR 20678 (9th Cir.), *cert. denied*, 114 S. Ct. 94 (1993); *see also* Michael D. Rappoport & John F. Cooney, *Visibility at the Grand Canyon: Regulatory Negotiations Under the Clean Air Act*, 24 Ariz. St. L.J. 627 (1992).

92. Governmental authority to obtain corporate information during an investigation is discussed in detail *infra*.

93. *See* Wilson v. United States, 221 U.S. 361 (1911).

94. *See, e.g.*, United States v. Bosse, 898 F.2d 113 (9th Cir. 1990); United States v. Tallmadge, 829 F.2d 767 (9th Cir. 1987).

95. 33 U.S.C. §1342, ELR Stat. FWPCA §402.

96. EPA has defined the FWPCA §204(k) permit shield as applying to three types of pollutants, provided they are clearly identified in the permit application: (1) pollutants specifically limited in the permit through indicator parameters; (2) pollutants for which the permit authority has not established limits, but that are specifically identified as present in discharges; and (3) pollutants not identified as present, but that are constituents of waste streams that were clearly identified during the permit process. Memorandum from Robert Perciasepe, Steven A. Herman, and Jean C. Nelson, to Regional Administrators and Regional Counsels, Policy Statement on Scope of Discharge Authorization and Shield Associated With NPDES Permits 2 (July 1, 1994) (reproduced in Appendix A of this book). By regulation, EPA has adopted a RCRA permit shield, under which compliance with a permit is considered compliance with all hazardous waste rules, except for subsequently enacted statutes. 40 C.F.R. §270.4(a). There is also a permit shield under the CAA. 42 U.S.C. §7661c(f), ELR Stat. CAA §504(f).

97. Pub. L. No. 101-549, Title V, 104 Stat. 2635 (1990).

to each source and by consolidating all applicable restrictions in one document.

Other aspects of the 1990 Amendments will require many sources to monitor emissions more intensively. In combination with the permitting system, these requirements will provide enforcement personnel with clear, plant-specific standards against which to measure compliance, as well as the data necessary to detect and prosecute violations.

Several innovations in the enforcement system created by the 1990 Amendments will facilitate the initiation of criminal prosecutions. These factors include:

- A requirement that in applying for a permit, each covered facility must submit a certification from a responsible corporate official either stating that the facility is in compliance with all applicable emission requirements or disclosing any violations that exist.[98] In order to avoid subjecting the certifying official to prosecution for submitting false statements, this provision will require each facility to conduct an extensive pre-submission audit of its operations to detect any violations. There is no permit application shield for such disclosures. Either EPA or an authorized state will be free to prosecute the plant for any existing violation it self-reports. And the permit application will provide a blueprint for enforcement officials on how to bring such a case.
- Creation of a bounty scheme, under which a person who reports a violation that leads to a criminal conviction under the Act may obtain a payment of up to \$10,000.[99] In May 1994, EPA issued proposed regulations to implement this provision, including a mechanism to hide the identity of whistleblowers.[100] Disgruntled plant employees are expected to be a major source of reporting permit violations under this program.
- Regulated facilities will bear the cost of the enforcement program. In order to obtain authorization of its air permit program, each state must demonstrate that the fees it receives from applicants for operating permits will be sufficient to make the state's clean air enforcement system self-supporting.[101] By essentially earmarking permit revenues to support enforcement programs, Congress has assured that there will be significantly more resources devoted to enforcement, and that state legislatures cannot undermine the program by underfunding state agencies.

Problems With the Regulatory and Permit Systems

The difficulty of prosecutorial decisionmaking is compounded by the fact that significant questions of interpretation remain in important EPA rules. Especially for the early sets of implementing regulations, EPA fashioned its rules to include within the permit system as many discharge streams as possible, as quickly as possible. Working under tight congressional deadlines, basic structural decisions about the regulatory scheme were poorly understood, "fudged," or compromised.[102] Little, if any, thought was given to criminal enforcement at the time. While EPA's understanding and precision in drafting have improved substantially in recent years, many of these problematic early rules remain in effect, with little clarification or correction.

For example, there are several recognized gaps in the definition of what constitutes a "hazardous waste," the central provision of the entire RCRA regulatory scheme. In order to qualify as "hazardous," a waste must first be classified as a "solid waste." A "solid waste" is a "discarded" material that is not excluded from regulation.[103] Recycled materials can be deemed discarded if they are recycled (or if they are accumulated, stored, or treated before recycling) in certain ways, and not discarded if they are recycled in other ways.[104] Over the last 15 years, EPA has had great difficulty in defining when "recycled" material will not be deemed hazardous.[105]

Similarly, some hazardous wastes are defined in functional, rather than chemical, terms. A used solvent that is further used as a commercial chemical product in manufacturing is not classified as hazardous, even though a chemically identical waste stream from the same production line may be subject to the full panoply of hazardous waste controls.[106] For these reasons, the hazardous waste rules are particularly difficult to enforce, a problem EPA has recognized for many years but has been unable to repair completely.

EPA's regulatory system includes many ambiguous provisions, which lie at the heart of the civil, and therefore the criminal, enforcement system. Prosecutors who investigate cases based on a common sense reading of the rules may learn about these ambiguities well after the fact. Indeed, an emerging feature of environmental criminal cases is that as Justice tries to prosecute substantive violations under more complicated EPA rules, both prosecutors and the courts are required to undertake a lengthy statutory and regulatory exegesis to define what the "crime" is. In pre-indictment negotiations, arguing that the regulations are ambiguous often may be the only way to persuade Justice not to prosecute. Defense counsel almost never deflect prosecution with arguments that the company or the individual is a solid citizen who would not and has not done anything wrong. Rather, if Justice is to be persuaded not to prosecute, counsel must point to a legal deficiency in the government's case. Interpreting EPA rules is often a battle of the regulatory experts. In these analyses, the prosecutor has to live with prior EPA statements, in preambles and guidance documents, about the rules' meaning. These documents frequently contain ambiguities or admissions that may be fatal to Justice's chances of obtaining a conviction.

---

98. 40 C.F.R. §70.5(c)-(d).

99. 42 U.S.C. §7413(f), ELR Stat. CAA §113(f).

100. U.S. EPA, Regulations Governing Awards Under Section 113(f) of the Clean Air Act, 59 Fed. Reg. 22795 (May 3, 1994) (notice of proposed rule).

101. 42 U.S.C. §7661a(b)(3), ELR Stat. CAA §502(b)(3).

102. *See Writing the Resource Conversation and Recovery Act Regulations, in* Marc K. Landy, Marc J. Roberts, & Stephen R. Thomas, The Environmental Protection Agency: Asking the Wrong Questions 89 (1990).

103. 40 C.F.R. §261.2(a)(1).

104. *Id.* §261.2(c).

105. *See, e.g.,* United States v. Self, 2 F.3d 1071, 23 ELR 21301 (10th Cir. 1993).

106. *See* 50 Fed. Reg. 614, 624 n.8 (Jan. 4, 1985); United States v. Recticel Foam Corp., 858 F. Supp. 726, 730-35, 25 ELR 20093, 20094-97 (E.D. Tenn. 1993).

The Crime of Knowing Endangerment

Facilities that generate highly toxic substances are subject to enhanced charges if environmental violations result in "knowing endangerment" of workers or the community. This regulatory scheme is proving to have unexpected ambiguities that make its application more difficult than Congress expected.

As ordinary environmental crimes were upgraded to felonies, Congress created the new crime of knowing endangerment, with significantly heightened penalties, to deal with particularly offensive conduct that directly threatens human life. Knowing endangerment has been added to each of the major federal environmental statutes since 1980.[107] The constitutionality and feasibility of knowing endangerment prosecutions have been demonstrated in court.[108] Nonetheless, Justice has experienced difficulty in determining when to use this weapon and in actually obtaining convictions. Because of the turbocharged nature of the penalties involved—for example, up to 15 years' imprisonment and a $250,000 fine for an individual under RCRA—Justice has given careful policy consideration to invoking the knowing endangerment charge.[109]

The knowing endangerment provisions impose substantial criminal penalties on a person who knowingly violates an environmental standard, and who knows at the time of the violation that he or she thereby places another person in imminent danger of death or serious bodily injury. Proof only of a risk of harm, and not actual harm, is required for conviction. An affirmative defense is available that the conduct was consented to by the person endangered and was a reasonably foreseeable hazard of an occupation.

The knowledge element for the predicate environmental offense is a general intent requirement, which is satisfied by evidence that the discharger knew it was dealing with a material that could harm humans or the environment. The second knowledge element requires a showing of specific intent, which ordinarily requires proof that the defendant was aware that the substance could pose a severe health hazard to anyone who came into contact with it. Evidence on the second knowledge element also may be provided in substantial part by the prior permitting of the pollutant, efforts by the regulatory authority to apply its rules to the substance, or safety practices followed by the facility with respect to the material.[110]

The more toxic the discharger's effluent—such as dioxin from paper mills, arsenic from metal operations, vinyl chloride or other volatile organic compounds from other industries—the lower the requisite factual threshold to justify a charge of knowingly exposing others to death or serious health risks. Thus, categorical discharges to surface waters and unauthorized disposal of hazardous wastes are likely to be held to a more stringent standard than, for example, violations at sewage treatment plants and discharges of non-process wastewater. As the air toxics program is implemented,[111] sources of hazardous air emissions will also be increasingly vulnerable to knowing endangerment charges. In addition, for highly toxic compounds, courts are likely to construe more broadly the zone of persons placed in "imminent danger," and to be less receptive to the defense that a discharger was unaware of the risk of death or serious health effects.

The knowing endangerment provision thus effectively establishes a higher standard of care for discharges of highly toxic substances. While Congress may or may not have intended this result, dischargers within this category must be aware that the knowing endangerment provisions are targeted against them.

Knowing Endangerment Prosecutions

The first major conviction for knowing endangerment under RCRA was *United States v. Protex Industries, Inc.*[112] The case involved charges that a drum recycling plant maintained woefully inadequate safety provisions to protect employees from the dangers of toxic chemicals to which they were exposed as a result of the plant's RCRA violations. The evidence at trial included results of a 1984 EPA investigation that found elevated levels of metals in the ground; physical documentation of earlier spills; corroded, leaking, and improperly stacked drums; and evidence of illegal dumping. Samples taken at the site in 1985 showed that RCRA hazardous wastes were present. EPA special agents witnessed a Protex employee dumping the contents of a barrel on the ground, and an employee told a special agent that drums were emptied, their contents diluted and then flushed off the property. Government experts testified that two Protex employees were suffering from some reversible and irreversible health effects (psychoorganic syndromes).

Justice argued at trial that to show knowing endangerment, it had to prove only that defendants acted voluntarily, with knowledge of their actions, and with an awareness that they were dealing with something dangerous, as opposed to something harmless. Justice also contended that such knowledge could be shown by contacts with environmental agencies about similar problems in the past. Justice argued successfully that it could show culpable knowledge through deliberate avoidance, reckless disregard, or lack of due diligence; that the corporation's knowledge could be inferred from its organizational indifference to violations; and that circumstantial evidence could be used to show individual defendants' knowledge based on their responsible positions or on the particular regulatory scheme.

On appeal of their convictions, the court rejected defendants' claim that the knowing endangerment provision was unconstitutionally vague in that it did not require that bodily

107. The first knowing endangerment provision was added to RCRA in 1980. 42 U.S.C. §6928(e), ELR Stat. RCRA §3008(e). In 1984, Congress relaxed several of the elements originally required for conviction because the original formula proved unworkable. *See* United States v. Greer, No. 85-105-Cr-Orl-18 (M.D. Fla. 1986), *judgments of acquittal on two counts rev'd*, 850 F.2d 1447, 18 ELR 21387 (11th Cir. 1988). Similar provisions were added to the FWPCA in 1987, 33 U.S.C. §1319(c)(3), ELR Stat. FWPCA §309(c)(3), and the CAA in 1990, 42 U.S.C. §7413(c)(5), ELR Stat. CAA §113(c)(5).

108. *See, e.g.*, United States v. Protex Indus., Inc., 874 F.2d 740, 19 ELR 21061 (10th Cir. 1989).

109. Knowing endangerment was one of the 10 priority areas reserved for prosecution by Washington in Justice's 1993 Bluesheet Revision, *supra* note 43. This suggests that knowing endangerment charges present sensitive policy issues.

110. *See* United States v. Rutana, 932 F.2d 1155, 21 ELR 21241 (6th Cir.), *cert. denied*, 112 S. Ct. 300 (1991). The knowing endangerment charges were later dismissed pursuant to a plea bargain.

111. *See* 42 U.S.C. §7412, ELR Stat. CAA §112.

112. 874 F.2d 740, 19 ELR 21061 (10th Cir. 1989)

injury be manifested immediately. The court concluded that evidence that the two employees had an increased risk of contracting cancer at some point in the future was sufficient to show that they had suffered serious bodily injury within the meaning of the statute.[113] Finally, the court specifically approved a jury instruction that defined "imminent danger" as "the existence of a condition or combination of conditions which could reasonably be expected to cause death or serious bodily injury unless the condition is remedied."[114]

Since *Protex*, Justice has experienced surprising resistance by courts and juries to returning convictions in knowing endangerment cases. For example, in *United States v. Borowski*,[115] a knowing endangerment conviction under the FWPCA was overturned on causation grounds, despite clear evidence that employees were put at risk by their company's violations of the Act and that the company president personally knew of this danger. The employees were placed in imminent danger of serious bodily injury when they illegally dumped chemical solutions into sinks that led to a treatment works, in violation of pretreatment standards. The court of appeals, however, read literally the statutory requirement that a defendant must know at the time of the violation that he *thereby* places another person in imminent danger.[116] The court reasoned that the danger to employees would have been identical if they had lawfully poured the chemicals into drums, or if the sinks had not led to a regulated treatment works. Accordingly, the court concluded that the violations were not properly linked by causation to the kind of endangerment for which Congress intended to impose criminal penalties. Rather, the court suggested that such charges should have been brought under RCRA or the Occupational Safety and Health Act (OSH Act).[117]

Similarly, in *United States v. Villegas*,[118] a district court acquitted an FWPCA defendant post-trial on knowing endangerment charges, despite the jury's verdict of guilty. The defendant had disposed of vials of blood, some of which contained hepatitis, from his medical testing laboratory by placing them in the Hudson River. Some of the vials later washed ashore and were traced to the laboratory. At trial, the government showed that the defendant knew the dangers of hepatitis and that some of the vials of blood he placed in the Hudson River were hepatitis-infected. The district court nevertheless ruled that the evidence did "not support the conclusion that when he placed the vials in the Hudson River, [the defendant] knew there was a high probability that he was thereby placing another person in imminent danger of death or serious bodily injury."[119] Rather, the evidence showed that the principal risk of hepatitis infection as a result of exposure to a vial of contaminated blood would arise if a vial were to break and a piece of glass were to penetrate the skin. An expert witness presented by the government testified that the risk of such an occurrence was "very low." Because there was no evidence showing that the defendant knew of this infection pathway when he dumped the vials into the river, or that he knew people would walk where they were hidden, the court overturned the jury's verdict.

These decisions suggest that Justice needs to exercise great care in setting potential knowing endangerment cases for prosecution.

State Criminal Enforcement

Under the dual sovereignty doctrine, both the federal and state governments may independently prosecute a person for environmental crimes without violating the Double Jeopardy or Due Process Clauses of the U.S. Constitution.[120] Counsel representing a facility in an environmental investigation must therefore be aware of the activities of state criminal enforcement personnel, and their potential for competition or cooperation with federal prosecutors. The role of state agencies is likely to expand in the future, as local prosecutors increase their expertise and federal resources are squeezed. The prosecutor's identity can be a crucial factor in determining whether a criminal charge is filed, because local officials are more likely to be responsive to local publicity and community expressions of concern.

State Program Examples

Many states have developed effective environmental criminal enforcement programs.[121] States are generally required to demonstrate the existence of criminal enforcement capacity in order to obtain EPA authorization to administer the RCRA, FWPCA, or CAA program locally. Until recent years, however, some of these programs had more nominal than actual capabilities. The high visibility and potential political attractiveness of some environmental cases, especially in the hazardous waste area, have led many state attorneys general and local prosecutors to give environmental cases a far higher priority than a decade ago.

Both state and local prosecutors now actively prosecute environmental crimes. New Jersey, Pennsylvania, and Ohio have long maintained criminal enforcement programs that are both well-organized and effective. For example, New Jersey has 35 criminal investigators devoted solely to environmental enforcement.[122] At the local level, Los Angeles County maintains its own interagency Environmental Crimes Strike Force with eight full-time investigators.[123]

Two of the most effective state programs are in California and Ohio. California's Environmental Protection Agency (Cal/EPA), created in 1991, has developed an integrated environmental enforcement program to coordinate the pre-

113. *Id.* at 743, 19 ELR at 21062.

114. *Id.* at 744, 19 ELR at 21062-63.

115. 977 F.2d 27, 23 ELR 20102 (1st Cir. 1992).

116. *Id.* at 30, 23 ELR at 20103.

117. *Id.* at 31, 23 ELR at 20103-04.

118. 784 F. Supp. 6, 22 ELR 21027 (E.D.N.Y. 1991), *conviction on other counts rev'd sub nom.* Plaza Health Labs., Inc. v. United States, 3 F.3d 643, 23 ELR 21526 (2d Cir. 1993), *cert. denied sub nom.* United States v. Villegas, 114 S. Ct. 2764 (1994).

119. 784 F. Supp. at 13, 22 ELR at 21031.

120. *See* Petite v. United States, 361 U.S. 529 (1960); *see also* DEPARTMENT OF JUSTICE MANUAL §9.2-142 (setting forth procedures for bringing prosecutions under the dual sovereignty doctrine).

121. New Jersey, Maryland, Ohio, New York, California, and Arizona have long had sophisticated environmental crimes programs. In recent years, EPA has spent considerable money and time training law enforcement authorities from almost every state at the Agency's training facility at the Federal Law Enforcement Training Center in Glynco, Georgia.

122. Block, *supra* note 26, at 35.

123. THEODORE M. HAMMETT & JOEL EPSTEIN, PROSECUTING ENVIRONMENTAL CRIME: LOS ANGELES COUNTY, NATIONAL INSTITUTE OF JUSTICE 10 (Aug. 1993). In 1990 alone, the program led to criminal charges against 107 defendants, of whom 75 percent were convicted. *Id.* at 20.

viously disjointed activities of many state and local agencies.[124] In particular, it attempts simultaneously to detect, investigate, and remediate all violations occurring at a facility. This integrated program is similar to a statewide "strike force" approach to enforcement. Cal/EPA pulls together administrative, civil, and criminal enforcement capability in all media. It gives special consideration to criminal prosecution in cases of intentional or reckless conduct, or actions that constitute serious threats to human health.

Cal/EPA has developed a centralized data management system to support its coordinated activities. A special Manifest Enforcement Unit targets significant or repeat violators. Further, the state agency promotes uniform enforcement by allocating resources to areas where local agencies are unable or unwilling to deal with significant violators. A number of specific illegal activities have been targeted, including mishandling of pesticides, failure to report leaking underground storage tanks, falsification of environmental documents, and illegal discharges that occur on federal facilities. Finally, Cal/EPA has concentrated resources in critical geographic areas, with special attention to the U.S.-Mexican border.

In Ohio, the enforcement effort has gradually shifted its target from midnight dumpers of hazardous waste to established businesses seeking to obtain a competitive advantage by keeping their disposal costs down. The program targets falsification of documents that sources are required to submit to the Ohio EPA. In addition, it seeks to identify and prosecute companies that intend to keep operating and that systematically violate environmental rules in search of greater profits. Such companies may simply regard civil penalties as a cost of doing business, and can be brought into compliance only through the individual deterrent effects of a criminal prosecution.[125]

Because of the increasing importance of state and local enforcement programs, in August 1994 Attorney General Reno directed all federal prosecutors to cooperate closely with their counterparts at other levels of government in reaching prosecutorial decisions on cases of common interest.[126]

State Authorization to Enforce Federal Laws

The three major federal environmental laws—RCRA, the FWPCA, and the CAA—provide that EPA may authorize a state to administer and enforce the federal regulatory program within its borders, upon EPA's determination that the state has a program in place that is the functional equivalent of the EPA program.[127]

Under all three statutes, the state assumes primacy upon authorization for implementing and enforcing the federal regulatory program, including such matters as permit issuance, receipt of monitoring reports, and civil enforcement. Each law also provides, however, that the federal government retains full, independent enforcement authority.[128] This provision is of crucial significance because it allows federal prosecutors to bring criminal cases if a state cannot or will not bring the case. In some instances, local prosecutors may refuse to proceed due to concern about the effects on a large local employer. In other situations, local politics—colloquially, the "good old boy network"—may lead state officials to derail efforts to remediate an important environmental violation. In such cases, federal enforcement—including criminal prosecution if warranted—may be the only method of breaking the local political impasse and responding to public complaints. Federal intervention is particularly dangerous for the offending facility, because state personnel whose earlier enforcement efforts were thwarted often have both the motivation and the information to assist federal prosecutors. Indeed, the history of fruitless, prior state efforts may be sufficient to prove the knowledge element under the federal statute at issue.

It is important to understand that federal environmental standards do not preempt state laws that contain "more stringent" or "broader" provisions than the federal counterpart. A more stringent state provision is deemed part of the approved federal program and may be enforced by Justice in a federal criminal prosecution. Federal prosecutors may not, however, enforce a broader state provision that lacks a counterpart in the federal program. Only the state may enforce that unique provision independently in a state criminal prosecution.[129]

EPA first issued implementing guidance on the limitations on federal enforcement authority in March 1982.[130] But EPA and the states continued to have difficulty determining which state rules should be deemed broader than the federal program. As a result, in May 1984, EPA issued further guidance, which established a two-part test for determining whether a state rule is broader in scope than the federal program, and therefore unenforceable at the federal level: (1) whether the state rule "increase[s] the size of the regulated community beyond that of the [f]ederal program"; and, if not, (2) whether the state requirement has "a direct counterpart in the [f]ederal regulatory program."[131]

Although originally drafted in the context of RCRA, EPA

---

124. James M. Strock & William W. Carter, *Cal/EPA's Integrated Enforcement Programs: State, Federal and Local Coordination*, *in* A.L.I.-A.B.A. Course of Study, Criminal Enforcement of Environmental Laws 53 (1993).

125. Lee Fisher, *Enforcement Trends and Developments in Ohio*, *in* A.B.A., Section on Natural Resources, Energy, and Environmental Law, 1993: The Year in Review 147-49.

126. 1994 Bluesheet Revision, *supra* note 44, at 6 (amending Department of Justice Manual §5-11.113).

127. 42 U.S.C. §6926, ELR Stat. RCRA §3006; 33 U.S.C. §1342(b), ELR Stat. FWPCA §402(b); 42 U.S.C. §7661a, ELR Stat. CAA §502. There are compelling policy rationales for devolving such authority, whenever possible. State regulators are closer to the regulated firms and may be better able to fine tune the application of rules to reduce compliance costs without compromising the level of environmental protection. And environmental restrictions may be more acceptable politically if imposed locally rather than by Washington.

128. 42 U.S.C. §6928(a)(2), ELR Stat. RCRA §3008(a)(2); 33 U.S.C. §1319(a)(3), ELR Stat. FWPCA §309(a)(3); 42 U.S.C. §7413(a)(3), ELR Stat. CAA §113(a)(3); *see also* Wyckoff Co. v. U.S. Environmental Protection Agency, 769 F.2d 1197, 16 ELR 20866 (9th Cir. 1986); United States v. Environmental Waste Control, Inc., 710 F. Supp. 1172, 20 ELR 20035 (N.D. Ind. 1989).

129. *See* 42 U.S.C. §6929, ELR Stat. RCRA §3009; 40 C.F.R. §271.1(i); United States v. Recticel Foam Corp., 858 F. Supp. 726, 740-43, 25 ELR 20093, 20100-01 (E.D. Tenn. 1993).

130. Memorandum from William A. Sullivan Jr., Enforcement Counsel, to Regional Administrators and Regional Counsels, EPA Enforcement of RCRA-Authorized State Hazardous Waste Laws and Regulations (Mar. 15, 1982) (available from the ELR Document Service, ELR Order No. AD-1203).

131. Memorandum from Lee M. Thomas, Assistant Administrator for Solid Waste and Emergency Response, to PIGs Addressees, Determining Whether State Hazardous Waste Management Requirements Are Broader in Scope or More Stringent Than the Federal Program 2 (May 21, 1984) (reproduced in Appendix A of this book).

now applies these memoranda to resolve the same issues under the FWPCA and the CAA.

The importance of state authorization will increase substantially with the implementation of the CAA's operating permit program. Section 502(b)(3) provides that in order to obtain authorization, the state permit program must provide for the assessment of user fees sufficient to finance an effective state air program, including its enforcement components.[132] Delegation of implementation authority is of compelling concern to the states, and EPA's proposed rule defining the CAA permit issuance process has been among its most controversial regulatory actions in many years.[133]

Legal Issues Created by the Cooperative Federalism Structure

Although the federal/state relationship has worked well, legal issues have arisen in anomalous cases in which the two programs have not meshed perfectly. The two most notable examples, which have arisen particularly in the context of RCRA, are: (1) when the underlying federal rule is invalidated; and (2) when there are enforcement gaps in the state authorization process.

☐ *When the Federal Rule Is Invalidated.* Experience in the aftermath of the demise of EPA's mixture rule under RCRA demonstrates how both pending federal and state criminal prosecutions based on a defective EPA rule may fail automatically.

The mixture rule is one of three pathways through which solid waste may become classified as hazardous waste under RCRA. Under EPA's 1980 RCRA implementing rules, a solid waste could be defined as hazardous if it were "listed";[134] if it exhibited at least one of the characteristics of ignitability, corrosivity, reactivity, or toxicity;[135] or, under the mixture rule, if it constituted a post-use mixture of a listed hazardous waste and another solid waste.[136]

From the beginning of the environmental crimes program, Justice has relied heavily on the mixture rule in RCRA prosecutions. The "listing" branch of the definition applies only to a relatively few, unmixed waste streams. And in order to demonstrate that the characteristic tests are satisfied, the government must take samples and conduct analyses of individual wastes on a case-by-case basis, which can be both expensive and subject to scientific challenge. On the other hand, the mixture rule is relatively easy and inexpensive to implement. Justice need only prove that a measurable quantity of a chemical was found in a mixed waste stream. If the government can prove that the source of that chemical was a listed hazardous waste, then the entire mixture is regarded as a hazardous waste. Reliance on the mixture rule thus eliminates the burdens involved in proving that the waste exhibits a hazardous characteristic.

In December 1991, the D.C. Circuit held in *Shell Oil Co. v. U.S. Environmental Protection Agency*[137] that the mixture rule was void from the date of its promulgation in 1980, because of procedural defects in its issuance. The Eighth Circuit subsequently held in *United States v. Goodner Bros. Aircraft, Inc.*, that the *Shell Oil* decision is fully retroactive in criminal cases, and that it bars prosecution for charges based on the mixture rule.[138]

After *Shell Oil* and *Goodner Bros.*, Justice and EPA attempted to salvage mixture rule prosecutions by generating novel arguments that the rule was somehow redundant of other RCRA provisions, and that its demise did not upset the basis for criminal or civil enforcement actions. These arguments were consistently rejected.[139]

Justice and EPA also attempted to shift the basis for pending prosecutions from the invalidated federal mixture rule to the counterpart state version. A state mixture rule was a mandatory element in every state that had been authorized to administer its own RCRA program. Reviewing courts found that in the absence of a federal mixture rule, the state mixture rule (even if still valid) would be broader than the federal law in effect at the time the conduct in question occurred. Applying EPA's own regulations and guidance documents, a district court held that the federal government may not lawfully enforce state rules that were broader than existing federal standards.[140]

☐ *Enforcement Gaps in the RCRA State Authorization Process.* RCRA provides that the grant of authorization to a state means that its program operates "in lieu of" the federal program.[141] As originally conceived, implementation of the state authorization process would not have been difficult. The state would submit an application describing the statutes and rules it had adopted, modeled on the federal provisions. EPA would analyze the state enactments and grant approval to state programs that were the functional equivalent of the federal counterpart. This approach might have worked effectively in a static world, where EPA adopted all RCRA rules at one time and updated them infrequently. In practice, however, the state authorization process worked poorly because EPA constantly adopted new rules that increased the scope of the RCRA program. States were aiming at a moving target,

132. 42 U.S.C. §7661a(b)(3), ELR Stat. CAA §502(b)(3).

133. *See* U.S. EPA, Federal Operating Permits Program, 60 Fed. Reg. 20804 (Apr. 27, 1995) (proposed rule; notice of opportunity for public hearing).

134. 40 C.F.R. §261.3(a)(2)(ii).

135. *Id.* §261.3(a)(2)(i).

136. *Id.* §261.3(a)(2)(iii).

137. 950 F.2d 741, 22 ELR 20305 (D.C. Cir. 1991, *amended* 1992).

138. 966 F.2d 380, 22 ELR 21201 (8th Cir. 1992), *cert. denied*, 113 S. Ct. 967 (1993). EPA repromulgated the mixture rule in March 1992. 57 Fed. Reg. 7628 (Mar. 3, 1992). The new rule thus applies to all waste streams disposed of after its effective date. But for wastes disposed of before March 1992, the rule is not a viable basis for prosecution.

139. *See* United States v. Recticel Foam Corp., 858 F. Supp. 726, 735-40, 25 ELR 20093, 20097-100 (criminal case); United States v. Bethlehem Steel Corp., 38 F.3d 862, 24 ELR 21499 (7th Cir. 1994) (civil enforcement).

140. *Recticel Foam Corp.*, 858 F. Supp. at 740-43, 25 ELR at 20100-01; *see also* In re Hardin County, Ohio, 1994 RCRA LEXIS 6, RCRA (3008) Appeal No. 93-1, ELR Admin. Mat. II 40313 (EPA EAB Apr. 12, 1994). Once it was established that federal enforcement was precluded, environmental prosecutors made a last-ditch effort to determine whether the state mixture rule could be enforced in an independent state prosecution. Analysis of the situation, however, revealed the possibility of unexpected state administrative law problems involving the process of adopting the state versions of federal rules that may preclude state prosecutions. *See* Equidae Partners v. Oklahoma State Dep't of Health, No. C-91-532 (D. Ct. Wash. County, Okla. Jan. 16, 1992) (state mixture rule falls with federal rule); New York State Coalition of Pub. Employers v. New York Dep't of Labor, 457 N.E.2d 785 (1983) (mere incorporation of federal rules into state rules is invalid).

141. 42 U.S.C. §6926(b), ELR Stat. RCRA §3006(b).

and could not update their proposed programs fast enough to keep up with EPA's frequent changes. As a result, the rate at which EPA could grant authorization to individual states lagged far behind schedule.

Congress attempted to solve this problem in the 1984 HSWA.[142] Congress amended RCRA §3006(b) to allow EPA to approve a state program that was the functional equivalent of the EPA program in place one year before submission of the state's application.[143] In addition to this one-year grace period, Congress enacted a new §3006(g)(1), which provided that any requirement imposed pursuant to HSWA shall take effect in each authorized state on the "same date as such requirement takes effect in other states."[144] In other words, any new EPA rule based on HSWA provisions would take effect in each authorized state on the effective date of the new EPA rule. In the interim, until an authorized state affirmatively adopts a new HSWA-based requirement, EPA enforces that provision directly.[145]

However, these two amended provisions have the unintended synergistic effect of creating the potential for an enforcement gap in authorized states regarding new rules that were: (1) issued after a state obtained final program approval; and (2) based on RCRA provisions that were in existence before passage of HSWA. As EPA has repeatedly conceded, new RCRA-based rules do not become effective in a previously authorized state until that state updates its program, submits an application for approval of that specific program element, and receives formal approval from EPA.[146] Consequently, until EPA grants separate approval for the update, the new rule is not federally enforceable in an authorized state, even though the EPA rule is fully effective in nonauthorized states.[147] This result occurs because the authorized state program continues to operate in lieu of the EPA program, but the state program does not yet contain the new rule.[148]

Thus, for rules based on RCRA (pre-HSWA) provisions, there is a risk that the intended grace period may become an inadvertent enforcement gap, in which no level of government can enforce a validly promulgated federal rule.[149] To avoid such gaps, EPA must be diligent in requiring states to update their programs in a timely fashion to incorporate new EPA rules. Congress gave EPA the authority to prevent such gaps by adding §3006(e), which empowers the Agency to withdraw its authorization for states that fail to submit program updates promptly.[150] But ensuring that authorized states updated their programs was a low priority at EPA during the 1980s. States routinely fell several years behind in applying and receiving EPA authorization for new RCRA program elements. EPA never revoked a final program approval for a state for delay in seeking approval for new RCRA elements. Under these circumstances, substantial enforcement gaps opened.

Where a gap exists, it gives the polluter a threshold legal defense to any prosecution based on the federal rule. Neither Justice nor the state had the authority to enforce the new RCRA-based rule under federal law, even though it was effective in nonauthorized states and in other authorized states that had updated their programs. In terms of federal enforcement, the gaps closed only when the state applied for and received program approval for that separate rule. The pattern is a crazy quilt, without rhyme or reason. The same rule may be federally enforceable in California during one year, but not in Texas, simply because it took the Texas legislature longer to adopt implementing legislation or because the state agency was slow in adopting its rules and applying for approval.

The enforcement gap problem is a potential obstacle that government prosecutors must look for before proceeding with criminal charges based on RCRA rules authorized by portions of the statute that were not added by HSWA in 1984.

The Knowledge Element in Environmental Crimes

Background

The "existence of a *mens rea* is the rule of, rather than the exception to, the principles of Anglo-American criminal jurisprudence."[151] The critical feature that distinguishes environmental crimes from other white-collar criminal offenses is the minimal proof of knowledge required, especially in light of the complexity and technical nature of the underlying violations. The major federal environmental statutes require proof that the defendant "knowingly" violated the law. The government need not prove premeditation or intent to violate the law. Rather, courts have interpreted these provisions to require only a showing of general intent for conviction. This minimal knowledge element has blurred the distinction between civil and criminal cases to the point that virtually every environmental violation is theoretically subject to criminal prosecution.

Using the "public welfare offense" doctrine,[152] courts

142. Pub. L. No. 98-616, 98 Stat. 3254 (1984).

143. 42 U.S.C. §6926(b), ELR STAT. RCRA §3006(b); 40 C.F.R. §271.21(e)(2).

144. 42 U.S.C. §6926(g)(1), ELR STAT. RCRA §3006(g)(1).

145. *See* Adam Babich, *Is RCRA Enforceable by Citizen Suit in States With Authorized Hazardous Waste Programs?*, 23 ELR 10536, 10538 (Sept. 1993). Babich correctly observes that "[i]f Congress had tried, it could hardly have made its 1984 amendments to RCRA's cooperative federalism scheme more confusing." *Id.*

146. For example, in adopting used oil management standards in September 1992, EPA stated:

> Today's rules . . . are promulgated under section 3014(a) for RCRA, *a provision that predates the 1984 amendments*. The rules will take effect in states that do not have final authorization six months from the date that this rule is published in the *Federal Register*. In authorized states, the rules will not be applicable *until a State revises its program to adopt equivalent requirements under State law*.

57 Fed. Reg. 41566, 41605 (Sept. 10, 1992) (emphasis added).

147. States, of course, may enforce their own laws and regulations without waiting for EPA approval. 42 U.S.C. §6929, ELR STAT. RCRA §3009.

148. By contrast, for rules based on the provisions added by HSWA, no enforcement gap can open. For HSWA-based regulations, the RCRA enforcement program operates much like the FWPCA and CAA state authorization programs. The federal rule is effective in all 50 states from its stated effective date. Thus, at least one jurisdiction—either the state or federal government—will always have authority to enforce the EPA rule at any given time.

149. As Babich notes, "the existence of a grace period (during which a regulatory change may go unimplemented) . . . depends not on when EPA promulgates the change but, instead, on when Congress amended RCRA to provide authority for it." Babich, *supra* note 145.

150. 42 U.S.C. §6926(e), ELR STAT. RCRA §3006(e).

151. United States v. U.S. Gypsum Co., 438 U.S. 422, 436 (1978).

152. *See* United States v. International Minerals & Chem. Corp., 402 U.S. 558 (1971). The public welfare offense doctrine is discussed in more detail *infra*.

have interpreted the term "knowingly" to require only general awareness that the defendant was dealing with a substance likely to be regulated and knowledge that a discharge was occurring. This standard will almost always be met by facilities that have obtained a discharge permit for their operations. Thus, environmental case law has been characterized as imposing a species of strict liability.[153]

As environmental felony prosecutions expand to include technical regulatory violations, substantial reconsideration is being given to whether the minimal intent element is appropriate, especially for charges of violating the terms of a permit.[154] The legal issue is whether the bare fact that an industrial process is subject to regulation provides sufficient notice to an operator of a particular action's illegality, when the substantive standards are frequently complicated and arcane. The policy concern is that courts have applied the lower knowledge standard in a manner that may ironically impose a de facto strict liability standard on companies that have made the greatest efforts to comply with their environmental obligations.

While reading the knowledge element expansively, courts have not expanded liability indiscriminately, however. In particular, courts have given cool reception to the government's argument that criminal liability might attach to senior corporate officials based solely on their positions in the company, without proof of their actual knowledge of, or involvement in, the illegal acts. Further, concerns about the appropriateness of criminal punishment, which might otherwise have found expression through a narrow reading of the knowledge element, are being articulated instead through strict judicial interpretations of the substantive elements of offenses.

Environmental Crimes as General Intent Offenses

All federal environmental laws except the Refuse Act prohibit "knowing" violations of their provisions, without further defining that term.[155] Consequently, courts have had to give the term meaning on a case-by-case basis. In the process, they have reduced the knowledge element to a minimum in the environmental area under the judicially created public welfare offense doctrine.

The Public Welfare Offense Doctrine

The public welfare offense doctrine applies when the substance involved is so inherently dangerous that the defendant's knowledge of legal issues can be presumed. The doctrine originated with substances such as drugs and munitions,[156] and was first extended to the environmental area in *United States v. International Minerals & Chemical Corp.*[157]

International Minerals involved a prosecution for knowing violation of an Interstate Commerce Commission rule that required a shipper to disclose the presence of hazardous chemicals on a container's label. The U.S. Supreme Court upheld the validity of a criminal information that failed to allege that the defendant had actual knowledge of the rule it allegedly violated. The Court stated that when "dangerous or deleterious devices or products or obnoxious waste materials are involved, the probability of regulation is so great that anyone who is aware that he is in possession of them . . . must be presumed to be aware of the regulation."[158]

The Court recognized two possible defenses under the public welfare offense doctrine. First, a factual defense is available if a "person think[s] in good faith that he was shipping distilled water when in fact he was shipping some dangerous acid . . . ."[159] Second, the Court recognized that products that are not obviously dangerous, such as "[p]encils, dental floss, [and] paper clips may also be regulated," and that "substantial due process questions" might be raised if the statute did not require that mens rea be present as to each ingredient of the offense for such materials.[160] But the Court concluded that the corrosive liquids involved in the information—sulfuric acid—were obviously dangerous. Therefore, the potential due process limiting principle was not implicated in *International Minerals*.

At this time, the public welfare offense doctrine is limited only by the Due Process Clause's requirement that the statute give the regulated entity due notice that an act has been made criminal.[161] To date, this concern has been more theoretical than real, as no environmental conviction has ever been overturned on this basis.[162]

The Knowledge Requirement in Nonenvironmental Cases

To understand the significance of applying the public welfare offense doctrine in environmental cases, it is important to contrast how courts have interpreted the knowledge requirement in nonenvironmental cases.

---

153. As Justice Thomas pointed out in *Staples v. United States*, use of the term strict liability is technically a misnomer. 114 S. Ct. 1793, 1798 n.3 (1994). Although courts have eliminated the requirement of mens rea, they do require that the defendant know that he or she is dealing with a "dangerous or deleterious substance." *Id.*

154. *See, e.g.*, Richard Lazarus, *A New Fault Line*—Mens Rea, ENVTL. F., May/June 1995, at 9.

155. The legislative history of environmental statutes rarely contains guidance as to what "knowingly" violates means. *See* United States v. Weitzenhoff, 35 F.3d 1275, 1283-84, 24 ELR 21504, 21506 (9th Cir. 1994), *cert. denied sub nom.* Mariani v. United States, 115 S. Ct. 939 (1995); *id.* 35 F.3d at 1295-96, 24 ELR at 21513-14 (Kleinfeld, J., dissenting). The exception is the Ocean Dumping Act, 33 U.S.C. §1411(a), for which the Senate Report provides that the term "refers to a conscious act or conscious omission . . . which amounts to a violation of law, regulation or permit." S. REP. No. 451, 92d Cong., 1st Sess. (1971), *reprinted in* 1972 U.S.C.C.A.N. 4234, 4249. On this basis, courts have held that the Ocean Dumping Act requires mere consciousness of the action, and not proof that the defendant had knowledge of the relevant statutory provision. United States v. Reilly, 827 F. Supp. 1076, 1078, 24 ELR 20097, 20098 (D. Del. 1993), *aff'd*, 33 F.3d 1396 (3d Cir. 1994).

156. *E.g.*, United States v. Freed, 401 U.S. 601 (1971) (possession of unregistered grenade); United States v. Balint, 258 U.S. 250 (1922) (possession of narcotics).

157. 402 U.S. 558 (1971).

158. *Id.* at 565.

159. *Id.* at 563-64.

160. *Id.* at 564.

161. *See* Kolender v. Lawson, 461 U.S. 352, 357 (1983); Jordan v. DeGeorge, 341 U.S. 223, 230 (1951); *International Minerals*, 402 U.S. at 558.

162. The knowledge issue has proved particularly difficult to resolve in cases that involve discharges from facilities possessing the requisite permits, when an individual may believe in good faith that he or she is acting in accordance with the provisions of those complex, technical documents. In such cases, the constitutional limit on the public welfare offense doctrine recognized in *International Minerals* may be implicated.

Under the doctrine of *Liparota v. United States*,[163] regulatory crimes outside the environmental area require proof of actual knowledge of illegality. *Liparota* concerned the mental element of the crime of knowingly possessing food stamps without authorization. The question before the Supreme Court was whether Congress intended to dispense with proof that the defendant knew that his possession was unauthorized. The Court recognized that defining the elements of a criminal offense is reserved to Congress. Absent evidence of contrary congressional intent in the statute's language or legislative history, the normal default setting for the knowledge element in criminal cases—as well as the rule of lenity—requires a showing that the defendant knew that his possession was unauthorized.[164] Because the statute in *Liparota* was silent, the Court held that proof of mens rea was required—especially because a rule that did not require knowledge of illegality would criminalize a broad range of apparently innocent conduct.[165]

In overturning the conviction, the Court rejected the government's argument for extending the public welfare offense doctrine to this crime. It noted that "[i]n most previous instances, Congress has rendered criminal a type of conduct that a reasonable person should know is subject to stringent public regulation and may seriously threaten the community's health or safety."[166] The Court concluded, however, that food stamps "can hardly be compared" to a hand grenade or drugs, materials to which the public welfare offense doctrine properly may apply.[167]

The reasoning in *Liparota* is unsatisfactory for two reasons. First, as a jurisprudential matter, the Court provided no justification for why—absent proof of congressional intent to apply a diminished knowledge requirement under a particular statute—federal courts should pick and choose among different criminal statutes with the same standing and change the default setting for the mens rea element, based on their subjective judgments that certain crimes should be placed in different categories. Second, the Court did not provide meaningful guidance as to how the lower courts should go about determining which crimes justify changing the default setting. For example, the FWPCA prohibits the unpermitted discharge of "pollutants" that range from known carcinogens to heat or sand.[168] The presumption of knowledge of regulation may fairly apply to many, but not necessarily all, of the covered substances. Under *Liparota*, however, the default setting may be changed as to all if *some* of the materials would provide actual notice of likely regulation.

In 1994, the Supreme Court decided four cases that defined the mens rea requirement of nonenvironmental statutes.[169] In each instance the Court imposed a heavier burden of proof on the knowledge element than the government believed was appropriate. In particular, the Court expressed a strong reluctance to dispense with a mens rea requirement for felony statutes, absent explicit congressional directions.[170] The Court observed, however, that notwithstanding the limits it had imposed, the public welfare offense doctrine remains viable and may be applied to "dangerous and deleterious devices that will be assumed to alert an individual that he stands in 'responsible relation to a public danger.'"[171]

Significant Decisions Construing the Knowledge Element

In assessing the adequacy of proof of the mental element of environmental crimes, courts have focused on whether the defendant must know: (a) that the conduct will violate the applicable law or regulation; (b) that the activity requires a permit; (c) of the underlying material facts; or (d) that the conduct will violate the terms and conditions of a permit. In order to sustain a criminal conviction, courts have required—with minor exceptions—proof only that the defendant was aware of his or her own activities.

Knowledge of the Law or Regulations

This issue has been litigated most frequently. It is well-established that the defendant need not have actual knowledge of the requirements of the statute or EPA implementing regulations in order to satisfy the "knowingly" element.

- *United States v. Frezzo Bros.*[172] The district court held, and the Third Circuit affirmed, that proof of specific intent is not required in order to sustain a conviction under FWPCA §§301 and 309(c) for willfully or negligently dumping pollutants into navigable waters without a permit.
- *United States v. Hayes International Corp.*[173] The defendants were convicted of illegally transporting hazardous waste in violation of RCRA §3008(d)(1).[174] Rejecting the proposed affirmative defense that the defendants misunderstood RCRA's implementing regulations, the court held that the knowledge element did not require proof that the defendants knew that the wastes were classified as hazardous under the regulations.[175] The court found, however, that the defendants must have knowledge of the permit status of the facility to which the waste was transported, and that the government proved sufficient knowledge by circumstantial evidence.[176]
- *United States v. Hoflin.*[177] The court held that interpreting RCRA §3008(d)(2)(A)'s knowledge requirement as a general intent provision was consistent with the express language of the statute. The prosecution could prove that the waste disposed of was hazardous by showing that the

163. 471 U.S. 419 (1985).
164. *Liparota*, 471 U.S. at 424-28.
165. *Id.* at 426.
166. *Id.* at 433.
167. *Id.*
168. 33 U.S.C. §1362(6), ELR STAT. FWPCA §502(6).
169. Ratzlaf v. United States, 114 S. Ct. 655 (1994); Posters 'N' Things Ltd. v. United States, 114 S. Ct. 1793 (1994); Staples v. United States, 114 S. Ct. 1793 (1994); United States v. X-Citement Video, Inc., 115 S. Ct. 464 (1994).
170. *Staples*, 114 S. Ct. at 1804.
171. *Id.* at 1801 n.6.
172. 546 F. Supp. 713, 12 ELR 21133 (E.D. Pa. 1982), *aff'd*, 703 F.2d 62, 13 ELR 20584 (3d Cir. 1983), *cert. denied*, 464 U.S. 829 (1983).
173. 786 F.2d 1499, 16 ELR 20717 (11th Cir. 1986).
174. 42 U.S.C. §6928(d)(1), ELR STAT. RCRA §3008(d)(1).
175. *Hayes International*, 786 F.2d at 1502-03, 16 ELR at 20718-19.
176. *Id.* at 1503-04, 16 ELR at 20719. *Compare* United States v. MacDonald & Watson Waste Oil Co., 933 F.2d 35, 21 ELR 21449 (1st Cir. 1991) (upholding convictions because the evidence supported the inference that the defendants knew that the waste was regulated under RCRA).
177. 880 F.2d 1033, 19 ELR 21140 (9th Cir. 1989), *cert. denied*, 493 U.S. 1083 (1990).

material "had the potential to be harmful to others or to the environment," and was not required to prove that the defendant knew the wastes were classified as hazardous under the regulations.[178]

• *United States v. Dee.*[179] The court upheld the defendants' convictions under RCRA §3008(d) for unpermitted disposal of hazardous waste, holding that a "knowing" violation of RCRA did not require a showing of specific intent to violate the law or that the defendants knew that the implementing regulations defined the material as hazardous waste.[180]

• *United States v. Buckley.*[181] In order to sustain a conviction for failure to notify authorities of an asbestos release under §103(b)(3) of the Comprehensive Environmental Response, Compensation, and Liability Act (CERCLA),[182] the government need only prove that the defendant knew of the release of more than one pound of asbestos. It need not prove that the defendant knew of the notification requirement or that asbestos was one of the substances whose release had to be reported.[183] Similarly, to justify a conviction under CAA §§112(c)(1)(B) and 113(c)(1)(C),[184] the government need only prove the defendant's knowledge of the asbestos emissions themselves, and not that the defendant knew that the emissions were illegal or that they presented hazards to human health or the environment.[185]

• *United States v. Baytank (Houston), Inc.*[186] Upholding a conviction under RCRA §3008(d)(2)(A) for illegal storage of hazardous waste, the court held that the government need not prove that the defendants knew that the wastes were defined as hazardous under RCRA. The court rejected the argument that the jury should have been instructed that the defendants must have known that the wastes were identified by EPA rules as hazardous.[187]

• *United States v. Dean.*[188] The court affirmed a plant manager's conviction under RCRA §3008(d)(2)(A) for illegal storage and disposal of hazardous waste, holding that the government did not have to prove that the defendant had knowledge of RCRA's permit requirements. Agreeing with *Hoflin*, the court held that the word "knowingly" in §3008(d)(2)(A) applied only to treatment, storage, and disposal of the hazardous waste, and not to the permit requirement for these activities.[189]

• *United States v. Goldsmith.*[190] The court upheld the defendant's convictions under RCRA §3008(d)(1) and (d)(2)(A) for transporting hazardous waste to an unpermitted facility and illegally storing waste without a permit, even though the government did not prove that the defendant actually knew that EPA defined the chemical as hazardous waste. The court held that an instruction requiring knowledge that the material in question had the potential to be harmful to humans or the environment was "sufficient to inform the jury that it must find that a defendant knew the substance he disposed of was hazardous."[191]

Knowledge of the Permit Requirement

This is the one area in which there is some divergence among the decisions. In particular, for conviction under RCRA §3008(d)(1) for knowingly transporting hazardous waste to an unpermitted facility, some courts require proof that the defendant had actual knowledge that the facility was unpermitted.

• *United States v. Johnson & Towers, Inc.*[192] The court held that in order to sustain an indictment under RCRA §3008(d)(2)(A) for illegal disposal of hazardous waste without a permit, the government must allege that the defendant had knowledge of each element of the offense. Thus, the indictment must assert that the defendant knew that it was required to obtain a permit and that the defendant knew that it did not possess a permit.[193] With respect to the defendant's knowledge of the law, however, the court held that "the government need only prove knowledge of the actions taken and not of the statute forbidding them."[194]

• *United States v. Speach.*[195] The court reversed a conviction under RCRA §3008(d)(1) for knowingly transporting hazardous waste to an unpermitted facility. The government failed to prove that the defendant knew or willfully failed to determine that the facility to which the hazardous waste was transported lacked a RCRA disposal permit. The court distinguished *Hoflin*, finding that the defendant there was in "the best possible position" to determine if the facility had a permit, so that it was reasonable to impose on him the risk of ascertaining the permit status of his own facility.[196] But because the allegedly illegal act in *Speach* involved knowledge of *another* entity's permit status, the court required proof of actual knowledge.

• *United States v. Laughlin.*[197] The court upheld a conviction under RCRA §3008(d)(2)(A) for illegal disposal of

178. *Id.* at 1039, 19 ELR at 21143. *Accord* United States v. Sellers, 926 F.2d 410, 21 ELR 20787 (5th Cir. 1991) (prosecution need not prove the defendant knew that the waste was classified as hazardous within the meaning of the RCRA rules).

179. 912 F.2d 741, 21 ELR 20051 (4th Cir.), *cert. denied*, 499 U.S. 919 (1991).

180. When "'dangerous . . . materials are involved, the probability of regulation is so great that anyone who is aware that he is in possession of them . . . must be presumed to be aware of the regulation.'" *Id.* at 745, 21 ELR at 20053 (quoting *United States v. International Minerals & Chem. Corp.*, 402 U.S. 558, 565 (1971)); *see also* text accompanying note 158 *supra*.

181. 934 F.2d 84, 21 ELR 21113 (6th Cir. 1991).

182. 42 U.S.C. §9603(b)(3), ELR Stat. CERCLA §103(b)(3).

183. *Buckley*, 934 F.2d at 89, 21 ELR at 21115.

184. 42 U.S.C. §§7412(c)(1)(B), 7413(c)(1)(C), ELR Stat. CAA §§112(c)(1)(B), 113(c)(1)(C).

185. *Buckley*, 934 F.2d at 88, 21 ELR at 21115.

186. 934 F.2d 599, 21 ELR 21101 (5th Cir. 1991).

187. *Id.* at 612, 21 ELR at 21107.

188. 969 F.2d 187, 22 ELR 21296 (6th Cir. 1992), *cert. denied*, 113 S. Ct. 1852 (1993).

189. *Id.* at 191, 22 ELR at 21297.

190. 978 F.2d 643, 23 ELR 20281 (11th Cir. 1992).

191. *Id.* at 646, 23 ELR at 20282.

192. 741 F.2d 662, 14 ELR 20634 (3d Cir. 1984), *cert. denied sub nom.* Angel v. United States, 469 U.S. 1208 (1985).

193. *Id.* at 669, 14 ELR at 20638.

194. *Id.*

195. 968 F.2d 795, 22 ELR 21498 (9th Cir. 1992).

196. *Id.* at 797, 22 ELR at 21500.

197. 10 F.3d 961, 24 ELR 20221 (2d Cir. 1993), *cert. denied sub nom.* Goldman v. United States, 114 S. Ct. 1649 (1994).

hazardous wastes, holding that the government need only prove that the defendant had a general awareness that he was performing the acts proscribed by the law. The court held that RCRA does not require proof that the defendant had actual knowledge of the lack of permit or that the specific waste involved was listed under RCRA.[198]

- *United States v. Wagner.*[199] The district court held that the government did not have to prove that the defendant had actual knowledge of RCRA's permit requirements. The Seventh Circuit affirmed, in a well-reasoned interpretation of RCRA §3008(d)(2)'s knowledge requirements:[200]

> The fact that [Congress] used "knowingly" in subsection (2) and subsidiary subsections (2)(B) and (2)(C) but omitted it from subsidiary subsection (2)(A), the permit requirement language at issue, is telling. To read "knowingly" as used in subsection (2) to apply to subsidiary subsections (A), (B), and (C) would render its use in (B) and (C) mere surplusage.[201]

Although this interpretation is consistent with prior environmental decisions, the necessary implication is that proof of a greater degree of mens rea than general intent should be required for a RCRA permit violation under §3008(d)(2)(B), which requires a "knowing violation" as well as proof of knowing treatment, storage, or disposal.

Knowledge of Material Facts

In upholding the general knowledge requirement, several courts have noted that *International Minerals* preserved the possible defense that the accused believed that he or she was dealing with an innocuous substance.[202] However, there has been little actual litigation concerning this theoretical "good-faith mistake of fact" defense. Perhaps the closest case is *Hayes International.* There, the issue was whether the defendants believed in good faith that the waste involved was being recycled, and thus exempt from the RCRA regulations. The court noted that "had the wastes been recycled, then no violation of the statute would have occurred."[203] The court found that once the defense of good-faith mistake is raised, the defendant bears the burden of persuasion. The government is "not required to disprove the [defendants'] mistake of fact defense."[204]

Violations of Permit Terms

The two leading cases in this area are *United States v. Weitzenhoff,*[205] and *United States v. Hopkins.*[206] They are discussed at length below. Two other decisions are significant:

- *United States v. Self.*[207] The court upheld the defendant's conviction under RCRA §3008(d)(2)(B) for illegally storing hazardous waste, holding that his knowledge of prior illegal storage constituted sufficient circumstantial evidence to satisfy the knowledge requirement. The court also held, however, that §3008(d)(2)(B) "ensures that a good faith belief that a permit allows a particular manner of treatment, storage or disposal of hazardous waste, when in fact [the permit] does not, is a defense to a criminal charge."[208]

- *United States v. Heuer.*[209] The court reversed a conviction under RCRA §3008(d)(2)(B) for illegal disposal of hazardous waste, because there was no express provision in the facility's permit that prohibited it from disposing of wastes generated at other facilities. The court held that the defendant facility manager could not be held guilty based on "implied conditions" allegedly included in the disposal permit.[210]

The Intent Element for Permit Offenses

Currently, the most hotly debated question in the environmental crimes area is whether the diminished knowledge requirement under the public welfare offense doctrine may be applied to charges of violating a discharge permit. The issues involved are clearly presented by the *Weitzenhoff* and *Hopkins* cases, in which the courts have affirmed criminal convictions while expressing some discomfort at the results.

United States v. Weitzenhoff

In *Weitzenhoff,* the managers of a sewage treatment plant were convicted of multiple felonies under the FWPCA for knowingly discharging partially processed sewage into the ocean, in violation of the plant's permit limits on discharging total suspended solids and biochemical oxygen demand.[211] While the pollutants the defendants discharged are certainly objectionable, they are not inherently toxic. Discharging these materials was illegal only because it exceeded by 6 percent over a 14-month period the quantities allowed under the plant's permit.[212]

---

198. The court suggested that in the future, the jury instruction should provide that the government must prove that the material the defendant stored or discarded did not have a *mere* potential to cause harm to humans or the environment, but that it had a *substantial* potential to be harmful. *Id.* at 967, 24 ELR at 20225.

199. 29 F.3d 264, 24 ELR 21353 (9th Cir. 1994).

200. RCRA §3008(d)(2) provides criminal penalties for any person who

> knowingly treats, stores or disposes of any hazardous waste identified or listed under this subchapter—
> (A) without a permit under this subchapter . . . ; or
> (B) in knowing violation of any material condition or requirement of such permit; or
> (C) in knowing violation of any material condition or requirement of any applicable interim status regulations or standards . . . .

42 U.S.C. §6928(d)(2)(A)-(C), ELR STAT. RCRA §3008(d)(2)(A)-(C).

201. *Wagner,* 29 F.3d at 266, 24 ELR at 21353.

202. *See, e.g.,* Staples v. United States, 114 S. Ct. 1793, 1798 n.3 (1994).

203. United States v. Hayes Int'l Corp., 786 F.2d 1499, 1506, 16 ELR 20717, 20720 (11th Cir. 1986).

204. *Id.*

205. 1 F.3d 1523, 23 ELR 21322 (9th Cir. 1993), *reh'g denied, opinion amended,* 35 F.3d 1275, 24 ELR 21504 (1994), *cert. denied sub nom.* Mariani v. United States, 115 S. Ct. 939 (1995).

206. 53 F.3d 533, 25 ELR 21178 (2d Cir. 1995).

207. 2 F.3d 1071, 23 ELR 21301 (10th Cir. 1993).

208. *Id.* at 1091, 23 ELR at 21309.

209. 4 F.3d 723, 23 ELR 21357 (9th Cir. 1993), *cert. denied,* 114 S. Ct. 1190 (1994).

210. *Id.* at 730-31, 23 ELR at 21359-60.

211. United States v. Weitzenhoff, 1 F.3d 1523, 23 ELR 21322 (9th Cir. 1993), *reh'g denied, opinion amended,* 35 F.3d 1275, 24 ELR 21504 (1994), *cert. denied sub nom.* Mariani v. United States, 115 S. Ct. 939 (1995).

212. 35 F.3d at 1294, 24 ELR at 21513 (Kleinfeld, J., dissenting).

The government proceeded on a conventional public welfare offense theory. The defendants argued that the phrase "knowingly violates" in FWPCA §309(c)(2)[213] differentiated this offense from other FWPCA criminal charges. They claimed that this phrase requires the government to prove that the defendants knew that the release violated permit limits.[214]

The defense also argued that the FWPCA is not a generic public welfare statute, but that Congress had enacted a specially tailored law under which the term "knowingly" must be interpreted to require proof of actual knowledge.[215] They argued that §309 establishes a six-tier hierarchy of enforcement provisions, including:

- two levels of administrative penalties;
- civil penalties enforceable in court;
- misdemeanor offenses;
- ordinary felonies; and
- aggravated felonies (knowing endangerment).[216]

Under this carefully calibrated scheme, all elements of the various levels of offense are essentially the same except for the mental element. No showing of intent is required for administrative penalties or civil penalties. The misdemeanor provision requires proof that the defendants "negligently" violated a permit,[217] whereas the aggravated felony provision requires proof of a "knowing" violation plus proof that the defendant "knows at the time that he thereby places another person in imminent danger."[218] The defendants argued that the FWPCA's structure thus suggests that the ordinary felony provision requires proof of some degree of mental intent beyond negligence.[219] In the context of the surrounding provisions, this standard would seem to require proof of some degree of actual knowledge that the action would exceed permit limits.

The district court denied the defendants' request for a jury instruction that would have required the government to prove that the defendants knew that their acts were unlawful. The court also refused to submit to the jury the defendants' proposed affirmative defense that they mistakenly believed that the permit authorized their behavior in order to avoid a catastrophic plant failure.[220]

In August 1993, a panel of the Ninth Circuit affirmed the convictions, finding that the district court had properly interpreted the phrase "knowingly violates" as requiring proof only that the defendants were aware that they were discharging pollutants, and not proof of actual knowledge that their acts violated the permit.[221] The panel concluded that the FWPCA felony provision was properly characterized as a public welfare offense, and that "*International Minerals* rather than *Liparota* controls" because §309(c) was intended to protect the public from the potential consequences of water pollution.[222]

The panel also held that the trial court had correctly refused to charge the jury on the proposed affirmative defense concerning the knowledge element. It found, however, that the district court had erred in admitting evidence about the meaning of the permit, because that was a pure question of law. The court nonetheless held that this "error was harmless because, under a proper interpretation of the permit, the discharges . . . necessarily violated the permit."[223]

The defendants petitioned for rehearing en banc, and the court held the matter under review for almost one year. In the interim, the Supreme Court decided *Staples v. United States*,[224] and two other cases interpreting nonenvironmental statutes[225] to require a stronger showing of intent than the government believed was required. In August 1994, the Ninth Circuit finally denied rehearing, over a strong, five-judge dissent.[226]

The panel substantially amended its prior opinion to deal with *Staples* and the other intervening decisions. It noted that the public welfare offense doctrine survived *Staples* and could justify dispensing with proof of knowledge in cases of products properly classified as "obnoxious waste materials."[227] The panel reasoned that the unregistered machine guns at issue in *Staples* were not covered by this rationale, but that the nonhazardous waste products discharged in *Weitzenhoff* were. The panel also noted that while the Supreme Court had expressed concern over the imposition of enhanced penalties for public welfare offenses, it had not prohibited application of the doctrine to felonies.[228]

The dissenters would have held that the phrase "knowingly violates" requires proof of actual knowledge. Their conclusion was based on the plain language of §309(c) and the structure of the Act, especially reading the felony provision in conjunction with the negligence standard for misdemeanors.[229] The dissenters also challenged the panel's finding that discharge of the pollutants involved could properly be classified within the ambit of the public welfare offense doctrine.[230] They contrasted offenses properly classified as public welfare offenses, which are

213. Under §309(c)(2), it is a felony to "knowingly violate . . . any permit condition or limitation implementing any of [certain enumerated] sections in a permit issued under [§402]." 33 U.S.C. §1319(c)(2), ELR STAT. FWPCA §309(c)(2).

214. In *United States v. Hopkins*, which is discussed *infra*, the court agreed that "[a]s a matter of abstract logic, it would seem that a statute making it unlawful to 'knowingly violate[ ]' a given statutory or permit provision would require proof that the defendant both violated and knew that he violated that provision." 53 F.3d 533, 537, 25 ELR 21178, 21179 (2d Cir. 1995).

215. *Weitzenhoff*, 35 F.3d at 1283, 24 ELR at 21506.

216. Petition for Writ of Certiorari at 19-23, Mariani v. United States, No. 94-6683 (filed Dec. 29, 1994).

217. 42 U.S.C. §1319(c)(1), ELR STAT. FWPCA §309(c)(1).

218. *Id.* §1319(c)(3), ELR STAT. FWPCA §309(c)(3).

219. *Weitzenhoff*, 35 F.3d at 1283-84, 24 ELR at 21506-07.

220. *Id.* at 1283, 24 ELR at 21506. The evidence would likely have permitted the government to obtain a conviction under either standard, because it showed that the defendants released the illegal material at night and instructed their employees to keep quiet. *Id.* at 1281-82, 24 ELR at 21505-06.

221. *Id.* at 1283-84, 24 ELR at 21506.

222. *Id.* at 1286, 24 ELR at 21508.

223. *Id.* at 1288, 24 ELR at 21509.

224. 114 S. Ct. 1793 (1994).

225. Posters 'N' Things Ltd. v. United States, 114 S. Ct. 1747 (1994) (Mail Order Drug Paraphernalia Control Act); Ratzlaf v. United States, 114 S. Ct. 655 (1994) (antistructuring provision of money-laundering statute).

226. United States v. Weitzenhoff, 35 F.3d 1275, 24 ELR 21504 (9th Cir. 1994).

227. *Id.* at 1280, 24 ELR at 21507.

228. *Id.* at 1281, 24 ELR at 21508.

229. *Id.* at 1293-95, 24 ELR at 21512-13 (Kleinfeld, J., dissenting).

230. *Id.* at 1296-98, 24 ELR at 21514-15 (Kleinfeld, J., dissenting).

unambiguously wrong, with the conduct involved here, which often was innocent and indeed explicitly lawful in many circumstances. The dissent argued that persons of good conscience could discharge 6 percent more pollutants than their permit allowed without recognizing the wrongfulness of the conduct when they engaged in it. Therefore, they would have found that *International Minerals* does not "justif[y] more aggressive criminalization without a plain statutory command."[231]

Because the Supreme Court ultimately denied certiorari, *Weitzenhoff* remains the leading case on applying the knowledge element to permit offenses.[232]

United States v. Hopkins

The other major case interpreting the intent element for permit offenses is *Hopkins*. The defendant in *Hopkins* was convicted, among other things, under FWPCA §309(c)(2)(A) for violating the restrictions of a permit with respect to zinc discharges, and under 18 U.S.C. §371 for conspiracy to violate §309(c)(2)(A). On appeal, the defendant argued that the jury should have been instructed that the government was required to prove that he knew he was acting in violation of the permit. The Second Circuit rejected this argument, finding that "the purpose and legislative history of [§309(c)(2)(A)] indicate that Congress meant that that section would be violated if the defendants' acts were proscribed, even if the defendant was not aware of the proscription."[233] Following circuit precedent in *Laughlin*, the panel applied the public welfare offense doctrine and its "presumption of awareness of regulation" to a permit violation.[234] The court noted that the "vast majority" of the substances to which the FWPCA applies "are of the type that would alert any ordinary user to the likelihood of stringent regulation. Moreover, the very fact that a governmental permit has been issued enhances the user's awareness of the existence of regulation."[235]

Hopkins completes the development of the knowledge element over the last 20 years. For facilities with discharge permits, environmental statutes are essentially strict liability offenses because the "enhanced awareness" of regulation implicit in receiving a permit virtually eliminates any possible knowledge defenses. The "enhanced awareness" factor may also mean that entities operating within the permit system are held to a higher standard than those operating outside the realm of environmental controls, a reversal of long-standing policy and prosecutorial guidance.

Developments Since *Weitzenhoff* and *Hopkins*

After the Ninth Circuit denied rehearing in *Weitzenhoff*, federal prosecutors took full advantage of the reaffirmation of the public welfare offense doctrine to advance pending cases. For example, in one FWPCA case pending in the Eastern District of California, the prosecution filed a superseding indictment that stripped out all references to the defendants' knowledge or state of mind that had been included in the prior indictment; submitted proposed jury instructions that would diminish the required knowledge element so that the government need prove only that the defendants knew that they operated a facility from which the discharges occurred; and sought jury instructions that the defendants could be convicted of conspiracy on the same showing of knowledge necessary for conviction of the underlying offense—that is, that the defendants could be convicted of conspiracy without proof that any one of them knew what the law required or that any one of them actually intended to violate the law.[236]

The de minimis nature of the knowledge requirement recognized in *Weitzenhoff* and *Hopkins* eliminates important defenses that companies generally rely on in the white-collar crime area. For example, good-faith reliance on the advice of counsel about what the EPA rules require is not a valid affirmative defense under the *International Minerals* doctrine. Similarly, reliance on the advice of environmental consultants or engineers about necessary steps to attain compliance is not a legally sufficient defense. Although these factors may be relevant to the prosecutor's decision whether to indict, they are irrelevant to the legal issues at trial, which focus only on whether an illegal discharge occurred.

In sum, as the case law has developed, the issue of knowledge has significance only for the prosecutor's decision whether or not to file criminal charges. Even then its role is discretionary, and its import may be outweighed by other factors. Once criminal charges are filed, however, the knowledge element has only a vestigial function in the case. Except in those isolated areas—such as RCRA transport charges and knowing endangerment cases—in which the statute contains a second knowledge element, proof of knowledge will not present a meaningful obstacle to the prosecution's ability to obtain a conviction.

Methods of Proving Knowledge

Corporate Defendants

Prosecutors can rely on several approaches to prove a corporation's guilty knowledge. Under the doctrine of respondeat superior, a corporation may be held criminally liable for the actions of its employees if the acts were done on

231. *Id.* at 1296, 24 ELR at 21514 (Kleinfeld, J., dissenting).

232. The defendants' petition for certiorari, *see supra* note 216, attracted substantial support from industry coalitions. The government filed a 27-page brief in opposition. The government's detailed legal arguments essentially said all that could be argued if review had been granted. This undertaking reflects the seriousness of the challenge presented to applying the public welfare offense doctrine.

233. United States v. Hopkins, 53 F.2d 533, 540, 25 ELR 21178, 21181 (2d Cir. 1995).

234. *Id.* at 538, 25 ELR at 21180.

235. *Id.* at 539, 25 ELR at 21180.

236. United States v. Liquid Sugars, Inc., No. S-93-302 (E.D. Cal. filed Dec. 16, 1994) (superseding indictment). The government's proposed jury instruction demonstrates the difficulty of defending against an environmental criminal charge on knowledge grounds. The proposed charge on the substantive offense provided that the government must prove only:

> First, that on the dates alleged in the indictment, the defendants knowingly operated a source by discharging or causing the discharge of pollutants;
> Second, that the defendants knew the general nature and character of the pollutants discharged . . . [; and]
> Third, that the pollutants discharged on those dates by the defendants in fact [violated the EPA rules]. . . .

Government's Supplemental Jury Instruction Re: Knowledge at 9 (Apr. 21, 1995).

behalf of the company and were within the scope of the employees' authority.[237] Criminal liability may be imputed even if the company has an explicit policy against the activity.[238] The company's establishment of an environmental policy, without diligent internal enforcement efforts, does not suffice to take the acts of the employee outside the scope of his or her employment.[239]

Under the doctrine of collective knowledge, the aggregate knowledge of all employees may be imputed to the corporation. Thus, a company may be found to have knowingly engaged in conduct constituting a crime based on proof that one employee knew facts relating to one element of the offense and other employees had knowledge relating to other essential elements, even though no one person had knowledge of all necessary facts.[240]

Individual Defendants

For individual defendants, prosecutors also have several avenues through which they can prove sufficient knowledge, including: (1) direct evidence, (2) willful blindness/conscious avoidance, (3) circumstantial evidence, and (4) the responsible corporate officer doctrine.

☐ *Direct Evidence.* The most effective means of proving criminal knowledge is through direct evidence that the individual personally was involved in the commission of the offense or personally aided and abetted the violation. A corporate officer who instructs his or her subordinates to perform acts that violate environmental laws is liable for such violations, even if the officer does not directly participate in the prohibited conduct. 241 For example, in *Hoflin*, the defendant was convicted of violating RCRA on proof that he instructed his employees to bury drums containing hazardous wastes after receiving warnings that such disposal would violate certain permits.[242] Similarly, in *United States v. Carr*,[243] the defendant was convicted under CERCLA for failing to report a release of a hazardous substance, based on evidence that he instructed workers to dump a truckload of paint cans into a pond, and then told the workers to dump earth into the pond.

237. *E.g.*, United States v. Marathon Dev. Corp., 867 F.2d 96, 19 ELR 20683 (1st Cir. 1989) (corporation found criminally liable for actions of a vice president who caused wetlands to be filled without a permit).

238. United States v. Hilton Hotels Corp., 467 F.2d 1000, 1004-07 (9th Cir. 1972), *cert. denied*, 409 U.S. 1125 (1973) (corporation liable for action of its agents even if they violated company policy in committing the act that constituted the crime).

239. United States v. Beusch, 596 F.2d 871, 877-78 (9th Cir. 1979) (corporation may be liable for acts of employees done contrary to express instructions and policies, but existence of such policies may be considered in determining whether employee in fact acted to benefit the corporation).

240. *E.g.*, United States v. Bank of New England, N.A., 821 F.2d 844, 856 (1st Cir.), *cert. denied*, 484 U.S. 943 (1987) (collective knowledge instruction for corporation; the aggregate knowledge obtained by corporate employees constitutes the corporation's knowledge).

241. *E.g.*, United States v. Johnson & Towers, Inc., 741 F.2d 662, 668, 14 ELR 20634, 20638 (3d Cir. 1984), *cert. denied*, 469 U.S. 1208 (1985).

242. United States v. Hoflin, 880 F.2d 1033, 19 ELR 21140 (9th Cir. 1989), *cert. denied*, 493 U.S. 1083 (1990).

243. 880 F.2d 1550, 19 ELR 21137 (2d Cir. 1989).

☐ *Willful Blindness/Conscious Avoidance.* The government may prove that the defendant intentionally avoided learning, or was willfully blind to, the truth. For example, in *Hayes International*, the court held that a corporate employee's willful failure to determine the permit status of a facility to which hazardous waste had been shipped satisfied the requirement of knowledge of permit status under RCRA.[244]

The government may also attempt to obtain a conviction by showing that the defendant consciously avoided learning the truth after receiving substantial warning signs, and therefore had the equivalent of knowledge. "A conscious avoidance charge is appropriate (a) when the element of knowledge is in dispute, and (b) the evidence would permit a rational juror to conclude beyond a reasonable doubt 'that the defendant was aware of a high probability of the fact in dispute and consciously avoided confirming that fact.'"[245]

☐ *Circumstantial Evidence.* Knowledge of environmental crimes can be proved by circumstantial evidence. For example, in *Hayes International*, a corporation and one employee were charged with knowingly transporting hazardous waste to an unpermitted facility in violation of RCRA §3008(d)(1). The government proved that the employee knew that the facility to which the paint waste was shipped derived no economic benefit from it, and that he failed to follow internal corporate procedures requiring disposal of wastes lacking resale value only at EPA-approved sites. Even though the government failed to present direct proof that the employee knew that the waste was not being recycled, the court held that this circumstantial evidence successfully proved guilty knowledge.[246] The court recognized, however, that the employee's good-faith belief that the material was being recycled, if proved, would be a valid affirmative defense.[247]

In particular, the knowing endangerment provisions of RCRA, the CAA, and the FWPCA expressly provide that in proving knowledge, circumstantial evidence may be used, including evidence that the defendant took affirmative steps to shield itself from relevant information.[248]

Other courts have permitted the inference of criminal knowledge to be based on what the defendant would have known through the exercise of reasonable diligence, when the defendant had some affirmative duty to know the facts or to investigate the situation. For example, in *Dee*, the court found that knowledge could be inferred with respect to one of the defendants from evidence that he was informed

244. United States v. Hayes Int'l Corp., 786 F.2d 1499, 16 ELR 20717 (11th Cir. 1986). In *United States v. Pacific Hide & Fur Depot, Inc.*, however, the Ninth Circuit reversed a conviction under TSCA, where the trial court's instructions had allowed the jury to convict the defendant of knowing violations on the basis of mere reckless conduct. 768 F.2d 1096, 15 ELR 20851 (9th Cir. 1985). The court held that although liability for knowing violations of TSCA could be based on willful blindness, "[i]t is not enough that [the] defendant was mistaken, recklessly disregarded the truth, or negligently failed to inquire." *Id.* at 1098, 15 ELR at 20853.

245. United States v. Hopkins, 53 F.3d 533, 542, 25 ELR 21178, 21181 (2d Cir. 1995) (citations omitted); *see also* United States v. Buckley, 934 F.2d 84, 88, 21 ELR 21113, 21115 (6th Cir. 1991).

246. *Hayes International,* 786 F.2d at 1506-07, 16 ELR at 20720-21.

247. *Id.* at 1506, 16 ELR at 20720.

248. 42 U.S.C. §6928(f)(2), ELR STAT. RCRA §3008(f)(2); *id.* §7413(c)(5)(B), ELR STAT. CAA §113(c)(5)(B); 33 U.S.C. §1319(c)(3)(B), ELR STAT. FWPCA §309(c)(3)(B).

by safety inspectors and employees of problems with stored chemicals. The defendant did not respond but merely "told staff to clean it up as best they could."[249] The court also found that knowledge could be inferred from evidence that the defendant was in charge of operations at the plant, had previously taken action with respect to the chemicals' storage, repeatedly ignored warnings, and took no actions to comply with RCRA.[250]

□ *Responsible Corporate Officers.* In cases in which the government has had difficulty proving knowledge through traditional means, Justice has occasionally relied on the responsible corporate officer doctrine as a substitute for proof of actual knowledge. Some courts have been receptive to the argument that showing that the individual occupied a supervisory position in the company might be sufficient to impute criminal knowledge from a subordinate employee with guilty knowledge to the supervising officer who was unaware of the violations. 251 The First Circuit has concluded, however, that the responsible corporate officer doctrine may provide an additional piece of circumstantial evidence with which to prove criminal knowledge, but does not, by itself, provide a conclusive means of imputing guilty knowledge to senior officials. 252 Justice policy announcements appear to have accepted as a matter of charging policy the substantive limitations on application of this doctrine established by the First Circuit.[253]

Congress has incorporated the responsible corporate officer concept into the criminal provisions of the CAA and the FWPCA without explaining how it is meant to apply.[254] In this vacuum, Justice has argued that the doctrine permits imposing criminal liability on (1) a corporate officer, (2) who is directly responsible within management for the conduct in question, and (3) who knew that the type of improper activity allegedly committed by his or her subordinates was occurring.[255] The government has claimed that corporate officers should be held criminally responsible for the misconduct of those who work under their supervision, even if the officers' knowledge of such conduct is minimal.

The specifics of the doctrine are discussed more fully below.

249. United States v. Dee, 912 F.2d 741, 747, 21 ELR 20051, 20054 (4th Cir. 1990).

250. *Id.* at 747-48, 21 ELR at 20054-55.

251. *See, e.g.,* United States v. White, 766 F. Supp. 873, 22 ELR 20050 (E.D. Wash. 1991); United States v. Brittain, 931 F.2d 1413, 21 ELR 21092 (10th Cir. 1991).

252. United States v. MacDonald & Watson Waste Oil Co., 933 F.2d 35, 21 ELR 21449 (1st Cir. 1991).

253. *See infra* note 285.

254. *See* 42 U.S.C. §7413(c)(6), ELR STAT. CAA §113(c)(6) (for purposes of criminal offenses, "the term 'person' includes . . . any responsible corporate officer"); 33 U.S.C. §1319(c)(6), ELR STAT. FWPCA §309(c)(6) ("responsible corporate officer" included within term "persons" for purposes of knowing endangerment provision). There appears to be no legislative history of the use of this term in the 1972 FWPCA. In the 1977 CAA Amendments, Congress simply based the language on a counterpart FWPCA provision. S. REP. No. 94-717, 94th Cong., 2d Sess. 40 (1976) ("[t]he Committee intends that criminal penalties be sought against those corporate officers under whose responsibility a violation has taken place, and not just those employees directly involved in the operation of the violating source").

255. *See* United States v. White, 766 F. Supp. 873, 894, 22 ELR 20050, 20060 (E.D. Wash. 1991); United States v. MacDonald & Watson Waste Oil Co., 933 F.2d 35, 53, 21 ELR 21449, 21455 (1st Cir. 1991).

The Responsible Corporate Officer Doctrine

Origins of the Doctrine

The responsible corporate officer doctrine developed from two Supreme Court cases decided under the Federal Food, Drug, and Cosmetic Act (FFDCA),[256] a strict liability statute whose violation is subject to misdemeanor penalties.

In *United States v. Dotterweich,*[257] the Supreme Court held that the president of a company could be convicted of illegally distributing adulterated drugs through acts committed by his subordinates. The Court held that no showing of mens rea was necessary to establish culpability under the FFDCA, a public welfare statute. It recognized that when applied to individuals acting on behalf of a company, the statute might be read to "sweep . . . within its condemnation any person however remotely entangled in the proscribed shipment."[258] The Court, however, narrowed the range of individuals subject to liability by finding that "[t]he offense is committed . . . by all who [have] a *responsible share* in the furtherance of the transaction which the statute outlaws."[259] But the Court declined to define the class of employees bearing a "responsible share" in the offense, leaving this definition to "the good sense of prosecutors, the wise guidance of trial judges, and the ultimate judgment of juries."[260]

Three Justices dissented, arguing that absent express congressional authority, it was improper to impose criminal liability on a corporate officer who did not participate in, and had no knowledge of, the offense.[261] In the dissent's view, although the stockholders could have sued the president for negligence and mismanagement, the imposition of vicarious criminal liability was unfounded.

In *United States v. Park,*[262] the chief executive officer (CEO) of a large national retail food operation was convicted of illegally distributing rodent-infested food, which had been discovered at a corporate warehouse. The evidence showed that the Food and Drug Administration had previously notified the officer of a similar problem at a different warehouse, and that he had notice of the problem at the warehouse where the contaminated food was found. The government also showed that one vice president was in charge of sanitation for both facilities, and that the defendant had previously conferred with that subordinate and other officers to ensure that corrective action would be taken.[263]

The CEO did not participate in the acts causing the violation, but was nonetheless convicted under this strict liability provision. On appeal, he claimed that he was denied due process by being convicted without proof of wrongful action on his part. The Court held that the government could establish liability by demonstrating "that the defendant had, by reason of his position in the corporation, responsibility and authority either to prevent in the first instance, or promptly to correct, the violation complained of, and that

256. 21 U.S.C. §§301-392.

257. 320 U.S. 277 (1943).

258. *Id.* at 284.

259. *Id.* (emphasis added).

260. *Id.* at 285.

261. *Id.* at 286-87 (Murphy, J., dissenting).

262. 421 U.S. 658 (1975).

263. *Id.* at 664.

he failed to do so."[264] The Court found that the conviction was proper because the defendant was aware that the company's internal system for ensuring the sanitary conditions was not working, but failed to restructure that system once notified that similar sanitary problems had arisen at two warehouses.[265] The Court recognized, however, that the officer could have raised an affirmative defense that he was powerless to prevent the violation, and that he could have sought a jury instruction requiring the government to prove beyond a reasonable doubt that he was capable of preventing the violation.[266]

As in *Dotterweich*, three Justices dissented. They argued that the jury was provided no meaningful guidance as to what constituted a "responsible relation" to the offense, and could have convicted based solely on the defendant's corporate position.[267] The dissenters were particularly concerned that the decision permitted imposing criminal liability on the officer for conduct that he was unaware of and did not participate in. They argued:

> The standardless conviction approved today can serve in another case tomorrow to support a felony conviction and a substantial prison sentence. However highly the Court may regard the social objectives of the [FFDCA], that regard cannot serve to justify a criminal conviction so wholly alien to fundamental principles of our law.[268]

Application of the Doctrine in Environmental Cases

Justice inevitably sought to apply the responsible corporate officer doctrine in environmental cases. First, courts have held these provisions to be public welfare laws, like the applicable statute in *Dotterweich* and *Park*. Second, the CAA and the FWPCA expressly include the term "responsible corporate officer" in their respective definitions of persons who can be liable.[269] The statutes, however, do not define the class of individuals that may be considered responsible corporate officers, and the legislative history does not provide any further guidance. As a result, courts have had difficulty translating the doctrine to the environmental area. Complications arise partly because federal environmental laws require a minimal showing of knowledge, and partly because of the ambiguous standards announced in *Dotterweich* and *Park*.

The most significant aspect of the doctrine is its potential for imposing liability on officials at corporate headquarters who have no direct responsibility for the operation of the offending facility. For example, in *United States v. Pennwalt Corp.*,[270] four corporate officers were indicted for FWPCA violations based on their failure to prevent the collapse of a chemical holding tank. The indictment charged that there was a known structural weakness in the tank, and that the officers knew of that defect and failed to respond to it. Three of the officers were based several thousand miles from the facility. They were nonetheless indicted under the responsible corporate officer doctrine, because they had received a memorandum identifying the defect and had failed to assure remedial action.[271]

In the environmental context, the critical question is whether the government may prove a corporate officer's criminal knowledge simply by showing that the officer would have known that environmental violations were occurring had the officer been properly fulfilling his or her duties. The question also arises whether this characterization of the responsible corporate officer doctrine could allow imposition of vicarious criminal liability for corporate negligence and mismanagement, thereby reading the requirement of criminal knowledge out of these laws.

The following three decisions apparently define the limits of the doctrine in environmental cases.

- *United States v. White.*[272] A company and several employees were indicted under RCRA and the Federal Insecticide, Fungicide, and Rodenticide Act for loading a truck with pesticide-contaminated water and then spraying the material on a field. One defendant was indicted under the responsible corporate officer doctrine on the ground that he "had direct responsibility to supervise the handling of hazardous waste by [corporate] employees. He is liable for the acts of all other agents and employees of [the company] in handling the hazardous waste at [its] facilities which he knew of or should have known of."[273]

The defendant moved to strike this charge, claiming that it would improperly permit the government to obtain a conviction based solely on a theory of respondeat superior. The court agreed and dismissed. It distinguished *Dotterweich* and *Park* on the basis that the statute at issue in those cases contained no mens rea requirement.[274]

- *United States v. Brittain.*[275] The defendant, who was a city's public utilities director with general supervisory authority over the operation of its wastewater treatment plant, was charged with two misdemeanor counts under FWPCA §§301(a) and 309(c)(1) for unlawful discharges into navigable waters. The evidence showed that staff had advised the director that pollutants were being discharged into a local creek in violation of permit limits. He also personally observed the discharges on two occasions, but instructed the plant supervisor not to report them to the EPA, contrary to the city's permit requirement.

The trial court rejected the government's argument that the director could be held criminally liable for the violations under the responsible corporate officer doctrine. Consequently, this theory of liability was not submitted to the jury.[276] On appeal

264. *Id.* at 673-74.
265. *Id.* at 678.
266. *Id.* at 676-77.
267. *Id.* at 679-80 (Stewart, J., dissenting).
268. *Id.* at 683 (Stewart, J., dissenting).
269. *See supra* note 254 and accompanying text.
270. No. 88-55T (W.D. Wash., *corporation sentenced* May 2, 1989; *manager sentenced* May 19, 1989).
271. Charges against these officers were ultimately dismissed on entry of the corporation's plea.
272. 766 F. Supp. 873, 22 ELR 20050 (E.D. Wash. 1991).
273. *Id.* at 894, 22 ELR at 20060.
274. The court also considered language in *United States v. Johnson & Towers, Inc.*, stating that criminal knowledge of each element of a RCRA offense "may be inferred by the jury as to those individuals who hold the requisite responsible positions within the corporate defendant." *Id.* at 895, 22 ELR at 20061 (citing *Johnson & Towers*, 741 F.2d 662, 670, 14 ELR 20634, 20638 (3d Cir. 1984), *cert. denied sub nom.* Angel v. United States, 469 U.S. 1208 (1985)). The court found that this statement was "clearly" dictum, and held that inclusion of the responsible corporate officer doctrine in the charge would improperly allow a conviction without the requisite intent. *White*, 766 F. Supp. at 895, 22 ELR at 20061.
275. 931 F.2d 1413, 21 ELR 21092 (10th Cir. 1991).
276. *Id.* at 1420 n.5, 21 ELR at 21095 n.5.

of his convictions, the director argued that there was no evidence that he personally caused the unlawful discharge, and the only proof of his involvement with the discharge was his relationship to the discharging entity. The director claimed, therefore, that he could not be held liable under the Act's definition of an "individual," and could only be found liable if the government proved that he was the permittee or a responsible corporate officer—a charge that had not been submitted to the jury on the defendant's objection.[277]

The Tenth Circuit affirmed the convictions, holding that the FWPCA's use of the term "responsible corporate officer" did not narrow the range of "individuals" subject to criminal liability.[278] Although the evidence would have permitted the court to treat the case as one in which the defendant was directly involved in the violation, the court chose to address the issue in responsible corporate officer terms:

> We think that Congress perceived this objective [restoration of the integrity of the nation's waters] to outweigh hardships suffered by "responsible corporate officers" who are held criminally liable in spite of their lack of "consciousness of wrongdoing." . . . Under this interpretation, a "responsible corporate officer," to be held criminally liable, would not have to "willfully or negligently" cause a permit violation. Instead, the willfulness or negligence of the actor would be imputed to him by virtue of his position of responsibility.[279]

Because the jury was charged on an actual knowledge theory, the broad language about imputation of willfulness or negligence is dictum. Further, the case involved misdemeanor convictions, not felonies, so its precedential significance may be limited for most environmental prosecutions. Nevertheless, *Brittain* is the strongest support to date for an aggressive interpretation of the responsible corporate officer doctrine.

• *United States v. MacDonald & Watson Waste Oil Co.*[280] A corporation and its president were convicted on two counts each of knowingly transporting hazardous waste to a facility that did not have a permit, in violation of RCRA §3008(d)(1). The evidence showed that hazardous waste had been illegally transported to an unpermitted site operated by the company, under the supervision of a corporate employee. The evidence further showed that the company president had participated in the day-to-day management of that site and had been warned on other occasions that his company had illegally disposed of hazardous waste. However, there was no direct evidence that the president knew of the particular unlawful shipment charged in the indictment.

The trial court issued the following instruction on the responsible corporate officer doctrine:

> When an individual defendant is also a corporate officer, the government may prove that individual's knowledge in either of two ways. The first way is to demonstrate that the defendant had actual knowledge of the act in question. The second way is to establish that the defendant was what is called a responsible officer of the corporation committing the act. In order to prove that a person is a responsible corporate officer three things must be shown.
>
> First, it must be shown that the person is an officer of the corporation, not merely an employee.
>
> Second, it must be shown that the officer had direct responsibility for the activities that are alleged to be illegal. Simply being an officer or even the president of a corporation is not enough. The government must prove that the person had a responsibility to supervise the activities in question.
>
> And the third requirement is that the officer must have known or believed that the illegal activity of the type alleged occurred.[281]

The First Circuit overturned the president's conviction, holding that the district court had improperly applied the responsible corporate officer doctrine "as a substitute means of proving the explicit knowledge element of this RCRA felony."[282] The court held that the charge was defective because it instructed the jury "that proof that [the president] was a responsible corporate officer would conclusively prove the element of his knowledge."[283] The court rejected the government's argument that the instruction merely permitted use of the doctrine to raise the inference of guilty knowledge, and observed that the instructions on willful blindness and circumstantial evidence

> would have sufficed had it merely been the court's purpose to point out that knowledge could be established by circumstantial evidence, although the court could, had it wished, have elaborated on the extent to which [the president's] responsibilities and duties might lead to a reasonable inference that he knew of the [illegal disposal].[284]

Thus, absent proof that the president had actual knowledge of the specific shipments charged in the indictment, the conviction had to be overturned.

In sum, *MacDonald & Watson* appears to have established that the responsible corporate officer doctrine provides an additional piece of circumstantial evidence to prove criminal liability. It does not, however, provide an independent means by which guilty knowledge may be imputed from an employee with direct responsibility for an environmental violation to a supervising employee or an officer at headquarters.[285]

277. *Id.* at 1419, 21 ELR at 21094.
278. *Id.*, at 1419, 21 ELR at 21094-95.
279. *Id.* at 1419, 21 ELR at 21095.
280. 933 F.2d 35, 21 ELR 21449 (1st Cir. 1991).
281. *Id.* at 50-51, 21 ELR at 21454 (capitalization modified).
282. *Id.* at 52, 21 ELR at 21455.
283. *Id.*
284. *Id.*
285. Justice apparently has accepted the holding in *MacDonald & Watson*, and has stated publicly that it will not bring indictments against corporate or municipal officials based solely on their line responsibility for supervising the employees who committed the knowing violations. In August 1993, Charles A. DeMonaco, Assistant Chief of the Environmental Crimes Section, announced at the Annual Meeting of the American Bar Association that as a matter of policy and notwithstanding the broader interpretation suggested by some courts, corporate officers would not be prosecuted for knowing violations of the environmental laws unless they met the liability standards of *MacDonald & Watson*. *Corporate Officer's Prosecution Should Rest on Real Knowledge, According to DOJ Official*, 23 Env't Rep. (BNA) 5 (Aug. 25, 1993). *See also* A.B.A., Section on Natural Resources, Energy, and Environmental Law, 1993: The Year in Review 145-46.

Practical Impact of the Doctrine

Although there are legal and policy limits on the reach of responsible corporate officer doctrine, it nonetheless continues to play a critical role in environmental investigations. The government's ability to use the doctrine as circumstantial proof of actual knowledge reduces the quantum of evidence otherwise necessary to prove actual knowledge on behalf of senior officials at corporate headquarters. It therefore constitutes a significant threat to senior corporate officials and a substantial weapon in the prosecutor's arsenal.

For example, members of the headquarters staff may receive reports or memoranda from plant officials indicating that violations have occurred at a facility. Under Justice policy, if corporate officials fail to investigate or take effective remedial action in response to such reports, they may be vulnerable to individual prosecution.[286] Their exposure is enhanced if their awareness is combined with other indicia of involvement, such as conversations with subordinates.

Even officials outside the division directly involved in the violation may be implicated under the responsible corporate officer doctrine. For example, a request for a capital allocation to redress an environmental violation might be reviewed by employees in the environmental compliance, finance, engineering, purchasing, and legal departments, as well as senior management. Few events can raise the level of concern within a corporation as effectively as subpoenas from the grand jury for testimony from these officials. And any headquarters official who demonstrably opposed a request to cure an environmental violation will be on perilous ground indeed if the official has to defend an investigation on the ground that he or she was not actually "responsible" for the employees who broke the laws, but merely had an advisory or policy formulation role.

Litigation Strategies Addressing the Reduced Intent Requirement

With the diminishment of the knowledge element, defense strategies in environmental cases tend to focus on difficulties in understanding how the complex regulatory schemes work and on challenges to the government's scientific proof.

At the appellate level, the following five cases stand out as examples of successful regulatory defenses.

- *United States v. Plaza Health Laboratories, Inc.*[287] The court held that the key definitional term "point source" in the FWPCA is ambiguous. Applying the rule of lenity, the Second Circuit held that a human being is not a point source and reversed criminal convictions under FWPCA §§301(a) and 309(c)(2) for disposing of vials containing tainted blood in navigable waters.

- *United States v. Heuer.*[288] The court reversed a conviction under RCRA §3008(d)(2)(B) for illegal disposal of hazardous waste, holding that in order "to support [criminal] liability under [§3008(d)(2)(B)] a condition, express or implied, must be clear on the face of a permit."[289] There was no express provision in the facility's permit that prohibited it from burning wastes that were generated at other facilities, and this condition could neither be implied from prior course of dealings between the regulator and the permit holder nor deemed incorporated by reference.

- *United States v. Self.*[290] The court found that EPA's RCRA regulations were ambiguous as to whether natural gas condensate burned as fuel was classified as a hazardous waste. The court interpreted the ambiguous language against the government and reversed several RCRA convictions predicated on this ground.

- *United States v. Goodner Bros. Aircraft.*[291] The Eighth Circuit overturned criminal convictions that had been premised on the RCRA mixture rule, which the D.C. Circuit had since invalidated based on EPA's failure to comply with the Administrative Procedure Act in promulgating the rule.[292]

- *Adamo Wrecking Co. v. United States.*[293] This case establishes a narrow exception to the CAA's preclusive review provision, which provides that the validity of EPA emissions standards may be challenged only by civil suits filed in the D.C. Circuit immediately after the rules are promulgated.[294] *Adamo* involved a CAA criminal prosecution in which the defendant challenged EPA's authority to issue a work practice standard for asbestos in place of a rule. The appellate court held that the preclusive review provision barred his defense that EPA had authority only to issue an emissions standard, not a work practice standard. The Supreme Court reversed, holding that the defendant's objection that the work practice standard was invalid was not subject to the preclusive review provision, and that the district court had jurisdiction to entertain this objection to the indictment.[295]

Although several such approaches have worked, broader lessons can be drawn from the more frequent cases in which courts have rejected proffered defenses. For example:

- *United States v. Louisville Edible Oil Products, Inc.*[296] The court rejected the double jeopardy argument that the federal government could not bring criminal charges against a company against whom a local environmental agency had already imposed large fines for violations of the CAA and CERCLA.

286. Use of this theory has not been limited to the private sector. Justice has argued that senior officials of federal departments could be subject to criminal prosecution under the same theory, if they fail to seek or approve increased appropriations to accelerate the cleanup of known environmental violations at federal facilities their agencies manage. Justice ultimately abandoned this argument when the Office of Management and Budget (OMB) offered to submit to Congress a supplemental appropriations for cleanup funds that would "bust" the President's budget and be characterized as mandatory spending pursuant to Justice's legal opinion.

287. 3 F.3d 643 (2d Cir. 1993), *cert. denied sub nom.* United States v. Villegas, 114 S. Ct. 2764 (1994).

288. 4 F.3d 723, 23 ELR 21357 (9th Cir. 1993), *cert. denied*, 114 S. Ct. 1190 (1994).

289. *Id.* at 731, 23 ELR 21360.

290. 2 F.3d 1071, 23 ELR 21301 (10th Cir. 1993).

291. 966 F.2d 380, 22 ELR 21201 (8th Cir. 1992), *cert. denied*, 113 S. Ct. 967 (1993).

292. *See* Shell Oil Co. v. Environmental Protection Agency, 950 F.2d 741, 22 ELR 20305 (D.C. Cir. 1991, *amended* 1992); *see supra* notes 137-38 and accompanying text.

293. 434 U.S. 275, 8 ELR 20171 (1978).

294. 42 U.S.C. §7607(b), ELR STAT. CAA §307(b).

295. *Adamo*, 434 U.S. at 285, 8 ELR at 20173.

296. 926 F.2d 584, 21 ELR 20690 (6th Cir.), *cert. denied*, 112 S. Ct. 177 (1991).

• *United States v. Mills.*[297] The court rejected the defendants' argument that Congress had unconstitutionally delegated to an administrative agency the power under the FWPCA to define "waters of the United States" as including "wetlands."

• *United States v. Ellen.*[298] The court rejected arguments that uncertainty over the definition of wetlands denied the defendant due process and violated the Ex Post Facto Clause.

• *United States v. Boldt.*[299] The court held that the FWPCA does not recognize a defense of economic or business necessity. Thus, the issue of whether the only alternative to noncompliance was closure of the plant could not be presented to the jury.

• *United States v. Marathon Development Corp.*[300] The court rejected arguments that provisions in the FWPCA authorizing states to impose more stringent water quality standards than those required by EPA denied criminal defendants equal protection of the law.

Finally, in several instances counsel have raised the defense of entrapment by estoppel, arguing that the defendant acted in reliance on instructions or guidance from a state or federal official about how to comply with the environmental rules governing the conduct that was the subject of the indictment. This is a familiar defense in other regulatory fields.[301] As far as can be determined, however, this defense has never been successfully invoked at the trial or appellate stage of an environmental case.

Conclusion

As long as environmental crimes continue to be subject to a de minimis knowledge requirement, defendants will have little prospect of defeating the government at trial on the issue of intent, which ordinarily is the centerpiece of a white-collar criminal case. This harsh reality gives prosecutors substantial leverage to compel targets to enter into plea agreements, either at the completion of the criminal investigation or before trial. Accordingly, in most cases the only realistic means of avoiding liability will be through successful defense of the investigation. It is in this area that seasoned environmental crimes counsel can make a significant difference in the outcome.

The Conduct of an Environmental Investigation

Background

How should a company respond when the government commences an environmental criminal investigation against it? At that point, all the company knows is that the government has preliminarily determined that a regulatory violation may present a significant risk of environmental damage or may have been committed deliberately. In particular, how does a potential target defend itself when the knowledge element in environmental crimes is so minimal?

There are several basic procedures that a regulated entity that becomes the target of an environmental criminal case should follow. The first and best line of defense is to have an effective environmental self-audit program to identify and resolve problems before they become serious. Environmental auditing is not used as frequently as it should be, however, due in part to governmental reluctance to give formal protection to internal documents generated during the audit process.

Once an adversarial investigation begins, the government has many different means by which it can extract from the regulated entity information relevant to its environmental practices. To protect itself, the company must mount its own internal investigation to obtain a complete understanding of what happened and who was involved, and to "reverse engineer" the government's investigation—that is, to determine what facts the prosecutor knows and what legal theories are being pursued. Experienced environmental criminal counsel can significantly contribute to the defense effort through imparting knowledge of the factors that will be relevant to the government's ultimate decision whether to indict and on what charges. Counsel can also assist a company in making the strategic decision whether to disclose to the government the results of the internal investigation in an effort to mitigate the civil regulatory consequences, or to be less forthcoming and preserve that evidence for trial.

In appropriate circumstances, the government may—but will not necessarily—simultaneously prosecute civil and criminal cases involving the same set of facts. If the civil action is delayed pending resolution of the criminal matter, the target must nevertheless conduct its own internal investigation with the constant understanding of the potential regulatory consequences and the impact the criminal resolution will have on future permit conditions and cleanup obligations.

Environmental Self-Audits—The First Line of Defense

The best method of avoiding an environmental investigation in the first instance is to establish a routine self-auditing program to detect pollution threats and correct minor problems before they become significant.

In developing an auditing program, corporate counsel should consider including the following elements:[302]

- attention to compliance issues and periodic reporting by line managers;
- formal integration of environmental policies, standards, and procedures in the company's operating procedures;

297. 817 F. Supp. 1546, 23 ELR 21096 (N.D. Fla. 1993).

298. 961 F.2d 462, 22 ELR 21282 (4th Cir. 1992).

299. 929 F.2d 35, 21 ELR 20998 (1st Cir. 1991).

300. 867 F.2d 96, 19 ELR 20683 (1st Cir. 1989).

301. *See, e.g.*, United States v. Brebner, 951 F.2d 1017 (9th Cir. 1991) (false statement on application to purchase firearm).

302. These elements are derived from Advisory Working Group on Environmental Sanctions, Proposed Federal Sentencing Guidelines for Organizations Convicted of Environmental Offenses (Nov. 16, 1993) §9D1.1(a) [hereinafter Draft Environmental Sentencing Guidelines]; *see* 58 Fed. Reg. 65764 (Dec. 16, 1993) (notice of public availability). *See infra* notes 503-15 and accompanying text. Counsel may also wish to consult the International Environmental Management Standards set forth in ISO 14000, developed by the International Standards Organization. Comprehensive guidance to the actual nuts and bolts of an effective environmental compliance and self-auditing program can be found in Frank B. Friedman, Practical Guide to Environmental Management (6th ed. 1995).

- creation of a system for auditing, monitoring, and reporting environmental problems and tracking resolution of compliance problems that are detected;
- establishment of effective environmental training programs for corporate employees and managers;
- creation of incentives that reward employee compliance efforts;
- imposition of disciplinary actions on employees who violate environmental obligations; and
- a commitment to continuing evaluation and upgrading of corporate environmental compliance and self-auditing programs.

Benefits and Risks of Environmental Self-Audits

From the regulated community's perspective, voluntary auditing and disclosure has many benefits. It helps:

- verify the environmental compliance of regulated facilities and evaluate the effectiveness of environmental management systems;
- detect potential problems and minimize pollution that does occur;
- prioritize compliance concerns and provide a method for allocating capital to address environmental problems;
- generate company protocols that help facilities better manage themselves and allow headquarters to monitor more effectively the performance of plant operations;
- provide a forum for employees to report information concerning violations;
- enhance the company's political and public relations; and
- anticipate and respond to emergency situations.

From the government's perspective, voluntary auditing helps enforcement authorities use their limited resources more efficiently by encouraging corporate vigilance regarding compliance and identification of violations without governmental intervention. Self-detection and reporting protects the environment and frees up enforcement resources to tackle the most egregious hidden problems.[303] And from the public's perspective, voluntary auditing and disclosure can create a cleaner environment and protect public health at less taxpayer expense.

The apparent risks of environmental audits, such as the government's potential use of audit findings against a company allegedly in violation of the law, fall directly on regulated entities. But the public also suffers if auditing is discouraged, insofar as pollution that could otherwise be prevented continues undetected due to the *in terrorem* threat of prosecution.

Companies must therefore conduct their audit programs with awareness that if the audit discovers violations that must be reported, or if the problems are not corrected immediately, there is a risk that criminal prosecutors may later use the audit documents as a road map for proving liability. Corporate officials have long complained that the risk of increasing their personal and institutional exposure has created disincentives to pursuing proactive audit programs that would clearly protect the environment.

Applicability of Common-Law Protections for Information Disclosed in Self-Audits

There are substantial doubts whether common-law doctrines such as the attorney-client, work product, or self-evaluation privileges protect documents generated in routine environmental audits from disclosure.[304]

The attorney-client privilege is likely inapplicable, because it protects only confidential communications between a lawyer and client that occur in the course of providing legal advice.[305] In order to extend the attorney-client privilege to routine audits, corporate counsel must specifically request each audit, the auditors must not communicate extensively with employees or regulators outside counsel's presence, auditors must address all written materials to counsel (marked as privileged), counsel must have direct control over the final audit report, and counsel must actually expend a significant amount of time participating in the auditing process and record that time in some fashion.[306] However, it is environmental consultants who often carry out many aspects of these audits; corporate counsel usually do not actively participate, because the expense and delay from their involvement are not cost-effective.[307] The con-

303. Congress clearly recognized these benefits in considering the criminal enforcement provision of the CAA Amendments of 1990, 42 U.S.C. §7413, ELR STAT. CAA §113:

> Nothing in subsection 113(c) is intended to discourage owners and operators of sources subject to this Act from conducting self-evaluations or self-audits and acting to correct any problems identified. On the contrary, the environmental benefits from such review and prompt corrective action are substantial and section 113 should be read to encourage self-evaluation and self-audits.
> Owners and operators of sources are in the best position to identify deficiencies and correct them, and should be encouraged to adopt procedures where internal compliance audits are performed and management is informed. Such internal audits will improve the owners' and operators' ability to identify and correct problems before, rather than after, government inspections and other enforcement actions are needed.

H.R. CONF. REP. NO. 952, 101st Cong., 2d Sess. 348 (1990).

304. By contrast, materials generated in a specific corporate audit after an actual environmental discharge generally are fully protected from disclosure under the work product doctrine, because such after-the-fact reviews are normally conducted by counsel "in anticipation of litigation." *See infra* note 315 and accompanying text.

305. *E.g.*, United States v. White, 950 F.2d 426 (7th Cir. 1991).

306. *See* Ohio-Sealey Mattress Mfg. Co. v. Kaplan, 90 F.R.D. 21, 28 (N.D. Ill. 1980).

307. Given the expense and delay of counsel's full involvement, some companies have devised practices that are less intensive but provide some degree of protection from the privilege. First, the moment a routine audit turns up a potential problem, it is made a separate project and counsel is involved. This puts the entity in a better position to claim attorney-client privilege, or even work product privilege, because legal advice is thereafter more clearly the focus of any future efforts related to the problem. Second, counsel reviews any final audit report carefully to make sure that the information is not framed in an unnecessarily inculpatory fashion. Third, some companies routinely destroy audit materials on a scheduled basis. Careful internal controls are necessary, however, because this activity could easily be construed as obstruction of justice if the material concerns a current investigation. Fourth, audit reports are distributed strictly on a "need to know" basis to avoid violating confidentiality requirements. The most important principle, however, is that the company must be prepared to disclose fully and voluntarily all violations that are discovered, pay the penalties, and remediate completely any resulting contamination.

fidentiality requirement is difficult to satisfy when courts view the consultants as invasive third parties, rather than as agents of the attorney. Even when attorneys are involved, courts may well conclude that a routine audit was intended to provide unprivileged "business" advice, rather than "legal" advice.[308] Case law examining application of the attorney-client privilege to routine environmental audits is sparse and inconsistent.[309] Furthermore, decisions considering the privilege in the context of other environmental compliance activities suggest that it may not protect audit materials.[310]

Similarly, there is little prospect of protecting audit materials under the common-law self-evaluative privilege. To qualify for protection under this privilege, the party asserting it must satisfy all of the following criteria:

- the information must result from a critical self-analysis undertaken by the party seeking protection;
- the public must have a strong interest in preserving the free flow of the type of information sought;
- the information must be of a type whose flow would be curtailed if discovery were allowed; and
- the information must be prepared with the expectation that it will be kept confidential and must, in fact, be kept confidential.[311]

With one exception,[312] courts have refused to apply this qualified privilege to routine environmental audits, even in litigation between private parties.[313] Outside the environmental area, decisions have uniformly held that the self-evaluative privilege applies only in private actions and not when the government seeks the material.[314] Thus, the doctrine would not seem to apply when EPA or Justice seeks environmental audit material through grand jury subpoenas, or the facts disclosed by those studies through regulatory reporting powers.

Finally, by definition, the work product doctrine cannot cover material produced in a routine environmental audit, as opposed to a specific audit, because the privilege protects only materials produced by or for an attorney "in anticipation of litigation."[315]

Steps Toward a Federal Policy on Self-Audits

Because of the enforcement risks associated with voluntary self-auditing, regulated industries have long argued that corrective federal policies are needed in order to foster environmentally beneficial and cost-effective audit programs, especially by small- to medium-sized companies. The regulated community has sought enforceable guarantees that audit documents will not be used against the disclosing company or individuals under any circumstances.

Ex ante, federal policy should encourage comprehensive corporate self-audits, because they directly protect the environment by preventing pollution. After a problem has occurred, however, prosecutors want to use audit documents to lessen the burden of proving their case, on both the fact of violation and knowledge. For over a decade, the federal policy process has been unable to resolve the difference in the before-the-fact and after-the-fact perspectives. EPA and Justice have hedged their bets by issuing policy statements that recognize the benefits of environmental audits while fully preserving prosecutors' ability to obtain and use these materials when necessary.

EPA's and Justice's first efforts to devise policies to encourage routine audits did not achieve their goals. The agencies failed to create legally enforceable rights to protect audit materials from disclosure or otherwise guarantee that companies would not be prosecuted or that penalties would be reduced for violations discovered and disclosed as a result of routine environmental audits.

☐ *EPA Policy.* EPA initially published a policy statement in 1986 that identified the three critical problems an environmental audit presents, but did not resolve them satisfactorily.[316]

- *Legal effect.* EPA issued the policy as agency guidance, rather than as a regulation that would be legally enforceable against the Agency in court.
- *Mitigation of punishment.* EPA stated that it would consider good-faith efforts by regulated companies to identify and correct environmental violations, but the language it used was equivocal: "When regulated entities take reasonable precautions to avoid noncompliance, expeditiously correct underlying environmental problems discovered through audits or other means, and implement measures to prevent their recurrence, EPA *may* exercise its discretion to *consider* such actions. . . ."[317]
- *Subsequent use in criminal prosecution.* EPA stated that it would not "routinely" request environmental audit reports for use in subsequent enforcement actions. But the Agency fully preserved

308. *See* Simon v. G.D. Searle & Co., 816 F.2d 397, 403 (8th Cir.) (business documents, such as internal risk-management estimates, sent to corporate officers and lawyers are not automatically privileged), *cert. denied*, 484 U.S. 917 (1987); *see also* 4 MOORE'S FEDERAL PRACTICE ¶26.11[2] at 175-77 (1995).

309. *See, e.g.*, United States v. Chevron, No. 88-6681, 1989 U.S. Dist. LEXIS 12267 (E.D. Pa. Oct. 16, 1989) (privilege rejected); Olen Properties Corp. v. Sheldahl, Inc., 24 ELR 20936 (C.D. Cal. Apr. 12, 1994) (privilege upheld).

310. *See, e.g.*, U.S. Postal Serv. v. Phelps Dodge Ref. Corp., 852 F. Supp. 156 (E.D.N.Y. 1994) (preparation of a waste management plan viewed as an "environmental" service, not a "legal" service, and therefore not protected); In re Grand Jury Matter, 147 F.R.D. 82 (E.D. Pa. 1992) (environmental studies of soil and remediation of property were not privileged even though in-house counsel participated substantially in the process, because many of the tasks could have been performed by nonattorneys).

311. Bredice v. Doctors Hosp., Inc., 50 F.R.D. 249, *aff'd on reh'g*, 51 F.R.D. 187 (D.D.C. 1970), *aff'd*, 479 F.2d 920 (D.C. Cir. 1973).

312. *See* Reichhold Chems., Inc. v. Textron, Inc., 25 ELR 20307 (N.D. Fla. 1994) (privilege upheld).

313. *See* Koppers Co. v. Aetna Casualty & Sur. Co., 847 F. Supp. 360 (W.D. Pa. 1994) (privilege denied); United States v. Dexter Corp., 132 F.R.D. 8 (D. Conn. 1990) (privilege denied).

314. *See, e.g.*, FTC v. TRW, Inc., 628 F.2d 207 (D.C. Cir. 1980); Emerson Elec. Co. v. Schlesinger, 609 F.2d 898 (8th Cir. 1979); United States v. Noall, 587 F.2d 123 (2d. Cir. 1978); Reynolds Metals Co. v. Rumsfeld, 564 F.2d 663 (4th Cir. 1977).

315. Hickman v. Taylor, 329 U.S. 495 (1946); *see generally* Jeffrey F. Ghent, Annotation, *Developments, Since* Hickman v. Taylor, *of Attorney's "Work Product" Doctrine*, 35 A.L.R.3d 412 (1971); *Depositions & Discovery*, 23 AM. JUR. 2d §55 (1983) (Statements of Reports Prepared in the Regular Course of Business). The work product doctrine can, however, apply to specific audits. *See supra* note 304.

316. U.S. EPA, Environmental Auditing Policy Statement, 51 Fed. Reg. 25004 (July 9, 1986).

317. *Id.* at 25007 (emphasis added).

its discretion to obtain and use a company's audit reports against it, including in a subsequent criminal investigation.[318]

Further, the guidance required companies to cooperate fully with the government and voluntarily disclose their audit materials in order to qualify for leniency and forbearance of subsequent use.[319] Such disclosure, however, might result in the disclosing entity's waiving its common-law privileges for purposes of private damage actions.[320]

Despite these problems, the 1986 audit policy was a useful step forward and served to frame the debate on this issue. Many companies—especially large firms—established audit policies for their own corporate reasons. Some of these companies have taken comfort in the guidance in discovering and reporting violations to regulators. Moreover, EPA applied the policy responsibly. The Agency generally honored its pledge not to initiate a criminal investigation of a company that voluntarily disclosed all materials related to a violation. It did, however, seek substantial civil penalties based on such disclosures.[321]

In 1993, several states began to respond to the regulated community's requests for greater protection for audit material.[322] To defuse these developments, EPA clarified its policy on audits in January 1994.[323] The update was somewhat more forthcoming than the Agency's 1986 guidance. EPA stated that self-auditing and full disclosure "should be considered as mitigating factors" and that violations "fully and promptly remedied as part of a corporation's systematic and comprehensive self-evaluation program generally [would] not be a candidate for the expenditure of scarce criminal investigative resources."[324] This articulation still reserved substantial discretion to EPA, however, and ultimately did not serve to head off the movement for greater certainty. As the momentum for an audit privilege built in the states, EPA published a restatement of its principles on auditing in June 1994[325] and commenced a series of meetings in July 1994[326] to determine how it should respond to concerns regarding its existing policy.

In March 1995, EPA issued an interim final revision of its audit policy that superseded the 1986 version and attempted to provide—without creating safe harbors that would hamstring enforcement—greater assurances to companies that wished to maintain effective self-audit programs.[327] The latest policy applies to environmental violations that are uncovered during self-evaluation, voluntarily disclosed, and promptly corrected, provided that the company complies with certain enumerated conditions.[328] In particular, the violator must commit to rectify any harms, adopt measures to prevent future violations, and cooperate with the regulator.[329] In addition, EPA may require the violator to enter into a written agreement or consent decree to assure that the conditions are satisfied.[330] Further, the policy provides that EPA will not refer a self-reported violation for criminal prosecution against the company unless the investigation shows a corporate practice of concealing or condoning environmental violations, high-level corporate involvement, blindness to the violation, or serious harm to human health or the environment.[331]

EPA's latest action is a welcome step forward because it adds real substance to the outline adopted in 1986 and commits the Agency to treating voluntary disclosures fairly. However, although the "body language" encourages audit programs, the text of the revised policy fails to resolve any of the major policy issues EPA identified in its earlier policy:

- *Legal effect.* Like the 1986 policy, the 1995 statement is guidance and thus is unenforceable against EPA in court. Further, the 1995 guidance does not even have the same standing within the Agency as the 1986 policy it replaced. The 1995 version was signed only by the Assistant Administrator for Enforcement; the Administrator issued the 1986 version. Finally, the statement itself provides that enforcement officials are free to "act at variance with the guidance" in specific cases.[332] It therefore fails to address the regulated community's concerns that reporting firms will always be exposed to demands for audit documents.

- *Mitigation of punishment.* The 1995 policy provides that for voluntary disclosures, EPA will elimi-

318. "EPA's authority to request an audit report, or relevant portions thereof, will be exercised on a case-by-case basis where the Agency determines it is needed to accomplish a statutory mission, or where the Government deems it to be material to a criminal investigation." *Id.*

319. *Id.*

320. Courts are divided over whether documents disclosed to the government in an enforcement action remain eligible for common-law privileges against disclosure to third parties in other actions. *See, e.g.,* Westinghouse Elec. Corp. v. Philippines, 951 F.2d 1414 (3d Cir. 1991) (privilege waived); In re Martin Marietta Corp., 856 F.2d 619 (4th Cir. 1988) (privilege waived); Permian Corp. v. United States, 665 F.2d 1214 (D.C. Cir. 1981) (privilege waived); Diversified Indus., Inc. v. Meredith, 572 F.2d 596 (8th Cir. 1977) (en banc) (upholding privilege on limited waiver theory). The implications of disclosure are discussed more fully *infra.*

Because waiver is a court-constructed doctrine, a change in *agency* rules or policy to allow for "limited waiver" would not be binding law. The only way to protect audit materials from third parties is either by EPA and Justice not requiring their disclosure in the first place or by Congress enacting a "limited waiver" statute. Thus, this risk is beyond the agencies' power to resolve, even with a binding rule.

321. There have been several important cases showing that the post-disclosure risk of civil punishment is real. *See, e.g., $1.05 Million Fine Against Coors May Deter Corporate Environmental Audits, Firm Says,* 24 Env't Rep. (BNA) 570 (July 30, 1993); United States v. Chevron, No. 88-6681, 1989 U.S. Dist. LEXIS 12267 (E.D. Pa. Oct. 16, 1989); United States v. Dexter Corp., 132 F.R.D. 8 (D. Conn. 1990); U.S. Postal Serv. v. Phelps Dodge Ref. Co., 852 F. Supp. 156 (E.D.N.Y. 1994). Similarly, a recent Price Waterhouse survey discovered 25 cases in which government agencies or third parties sought confidential audit information to prove a company's liability. Jim Moore & Nancy Newkirk, *Not Quite a Giant Step,* ENVTL. F., May/June 1995, at 16.

322. *See infra* notes 343-47 and accompanying text.

323. Devaney Memorandum, *supra* note 37.

324. *Id.* at 6.

325. U.S. EPA, Notice of Public Meeting on Auditing, 59 Fed. Reg. 31914 (June 20, 1994) (noting that Colorado, Indiana, Kentucky, and Oregon had enacted "self-evaluative" privileges for audit reports).

326. U.S. EPA, Restatement of Policies Related to Environmental Auditing, 59 Fed. Reg. 38455 (July 28, 1994) (notice).

327. U.S. EPA, Voluntary Environmental Self-Policing and Self-Disclosure Interim Policy Statement, 60 Fed. Reg. 16875 (Apr. 3, 1995).

328. *Id.* at 16876-77.

329. *Id.* at 16877.

330. *Id.* The policy sets forth the conditions a company must satisfy to enjoy the policy's two principal benefits—reduced civil penalties and nonreferral for criminal prosecution. *Id.* at 16877-78.

331. *Id.*

332. *Id.* at 16879.

nate or substantially reduce (up to 75 percent) the gravity component of the civil penalty, unless the violation constitutes "criminal conduct by the regulated entity or any of its employees."[333] This is a significant improvement over the former policy. This incentive, however, "does not apply to criminal acts of individuals managers or employers."[334] Thus, the 1995 policy does not protect individuals from prosecution under any circumstances. Nor does it mitigate the economic benefit/unjust enrichment component of civil penalties.[335]

• *Subsequent use in criminal prosecutions.* The 1995 policy provides that EPA will not request an environmental audit report unless a criminal or civil investigation is already underway based on information derived independently of the audit. This concession is not significant, however, because Justice retains full discretion to initiate a criminal prosecution when a violation is brought to its attention.

In sum, although the 1995 policy is an improvement on the former version, EPA's insistence on preserving its enforcement discretion through multiple exceptions to the guidelines guarantees that the issue will continue to simmer.

☐ *Justice Policy.* In July 1991, Justice issued the first comprehensive guidance on its policy toward prosecution in the case of voluntary disclosure of environmental problems.[336] The guidance provides that it is Justice's policy "to encourage self-auditing, self-policing and voluntary disclosure of environmental violations by the regulated community by indicating that these activities are viewed as mitigating factors in the Department's exercise of criminal environmental enforcement discretion."[337]

The guidelines detail, through extensive practical examples, factors that mitigate in a company's favor, such as voluntary disclosure and full cooperation. But the policy fails to offer clear guidance on when these factors will lead to a decision not to prosecute criminally, or on how much they can mitigate the charges or punishments Justice will seek.[338]

The principal factors Justice will consider are:

• whether the person "made voluntary, timely and complete disclosure" and whether the disclosure "substantially aided the government's investigatory process";

• whether the person gave full and prompt cooperation and made all relevant information available, "including the complete results of any internal or external investigation and the names of all potential witnesses"; and

• "the existence and size of any regularized, intensive, and comprehensive environmental compliance program," including an environmental compliance audit, which demonstrates a strong institutional commitment to environmental compliance.[339]

Other relevant factors include the persuasiveness of the noncompliance, effective internal disciplinary programs for environmental violations, and the promptness and completeness of actions taken to address the violation and remedy the environmental harm.[340]

Justice's enforcement policy has several problems. It reserves Justice's discretion to use audit documents when necessary to prove its case, regardless of whether the disclosure is voluntary and complete. The policy is not binding on the states, which have independent enforcement authority in most cases. Moreover, to the extent that it provides assurances, the policy is simply a guidance document, which is not legally binding against the agency.[341] In addition, with the delegation of greater enforcement discretion to the U.S. Attorneys, the policy against seeking access to audit documents except in extraordinary cases will no longer be centrally directed.[342] Finally, concerns about the potential for criminal liability have grown with the expansion of the federal enforcement program and the practical elimination of a meaningful knowledge element for criminal offenses.

In sum, current EPA and Justice enforcement policies require entities that self-audit and report to place an enormous

333. *Id.* at 16878. The policy also includes the Agency's intended response to a company's good-faith efforts to disclose and rectify environmental problems. *Id.* at 16876-77.

334. *Id.* at 16878.

335. There are at least two reasons why this approach fails to resolve industry concerns. First, the de minimis intent element for criminal violations means that virtually all violations may be prosecuted criminally. Thus, the "criminal conduct" exception can be read as swallowing the leniency the guidance suggests. Second, the policy applies only to disclosures that are not otherwise required by law. For companies that have obtained permits and are covered by reporting requirements, this exception would take away many of the policy's apparent benefits. In addition, there are numerous other reporting obligations under a wide array of environmental statutes that are outside the policy's scope. Thus, this approach may inadvertently treat more harshly companies that are doing their best to comply with the law.

336. Factors in Decisions on Criminal Prosecutions, *supra* note 42.

337. *Id.* at 1.

338. The proposed environmental sentencing guidelines for organizations set forth in detail the criteria for a model environmental compliance and auditing program. Draft Environmental Sentencing Guidelines, *supra* note 302. They provide for substantial mitigation of a criminal fine for a company that is convicted despite having such a program in place. This serves as small consolation to most companies, whose good-faith efforts ought to protect them from any criminal prosecution to begin with. Furthermore, the proposed guidelines do nothing to address companies' other major disincentive to voluntary auditing and disclosure—the prospect of sizeable civil penalties.

339. Factors in Decisions on Criminal Prosecutions, *supra* note 42, at 4-5.

340. *Id.* at 5-6.

341. *Id.* at 14-15; *see also* United States v. Caceres, 440 U.S. 741 (1979) (violation of Internal Revenue Service internal regulation not a basis for excluding tape recordings from evidence when neither Constitution nor federal law requires compliance with regulation). Like EPA's policy, Justice's guidance is not legally enforceable in court. It also requires companies to "cooperate" completely and to disclose audit materials in order to retain any hope of leniency. Compliance with this requirement effectively constitutes a waiver of common-law privileges if private parties seek access to internal investigation materials that companies have turned over to prosecutors. *See* United States v. Billmyer, 57 F.3d 31, 36-37 (1st Cir. 1995).

342. Even before this delegation of power, however, individual prosecutors occasionally used the threat to seek access to audit material as leverage to force plea bargains. Under the January 1993 bluesheet revision to the U.S. Attorneys Manual, review of requests for access to audit documents was one of the priority areas reserved for centralized review in Washington. *See* 1993 Bluesheet Revision, *supra* note 43. This policy was subsequently reversed by Attorney General Reno. *See* 1994 Bluesheet Revision, *supra* note 44. Under the new policy, main Justice has no formal role in such decisions by U.S. Attorneys.

amount of trust in investigators and prosecutors. These officials retain broad discretion to determine if compliance efforts have been adequate and may seek to bypass the stated policy as they see fit. Further, the reporting party has no recourse to judicial review concerning the policies' implementation.

Efforts to Adopt a Statutory Audit Privilege

While federal agencies have reacted grudgingly on the self-audit issue, the states have plunged ahead. Since Oregon's passage of an audit privilege law in July 1993, as of this writing, at least 14 states have enacted laws providing a qualified privilege for environmental audits.[343] At least 20 other states are considering enacting such laws.[344]

The audit privilege varies somewhat from state to state. In general,[345] it provides a qualified privilege that applies only when the audit was not required by law, the audit was not fraudulent, the company has responded properly to any noncompliance it has discovered as a result of the audit, and the company cooperates fully with enforcement personnel. In civil proceedings, the privilege is usually absolute. In criminal proceedings, audit material is typically available to a prosecutor who demonstrates a compelling need for the information through a showing similar to that necessary to obtain access to attorney work product material.[346] The privilege protects from disclosure most materials related to the audit, not just the final report. In most instances, this includes all analyses of the primary report and any documentation implementing the report.

The state legislation has created a substantial political problem for EPA, in terms of its ability to resist such legislation at the federal level and its enforcement of current programs. For states to which EPA has delegated authority to administer and enforce a federal environmental program, adoption of a self-audit privilege arguably makes the state program less effective than the federal counterpart, and thus provides a possible basis for revoking state authorization. However, the political consequence to EPA of revoking state program authorization—not to mention the strain on its resources—could be severe. Accordingly, EPA has followed a "jawboning" strategy, announcing its opposition to the privilege approach and its intention to review actual enforcement decisions carefully in states with privilege laws.[347] But it has yet to initiate the revocation process against any state. The Agency has also threatened to "overfile" by initiating its own enforcement action when a state forgoes enforcement against a violator that has invoked a state statutory audit privilege. This threat is largely hollow, however, given EPA's limited enforcement resources, and is increasingly unlikely to be implemented as more states adopt audit privileges.

As of this writing, the 104th Congress is also considering legislation that would provide protection for environmental audit materials and mitigation of penalties for voluntarily disclosed violations. In the House, H.R. 1047,[348] introduced by Rep. Joel Hefley (R-Colo.), closely tracks the Colorado statute.[349] It would provide a qualified privilege that would presumptively protect audit materials and provide substantial immunity for voluntary disclosures of violations. In the Senate, S. 582,[350] introduced by Sens. Mark Hatfield (R-Or.) and Hank Brown (R-Colo.), would offer an audit privilege similar to that of H.R. 1047, as well as substantial immunity to companies that voluntarily disclose violations discovered as a result of routine audits.

The Future of the Audit Privilege

The first principle of environmental enforcement should be how society can obtain the maximum reduction in pollution with the resources it has available. Systematic corporate self-audits could play an important role in that equation. The question is how can an audit policy and enforcement program work together to maximize environmental compliance and minimize actual pollution discharges? Such a policy should neither relax ongoing regulatory compliance and reporting obligations nor provide total immunity for violations reported.

Audits are one field in which the enforcers' desire to make certain that marginal violations do not escape enforcement may well be interfering with progress in the large universe of firms trying to comply with the law. In practice, EPA and Justice rarely rely on environmental audit materials to prosecute a criminal matter, except in extreme cases. The underlying facts surrounding a violation are discoverable, regardless of the audit, and all applicable compliance and reporting obligations remain in full force. In most cases, access to audit materials simply reduces the burden on enforcement staff and presents a useful checklist to make certain that the agency has not missed any available proof.

Under these circumstances, EPA and Justice policy officials need to ask themselves how much of an administrative burden would be involved in finally agreeing to forego access to self-audit materials in marginal cases. They need to compare the effect of reduced efficiency in those cases against the likely environmental protection benefits if more companies are encouraged to pursue routine and secure audit practices.

Governmental Authority to Obtain Corporate Information During an Investigation

Despite the best intentions and the most comprehensive self-audit programs, environmental violations may occur at

343. *See* 1995 Ark. Acts 350; Colo. Rev. Stat. §13.25-126.5 (1994); 1995 Idaho Sess. Laws 359; Ill. Ann. Stat. ch. 415, para. 5/52.2 (Smith-Hurd 1994); Ind. Code §13-10-3-1 (1994); 1995 Kan. Sess. Laws 204; Ky. Rev. Stat. Ann. §224.01-040 (Baldwin 1994); 1995 Minn. Sess. Law Serv. 168 (West); 1995 Miss. Laws 627; Or. Rev. Stat. §468.963 (1993); 1995 Tex. Sess. Law Serv. 219 (Vernon); 1995 Utah Laws 304; 1995 Va. Acts 564; 1995 Wyo. Sess. Laws 58. On April 19, 1995, the Governor of Arizona vetoed an audit privilege bill (S.B. 1290), which the state legislature had passed. *Arizona Governor Vetoes Audit Legislation*, 25 Env't Rep. (BNA) 2544 (Apr. 28, 1995).

344. *More States Adopt Audit Privilege Laws; EPA Calls Federal Legislation Ill-Advised*, 25 Env't Rep. (BNA) 2186, 2188 (Mar. 10, 1995).

345. *See, e.g.*, Colo. Rev. Stat. §13.25-126.5; Or. Rev. Stat. §468.963.

346. *See, e.g.*, Or. Rev. Stat. §468.963.

347. *No Audit Privilege in Interim EPA Policy; Lack of Prosecution, Punitive Fines Possible*, 25 Env't Rep. (BNA) 2411, 2412 (Apr. 7, 1995).

348. H.R. 1047, 104th Cong., 1st Sess. (1995). The bill was cosponsored by, among others, Minority Whip Tom DeLay (R-Tex.), Judiciary Committee Chairman Henry Hyde (R-Ill.), and Natural Resources Committee Chairman Don Young (R-Alaska).

349. Colo. Rev. Stat. §13.25-126.5.

350. S. 583, 104th Cong., 1st Sess. (1995).

even the best-managed facilities. Once a criminal investigation of a violation is initiated, there are six basic methods by which the government can obtain information from a corporation: (1) recordkeeping and reporting obligations; (2) informal visits or consensual inspections; (3) items in "plain view"; (4) inspections pursuant to administrative warrant procedures; (5) grand jury subpoenas; and (6) search warrants. Each mechanism involves applying familiar principles of probable cause or exceptions to the warrant requirement specifically in the environmental context. The company under investigation should be prepared to respond in a manner that is cooperative and does not obstruct the prosecution, while simultaneously fully preserving its rights to protect privileged information from disclosure.

Recordkeeping and Reporting Obligations

Many environmental statutes require regulated entities to maintain records and produce them for inspection.[351] These recordkeeping and production obligations have been upheld against due process challenges,[352] and are enforceable by civil and criminal penalties.[353] In addition, several statutes, including the CAA, contain provisions that allow EPA to demand production of information necessary to fulfilling its regulatory functions.[354] This authority may be used to request information from a single company or on an industrywide basis, as a prelude to a broad investigation.

Informal Visits or Consensual Inspections

An EPA inspector normally will not secure a warrant prior to visiting a site to make an inspection. Only in exceptional circumstances—such as when EPA considers a surprise inspection crucial to its enforcement goals—will the inspector attempt to obtain a warrant before seeking the company's consent to an inspection. Instead, the inspector will initially present his or her credentials and seek the consent of the owner or the person in charge. Consensual searches do not violate the Fourth Amendment's prohibition against unreasonable searches.[355] By eliminating the need to prepare papers showing probable cause, this approach conserves EPA's administrative resources. If consent is refused, then the inspector will seek an administrative warrant in court.[356]

Policy developments at EPA over the past several years may make these administrative inspections more intimidating to regulated entities than they used to be. Since approximately 1990, EPA policy has increasingly emphasized a multimedia approach that analyzes a facility's overall pollution impact rather than focusing separately and sequentially on air, water, and hazardous waste emissions as if they had no relation to one other. Further, EPA and the states are attempting to minimize the burden they impose on regulated entities by cross-training personnel to conduct inspections under multiple environmental statutes. In combination, these factors may mean that a consensual administrative inspection will turn into an expansive multimedia review of a plant's entire operations, which may trigger unwarranted alarm in operating personnel who had become accustomed to a narrower, medium-specific review.

"Plain View" Searches

Under the plain view doctrine,[357] EPA need not obtain a warrant to inspect things that are observable to the public or the naked eye of an investigator who has been lawfully admitted onto a facility to conduct an inspection.[358] For example, in *Dow Chemical Co. v. United States*,[359] the Supreme Court held that EPA's taking of aerial photographs of a company's premises without a warrant was lawful. The company had denied EPA's request for an on-site inspection of its 2,000-acre chemical plant. Rather than obtain an administrative warrant, EPA hired a photographer to take pictures of the plant from various altitudes. The Court held that no warrant was required, because the aerial observation involved no physical entry and the company had no reasonable expectation of privacy in the photographed area.[360]

Administrative Inspections

Each major federal environmental statute provides for administrative inspections of regulated facili-

351. For example, CERCLA requires maintenance of records relating to the location and condition of a facility where hazardous waste has been stored, plus the identity and characteristics of such waste. 42 U.S.C. §9603(d), ELR STAT. CERCLA §103(d). FIFRA requires pesticide producers to maintain certain records regarding their operations and products. 7 U.S.C. §136f(a), ELR STAT. FIFRA §8(a). The FWPCA requires regulated facilities to maintain records as a condition to obtaining a discharge permit. 33 U.S.C. §1318(a), ELR STAT. FWPCA §308(a). TSCA requires chemical manufacturers to maintain records relating to the environmental and health effects of the chemical substances they produce, plus records of significant adverse environmental or physical reactions alleged to be caused by their chemicals. 15 U.S.C. §2607, ELR STAT. TSCA §8.

352. *See, e.g.*, United States v. Tivian Labs., Inc., 589 F.2d 49, 9 ELR 20008 (1st Cir. 1978).

353. During the 1980s and early 1990s, EPA allowed the clearances for many of its record retention obligations to lapse, in violation of the Paperwork Reduction Act. Under the Act's public protection provision, EPA cannot bring enforcement actions for violations of paperwork requirements whose OMB clearance numbers have lapsed. 44 U.S.C. §3512. This led to the demise of several pending cases and the non-institution of many others.

354. *See* 42 U.S.C. §7414(a), ELR STAT. CAA §114(a) (EPA may require emission sources to establish and maintain records, to file reports, to install and use monitoring devices, and to provide such other information as the Agency may reasonably require).

355. Schneckloth v. Bustamonte, 412 U.S. 218 (1973).

356. Indeed, an investigator's proposal to obtain prior judicial authorization requires preapproval from the appropriate EPA regional office. Memorandum from Assistant Administrator for Enforcement, to Regional Administrators et al., Conduct of Inspections After the *Barlow's* Decision 2 (Apr. 11, 1979) (available from the ELR Document Service, ELR Order No. AD-869) [hereinafter Memorandum on Conducting Inspections]. The memorandum refers to the Supreme Court's decision in Marshall v. Barlow's, Inc., 436 U.S. 307, 8 ELR 20434 (1978). *See infra* notes 367-70 and accompanying text.

357. *See* Coolidge v. New Hampshire, 403 U.S. 443 (1971) (in arresting defendant, police did not require a warrant to seize automobiles in plain view in driveway); Horton v. California, 496 U.S. 128 (1990) (seizure of evidence not described in warrant but in plain view is permissible, even though discovery of the evidence was not inadvertent).

358. "[A]n inspector's observations from the public area of a plant or even from certain private property not closed to the public are admissible. Observations made before presentation of credentials while on private property which is not normally closed to the public are admissible." Memorandum on Conducting Inspections, *supra* note 356, at 12 n.18.

359. 476 U.S. 227, 16 ELR 20679 (1986).

360. *Id.* at 237-38, 16 ELR at 20682-83.

ties.[361] These provisions give EPA a cost-effective means of auditing the accuracy of required reports and following up on reports of violations.[362]

Courts have repeatedly upheld against statutory and constitutional challenges the Agency's broad authority to conduct administrative inspections under these provisions. For example, in *In re An Order Pursuant to Section 3013(d) RCRA, 42 U.S.C. §6934(d)*,[363] the court upheld the constitutionality of RCRA's administrative inspection provision against a Fourth Amendment challenge. The court rejected the defendant's motion to quash an ex parte administrative warrant, noting Congress' recognition of the "'clear danger to the health and safety of the population and to the quality of the environment'" that hazardous wastes pose.[364] And in *National-Standard Co. v. Adamkus*,[365] the court rejected an argument that under RCRA §3007(a), EPA could only enter places where it *knew* hazardous waste was being or had been stored. The court held that "'[t]he main purpose of an inspection and sampling visit is to detect the presence of hazardous wastes. If EPA could not inspect an area unless it knew hazardous wastes were stored there, EPA would be rendered effectively powerless.'"[366]

The scope of EPA's administrative inspection authority is defined by *Marshall v. Barlow's, Inc.*,[367] which involved an analogous administrative inspection provision under §8(a) of the OSH Act.[368] There, the Supreme Court noted that administrative inspections are "searches" for Fourth Amendment purposes and that the Fourth Amendment applies to searches of commercial buildings.[369] An administrative search warrant may therefore issue only on a showing of "probable cause." However, "probable cause" for purposes of issuing such a warrant substantially differs from that needed to obtain a criminal search warrant. Under *Barlow's*, probable cause for an administrative search warrant may be based on either specific evidence of an existing violation or a showing that the inspection is being conducted pursuant to a neutral enforcement scheme.[370] According to EPA guidance, an employee's complaint or a competitor's tip may provide "specific evidence" constituting probable cause.[371] "Neutral scheme" probable cause may be established by a showing that the premises are being inspected pursuant to a regularly imposed schedule.[372] EPA has prepared descriptions of the particular neutral administrative schemes under which inspections pursuant to each of its programs are to be conducted.[373]

The warrant requirement established in *Barlow's* is not absolute. The Supreme Court has held that in emergencies and in truly "exigent circumstances," the Fourth Amendment does not require a warrant for an entry and administrative search.[374] According to EPA guidance, emergency situations include those involving potential imminent health hazards or the potential for the destruction or dissipation of evidence.[375] No appellate decision has yet construed the scope of this emergency/exigent circumstances exception in the environmental law context.

Grand Jury Subpoenas

A company may first learn that its conduct is under criminal investigation when the government serves it a grand jury subpoena for the production of documents. Environmental prosecutors frequently issue subpoenas at the early stages of an investigation because the breadth of the grand jury's power enables them to obtain a wide range of books and records, including financial data and internal memoranda. The grand jury power complements, and does not supersede, EPA's administrative authority to demand production of documents.[376]

The rules governing a subpoena duces tecum are the same in the environmental area as elsewhere. The subpoena must be both reasonable and specific.[377] A subpoena that designates the types of documents with reasonable particularity is adequate. Objections to subpoenas may be raised prior to compliance through a motion to quash. Courts, however, accord environmental prosecutors broad discretion in fashioning subpoenas. They will seldom grant a motion to quash in the face of an assertion by the government that the material sought is reasonably related to a matter under investigation. At best, the court will narrow the scope of a subpoena that is unreasonable or oppressive under the power granted by Fed. R. Crim. P. 17(c).

There are numerous grounds for moving to quash to a subpoena in the environmental area. Objections may challenge relevance[378] or the fact that the subpoena requests documents that cover an unreasonable period of time.[379] A subpoena may also be challenged when it calls for privileged materials, including those covered by the attorney-client

361. *See* 42 U.S.C. §6927(a), ELR Stat. RCRA §3007(a); *id.* §9604(e), ELR Stat. CERCLA §104(e); *id.* §7414(a), ELR Stat. CAA §114(a); 33 U.S.C. §1318(a), ELR Stat. FWPCA §308(a); 15 U.S.C. §2610, ELR Stat. TSCA §11; 7 U.S.C. §136g, ELR Stat. FIFRA §9.

362. The times at which these inspections may be performed are left to the Agency's reasonable discretion. For example, CERCLA authorizes EPA to enter facilities "at reasonable times." 42 U.S.C. §9604(e)(3), ELR Stat. CERCLA §104(e)(3). RCRA provides for mandatory biennial inspection of all permitted facilities and authorizes permissive administrative inspections "at all reasonable times." 42 U.S.C. §6927(a) and (e), ELR Stat. RCRA §3007(a) and (e).

363. 550 F. Supp. 1361, 13 ELR 20370 (W.D. Wash. 1982).

364. *Id.* at 1363, 13 ELR at 20371 (quoting H.R. 1491, 94th Cong., 2d Sess. 3, *reprinted in* U.S.C.C.A.N. 6238, 6241).

365. 881 F.2d 352, 19 ELR 21144 (7th Cir. 1989).

366. *Id.* at 360, 19 ELR at 21148 (quoting the district court's opinion in National-Standard Co. v. Adamkus, 685 F. Supp. 1040, 1049, 18 ELR 21455, 21460 (N.D. Ill. 1988)).

367. 436 U.S. 307, 8 ELR 20434 (1978).

368. 29 U.S.C. §657(a).

369. *Barlow's*, 436 U.S. at 311-15, 8 ELR 20434 at 20435-36.

370. *Id.* at 320-21, 8 ELR at 20437.

371. Memorandum on Conducting Inspections, *supra* note 356, at 7.

372. *Id.*

373. *Id.* at 11.

374. *See* Michigan v. Clifford, 464 U.S. 287, 293 (1987) (aftermath of a fire presents exigencies that do not tolerate the delay necessary to obtain an administrative search warrant).

375. Memorandum on Conducting Inspections, *supra* note 356, at 5.

376. *See* 42 U.S.C. §7414(a), ELR Stat. CAA §114(a); 33 U.S.C. §1318(a), ELR Stat. FWPCA §308(a).

377. Hale v. Henkel, 201 U.S. 43 (1906); United States v. Reno, 522 F.2d 572 (10th Cir. 1975); 2 Charles A. Wright, Federal Practice and Procedure: Criminal §275 (2d ed. 1982).

378. United States v. Reed, 726 F.2d 570 (9th Cir.), *cert. denied*, 469 U.S. 871 (1984).

379. United States v. Lieberman, 608 F.2d 889, 904 (1st Cir.), *cert. denied*, 444 U.S. 1019 (1979).

privilege or work product doctrine.[380] When documents are sought from individuals, the Fifth Amendment privilege against self-incrimination may be invoked.[381] Finally, objections may be raised if the prosecutor uses the grand jury after indictment for the sole purpose of gathering and preparing evidence for trial.[382]

In responding to a subpoena, the company should designate one responsible officer to ensure that the response will be accurate and timely.[383] The officer should contact in-house counsel immediately, and counsel should initiate a careful review of the request to determine the focus of the investigation. The government is not obligated to—and, if asked, will not—reveal the focus or scope of its investigation. However, analysis of the request may reveal the direction of the investigation and enable the company to determine what triggered the government's interest. It may also help the company decide which of its employees to interview. If the company determines that it is the target of the investigation, it should immediately hire experienced outside counsel to defend the investigation.

Counsel should then meet with the assigned prosecutor to discuss the investigation. This meeting can provide an opportunity for counsel to establish a working relationship with the prosecutor and the investigators, and to demonstrate the corporation's willingness to be forthcoming with information. Counsel can also attempt, often successfully, to narrow the scope of the subpoena and obtain additional time to comply.

Next, counsel should meet with senior management and those directly involved with the division, facility, activity, or program described in the subpoena to identify all sources of documents responsive to the government's demand and the places in which such documents are likely to be located. The company should circulate a memorandum formally designating the officer responsible for collecting responsive documents and assigning specific employees the task of searching for and delivering these documents. The memorandum should also establish a deadline for completing the document search and designate a location to which responsive documents are to be delivered. In addition, the memorandum should clearly state that no requested documents are to be destroyed or sent to records retention, and that the government will likely perceive failure to produce responsive documents—whether intentional or not—as obstruction of justice.

After compiling all potentially responsive documents, counsel and the designated official should review each file to identify documents that must be submitted. Discovering responsive documents after production has been made is, at best, embarrassing and, at worst, can lead to obstruction of justice charges. If a large volume of material is involved, the responsive documents should be numbered and a computer database created to identify each document by number, author, recipient, date, and summary of content. The document database is particularly useful during an ongoing investigation in which the government serves more than one subpoena.

All responsive documents should be closely reviewed to determine whether they contain privileged communications or attorney work product. The protected documents should not be produced; rather, a "Vaughn" index should be submitted that identifies and describes the documents withheld, without revealing their contents.[384]

If subpoenaed documents include confidential trade secrets, the company should request an agreement with the government to avoid disclosure of such material to a competitor. These documents should be clearly stamped and identified as to their sensitive nature. Finally, no document should be produced before it has been copied. Counsel should retain a complete set of all documents produced.

From counsel's perspective, document production provides the opportunity to learn the nuts and bolts of the company's operations, its chain of command, and where the government's case may be strongest. Careful review of the documents will expose some of the company's vulnerabilities and allow counsel to target the internal investigation and defense effort.[385] Thus, the process of responding to the subpoena may actually provide a rare opportunity to catch up with, and then move ahead of, the government in defending the case.

Search Warrants

A search warrant provides no advance notice to the corporation or facility staff that their environmental practices are under criminal investigation.[386] Thus, it prevents the destruction of evidence. Unlike subpoenas for documents, search warrants do not allow the party being searched to assert privileges creatively to protect materials. The confusion that executing a search warrant causes also allows the government better access to interview flustered, unprepared employees.

As soon as agents arrive to execute a search warrant, they will provide a copy to the facility manager. The company should immediately contact counsel. Either the facility manager or counsel should attempt to secure the affidavit supporting the warrant, either by asking the agents for a copy or, if the agents refuse, by obtaining a copy from the court. In federal investigations, however,

380. Upjohn Co. v. United States, 449 U.S. 338 (1981); In re Grand Jury Subpoenas Duces Tecum, 773 F.2d 204 (8th Cir. 1985).

381. Braswell v. United States, 487 U.S. 99 (1988); *see also* Fisher v. United States, 425 U.S. 391 (1976). Only an individual may assert the Fifth Amendment privilege against self-incrimination as grounds for objecting to a subpoena that calls for the production of documents; the privilege is not available to corporations, partnerships, or even sole proprietorships.

382. United States v. Gibbons, 607 F.2d 1320 (10th Cir. 1979); United States v. Beasley, 550 F.2d 261 (5th Cir.), *cert. denied*, 434 U.S. 938 (1977).

383. With respect to the Fifth Amendment privilege against self-incrimination, the Supreme Court has recognized the testimonial aspects of producing even corporate documents. Under *United States v. Doe*, 465 U.S. 605 (1984), the actual production of documents by an individual is testimonial in nature. Any incriminating information in the documents produced may thus be imputed to the individual producing the documents, waiving any privilege against self-incrimination as to that information. *See* In re Grand Jury Subpoena Duces Tecum Dated June 13, 1983 and June 22, 1983, 722 F.2d 981 (2d Cir. 1983). Therefore, when designating a custodian of records in order to authenticate corporate documents, counsel must first assess the officer's potential personal liability.

384. *See* Vaughn v. Rosen, 484 F.2d 820 (D.C. Cir. 1973), *cert. denied*, 415 U.S. 977 (1974).

385. Conducting an internal investigation and defending against a governmental investigation is discussed more fully *infra*.

386. *See generally* JUDSON W. STARR, THE KNOCK ON THE DOOR: PREPARING FOR AND RESPONDING TO A CRIMINAL INVESTIGATION (Chemical Manufacturers Association 1991).

affidavits may be filed under seal and often may not be released if the government can convince the magistrate to keep the affidavit confidential.

There are two general rules regarding search warrants in environmental criminal law: (1) the allegations contained in the search warrant usually do not form the basis for the criminal charges contained in the indictment; and (2) once on the property, the government always finds some violations. Therefore, to be effective, counsel hired to defend a company needs to be experienced in what to do and how to react. Once the warrant is served, the company cannot afford to have counsel who is still on the learning curve.

Counsel should copy and carefully review the warrant itself to determine that it is specific in describing the location to be searched and the inspection functions to be performed. The company may lawfully deny government agents access to areas not specifically set forth in the warrant.[387] Counsel or a designated corporate response coordinator should establish with government agents and company employees that all inquiries arising during the inspection be directed to him or her. The designated official should escort the agents at all times and note whether the agents confine their search to the areas defined in the warrant.

A unique feature of environmental cases is that much of the government's case is driven by what is found in the soil and water on the company's property. For example, in order to prove the illegal disposal of a hazardous waste under RCRA, the government will try to demonstrate that constituents of hazardous wastes that should have been disposed of at a permitted facility are found in the soil on the entity's property. Items seized will often include soil and water samples, as well as documents and other more common forms of evidence. In order to represent the company adequately, counsel needs to record the number of samples and location from which they were taken, and if possible, to videotape the sampling. If videotaping is impractical, a designated company official or an environmental consultant should follow the government agents to photograph or otherwise record the location. Government agents may refuse to allow company representatives to follow them as they search, but most agents will allow observation from a distance.

In addition, counsel for the corporation should demand: (1) a receipt describing the samples obtained by government agents; (2) "split samples"—a portion of each sample equal in volume or weight to the portion retained by the government agents; and (3) a description of the tests that the government agents intend to perform on the samples. Although EPA has taken the position that providing split samples is not required during a criminal search, its policy is to furnish such samples.[388]

The company's split sample should be sent to a qualified laboratory and subjected to the same tests that the government intends to perform. Analysis of these samples may show whether the government can establish that a substance is a "hazardous waste" or "pollutant" under the relevant laws. Additionally, if the two sets of test results differ substantially, the company may be able to contest the accuracy of the government's evidence. Because the sample's age may affect the testing, the material should be obtained on the spot or in a timely fashion, so that the company's testing can yield accurate results. If the agents refuse to provide the company with split samples, counsel should contact the Assistant U.S. Attorney whose name appears on the search warrant affidavit and request the splits. If that request is refused, the company should request a hearing before the magistrate or emergency judge.[389]

As soon as possible—preferably during execution of the search warrant—the company should retain an environmental consultant to assist counsel. An environmental expert can identify a laboratory to analyze the split samples and can aid in determining the locations from which the samples were obtained. He or she can help explain the facility's technical processes and identify the various waste streams involved. The consultant can also assess whether the facility is in compliance with applicable regulations. With his or her specialized knowledge of environmental issues, the consultant may, by viewing the government search, be able to determine what the prosecutor is looking for. A consultant may also facilitate a response to any regulatory deficiencies detected during the search.

In executing the search warrant, government agents will attempt to interview company employees. Most employees mistakenly believe that it is a crime to refuse to be interviewed by a government agent. One of counsel's most valuable functions during a search is to inform employees of their rights. Employees may lawfully refuse to speak to government agents, agree to be interviewed by the agents, or agree to be interviewed with the assistance of counsel. Government agents rarely explain these options to employees and, given a choice, most employees will opt for representation of counsel.

Counsel should also caution employees not to volunteer information to the investigators, while reminding them not to interfere with the search or otherwise take any actions that might obstruct justice, such as hiding or destroying documents. If the government interviews employees, counsel should debrief them promptly to understand the government's areas of interest and legal theories. Finally, while the warrant is being executed, counsel should identify privileged attorney-client communications or materials potentially covered by the government's audit policy.

Conducting an Internal Investigation

Once a company learns that the government has initiated a criminal investigation of its environmental compliance, management will often seek an independent examination by outside counsel, as well as consultants retained by

387. United States v. McCain, 677 F.2d 657, 660 (8th Cir. 1982).

388. The law is narrower; it does not require EPA to share the actual samples so that the owner can perform independent testing to detect pollutants. If any analysis is made of samples taken at a site, "the *results* of such analysis shall be furnished promptly to the owner [or] operator. . . ." 42 U.S.C. §6927(a), ELR STAT. RCRA §3007(a) (emphasis added); *see also* United States v. Protex Indus., Inc., 874 F.2d 740, 745-46, 19 ELR 21061, 21063 (10th Cir. 1989) (government's failure to provide defendant with the results of laboratory analyses provides no defense to criminal charges under RCRA).

389. In any criminal investigation, it is difficult to determine the government's focus and ability to prove its allegations because of grand jury secrecy rules and limited discovery available to the target before indictment. In the environmental area in particular, if the corporation does not obtain the split samples from the search and quickly follow up with any employees whom the government contacted, it will never be able to keep pace with the investigation.

counsel, to define the company's potential legal exposure and identify potential remediation options.[390] The conduct of internal environmental investigations is similar in many respects to those in other white-collar areas, such as securities and antitrust. The principal difference is that at the end of the review, counsel must advise the company as to how forthcoming it should be in disclosing the results to EPA, multiple state regulatory entities, and Justice—all of whom may already have access to continuing, mandatory environmental reports the company has submitted.

The Role of Counsel

Experienced environmental counsel can add significant value to the internal investigatory process by understanding the factors relevant to Justice's decision whether to seek an indictment. By "reverse engineering" the government's investigation, counsel can assess whether Justice is likely to decide to prosecute and what information or arguments might affect that decision. Counsel can also judge whether extensive disclosure of the internal review results might reduce the charges filed or turn the investigation toward a civil resolution. Moreover, counsel may be able to determine the optimal method of maintaining a viable criminal defense, while avoiding alienating the regulatory agencies that will continue to exercise material influence over the economic fortunes of the facilities involved. Finally, with an understanding of the nuances of criminal and civil enforcement and the tradeoff in the prosecutor's mind between criminal conviction and environmental cleanup, counsel may be able to engineer a "global settlement" that comprehensively resolves the company's civil and criminal liability.[391]

If counsel concludes that the case is likely to be resolved civilly, the company will want to be more cooperative with the government. Counsel will try to use the fact of cooperation to shift the discussion to the kind of cleanup that will be necessary; maximize the amount of (tax-deductible) money spent on actual remedial work, rather than the deadweight loss of a fine; attempt to preserve operational flexibility for the facility; and seek favorable exercise of regulatory discretion on such issues as the levels to which pollution must be cleaned up, the compliance schedule, and the terms of new discharge permits. On the other hand, if counsel concludes that the case is likely to be prosecuted criminally, the company will want to be less forthcoming and operate more in the traditional mold of a criminal target.[392]

☐ *Retaining Outside Counsel.* Early in the course of organizing the internal investigation, the company will have to decide whether to hire outside counsel or rely on its own attorneys to conduct the review. In-house counsel have knowledge about the company's history, structure, and employees that is invaluable in identifying sources of information and assessing allegations. On the other hand, outside counsel usually have greater expertise in criminal matters and a higher level of detachment and objectivity. Further, for purposes of negotiation, prosecutors are more likely to recognize the detachment of outsiders and discount the independence and validity of the insiders' analyses.

The governing principle in most white-collar criminal investigations is that the company's general counsel should stay as far away as possible from the actual conduct of the investigation. This distance minimizes the risk that personal and political relations within the company could affect the results. Further, the review may conclude that individuals within the company are personally responsible for the violation at issue. This task—which is never easy—is nonetheless more likely to be performed dispassionately, and its results more readily accepted as valid, when impartial outsiders have drawn the adverse conclusions. Finally, retaining outside counsel minimizes in-house counsel's personal exposure if tough calls are required during the investigation about whether information must be disclosed to the prosecutor.

When there is evidence of a continuing environmental violation, however, in-house counsel may need to become personally involved in the conduct of the investigation. In-house counsel's greater familiarity with the company's operations and its personnel can be a significant asset in identifying problems, defining the business and regulatory risks, devising cost-effective remedial options, and shaping the corporate business response.

Conducting Employee Interviews

One of the most important parts of an internal investigation is to determine why the government has targeted the company, by interviewing the employees whom the government has questioned and by talking to other employees with knowledge of the facts. Thus, after deciding whether to use in-house or outside counsel, the company's first step in conducting the internal investigation should be for management to issue a memorandum to employees authorizing the internal investigation and informing them that they should cooperate with investigating counsel.

When conducting employee interviews, counsel should observe the following procedures:

- The attorney should explain the purpose of the investigation and request the employee's cooperation.
- The interview must be voluntary. The employee should be informed that he or she need not agree to an interview and may stop it at any time.
- The employee should be informed that the interview is presumptively confidential and privileged.
- The employee should be informed that the attorney conducting the interview represents the company, not the individual employee, and that the employee has the right to hire separate counsel. The employee should be clearly advised that the company may assert or waive the attorney-client privilege with respect to the interview's contents. The employee should acknowledge his or her understanding that the company has the right to decide to disclose the contents of the

390. *See generally* STARR, *supra* note 386.

391. Negotiating global settlements is discussed more fully *infra*.

392. Outside counsel may well assume the worst about the government's intentions. However, in-house counsel, who bear the responsibility for both regulatory affairs and criminal matters, will likely hesitate to conclude prematurely that prosecution is inevitable because of greater sensitivity toward the operational consequences of taking an adverse posture toward the government.

interview to senior managers or the government.

• The attorney should not ask the employee to review or sign any memorandum of the interview, nor should the interview be tape recorded. If the matter proceeds to trial, the government may obtain all statements of testifying witnesses. The employee's signature creates a risk that the memorandum constitutes a statement that the employee witness has adopted.

• Counsel should terminate the interview if it appears that the employee's personal interests could be adverse to the company's interests, e.g., if the employee admits to document destruction or bypassing pollution controls.

☐ *Issues Concerning Multiple Representation.* The conduct of individual officers and employees is always an issue in the investigation of a company. Hence, one of the most difficult questions in defending an investigation is whether these individuals should be represented by their own counsel.[393] Potential conflicts of interest arise frequently during investigations and run in both directions. For example, if the facts indicate that the employee has criminal exposure, the corporation may want to distance itself from that person. On the other hand, the employee may want to cooperate with the government and give testimony against other workers or supervisors who directed the employee's activities. In each instance, an attorney would have a conflict of interest in representing two parties with opposing interests. Therefore, separate counsel for the individual would be required.[394]

The need for separate representation may be apparent at the outset or may emerge only after the facts are further developed. In some cases, it may be in the corporation's best interests to provide separate counsel for employees at the company's expense, even if separate counsel is not ethically required. For example, the government may object to corporate counsel's presence at an employee's interview and may assert the potential for conflict of interest; this objection cannot be raised if the witness is separately represented. Further, the government is less likely to suspect a corporation of obstructing the investigation if an employee is separately represented. And counsel for the employee may, consistent with its exclusive ethical obligations to the employee, be able to provide the company with information about the direction of the government's investigation. Absent an actual conflict of interest among employees, the same lawyer may be able to represent multiple workers with a common interest.[395]

Once an employee is represented by independent counsel, corporate counsel should consider whether to enter into a joint defense agreement with the employee.

☐ *Joint Defense Agreements.* **Many environmental investigations cover activities that involve multiple corporations and/or multiple individuals. Often, each of the persons under scrutiny can gain from sharing information with the other potential targets through a joint defense agreement. This arrangement allows attorneys for the various parties to exchange information without waiving the attorney-client or work product privileges. Pooling of information can allow defense counsel to extend their information-gathering network, obtain factual and legal suggestions, and take advantage of each others' expertise, at considerable cost and time savings.**

Courts have long recognized the joint defense privilege contained in agreements among groups of defendants or subjects of investigations.[396] Certain core elements are required to maintain the privileged status of the information exchanged: (1) the parties must share a common interest; (2) the information must have been exchanged in order to facilitate the parties' representation; and (3) the materials must still qualify as confidential at the time one attorney shares them with the group.[397] Although the agreement need not be written to be legally valid, a written arrangement clarifies each party's objectives, reduces the chances of conflicts of interest, and better protects against governmental challenges to the privilege.

All joint defense agreements must be tailored to the facts of a particular investigation and should cover both the attorneys and the clients. The agreement should include all materials shared, acknowledge that each lawyer's obligations to his or her client may prevent the sharing of all information, and provide for procedures for withdrawing from the agreement and returning documents. The agreement should extend to debriefing memoranda of witness interviews and work product generated during the investigation, and allow no disclosure of any covered documents to the government by one party without the permission of all other parties. Confidential protection should continue to apply to any material previously provided to a member who later withdraws. Finally, the agreement should preserve the right of cross-examination at trial if one of the parties later becomes a defendant and the others become witnesses against that party.[398]

Protecting Privileged Information

Issues of attorney-client privilege and work product protection arise repeatedly in the course of environmental investigations. For example, a subpoena may seek production of internal investigative reports or documents generated by an expert a company retains after a governmental search. Privilege issues are particularly important with respect to environmental consultants. Documents they prepare relating to the facility's compliance with environmental regulations will be submitted to the regulator and, thus, are not privileged. Other documents

393. This issue may arise in both the government's investigation and the company's internal investigation.

394. *See, e.g.,* Wheat v. United States, 486 U.S. 153 (1988) (district court properly refused to permit lawyer with a potential conflict of interest to represent criminal defendant, even though the client was willing to waive the conflict arising from multiple representation of persons indicted for one conspiracy); *see also* MODEL RULES OF PROFESSIONAL CONDUCT Rule 1.13(d).

395. FED. R. CRIM. P. 44(c); *see also Wheat,* 486 U.S. at 163 (trial court has substantial latitude in refusing waivers of conflicts of interest, even in cases in which "a potential for conflict exists which may or not burgeon into an actual conflict as the trial progresses").

396. *See, e.g.,* United States v. Schwimmer, 892 F.2d 237 (2d Cir. 1989), *cert. denied,* 112 S. Ct. 55 (1991).

397. Hunydee v. United States, 355 F.2d 183 (9th Cir. 1965); Continental Oil Co. v. United States, 330 F.2d 347 (9th Cir. 1964).

398. *See, e.g.,* United States v. Anderson, 790 F. Supp. 231 (W.D. Wash. 1992) (defendant's participation in joint defense agreement that limited counsel's access to confidential information on cross-examination did not present conflict of interest requiring counsel's disqualification).

they prepare, however, may be directed toward defense of litigation and, thus, may be privileged. It is therefore important for the company to understand from the outset how the attorney-client privilege and work product protections apply to different classes of records.

In *Upjohn v. United States*,[399] the Supreme Court held that the attorney-client privilege applies to communications made by corporate employees to corporate counsel in the context of an internal investigation. The company's in-house and outside counsel had initiated an investigation after receiving reports that its foreign subsidiary was engaging in illegal conduct. The government subsequently sought production of documents generated during the course of that investigation. The Sixth Circuit held that the privilege did not attach to communications made by employees who were "not responsible for directing Upjohn's actions in response to legal advice," but applied only to officials in the "control group."[400] The Supreme Court reversed, rejecting the "control group" test and ruling that the privilege protects communications of even low-level employees.[401] In order to qualify for the privilege, however, the disclosures must be made within the scope of employees' duties and when the employees are aware that they are being questioned "in order that the corporation [may] obtain legal advice."[402]

The work product doctrine insulates from discovery an attorney's mental impressions, conclusions, opinions, or legal theories contained in materials prepared "in anticipation of litigation."[403] Subject to waiver on a showing of substantial need, the work product doctrine will protect the confidentiality of materials generated by attorneys and by nonattorneys hired by counsel, if such materials are prepared in anticipation of civil or criminal litigation.

A number of safeguards are advisable to ensure the confidentiality of information generated as part of an internal investigation.[404] These include generating a formal corporate resolution establishing that counsel will be conducting an investigation for the purpose of obtaining legal advice; marking all documents pertaining to the investigation as "privileged and confidential"; and ensuring that all outside experts and investigators are retained by, and report directly to, counsel. Finally, internal investigation reports should not be distributed beyond the senior management privy to the review process. Only a few copies of the reports should be made, the copies numbered, and their whereabouts known at all times.

Disclosing the Results of the Internal Investigation

At some stage during the internal investigation, counsel should request a meeting with the prosecution to discuss its view of the case or to attempt to persuade the government that it should not charge the client with a criminal offense. Such precharging meetings are indispensable prerequisites to effective representation; counsel simply cannot wait until the client is indicted to discover the government's case.

In conducting these meetings, defense counsel must walk a fine line between revealing too little—and thereby failing to apprise the prosecutor of problems with the case—and revealing too much—and thereby eliminating the element of surprise and giving the prosecutor a road map to the case. Disclosing part of an internal investigative report may constitute a waiver of the attorney-client privilege or work product protection. Courts have held that once a company shares some of its investigatory material with the government, the privilege may be waived for all related materials if the information provided presents an unfair or skewed perspective.[405]

The leading case on waiver is *In re Martin Marietta*.[406] During a meeting with the government, company counsel had submitted a position paper arguing against indictment of the corporation. The paper quoted directly from materials compiled during an internal investigation, including statements of employee witnesses. The court ruled that by revealing the statements of its employees, counsel had waived the attorney-client privilege.[407]

In light of *Martin Marietta*, if the entity under investigation elects to make a written submission to the government, counsel should, at a minimum, obtain a prior express agreement from the prosecutor that the submission will not waive the attorney-client privilege or work product protection for any material disclosed. If possible, information should be presented orally because written statements are more likely to be found to constitute a waiver and be admissible at trial. Finally, counsel should attempt to bring all remarks under the protection of Fed. R. Crim. P. 11(e)(6)(D), which generally prohibits the admission of statements made in the course of plea discussions. In order to qualify for this protection, counsel should at least mention the possibility of a plea agreement as a means of resolving the investigation.

In addition, counsel should be aware of the risk that third parties in a derivative action or a related proceeding may subsequently seek disclosure of confidential material by arguing that the company waived the attorney-client privilege and/or work product protection when it shared the information with the prosecutor.[408] For example, in *Westinghouse Electric Corp. v. Philippines*,[409] the Third Circuit held that disclosure of a privileged internal investigative report to the Securities and Exchange Commission

399. 449 U.S. 383 (1981).

400. The court of appeals found that the privilege applied only to communications with the "control group"—those "officers and agents . . . responsible for directing [the company's] actions in response to legal advice." United States v. Upjohn Co., 600 F.2d 1223, 1225 (6th Cir. 1979).

401. *Upjohn*, 449 U.S. at 394.

402. *Id.*

403. Hickman v. Taylor, 329 U.S. 495, 508 (1947).

404. *See generally* Richard Marmaro, *Protecting the Results of Internal Corporate Investigations*, 1 White Collar Crime Rep. No. 4, July/Aug. 1987.

405. *See, e.g.*, Westinghouse Elec. Corp. v. Philippines, 951 F.2d 1414, 1426 n.12 (3d Cir. 1991) ("When a party discloses a portion of otherwise privileged materials while withholding the rest, the privilege is waived only as to those communications actually disclosed, unless a partial waiver would be unfair to the party's adversary.").

406. 856 F.2d 619 (4th Cir. 1988), *cert. denied*, 490 U.S. 1011 (1989).

407. *Id.* at 623-26.

408. *See, e.g.*, United States v. Billmyer, 57 F.3d 31 (1st Cir. 1995) (disclosing to the government results of an internal investigation conducted by counsel waived the privilege and therefore compelled the company to produce the documents in response to a subpoena served by former corporate employees who were indicted based in part on that disclosure).

409. 951 F.2d 1414 (3d Cir. 1991).

(SEC) and Justice waived the attorney-client privilege and work product protection, even though the agencies had agreed to maintain the confidentiality of the material submitted. The court indicated, however, that if the disclosure had been compelled and the company had fully contested the subpoena in court, there might have been no waiver.[410] Thus, after *Westinghouse*, the production of an internal investigative report without contesting the subpoena apparently would not be considered compulsory disclosure, and therefore may waive the privileges in private litigation as well.

Global Settlements

A company under environmental criminal investigation often finds it advantageous to seek a simultaneous, comprehensive settlement of its criminal and civil liabilities with both the federal and state governments. By resolving all potential obligations in one proceeding, a company can put the problems behind it and focus on the future, with defined limits on its financial outlays and a compressed period of negative publicity.

Whether to seek a global settlement is a strategic decision that the company must make, based on its evaluation of criminal and civil liability at the conclusion of a thorough internal investigation. This decision calls for the exercise of fine judgment by counsel, especially when the government demands pleas to criminal charges from individuals to resolve the matter. When the liberty and careers of employees are in jeopardy, corporate counsel must incorporate these emotionally charged factors into the calculus of whether a settlement is fair and advisable.

One of the most valuable functions environmental criminal counsel can serve is assessing the prospects for settlement on both the criminal and civil sides at all levels of government, and then successfully negotiating and managing the multiple independent settlements that are necessary to accomplish a complete resolution of the problem. Counsel must be aware that the government will not affirmatively seek a global settlement; the corporate defendant must initiate, negotiate, and close the agreement. Also, the window for negotiating such a resolution is limited. The prosecutor will not agree to release any claims until the government has completed its investigation of all potential charges against the company and responsible individuals. Seeking a global settlement may compel the prosecution to open up other areas it had no previous interest in investigating. Further, the government will be both reluctant to waive its civil remedies and adamant about the corporation's obligation to remediate fully the effects of the pollution for which it is responsible.

A major impediment to achieving a global settlement is the number of governmental bodies the company must deal with, each of which has its own interests and priorities. Left to their own devices, these components make little effort to coordinate their responses. For example, the criminal prosecutors typically are not the same persons as those responsible for civil penalty actions. On the regulatory side, the official dealing with clean air issues usually is not responsible for hazardous waste issues, and may have little understanding of how RCRA works or how a solution that makes sense from a discrete "air" perspective may exacerbate hazardous waste problems. Further, different levels of government may be responsible for the judicial and regulatory parts of the problem. Indeed, there may be competition for primary jurisdiction, both among federal and state enforcement personnel and between EPA and state regulators. Accordingly, the indispensable prerequisite for a successful global settlement is for the target to accept these facts of life and take full responsibility for making the settlement happen.

During negotiations to resolve a criminal case, the target must also address the question of civil liability. An admission of guilt may be used as evidence against the company in a subsequent civil case and may have conclusive collateral estoppel effects.[411] For example, a plea of guilty to the illegal disposal of hazardous waste in a criminal case may expose a company to significant costs in a subsequent civil case to remediate the waste site, as well as to claims by citizen groups or injured employees.

Prosecutors engaged in negotiating a criminal plea cannot formally agree to terms that would bind a federal regulator with jurisdiction over a facility. Individual prosecutors vary widely in their willingness and persuasiveness in attempting to interest the regulator in a resolution acceptable to the company. Moreover, while a federal prosecutor may have good relations with state prosecutors and may be able to work out a resolution of all possible criminal charges at all levels, the federal prosecutor may have greater difficulty helping the company close a deal with independent state regulators.

The corporate target needs to understand that negotiating a global settlement can be time-consuming and expensive. The company must harmonize the priorities and bureaucratic interests of every government agency involved and bring each separate investigation to simultaneous completion. There may be some advantages in pursuing such an approach. The environmental prosecutor may consider reducing or dropping the charges in return for significant environmental cleanup commitments or agreements to install pollution control equipment enforceable through a revised permit. Once the outline of a plea agreement is reached, however, the prosecutor may have little patience with the time necessary for the company to complete negotiations with regulators. Understanding this fact, civil regulators might not hesitate to exploit the enhanced leverage it gives them over the target. Counsel cannot expect the prosecutor to serve as the "closer" within the government; counsel must perform that function.

One example of a successful global settlement involving the federal and two state governments is *United States v. Exxon Corp.*,[412] which involved an oil pipeline rupture that discharged 567,000 gallons of heating oil into New York Harbor. The states of New York and New Jersey joined the United States in a memorandum of agreement (MOA) with

410. *Id.* at 1427 n.14. Following the reasoning in *Permian Corp. v. United States*, 665 F.2d 1214 (D.C. Cir. 1981), the Third Circuit explicitly rejected the holding in *Diversified Indus., Inc. v. Meredith*, 572 F.2d 596 (8th Cir. 1978) (en banc), that voluntary disclosure to the government constitutes only a limited waiver of the attorney-client privilege. *Westinghouse*, 951 F.2d at 1423-27.

411. The possible collateral civil consequences of a criminal conviction are discussed in detail *infra*.

412. No. 91-131 (D.N.J. Mar. 20, 1991) (commonly known as the *Exxon Bayway* case). *See infra* notes 536-37 and accompanying text.

the defendant, setting out the fines that the company would pay to the three sovereigns following its guilty plea to an FWPCA violation. Under the MOA, the company agreed to pay $15 million in criminal and civil fines and restitution to the three governments. In return, New York and New Jersey agreed to bring no criminal charges. In a separate plea agreement with the United States alone, the company pleaded guilty to a single misdemeanor charge of negligent violation of the Act.

Parallel Proceedings

Defending an environmental criminal investigation is sufficiently complicated to test any lawyer's skill when all violations are long past. When the problems are ongoing, however, counsel may be confronted from the outset with defending parallel criminal and civil proceedings, each of which presents serious risks to the client.

Parallel proceedings are simultaneous criminal and civil actions against the same defendant that arise out of a single set of facts. Parallel proceedings questions arise frequently in the environmental area, due to ongoing compliance obligations and the easy cross-over from civil to criminal enforcement resulting from the de minimis intent requirement. No appellate case has yet addressed these issues in the environmental context, in part because EPA and Justice have long had policies in place that restrict the circumstances under which their staffs may institute parallel proceedings.

Parallel proceedings are a double-edged sword creating procedural and substantive problems for both the government and the entity under investigation. These problems arise when the government wishes to file a civil action to enjoin long ongoing environmental violations and accelerate the remediation process, while simultaneously conducting an investigation to determine if the infractions should be prosecuted criminally. Civil discovery is far broader and less restrictive than criminal investigation, and there is substantial basis for concern that the government could use civil discovery as a means of avoiding the many protections afforded in criminal cases. The differences between the criminal and civil investigatory mechanisms create substantial tactical questions for counsel and concerns about due process for defendants.

Difficulties Created by Parallel Proceedings

For the Entity Under Investigation

For the target, some problems from overlapping investigations are obvious from the outset, while others take some time to surface.

First, the company must be prepared to negotiate and litigate on multiple fronts. Responding to the demands of several agencies is expensive and ties up corporate staff time. Second, information released or witness statements made in one context, either voluntarily or due to regulatory reporting obligations, may have adverse effects in the other context. Third, strategies that are appropriate in the criminal area may hurt efforts on the civil side, and vice versa. For example, both Justice's voluntary disclosure policy[413] and the Sentencing Commission's proposed sentencing guidelines for organizations[414] provide incentives to disclose and benefit from leniency on the criminal side, but this may constitute a near confession of judgment in any civil suit the regulator may choose to bring.

RCRA provides a good example of how a company's regulatory compliance obligations may affect its response to a grand jury investigation. A plant's continued operations may be jeopardized if the regulator uses its authority to suspend or revoke the company's permit based on an alleged violation. Thus, even before a determination has been made regarding the legality of its past environmental practices, civil enforcement authorities may pressure or legally require the company to remediate a situation, change its disposal method, or obtain a new or revised permit.

The repercussions of these actions could be significant on both the civil and criminal sides. For example, the defense in the criminal case may well be that the waste generated at the facility is not hazardous waste at all. If it is hazardous, however, the company must obtain a manifest and an EPA identification number, and must ship the waste to a permitted hazardous waste facility. Once a dispute arises about the proper characterization of the waste, the conservative approach is to satisfy the civil regulator and manifest the waste as hazardous. But on the criminal side, the changes necessary to resolve all doubts about continuing compliance may be interpreted by the government as an admission that the prior conduct was illegal. The prosecutor may subpoena information relevant to the modifications and use it against the company before the grand jury and at trial.[415]

On the other hand, voluntary remediation has many benefits. It demonstrates a positive corporate environmental stance, and thus may be an important factor in demonstrating why no criminal charges should be filed. It may also lessen the chances of the government instituting injunctive action. How to strike the proper balance between these risks is a difficult question in every case, as a matter of both business judgment and legal strategy.

To complicate the problem, EPA or the state authorities overseeing the ongoing compliance and remediation efforts may not be directly involved in the criminal prosecution. Moreover, the corporate officials responsible for managing the cleanup may not be the ones responsible for working with criminal counsel. This division of authority can result in statements or actions that compromise the company's efforts to assert its legal rights in the criminal proceeding. For example, employees involved in the civil cleanup effort may be willing to answer leading questions or respond to hypothetical questions in a manner that may produce devastating admissions on the criminal side.

Thus, companies involved in parallel proceedings need to coordinate their responses carefully. It is particularly important that counsel involved in the criminal matter reviews any reports or certifications before they are submitted to civil regulators. In such circumstances, counsel must make certain that a response is truthful but does not inad-

413. FACTORS IN DECISIONS ON CRIMINAL PROSECUTIONS, *supra* note 42, at 3-4.

414. DRAFT ENVIRONMENTAL SENTENCING GUIDELINES, *supra* note 302, proposed §9C1.2(a).

415. In the authors' experiences, several months into criminal investigations, prosecutors have subpoenaed all documents that reflect any changes in the method of operation of the specific environmental practice that is the subject of the grand jury investigation. *See* FED. R. EVID. 407.

vertently create further problems, given the difference in perspective between the two enforcement schemes.

Another important difference between criminal and civil proceedings involves application of the Fifth Amendment privilege against self-incrimination. The Supreme Court has held that the fact that an individual has invoked the privilege and declined to answer questions may not be used against that individual in a criminal case.[416] Thus, no prosecutor, judge, or jury may draw an inference that a person is guilty from the fact that he or she has invoked the privilege. A litigant in a civil case is not accorded the same level of protection, however. Although a person retains the absolute right to decline to answer questions, the fact finder in a civil case may draw an adverse inference from the person's silence.[417]

The difference between the two systems places the subject of parallel proceedings on the horns of a dilemma. In a civil case, the privilege against self-incrimination may be waived if not invoked.[418] Statements an individual makes in the civil (or administrative) proceeding could then be used in the criminal case as evidence against the individual or his or her employer. But if the individual invokes the right to decline to answer questions, that silence could be the basis of a negative inference in the civil proceeding, and thus a significant factor in the determination whether to impose a penalty and cleanup obligations.

For the Government

At first glance, parallel proceedings would appear to have several attractive features for the government. They can promote environmental compliance through civil injunctions and large monetary penalties, accelerate the start of remediation and mandate cleanup terms, and deter future violations by imposing criminal sanctions. Thus, whenever the environmental problem sparking a criminal investigation is ongoing, the government will almost always start from the assumption that it should also bring a civil case. Indeed, a criminal prosecutor might encourage the filing of an injunctive action to demonstrate that the environmental harm is substantial.

On the other hand, there are several significant reasons why the government may decide—from a tactical viewpoint as well as from concern with fairness to the potential defendants—not to institute a parallel proceeding:

- in the case of a small violation, instituting two cases may be an inefficient use of scarce enforcement resources;
- the defense may use civil discovery to gain information about the criminal investigation;
- the need to create a wall between civil and criminal proceedings, and the documentation of the civil discovery process necessary to avoid problems under Fed. R. Crim. P. 6(e),[419] may inappropriately delay and complicate the proceedings;
- additional delay may be encountered if the defendant files a motion seeking dismissal on the ground of bad-faith use of compulsory processes;
- prior imposition of large civil penalties may lead to dismissal of an indictment on double jeopardy grounds; and
- the prosecutor will have to guard against potential constitutional violations, which are always a possibility in parallel proceeding situations.[420]

At bottom, most of the problems stem from the fundamental differences in the fact-gathering mechanisms of criminal investigation and civil discovery. Criminal investigations are conducted by grand juries. The law imposes substantial secrecy obligations on these investigations in order to preserve the integrity of the process and witness confidentiality. These restrictions place substantial limitations on the ability of government investigators to disclose information obtained in the grand jury process to other federal officials. These constraints also prevent counsel for potential defendants from determining directly what information the government is presenting to the grand jury, and thus shield the government's theory of the case from disclosure. On the other hand, civil enforcement actions are conducted under the ordinary rules of discovery. These rules provide for early, mutual release of information and do not place significant limits on the extent to which federal personnel may share material obtained through discovery with other law enforcement agents.

The adverse effect that the principle of grand jury secrecy can have on parallel environmental proceedings was demonstrated in *United States v. Gold*,[421] where criminal charges of falsifying registration material for a pesticide were dismissed because of prosecutorial misconduct. A single government attorney acted as an EPA staff attorney, a special attorney for Justice, and a grand jury witness. The court found that the attorney's presence in the grand jury room compromised its secrecy, due to the conflict of interest arising from his various roles. This defeat taught EPA and Justice a lesson about criminal procedure and maintaining separate roles for their personnel.

Agency Procedures Governing the Institution of Parallel Proceedings

In recognition of the difficult tactical and legal questions that a decision to institute parallel proceedings presents, Justice and EPA have long maintained policies on when such proceedings may be authorized. The policies are largely intended to prevent errors that inadvertently lead to limitation or dismissal of criminal charges, and are of particular importance to entities under investigation.

---

416. Kastigar v. United States, 406 U.S. 441 (1970).

417. Baxter v. Palmigiano, 425 U.S. 308, 316-20 (1976) (drawing an adverse inference in a civil case is not an impermissible consequence of the exercise of the privilege against self-incrimination).

418. United States v. Kordel, 397 U.S. 1 (1970).

419. Rule 6(e) generally prohibits the disclosure of matters occurring before a grand jury.

420. *See, e.g.*, United States v. Fields, 592 F.2d 638, 643 (2d Cir. 1978), *cert. denied*, 442 U.S. 917 (1979) (exploitation of evidence from one proceeding to benefit another); *Kordel*, 397 U.S. at 11-12 (Food and Drug Administration's insistence that defendant answer interrogatories while grand jury investigation was underway did not violate Fifth Amendment right against self-incrimination); United States v. LaSalle Nat'l Bank, 437 U.S. 298 (1978) (parallel civil and criminal investigations in tax area are valid).

421. 470 F. Supp. 1336, 9 ELR 20713 (N.D. Ill. 1979).

Justice Guidelines

Justice will not institute parallel proceedings unless there are compelling reasons why both civil and criminal sanctions are appropriate.[422] It takes the position that an environmental criminal proceeding generally should be brought and resolved before a civil action, because the criminal charges entail greater punishment and have more of a deterrent effect. The agency wants to avoid circumstances in which a court gives a more lenient sentence so as not to compound a large prior civil penalty. Moreover, the Speedy Trial Act[423] dictates that criminal cases must be tried expeditiously; on the other hand, civil proceedings may—and often do—lag. Finally, a criminal conviction may have collateral estoppel effect in a subsequent civil case against the defendant.[424]

For these reasons, Justice policy prescribes that civil cases ordinarily should not proceed at the same time as a criminal investigation, unless one of the following factors is present:

> 1. The civil violations are ongoing and of such concern to the public health or to the environment as to call for preliminary or accelerated permanent injunctive or cost recovery relief.
> 2. The assets of the defendant are in danger of dissipation. . . .
> 3. There is only a marginal relationship between the civil violations and the illegal conduct that is the subject of the criminal proceeding.
> 4. There is an imminent statute of limitations deadline for the filing of a civil action.[425]

If the government chooses to pursue parallel proceedings, it must conform to Fed. R. Crim. P. 6(e), which prohibits, with few exceptions, the disclosure of matters occurring before a grand jury. Although civil use of grand jury materials is not per se illegal, the Supreme Court has interpreted Rule 6(e) to prohibit federal prosecutors from disclosing grand jury matters to other Justice attorneys for use in a civil suit, unless the government can demonstrate a particularized need for the materials on the civil side.[426] Therefore, Justice's policy requires that evidence be obtained through channels other than the grand jury subpoena, such as searches, interviews, and administrative Inspector General subpoenas issued through EPA.[427]

Matters uncovered in administrative inquiries or produced in civil discovery are not subject to the same limitations on subsequent use. As long as the investigation was "objectively reasonable" or civil discovery was not used exclusively as an information-gathering device for a criminal prosecution, Justice or EPA litigators may share civil investigative information with criminal prosecutors without limitation.[428] There is no bar to sharing the fruit of civil discovery with a federal or state prosecutor if there was "a good faith civil or administrative basis for conducting the discovery."[429] Similarly, information gathered from an administrative inspection may be shared with prosecutors, so long as the inspection was "objectively reasonable" under *Camara v. Municipal Court*[430] and *Barlow's*.[431] Furthermore, if the government has obtained the civil information without using any formal discovery or compulsory means, e.g., by voluntary production or proffer, it may share the material "regardless of whether there was a 'good faith' basis for seeking the information, as long as the government did not deceive the defendant about its intentions" for using the information.[432]

EPA Policy

EPA's policy on parallel proceedings provides that "the pendency of a criminal proceeding is not necessarily a sufficient reason to fail to seek appropriate" injunctive relief when necessary to obtain compliance with the law or impose remedial obligations.[433] When a criminal proceeding is contemplated or pending, both the regional counsel and the head of the region's Criminal Investigative Division must agree before a parallel civil enforcement proceeding may be filed. However, if the civil action is to be filed in federal district court, rather than as an agency administrative action, EPA policy "continues to require that the request for referral of a parallel proceeding to the Department of Justice be routed through EPA-[Headquarters] for Assistant Administrator approval."[434]

EPA policy also cautions that for double jeopardy reasons, it is preferable to avoid assessing federal civil penalties against a person who is likely to be prosecuted criminally. Normally, a civil penalty claim should be stayed, i.e., not assessed or collected, against a person who is a target of a criminal investigation until the criminal matter is resolved.[435]

---

422. U.S. DOJ, LAND AND NATURAL RESOURCES DIVISION, DIRECTIVE No. 5-87, GUIDELINES FOR CIVIL AND CRIMINAL PARALLEL PROCEEDINGS (Oct. 13, 1987), ELR ADMIN. MAT. I 35159 (reproduced in Appendix A of this book) [hereinafter DIRECTIVE No. 5-87]. Institution of parallel procedures was one of the issues specifically reserved for resolution by Washington in the 1993 BLUESHEET REVISION, *supra* note 43, which was later superseded by the 1994 BLUESHEET REVISION, *supra* note 44.

423. 18 U.S.C. §§3161-3174.

424. *See infra* notes 517-23 and accompanying text.

425. DIRECTIVE No. 5-87, *supra* note 422, at 2, ELR ADMIN. MAT. I at 35159.

426. United States v. Sells Eng'g, Inc., 463 U.S. 418 (1983); United States v. Doe, 481 U.S. 102 (1987).

427. DIRECTIVE No. 5-87, *supra* note 422, at 3, ELR ADMIN. MAT. I at 35159.

428. *Id.* at 4, ELR ADMIN. MAT. I at 35159.

429. *Id.*; *see also* United States v. LaSalle Nat'l Bank, 437 U.S. 298 (1978).

430. 387 U.S. 523 (1967).

431. Marshall v. Barlow's, Inc., 436 U.S. 307, 8 ELR 20434 (1978); DIRECTIVE No. 5-87, *supra* note 422, at 4, ELR ADMIN. MAT. I at 35159.

432. DIRECTIVE No. 5-87, *supra* note 422, at 5, ELR ADMIN. MAT. I at 35159. The directive also notes that "*Miranda* warnings are unnecessary during civil discovery." *Id.* Therefore, it instructs government attorneys to give the following standard response to witness inquiries about criminal liability: "[T]he United States is free to choose civil, criminal or administrative enforcement and any decision to take one type of action does not preclude another type of action." *Id.*, ELR ADMIN. MAT. I at 35160; *see also* United States v. Mitchell, 966 F.2d 92, 22 ELR 21291 (2d Cir. 1992) (statements made to EPA investigators may be suppressed in a criminal case only if defendant shows by clear and convincing evidence that agents affirmatively misled him as to the true nature of the investigation).

433. Memorandum from Steven A. Herman, Assistant Administrator, to All Assistant Administrators et al., Parallel Proceedings Policy (June 24, 1994), ELR ADMIN. MAT. I 35599 (reproduced in Appendix A of this book).

434. *Id.* at 3 n.3, ELR ADMIN. MAT. I at 35599 n.3. The policy also notes that "DOJ policy affects the Agency's ability to pursue a civil judicial action that is related to a pending investigation." *Id.*

435. *Id.* at 4, ELR ADMIN. MAT. I at 35599.

Protection Against Abuse of Parallel Proceedings

If the government institutes parallel proceedings the potential defendants usually will be powerless to overturn that decision or stop the civil action altogether. There are, however, means available to mitigate the possible adverse effects.

Stays

The preferred defense strategy is to seek a stay or postponement of the civil action, pending resolution of the parallel criminal matter.[436] Even at the investigatory stage of the criminal proceedings, the argument can be made that a stay is required to avoid presenting individuals with the Hobson's choice of either waiving the Fifth Amendment privilege against self-incrimination by answering civil discovery and thereby prejudicing defense of the criminal action, or invoking the privilege and thereby prejudicing defense of the civil action.[437] Thus, an alternative approach is for the target to seek a stay of civil discovery until the government decides whether to indict.[438]

Decisions in other regulatory areas, such as securities and antifraud, demonstrate courts' hesitancy to restrict the government's ability to enforce the law based only on an anticipatory claim that a subsequent action by the government might conceivably harm the defendant's rights.[439] In these areas, the party seeking a stay must demonstrate a clear hardship or inequity arising out of the need to go forward on both fronts. In reaching its decision, a court will balance the harm to the moving party in the absence of the stay against the harm that may result from granting the stay.[440] Those seeking a stay must show that a criminal investigation is active or that indictment is likely, and must clearly demonstrate how continuation of civil or administrative discovery would compel them to assert the Fifth Amendment privilege. Any evidence of actual government misconduct in the two matters to date can be an effective factor in persuading a court to stay the civil matter.[441]

Double Jeopardy Constraints

The aspect of the Double Jeopardy Clause that prohibits multiple punishments for the same act provides some protection against civil sanctions that are imposed for punishment purposes after final judgment has been entered in a criminal case.

The Supreme Court has ruled that the Double Jeopardy Clause does not preclude the government from imposing both civil and criminal sanctions based on the same behavior, as long as the civil sanction serves only a remedial purpose.[442] The same sovereign may not, however, impose multiple punishments for the same offense if the purported civil sanction actually serves the criminal purpose of punishment.[443]

Although a court will generally allow civil penalties that are greater than the loss the defendant's action caused, a penalty may be so excessive as to constitute a second punishment. In *Halper v. United States*,[444] the Supreme Court held that a civil penalty that was not rationally related to the government's actual damages constituted criminal punishment and, thus, was barred by the Double Jeopardy Clause.[445] The Court concluded that the post-conviction civil penalty of 220 times the government's actual loss did not serve a remedial purpose, but inappropriately furthered the criminal goal of punishment.[446]

The *Halper* prohibition against double punishment does not apply to suits by private entities or to penalties imposed sequentially by a state and the federal government.[447] Under the dual sovereignty doctrine, the Double Jeopardy Clause does not apply to suits brought by separate sovereigns.[448] For these reasons, in order to minimize the risk that a sizable settlement in an administrative action might be construed to bar subsequent criminal penalties, government counsel negotiating a civil settlement often insist that the agreement explicitly recognize the possibility of subsequent criminal proceedings.

Consequences of an Environmental Criminal Conviction

Entry of a judgment of guilty, whether by plea or after trial, does not end the defendant's ordeal; in many respects, a determination of guilt represents only the mid-point in the process. The consequences of conviction are potentially severe, in terms of the sentence that may be imposed on the individual or corporation, the costs of the remedial

436. The intermediate strategy of allowing the civil matter to go forward but imposing a protective order on its fruits to prevent their use in the criminal case was recognized in *Martindell v. ITT Corp.*, 594 F.2d 291 (2d Cir. 1979), but later disapproved in *In re Grand Jury Proceedings*, 995 F.2d 1013 (11th Cir. 1993).

437. *See, e.g.*, SEC v. Dresser Indus., Inc., 628 F.2d 1368 (D.C. Cir.) (en banc), *cert. denied*, 449 U.S. 993 (1980) (the SEC's use of civil investigative warrants was lawful even though it had previously referred allegations about the company to Justice for criminal investigation).

438. *See* In re Grand Jury Proceedings, 995 F.2d at 1018 n.11 (The "civil trial court may stay discovery until the grand jury investigation is completed.").

439. *See, e.g., Dresser Indus.*, 628 F.2d at 1368.

440. *See, e.g.*, Golden Quality Ice Cream Co. v. Deerfield Specialty Papers, Inc., 87 F.R.D. 53, 56 (E.D. Pa. 1980) (resolution of stay issue requires balancing "the interests of the public in the pending civil and criminal litigation" against other factors, including defendant's Fifth Amendment rights).

441. If the government seeks a stay, however, a court is likely to grant it. *See, e.g.*, United States v. Hugo Key & Son, Inc., 672 F. Supp. 656, 18 ELR 20272 (D.R.I. 1987) (staying proceedings in a civil CAA case pending resolution of parallel criminal investigation so as to prevent harm to paramount government interest, including protecting informants' identity against disclosure in civil discovery). The government's arguments for a stay would appear stronger if a stay is necessary to prevent the statute of limitations from expiring on civil charges pending resolution of the criminal matter.

442. Helvering v. Mitchell, 303 U.S. 391 (1938).

443. *E.g.*, United States v. Morgan, 51 F.3d 1105 (2d Cir. 1995) (double jeopardy protection attaches only if civil sanction is "overwhelmingly disproportionate" and "bears so little relationship to making the government whole as to shock the conscience of the court").

444. 490 U.S. 435 (1989).

445. In a prior criminal case, the defendant had pleaded guilty to 65 false claims for Medicare reimbursement overcharges of $9 each. Invoking the doctrine of collateral estoppel, the district court granted summary judgment to the government in a subsequent civil false claims case. The civil statute provided for a penalty of $2,000 per violation.

446. *Halper*, 490 U.S. at 451.

447. United States v. Louisville Edible Oil Prods., Inc., 926 F.2d 584, 21 ELR 20690 (6th Cir.), *cert. denied*, 112 S. Ct. 177 (1991) (*Halper* doctrine does not apply when different sovereigns impose sanctions under their respective laws for the same act).

448. Petite v. United States, 361 U.S. 529 (1960). *See supra* note 120 and accompanying text.

obligations it will be required to undertake, and the collateral effects on its ability to conduct its future affairs. Individuals convicted of an environmental crime face a high probability of a significant term of imprisonment, even for a first offense. Prosecutors are well aware of the stringency of these penalties, and they effectively use these threats to persuade environmental violators to enter into plea agreements.

Remedial Obligations and Negotiated Pleas

An entity that is found guilty of an environmental crime will be compelled to clean up any pollution remaining from the violation. The costs of remediation frequently exceed the fines involved, often by substantial amounts.[449] A corporation will inevitably be required to make large capital expenditures upon conviction, whether as part of the criminal sentence or as a consequence of a subsequent civil suit. This consideration often plays a substantial role in both the company's decision whether to seek a plea agreement and the prosecutor's charging decision.

During an environmental investigation, the government will likely seek evidence of all pollution generated by the facilities involved or disposed of on those sites. Both the prosecutor and the civil regulatory agency will be interested in cleaning up all the contamination detected, whether or not it forms the basis of the criminal charges. Further, an environmental prosecutor, as distinguished from a conventional prosecutor, may seek to maximize the combination of criminal penalties and cleanup benefits, rather than focusing strictly on sentence length and fine amount. An environmental prosecutor may thus be willing to trade a significantly greater cleanup commitment than could be required by law in return for foregoing criminal charges against the company and/or individuals, or reducing the severity or number of counts filed.

Accordingly, corporations and municipalities faced with the inevitability of cleaning up the pollution they have caused may decide to "make a virtue of necessity" and seek a negotiated resolution, based on their willingness to undertake a comprehensive remediation program. The prosecutor may be attracted to such a resolution if it benefits the environment directly, through prompt elimination of contaminants, rather than indirectly through deterrence of potential violators. The prosecutor does not act with a free hand, however, and may need the concurrence of federal and state civil regulators on many of the cleanup terms that have critical cost implications.

For the polluter, the principal attraction of this approach—besides the possibility of reduced charges—is the greater flexibility that may be afforded in the plea context on such critical terms as the level of cleanup, cleanup techniques, the timetable, and post-closure obligations. A negotiated plea agreement provides opportunities for substantial cost savings vis-à-vis an adverse judgment entered after litigation. Further, with the prosecutor's cooperation, it may be possible to structure the agreement in a manner that makes most, if not all, of the out-of-pocket costs tax deductible.[450] The company must realize, however, that all aspects of its environmental performance will be in play in these discussions, including prior disposals, other operations, or discharges to other media that are not part of the contemplated charges or included in the criminal complaint.

The degree of cooperation the company demonstrates during the investigative process may significantly affect the prosecutor's willingness to consider a consensual resolution. None of these benefits is likely to be achieved unless the prosecutor is convinced of the company's good faith and the permit writer has confidence in the company's reliability. Effective environmental criminal counsel must therefore understand the difficult balancing act it must play in conducting the defense of the investigation. Counsel must organize the defense in a manner that fully presents the company's position on the merits, without turning either the prosecutor or the civil regulator against the client. To preserve opportunities to turn the solution toward negotiations over the scope of the cleanup and the terms of the permit governing future operations, relations must not have been cast in an adversarial, scorched-earth posture.

Finally, because settlement must be reached with all federal and state criminal and regulatory agencies, counsel must eliminate the risk that the cleanup resolution may later be undone by another enforcement authority initiating proceedings on the same issues.

Criminal Sentences

Individuals and organizations convicted of federal environmental crimes are sentenced pursuant to sentencing guidelines[451]—mechanical formulas whose purpose is to deny judges discretion in sentencing and to produce uniformity in punishments imposed for similar crimes.[452]

The Sentencing Commission issued guidelines for the sentencing of individuals convicted of criminal offenses, including environmental crimes, in 1987.[453] The guidelines have broken down judges' former reluctance to imprison individuals convicted of environmental offenses and have produced significantly longer sentences than the few imposed before the guidelines' issuance. Experience under the guidelines demonstrates that even first-time offenders can expect to serve significant prison terms. Thus, if indicted, individuals have relatively greater incentives to fight the charges through trial because they are likely to be imprisoned if they plea bargain. On the other hand, companies with operating facilities have significant incentives to settle, because of both the cost of litigation and the importance of maintaining working relations with the civil regulator.

Defense counsel still has an important, if diminished, role to play at the sentencing stage. It is important for the lawyer

449. For example, in the *Exxon Valdez* case, the company made $100 million in restitutionary payments earmarked for restoration projects in Alaska related to the oil spill for which it pleaded guilty to violations of FWPCA §§301(a) and 309(c)(1)(A), 33 U.S.C. §§1311(a) and 1319(c)(1)(A); the Refuse Act, 33 U.S.C. §§407 and 411; and the Migratory Bird Treaty Act, 16 U.S.C. §§703 and 707(a). United States v. Exxon Corp., No. A91-015CR (D. Alaska Mar. 22, 1991).

450. The tax deductibility of criminal penalties is discussed more fully *infra*.

451. SENTENCING GUIDELINES, *supra* note 41.

452. "[T]he Guidelines bind judges and courts in the exercise of their . . . responsibility to pass sentence in criminal cases." Mistretta v. United States, 488 U.S. 361, 391 (1989).

453. Despite intensive efforts over the last eight years, however, the Commission has not yet been able to devise comparable guidelines for the fines that should be imposed on corporations convicted of environmental crimes, due to the difficulty of adapting general sentencing principles to crimes that involve economic externalities and a de minimis mental element. *See infra* note 491.

to advise his or her client before indictment or trial about the guidelines' likely impact on a conviction and how that factor can influence the prosecutor's negotiating strategy. This advice can prove essential in helping a client decide whether to cooperate with an investigation, seek a plea agreement, or negotiate a global settlement.

Criminal Sentences for Individuals

The sentencing guidelines for individuals provide for assigning a numerical value to a crime through a three-step process that considers (1) a base offense level, (2) specific offense characteristics, and (3) adjustments for other factors. Adding and subtracting numbers derived at each step leads to a final offense number, which corresponds to a narrow range of sentences on a grid that applies equally to all types of criminal offenses. The district judge is generally obliged to sentence a defendant convicted of an environmental crime to a specific term of imprisonment within the narrow confines allowed for the offense level calculated under the formula.[454] Downward departures from the guidelines are permitted under very limited circumstances, and Justice may appeal the court's application of any downward departure.[455]

☐ *Base Offense Level.* The first step in determining the sentence is selecting the most appropriate offense category and its associated base offense level. There are six general types of offenses listed for environmental crimes, only three of which are broadly applicable:[456]

- Knowing endangerment resulting from mishandling hazardous or toxic substances, pesticides or other pollutants: Base offense level 24;[457]
- Mishandling of hazardous or toxic substances or pesticides: Recordkeeping, tampering, and falsification: Base offense level 8;[458] and
- Mishandling of other environmental pollutants: Recordkeeping, tampering, and falsification: Base offense level 6.[459]

For example, if the offense involved illegal disposal of polychlorinated biphenyls, a hazardous substance, the base offense level would be eight, the level prescribed under §2Q1.2 for violations involving hazardous or toxic substances or pesticides. If, on the other hand, the offense involved the illegal disposal of oil or petroleum byproducts, the base offense level would be six, as prescribed under §2Q1.3 for mishandling of "other pollutants."

☐ *Specific Offense Characteristics.* The base offense level is then typically increased by a certain number of levels if there are "specific offense characteristics"—i.e., aggravating circumstances—involved.[460] These characteristics include ongoing, continuous, or repetitive discharges of the substance;[461] substantial likelihood of death or serious bodily injury as a result of the wrongdoing;[462] the requirement of a substantial expenditure for cleanup;[463] or the failure to obtain a permit.[464] For example, if a person convicted of mishandling hazardous wastes is found to have created a substantial likelihood of death or serious injury, the offense level would be increased by nine,[465] which could translate into a several-month increase in the required sentence.

☐ *Adjustments for Other Factors.* After the base offense level is calculated and any points for specific offense characteristic are added, the guidelines allow for downward or upward "departures" from the offense level.[466] Departures under Chapter 2 of the guidelines may be appropriate if, for example, the violation resulted from negligent rather than knowing behavior (downward departure);[467] the offense involved highly hazardous substances (upward departure);[468] or the offense resulted in a substantial cleanup expense (upward departure).[469] In addition, on motion of the government stating that the defendant provided substantial assistance in pursuing other persons who committed a crime, the court may depart downwardly from the guidelines.[470]

Once the Chapter 2 adjustments are applied, additional adjustments are possible. Chapter 3 provides for adjustments

454. The court "shall impose a sentence of the kind, and within the range" established by the applicable guidelines. 18 U.S.C. §3553(b).

455. The general "departure" guidelines, which apply to all the guidelines, are found at SENTENCING GUIDELINES, *supra* note 41, §8K. The application notes following each of the specific environmental offenses list possible departures applicable to each. *See* application notes accompanying *id.* §§2Q1, 2Q1.1, 2Q1.2.

456. The other three offenses are tampering or attempted tampering with public water system, threatened tampering with public water system, and hazardous or injurious devices on federal lands. *See id.* §§2Q1.4, 2Q1.5, 2Q1.6.

457. *Id.* §2Q1.1.

458. *Id.* §2Q1.2.

459. *Id.* §2Q1.3.

460. In very limited circumstances, application of specific offense characteristics might decrease the base offense level. For example, under §2Q1.2, if a person mishandles a hazardous or toxic substance but the offense is merely a recordkeeping or reporting violation, the base level may be decreased by two levels. *Id.* §2Q1.2(b)(6).

461. *Id.* §§2Q1.2(b)(1)(A) (hazardous waste), 2Q1.3(b)(1)(A) (nonhazardous waste). *See* United States v. Suarez, 15 F.3d 1094 (9th Cir. 1994) (trial court required to impose either a six-level increase under §2Q1.3(b)(1)(A) for an "ongoing, continuous or repetitive discharge," or a four-level increase under §2Q1.3(b)(1)(B) "if the offense otherwise involved a discharge"). *Compare* United States v. Strandquist, 993 F.2d 395, 23 ELR 21429 (4th Cir. 1993) (actual environmental contamination not required for "ongoing, continuous or repetitive" discharge under §2Q1.3(b)(1)(A)) *and* United States v. Goldfaden, 959 F.2d 1324, 22 ELR 21069 (5th Cir. 1992) (actual environmental contamination not necessary under §2Q1.2(b)(1) to increase offense level for repetitive discharges), *conviction on remand aff'd*, 987 F.2d 225, 23 ELR 20774 (5th Cir. 1993) *with* United States v. Ferrin, 994 F.2d 658, 23 ELR 20854 (9th Cir. 1993) (no enhancement under §2Q1.2(b)(1) for discharge that did not cause environmental contamination).

462. SENTENCING GUIDELINES, *supra* note 41, §§2Q1.2(b)(2), 2Q1.3(b)(2).

463. *Id.* §§2Q1.2(b)(3), 2Q1.3(b)(3).

464. *Id.* §§2Q1.2(b)(4), 2Q1.3(b)(4).

465. *Id.* §2Q1.2(b)(2).

466. These adjustments are found in the application notes that follow each subpart. Commentary that interprets or explains a guideline is authoritative and binding on a court, much like an agency's interpretation of its own rules, unless the commentary violates the U.S. Constitution or a federal statute, or is inconsistent with, or a plainly erroneous reading of, the guideline. Stinson v. United States, 113 S. Ct. 1913, 1915 (1993).

467. SENTENCING GUIDELINES, *supra* note 41, §2Q1.2, Application Note 4.

468. *Id.*, Application Note 8.

469. *Id.*, Application Note 7.

470. *Id.* §5K1.1.

to the offense level to take into account other factors, which apply to all offenses, not just environmental crimes. These factors account for the defendant's role in the offense. The sentence can be adjusted upwardly if the defendant was an organizer or leader of the offense,[471] or impeded the investigation, prosecution, or sentencing of the offense,[472] or downwardly, if the defendant accepted responsibility for his or her actions.[473] Finally, Chapter 5 determines the actual sentence by applying a criminal history number (from I to VI) to the offense levels on a sentencing table.[474]

☐ *Determining the Sentence.* The base offense level, specific offense characteristics, and adjustments are then totaled, and the corresponding sentencing range is determined from a chart.[475] Sentences run from 0 to 6 months for crimes with a total offense level of 1; to 6 to 30 months for crimes with a total offense level of 10; to life imprisonment for crimes with a total offense level of 43. Most environmental violations receive sentences toward the lower end of the sentencing table. However, environmental offenders are being sent to prison at a much greater rate and for longer periods of time than before the guidelines were promulgated. A fine table determines the nature of the criminal fine to be imposed, which is calculated from the base level as adjusted.[476] The court is required to impose a fine on an individual defendant in all cases unless the violator establishes that he or she is unable to pay.[477]

☐ *Probation and Restitution.* The sentencing judge may also determine, in accordance with Chapter 5 of the guidelines, to impose probation and full restitution to the victims of the offense.[478] Probation, however, may be imposed only if the offense falls within Zone A of the sentencing table (up to offense level eight for a defendant with a criminal history level of I). Similarly, the court has discretion to sentence a violator to probation plus some type of nonprison confinement, such as home detention, only if the offense falls within Zone B (up to offense level 10 for a defendant with a criminal history level of I). In the limited circumstances in which probation is available, the court may impose a broad range of conditions.[479] However, probation is never available for crimes classified in Zones C and D (minimum sentence of eight months).[480]

For environmental crimes, the base offense levels under subpart 2Q are comparatively low—six to eight for offenses other than knowing endangerment.[481] After specific offense characteristics and adjustments—which can increase the base offense level by up to 17 levels—are applied, however, many defendants are not eligible for probation. If the offense level is nine or above, under the sentencing table the court must sentence the offender to prison. Thus, even first-time offenders are now exposed to significant jail time for environmental crimes.[482]

☐ *Double Counting.* The guidelines allow for "double counting," which occurs when base offense levels and specific offense characteristics incorporate the same elements.[483] Double counting happens frequently for environmental crimes. For example, a base offense level of six is associated with an FWPCA felony conviction for discharging a pollutant without a permit; a specific offense characteristic, which increases the offense level by four, may also apply to failure to obtain a permit.[484] Thus, the same activity may simultaneously determine the offense level and constitute an aggravating factor that increases that level. And the increase in offense level from 6 to 10 for a person with a criminal history category of I would produce an increase in the jail sentence from 0-6 months to 6-12 months.[485]

---

471. *Id.* §3B1.1(a); *see also* United States v. Goldsmith, 978 F.2d 643, 23 ELR 20281 (11th Cir. 1992) (upholding two-level increase because defendant was a supervisor, even though three men working for him were not prosecuted); United States v. Dean, 969 F.2d 187, 22 ELR 21296 (6th Cir. 1992) (affirming enhancement of sentence under §3B1.1(b) because defendant was a manager or supervisor of criminal activity involving five or more participants; "participants" included those on an equal footing with defendant or his superiors, and not merely his subordinates), *cert. denied*, 113 S. Ct. 1852 (1993); United States v. Irby, 944 F.2d 902 (4th Cir. 1991) (affirming two-level increase under §3B1.1(c) because defendant supervised an employee whom he directed to discharge raw sewage illegally).

472. SENTENCING GUIDELINES, *supra* note 41, §3C1.1; *see also* United States v. Weitzenhoff, 1 F.3d 1523, 23 ELR 21322 (9th Cir. 1993), *reh'g denied, opinion amended*, 35 F.3d 1275, 24 ELR 21504 (1994) (two-level enhancement for obstruction of justice based on perjury during trial), *cert. denied sub nom.* Mariani v. United States, 115 S. Ct. 939 (1995).

473. SENTENCING GUIDELINES, *supra* note 41, §3E1.1.

474. *Id.* §5, Part A. A defendant's Criminal History Category is determined by the total criminal history points calculated from *id.* §4, Part A.

475. *Id.* §5A.

476. *Id.* §5E1.2. In addition, under the Alternative Fines Act, the government has the option of seeking, instead of the maximum permitted by the environmental statutes, fines of up to twice the profits realized by the defendant as a result of noncompliance, and/or twice the harm caused to injured parties. 18 U.S.C. §3571. The most prominent use of this statute was in the case involving the Ashland Oil tank collapse. Over the government's objection, the court accepted a nolo contendere plea and imposed a fine of $2.25 million. United States v. Ashland Oil, Inc., No. 88-146 (W.D. Pa. Mar. 9, 1989); *see also* United States v. Ashland Oil, Inc., 20 ELR 20399, 20399 n.1 (W.D. Pa. June 19, 1989).

477. SENTENCING GUIDELINES, *supra* note 41, §5E1.2(a).

478. *Id.* §§5B (probation), 5E1.1 (restitution).

479. *Id.* §§5B1.3, 5B1.4. Probation may not be imposed in lieu of imprisonment for Class A and B felonies, or if the statute establishing the offense precludes probation. *Id.* §5B1.1(b). A Class A felony is punishable by death or life imprisonment; a Class B felony is punishable by imprisonment for 25 years or more. 18 U.S.C. §3559.

480. SENTENCING GUIDELINES, *supra* note 41, §5B1.1, Application Note 2.

481. *See* United States v. Goldfaden, 959 F.2d 1324, 22 ELR 21069 (5th Cir. 1992) (trial court improperly applied a base level of eight under §2Q1.2 for the mishandling of "hazardous and toxic substances," since the conviction was for discharge of industrial waste, which should have been considered "other environmental pollutants" with a base level of six under §2Q1.3), *conviction on remand aff'd*, 987 F.2d 225, 23 ELR 20774 (5th Cir. 1993).

482. *See* United States v. Weitzenhoff, 1 F.3d 1523, 23 ELR 21322 (9th Cir. 1993), *reh'g denied, opinion amended*, 35 F.3d 1275, 24 ELR 21504 (1994) (first-time offenders sentenced respectively to 33 and 21 months imprisonment), *cert. denied sub nom.* Mariani v. United States, 115 S. Ct. 939 (1995); *Goldfaden*, 959 F.2d at 1324, 22 ELR at 21069 (first-time offender sentenced to 33 months imprisonment); United States v. Irby, 944 F.2d 902 (4th Cir. 1991) (first-time offender sentenced to 33 months imprisonment).

483. The practice of double counting has been frequently criticized on policy grounds. In 1992, the Sentencing Commission published a proposed amendment to the guidelines to eliminate this practice. *See* 57 Fed. Reg. 97 (Jan. 2, 1992). The amendment was never enacted.

484. *See, e.g.*, United States v. St. Angelo, 993 F.2d 229 (4th Cir. 1993); United States v. Mills, 904 F.2d 713 (11th Cir. 1990).

485. SENTENCING GUIDELINES, *supra* note 41, §5, Part A (sentencing table).

Courts have upheld the double-counting characteristic against constitutional challenges in environmental cases. For example, in *United States v. Goldfaden*,[486] the Fifth Circuit allowed a four-level addition to the defendant's offense level for an FWPCA felony conviction for discharging hazardous and industrial waste into a city sewer system without a permit. The appellate court found that the sentencing court had appropriately followed the relevant guideline provision when it added the four levels. The Fourth Circuit reached the same conclusion in *United States v. Ellen*,[487] finding that "'the Sentencing Commission plainly understands the concept of double counting, and expressly forbids it where it is not intended.'"[488] Because "'the Guidelines are explicit when double counting is forbidden . . . [a]n adjustment that clearly applies to the conduct of an offense must be imposed unless the Guidelines expressly exclude its applicability.'"[489]

Criminal Sentences for Organizations

☐ *General Organizational Guidelines.* In November 1991, the Sentencing Commission added a new Chapter 8 to the guidelines to address situations in which fines, restitution, and probation may appropriately be applied to corporations convicted of criminal offenses.[490] The organizational guidelines specifically exempt environmental crimes from their financial penalty provisions because the Commission needed to give further consideration to the problems of adapting its neutral sentencing principles to this context.[491] The parts of the organizational guidelines concerning restitution, remediation, community service, and notice to victims do, however, apply to companies convicted of environmental crimes.[492]

Although the financial penalty section of the organizational guidelines does not currently apply to environmental crimes,[493] these provisions do apply to convictions for false statements, conspiracy, and mail or wire fraud, which may be charged in conjunction with, or in lieu of, environmental offenses. Further, the restitution and probation sections are applicable to environmental crimes committed on or after November 1, 1991.[494] The degree of latitude the probation provision affords sentencing courts is so great that some corporate violators may find the terms of probation more onerous than the fines. The guidelines allow the sentencing court to impose, as a condition of probation lasting up to five years,[495] a requirement that the organization publicize the nature of its offense;[496] periodically submit information regarding remedial programs to the court;[497] be assigned probation officers to monitor its operations;[498] develop a compliance program;[499] submit to regular or unannounced examinations of its books, records, and premises;[500] or perform community service.[501]

A recent case illustrates how the organizational guidelines might be applied to sentence companies convicted of environmental offenses. A cruise ship line prosecuted for discharging oil from its vessels in violation of the FWPCA reached a plea agreement in which it explicitly acknowledged the applicability of the organizational guidelines (except the fine provisions). Along with imposing a $500,000 fine, the plea agreement placed the company on organizational probation for five years and required it to

486. 959 F.2d 1324, 22 ELR 21069 (5th Cir. 1992), *conviction on remand aff'd*, 987 F.2d 225, 23 ELR 20774 (5th Cir. 1993).

487. 961 F.2d 462, 22 ELR 21282 (4th Cir.), *cert. denied*, 113 S. Ct. 217 (1992).

488. *Id.* at 468, 22 ELR at 21285 (quoting the nonenvironmental case of United States v. Williams, 954 F.2d 204, 208 (4th Cir. 1992)).

489. *Id.* (quoting *Williams*, 954 F.2d at 207).

490. SENTENCING GUIDELINES, *supra* note 41, §§8B1.1 (restitution), 8C (fines), 8D (probation).

491. *Id.* §8C2.1 (background); *see also* Ilene H. Nagel & Winthrop M. Swenson, *The Federal Sentencing Guidelines for Corporations: Their Development, Theoretical Underpinnings, and Some Thoughts About Their Future*, 71 WASH. U. L.Q. 205, 256 (1993).

Three major policy problems make it difficult for the Commission to determine the amount of the fine that should be imposed on a corporation convicted of an environmental offense. First, defining and computing the amount of loss—a key factor in assessing the seriousness of an offense under the organizational guidelines—is extremely difficult for environmental crimes. Unlike other white-collar crimes such as securities fraud, there is not necessarily a correlation between the gain to the defendant and the loss to society from an environmental crime. The economic rationale for regulation of pollution is based on externalities, i.e., the costs that pollution imposes on the society that are not reflected in the cost of the product to its owner. Externalities dominate the penalty calculus as well. Environmental violations that produce small economic gains to the defendant may result in large harm to the public. The costs of remediating an illegal discharge are often many times greater than what it would have cost the defendant to dispose of the waste legally. The sentencing principles break down in the face of these environmental externalities.

Second, the intent element is also an important factor in the principles that the guidelines ordinarily apply in determining the appropriate amount of a fine for an organization. However, the degree of knowledge necessary to obtain an environmental criminal conviction is minimal. Further, the environmental harm caused by the violation is often disproportionate to the defendant's mental state. For example, a negligent violation such as the *Exxon Valdez* spill can cause massive environmental degradation, whereas a willful violation may not result in any environmental harm at all.

Third, environmental violations are subject to overlapping enforcement schemes and greater collateral sanctions than are violations of other laws. An extensive system of civil enforcement exists at both the state and federal levels. This system attempts to capture directly, through the "economic benefit to the violator" part of the civil penalty calculus, the monetary gain the violator realizes from failing to comply with the law. Further, because the government can obtain extensive remedial relief, including money damages, the harm to the environment often can be largely corrected through civil enforcement. And because the cost of cleanup may greatly outweigh the initial cost of compliance, the threat of civil liability works as an effective deterrent in the environmental area. Finally, the collateral consequences of an environmental conviction are substantial and contribute to an effective degree of deterrence and punishment as well.

492. SENTENCING GUIDELINES, *supra* note 41, §8C2.1 (commentary).

493. *Id.* §8C2.1 (background).

494. *Id.* §8A1.1, Application Note 1.

495. *Id.* §8D1.2.

496. *Id.* §8D1.4(a) (policy statement).

497. *Id.* §8D1.4(c)(3).

498. *Id.* §8D1.4(b)(1) (policy statement).

499. *Id.* §8D1.4(c)(1) (policy statement). The guidelines place substantial emphasis on the development of an effective compliance program. Indicators of such a program include compliance standards and procedures reasonably capable of reducing the prospect of criminal conduct, assignment of a high-level employee with responsibility to oversee these standards, steps to communicate standards and procedures effectively, and consistent enforcement of the standards. *Id.* §8A1.2, Application Note (k). This is of particular importance in the environmental crimes area because the existence of an effective compliance program may substantially mitigate any potential fine that might be imposed under the court's current discretionary authority.

500. *Id.* §8D1.4(b)(2) (policy statement).

501. *Id.* §8D1.3(b).

establish and maintain an effective environmental compliance program (including hiring an independent environmental and maritime consultant); to make quarterly reports on the program to the court; and to assume all costs associated with implementation, maintenance, and court oversight of the program.[502]

☐ *Proposed Federal Sentencing Guidelines for Organizations Convicted of Environmental Offenses.* In December 1991, after several failed attempts to formulate appropriate organizational guidelines for environmental crimes, the Sentencing Commission appointed an Advisory Working Group (AWG) on Environmental Sanctions to consider further how general principles governing criminal punishment could be applied to organizational fines. On March 5, 1993, the AWG released a working draft of recommendations concerning guidelines for organizations convicted of environmental crimes.[503] After extensive public comment, the AWG released a second draft on November 16, 1993, which was sent to the full Commission for consideration.[504]

The AWG's proposed guidelines, which would be a new Chapter 9 of the existing sentencing guidelines, contain both fine and probation sections.[505] The fine provisions are completely new, whereas the probation provisions will replace the probation provisions in Chapter 8 that currently apply to crimes committed by organizations.

The draft guidelines use the maximum statutory fine as the starting point in determining the criminal fine. They provide for possible downward adjustment depending on the elements and the characteristics of the offense and the presence of any mitigating factors. However, the presence of aggravating characteristics will limit the downward adjustment, if any. For the most part, the procedure of determining fines under the draft guidelines closely follows that of Chapter 2 of the current guidelines. Courts will have less discretion, however, to depart upwardly or downwardly from the draft guidelines.

Under the draft guidelines, the first step generally is to determine the primary offense level by applying specific offense characteristics to the base offense level for each listed violation.[506] This requires determining the type of environmental offense.[507] As under Chapter 2 of the current guidelines, numerical values—or levels—are assigned to the types of offenses and to the specific offense characteristics. The level assigned to each type of offense is referred to as the "base offense level."[508] The facts of each offense determine how these levels will be added. The values of specific offense characteristics may change depending on the type of offense, and certain specific offense characteristics do not apply to all types of offenses.[509]

Once the primary offense level has been determined, courts should apply culpability factors, which include both aggravating and mitigating factors.[510] These factors are also assigned numerical values that are added to, or subtracted from, the primary offense level. Aggravating factors include management involvement in the offense, an organization's criminal and civil compliance histories, violations of orders, concealment, and the absence of a corporate compliance program or other organized effort to comply with environmental requirements.[511] Mitigating factors include a corporate commitment to environmental compliance, cooperation and self-reporting of the violation, and remedial assistance.[512] Application of aggravating and mitigating factors to the primary offense level results in the total offense level for the violation.

To calculate the fine, the draft guidelines set up a fine table in which each offense level corresponds to a percentage of the maximum available statutory fine.[513] An offense level of 24 or more requires the court to sentence an organization to 100 percent of the maximum statutory fine, while an offense level of 0 to 6 requires the court to sentence an organization to 10 percent of the maximum statutory fine. Thus, for example, the court could sentence an organization whose conduct resulted in an offense level of 20 to between 70 and 90 percent of the maximum statutory fine. The draft guidelines, however, generally limit mitigation to 50 percent of the offense level.[514]

The probation section of the draft guidelines largely mirrors that of the current organizational guidelines. The draft guidelines, however, allow courts to impose more stringent and detailed remedial programs and to order violating organizations to publicize their offense and the punishment imposed.[515]

---

502. United States v. Palm Beach Cruises, S.A., No. 94-8049 (S.D. Fla. Aug. 30, 1994) (plea agreement).

503. *See* Memorandum from Advisory Working Group on Environmental Sanctions to Interested Members of the Public, Working Draft Recommendations (Mar. 5, 1993) (releasing and soliciting public comment on the working draft).

504. DRAFT ENVIRONMENTAL SENTENCING GUIDELINES, *supra* note 302. The Commission, however, was unable to resolve this issue and, thus, has never acted. Accordingly, sentencing judges still apply criminal fines to corporations based on their discretion within the range permitted by the statute under which the corporation was convicted or under 18 U.S.C. §§3553 and 3572, rather than under a uniform formula devised by the Commission. As long as this state of affairs persists, defense counsel will continue to play an important role in attempting to persuade the court to use this power as lightly as possible.

505. DRAFT ENVIRONMENTAL SENTENCING GUIDELINES, *supra* note 302, proposed §§9E and F.

506. *Id.*, proposed §9A1.2(a)(2). If the organization is operated primarily for a criminal purpose or primarily by criminal means, courts should not apply offense levels and should determine a fine sufficient to divest the organization of all of its net assets. *Id.*, proposed §§9A1.2(a)(1) and 9B1.1.

507. *Id.*, proposed §9B2.1(a).

508. For example, the base offense level for the mishandling of hazardous or toxic substances is eight. *Id.*, proposed §9B2.1(b)(2)(A). This same base offense level applies to the mishandling of hazardous or toxic substances under §2Q1.2 of the existing guidelines.

509. For example, as under Chapter 2 of the existing guidelines, if a person mishandles a hazardous or toxic substance and the offense results in a substantial likelihood of death or serious bodily injury, nine levels would be added to the base offense level. *Id.*, proposed §9B2.1(b)(2)(B)(ii). Thus, the proposed provision would produce the same result as existing §2Q1.2(b)(2).

510. *Id.*, proposed §9C.

511. *Id.*, proposed §9C1.1.

512. *Id.*, proposed §9C1.2. To grant mitigation under §9C1.2(a) for environmental compliance, the sentencing court must conclude that each of the following seven factors was substantially satisfied: (1) line management's attention to compliance; (2) integration of environmental policies, standards, and procedures; (3) auditing, monitoring, reporting, and tracking systems; (4) regulatory expertise, training, and evaluation; (5) incentives for compliance; (6) disciplinary procedures; and (7) continuing evaluation and improvement. An organization can obtain additional mitigation if, in addition to meeting the above factors, it has implemented additional programs or components that demonstrate its commitment to environmental compliance. *Id.*, proposed §9D1.1.

513. *Id.*, proposed §9E1.1.

514. *Id.*, proposed §9E1.2(b).

515. *Id.*, proposed §9F.

Although the draft organizational guidelines were released some time ago, as of this writing, the Sentencing Commission has taken little action on the proposal and has not focused on the issue in some time. Thus, it is unlikely that the Commission will submit a final proposal to Congress in the foreseeable future. Should the draft guidelines become effective in a form that resembles the current version, however, companies convicted of an environmental crime will ultimately face tougher financial penalties.

Collateral Consequences

Consequences collateral to an environmental conviction may have more significant adverse effects on a corporation than the criminal penalties, particularly for companies that have federal government contracts. A corporation charged with an environmental crime must consider the potential negative effects of conviction on several fronts, including: collateral estoppel effects in subsequent civil litigation regarding the environmental cleanup; mandatory "blacklisting" for future federal contracts under the FWPCA and the CAA; suspension and debarment from government contracts; federal tax consequences; SEC disclosure obligations; and potential disqualification from holding environmental operating licenses under state "bad actor" statutes. These impacts can be so devastating to the future conduct of a business that prosecutors have substantial leverage to compel companies to accept a criminal plea in the hope of receiving favorable exercise of discretion on these other matters. A corporation defending against environmental criminal charges must be aware of these potential collateral effects from the onset of the government's investigation and should immediately look for opportunities to minimize their adverse effects.[516]

Collateral Estoppel Effects in Subsequent Civil Litigation

Under the common-law doctrine of collateral estoppel, a party may not relitigate an issue that has been decided in a prior action in which the question was necessarily determined by final judgment.[517] Once a defendant is convicted of a criminal offense, collateral estoppel generally will prevent it from relitigating the facts underlying the essential elements of the offense in any subsequent civil action.[518]

Most environmental statutes provide ample grounds for civil damages actions seeking restitution, cleanup of pollution, and restoration of the natural environment resulting from the acts that led to criminal conviction.[519] Federal and state governments may bring such actions themselves, and many statutes authorize citizen suits for damages. In either case, a defendant convicted of an environmental crime is subject to "offensive" use of collateral estoppel, which would preclude it from relitigating the facts that established the environmental violation. For example, a party whose property was harmed by an illegal disposal of hazardous waste could invoke collateral estoppel in a civil action against a party convicted of that disposal, to prevent the defendant from litigating most issues relevant to the determination of liability.[520] Further, collateral estoppel can be used "defensively" by third parties to defeat any lawsuits that a convicted polluter brings against them for the events giving rise to the conviction.[521]

The collateral estoppel effect of criminal judgments is often the decisive factor in a corporation's decision to plead guilty to a criminal charge and to seek a global settlement. Several tactics have emerged to attempt to lessen the collateral estoppel effects of a plea, but their success depends entirely on the cooperation of the prosecution in its charging decision. For example, conviction on a plea of nolo contendere, rather than a plea of guilty, will reduce the collateral estoppel consequences because a nolo plea is generally inadmissible in a subsequent federal civil or criminal proceeding.[522] Prosecutors are rarely satisfied with a nolo plea, however, and such a disposition may be available only in unusual cases.[523]

---

516. *See generally* David T. Buente Jr. et al. *The Civil Implications of Environmental Crimes*, *in* A.L.I.-A.B.A., CRIMINAL ENFORCEMENT OF ENVIRONMENTAL LAWS 395 (1994).

517. *See, e.g.*, Montana v. United States, 440 U.S. 147, 153 (1979). This doctrine applies only to issues necessarily decided by the adjudication of liability, not to factual determinations made by the judge at sentencing to support a restitution order. United States v. Palma, 760 F.2d 475 (3d Cir. 1985).

518. Even if collateral estoppel does not apply, a prior bad act may be admissible in a subsequent federal case under Fed. R. Evid. 404(b), which permits evidence of a prior crime, wrong, or act to be admitted to prove motive, opportunity, intent, preparation, plan, knowledge, identity, or absence of mistake or accident. Fed. R. Evid. 609 also allows for impeachment of a witness by evidence of conviction of a felony.

519. *See, e.g.*, 33 U.S.C. §1321(b), (c), ELR STAT. FWPCA §311(b), (c); 42 U.S.C. §§6924(u), 6928(h), ELR STAT. RCRA §§3004(u), 3008(h).

520. In addition, the Victim and Witness Protection Act provides that a defendant convicted of an offense for which restitution has been ordered is estopped from denying the essential allegations of the offense in a subsequent action for damages brought by the victim. 18 U.S.C. §3664(e).

521. Many federal environmental statutes authorize states to administer and enforce federal requirements, resulting in concurrent state and federal authority. *See, e.g.*, 33 U.S.C. §1342(b), ELR STAT. FWPCA §402(b); 42 U.S.C. §6926, ELR STAT. RCRA §3006; *id.* §7410, ELR STAT. CAA §110. The question is periodically raised whether under the state authorization process of federal environmental laws, the United States and state enforcement authorities should be considered in privity with each other, so that the defendant may assert collateral estoppel against a subsequent federal action based on the same facts as an unsuccessful prior state enforcement action. *See* United States v. ITT Rayonier, Inc., 627 F.2d 996, 10 ELR 20945 (9th Cir. 1980); William D. Benton, *Application of Res Judicata and Collateral Estoppel to EPA Overfiling*, 16 B.C. ENVTL. AFF. L. REV. 199 (1988). *But see* Aminoil U.S.A., Inc. v. California State Water Resources Control Bd., 674 F.2d 122, 12 ELR 20594 (9th Cir. 1982). The issue arose recently in *In re Beaumont Co.*, No. RCRA-III-238 (EPA Oct. 20, 1994), in which an EPA administrative law judge held that pursuant to RCRA §3006(d), the state was EPA's representative in the prior state enforcement proceeding, so that EPA was collaterally estopped from pursuing RCRA charges against a company after resolution of a state proceeding that resulted in minimal sanctions.

In the civil context, invoking collateral estoppel against the federal government would appear clearly wrong under statutes such as the FWPCA, where parallel EPA and state programs are in force at all times, and highly questionable even under statutes such as RCRA, where the state program operates "in lieu of" the federal program. In the criminal context, the dual sovereignty doctrine appears to preclude any use of collateral estoppel to block a subsequent criminal action by the other level of government. *See* United States v. Louisville Edible Oil Prods., Inc., 926 F.2d 584, 21 ELR 20690 (6th Cir.), *cert. denied*, 502 U.S. 859 (1991).

522. FED. R. CRIM. P. 11(e); FED. R. EVID. 410. The laws of many states, however, do permit introduction of nolo pleas as evidence of guilt.

523. Justice's policy against accepting nolo pleas was established in a directive issued by Attorney General Herbert Brownwell in 1953. *See* DEPARTMENT OF JUSTICE MANUAL §9-16.010 (1993 Supp.). Although a court may accept such a plea over Justice's objections, it will not do so when it would not serve the public interest. *See* United States v. American Bakeries Co., 284 F. Supp. 871, 873-74 (W.D. Mich. 1968).

Another strategy to lessen the collateral estoppel effect is to negotiate a plea to a strict liability crime, where possible, to avoid preclusion on the issue of negligence in a subsequent private damages action. Conviction of a strict liability crime establishes the fact of the occurrence, but not any intent, because the crime has no mental element.

Mandatory "Blacklisting" Under the FWPCA and the CAA

The FWPCA and the CAA prohibit federal agencies from entering into new contracts with, or issuing any grants to, an entity convicted of crimes under those statutes, pursuant to a mandatory blacklisting procedure.[524] The listing applies for a finite period of time and operates prospectively, not retroactively. Accordingly, a criminal conviction does not require cancellation of contracts, grants, or other forms of assistance already awarded to the facility, but does preclude all federal agencies from entering into new arrangements until EPA removes the listing.

FWPCA §508(a) prohibits all federal agencies from entering into any contract with any person who has been convicted of a criminal offense under FWPCA §309(c) "if such contract is to be performed at *any facility* at which the violation which gave rise to such conviction occurred, and if such *facility* is owned, leased, or supervised by such person . . . ."[525] Listing under §508(a) applies only to the particular facility involved, and not to the entire division or company to which the facility belongs.

CAA §306[526] contains a similar provision, based on the FWPCA, that requires mandatory listing for a criminal conviction under §113(c). The 1990 CAA Amendments give EPA discretion to extend the listing beyond the facility at which the violation occurred and apply it to other facilities owned or operated by the convicted person or entity.[527] No similar discretionary authority exists under the FWPCA.

The listing program is administered by the EPA Assistant Administrator for Compliance, the official responsible for the original criminal referral to Justice. The EPA regulations implementing the FWPCA and the CAA[528] provide for maintenance of a List of Violating Facilities, which is published in the *Federal Register* and disseminated to all federal agencies monthly. Publication on the list bars the facility or broader entity from receiving any new federal contract or subcontract. This exclusion is enforced by a federal acquisition regulation (FAR) that requires each bidder for a contract to certify, subject to the provisions of the False Statements Act,[529] that the bidder is not ineligible to receive the award.[530]

In order to remove a facility or entity from the list, the Assistant Administrator must certify that the necessary remedial action has been taken to correct the conditions giving rise to the violation.[531] Removal action may be initiated by the company or by the listing official.[532] After receiving a delisting request, the Assistant Administrator will request a review and recommendation from the applicable EPA regional office before making a final decision. If the listing official refuses to remove the facility from the list, the facility's owner or operator may request a removal hearing, at which it must demonstrate by a preponderance of the evidence that the condition giving rise to the listing has been corrected.[533]

Under a 1991 EPA policy statement, correction of the "conditions giving rise to the violation" requires the adoption of an appropriate "corporate attitude" toward future compliance with environmental laws and regulations.[534] The policy identifies several criteria EPA will consider in determining whether such an attitude exists, including:

- the existence of written procedures defining the company's environmental standards, which are consistently enforced through disciplinary mechanisms;
- an effective program to apply these standards, such as a monitoring and auditing system, and methods by which employees can report environmental problems without retribution; and
- a program for prevention and immediate correction of future environmental problems, which may include an independent environmental audit to ensure that there are no other problems at the facility.[535]

Through these "attitude adjustment" factors, EPA seeks to assure, as consideration for release from the list, that the violator will adopt prospective environmental practices that are more stringent than EPA can require under its ordinary statutory powers.

524. 33 U.S.C. §1368(a), ELR STAT. FWPCA §508(a); 42 U.S.C. §706, ELR STAT. CAA §306. Under Agency rules, EPA also has discretion to list a facility even in the absence of a criminal conviction, but has rarely exercised this power. Discretionary listing is based on a determination that there is a record of continuing or recurring noncompliance with federal, state, or local clean water or air standards. 40 C.F.R. §15.11. The effect of listing is generally the same, regardless of whether it occurs automatically by operation of law or by exercise of discretion. EPA rules do, however, provide procedures to challenge a proposed discretionary listing. *Id.* §15.12.

525. 33 U.S.C. §1368(a), ELR STAT. FWPCA §508(a) (emphasis added). This provision also prohibits participation in any federal loan, loan guarantee, grant, or other assistance program.

526. 42 U.S.C. §7606, ELR STAT. CAA §306.

527. *Id.* §7606(a), ELR STAT. CAA §306(a). The term "facility" is defined expansively in 40 C.F.R. §15.4 to give the EPA Assistant Administrator authority to consider all operations at one location or site that are part of the same facility. EPA has not issued a regulation to define how and when it will exercise its authority under the CAA to extend listing beyond the particular facility involved in a violation.

528. 40 C.F.R. pt. 15.

529. 18 U.S.C. §§1001-1027.

530. 48 C.F.R. §52.209-5. EPA's rules explicitly apply the listing sanction to subcontracts as well. 40 C.F.R. §15.4. Federal agency heads have authority to exempt certain contracts or grants from the listing disqualification, based on the "paramount" interests of the United States. *Id.* §15.51(c)(2). Such exemptions are rare and must be reported to Congress.

531. 40 C.F.R. §§15.20, 15.22(b).

532. *Id.* §15.22(a).

533. *Id.* §15.24. Even if the conditions creating the violation have been completely corrected by the time of conviction, the facility must still be listed for some period of time. As a matter of policy, EPA has refused to entertain any request to be removed from the list, or to review corrective actions regarding the violation, prior to placing the facility on the list. The policy of not considering remedial actions before the date of listing, coupled with a period of observation necessary to determine whether the proper "corporate attitude" exists, means that upon conviction of an FWPCA or CAA violation, the offending facility will spend a minimum of four to six months on the list, even if it cures the problem immediately and demonstrates an exemplary attitude.

534. U.S. EPA, Policy Regarding the Role of Corporate Attitude, Policies, Practices, and Procedures, in Determining Whether to Remove a Facility from the EPA List of Violating Facilities Following a Criminal Conviction, 56 Fed. Reg. 64785, 64786, ELR ADMIN. MAT. I 35411 (Dec. 12, 1991).

535. *Id.* at 64787, ELR ADMIN. MAT. I at 35412.

The *Exxon Bayway* case demonstrates the extensive steps that may be required before a major facility is delisted. This oil pipeline was listed in March 1991 as a result of its plea to an FWPCA misdemeanor for a major oil spill.[536] The facility was delisted 10 months later, after the company spent $18 million to remove the spilled oil, settled federal and state civil and natural resource damage claims for $10 million, paid $5 million in criminal fines, closed the facility for 3 months, and conducted a $25 million environmental study that led to initiation of a host of safeguards to prevent future oil spills.[537]

In sum, a company facing an FWPCA or CAA criminal charge must consider the practical consequences of the facility's inability to receive federal contracts or grants for a period of time. This concern can play an instrumental role in any plea negotiations. In particular, a company contemplating a plea will want to determine if EPA will discuss how the "facility" subject to mandatory listing would be defined. For CAA pleas in particular, the company also must determine whether EPA will forego exercise of its discretion to extend the listing beyond the offending facility.

Suspension and Debarment From Government Contracts

Federal agencies (and each state) have authority to suspend and debar companies from receiving future contracts and grants when the contractor's responsibility is deemed compromised, even if no criminal conviction occurs. Thus, environmental violations can have significant adverse economic effects on a government contractor, even if the violations do not result in criminal charges. Imposition of such sanctions is virtually assured, however, if a company is convicted of an environmental crime.

Suspension is an interim refusal to deal with a contractor pending receipt of further information. It temporarily disqualifies a contractor from receiving government contracts or having contracts renewed or extended until the basis for the suspension is resolved. Although it is typically based on the return of an indictment, suspension can occur whenever evidence exists to believe that a contractor has committed an offense that may give rise to debarment.[538] If a company is indicted for an environmental crime, it will likely be suspended until the indictment is resolved.

Debarment is the disqualification of a contractor for a set period of time—typically from one to three years. Thus, the debarment period may be longer than the listing period. The decision to debar and the length of the sanction are within the discretion of the debarring official. The length is based on the nature of the basis for debarment, any mitigating circumstances, and any remedial actions that the contractor has taken. If a company is convicted of an environmental crime, it will likely be proposed for debarment. If the company has not already been suspended, the notice of proposed debarment will bar the company from receiving contracts until a final decision is made by the debarring official. Debarment may apply to all of the company's activities, not just to the offending facility.

Suspension and debarment are discretionary administrative procedures to protect the government from undesirable contractors, by excluding the entities from receiving new federal contracts or participating in federal assistance programs based on evidence that the contractor lacks "present responsibility."[539] Suspension and debarment by any one agency is effective throughout the federal government, and results in the entity's disqualification from all new federal awards during the period the action is in effect.[540] The contractor's name is placed on a consolidated list that is circulated to all federal agencies monthly and is available on-line. The prohibition against awarding a new contract, consenting to a subcontract, or renewing an existing contract with the disqualified entity is enforced through the FAR certification requirement.[541] While the action's effect is governmentwide, its scope may be limited to particular organizational elements, or extend to the entire company, depending on the facts and the policy of the agency taking the action.[542]

The suspension and debarment regulations recommend that when multiple agencies have an interest in a particular company, one agency should be designated as the lead agency to consider suspension or debarment action.[543] There are no set rules, however, for determining which agency will take the lead in a particular case. Normally, considerations such as primary contacts—either through contracts or federal assistance programs with a particular federal agency—or a particular interest arising out of the underlying actions giving rise to the potential suspension or debarment, are determinative in designating the lead agency.

In the last several years, EPA has become increasingly aggressive in taking suspension or debarment actions against companies that have been accused or convicted of environmental crimes. If the violation does not arise out of a particular government contract or program, but exclusively concerns the violation of an environmental law or regulation, EPA has consistently taken the lead agency role. In such a context, other federal agencies will typically defer to EPA's Assistant Administrator for Compliance.

The decision to suspend or debar can be limited to the particular organizational element responsible for the offense, extended to other organizational components, or applied to the entire corporation.[544] The debarring agency will normally limit the scope of the sanction to the organizational element responsible for the misconduct, unless the evidence shows that other elements or corporate headquarters were involved in the events leading to debarment.

536. *See supra* note 412 and accompanying text.

537. In re Exxon Corp. (*Exxon Bayway*), No. 02-91-L034 (EPA Feb. 4, 1992) (delisting determination).

538. *See* 48 C.F.R. §9.407-2.

539. *Id.* §§9.104-1(d), 9.406-2(a)(5), 9.407-2(a)(5).

540. EPA has suspension and debarment authority over a company's procurement and nonprocurement relationships with the federal government. *Id.* subpt. 9.4 (procurement), 40 C.F.R. pt. 32 (nonprocurement).

541. The regulations permit an agency to contract with a suspended or debarred entity only if "the acquiring agency's head or a designee states in writing the compelling reasons" for doing so. 48 C.F.R. §9.405-2(a).

542. These sanctions apply to "all divisions or other organizational elements of the contractor, unless the . . . decision is limited by its terms to specific divisions, organizational elements, or commodities." *Id.* §9.406-1(b). Like many other agencies, EPA has shown a preference for taking action against the lowest possible operating unit or division involved in the criminal action.

543. *Id.* §9.402(c); 40 C.F.R. §32.115(c).

544. 48 C.F.R. §9.406-1(b).

If other elements of the corporation remain eligible to receive contracts, however, they may not contract with the debarred component.

The company may present argument and evidence in opposition to the proposed debarment before a final decision is reached.[545] A final agency decision to debar is reviewable in federal court, although judicial relief is rarely granted. In certain circumstances, the agency may entertain a petition to reduce the length of a debarment.[546] For example, a post-violation change in the ownership of the facility responsible for the wrongdoing is an acceptable ground for discretionary reduction of the term of debarment.[547]

A company facing an environmental criminal charge should carefully consider the effects of suspension and debarment on its business. EPA and most other federal agencies will negotiate with a company under investigation to resolve the government's concerns regarding the company's integrity without using suspension or debarment; this is not so with listing. The government may be willing to forego suspension and debarment procedures if it is assured of the company's "present responsibility" through other means, such as a settlement agreement that imposes certain conditions on the business. The lead agency may require the company's agreement to operating restrictions, removal or discipline of those responsible for the wrongdoing, and implementation of training and compliance programs. Consequently, settlement discussions in the criminal case and the debarment action may proceed on separate tracks. However, many settlement discussions begin only after a post-indictment suspension has been imposed, which significantly reduces the company's bargaining leverage.

Federal Tax Consequences

A criminal fine, including a fine paid pursuant to a plea of nolo contendere, is not deductible from gross income as an ordinary and necessary business expense under §162(a) of the Internal Revenue Code.[548] However, federal tax regulations provide that amounts paid to the government as "compensatory damages" do not constitute fines or penalties and thus are deductible.[549]

The case law provides conflicting guidance on the factors that allow a restitutionary payment in a criminal case to be treated as tax deductible. Deductibility determinations are fact-specific and depend on whether the payment is characterized primarily as punitive or compensatory.[550] Thus, the terms of a plea agreement or sentence may affect the deductibility of a restitutionary payment. With the prosecutor's cooperation, the defendant may be able to structure a restitutionary payment to increase the likelihood of deductibility.[551] The prosecutor's ability to affect the extent to which a payment is deductible or a deadweight loss to the company is both an inducement to the business to enter a plea and a source of significant leverage for the government in negotiations.

In *Stephens v. Commissioner*,[552] the deductibility analysis turned on whether the restitutionary payment was ordered instead of, or in addition to, punishment. The Second Circuit held that when restitution is imposed in addition to a specific fine and prison sentence, an inference is raised that the primary purpose of the restitution is compensatory.[553] Thus, the payment at issue was deductible.

In contrast to *Stephens*, the Sixth Circuit in *Kraft v. United States*[554] denied a deduction for a restitutionary payment, notwithstanding the fact that it was in addition to a sentence of imprisonment and the imposition of a fine. The plea agreement required the taxpayer to pay restitution to a private party. The court held that because the payments arose out of a criminal proceeding, they constituted a penalty and were not deductible.[555] If, as *Kraft* implies, the criminal nature of the underlying proceeding alone is sufficient to result in a determination of nondeductibility, then a defendant facing an environmental criminal charge should attempt to arrange for the restitutionary payment to be made in the context of a parallel civil damages action.

In *Allied-Signal, Inc. v. Commissioner*,[556] the Tax Court held that a restitutionary payment made before sentencing, with the firm expectation of a lower sentence as a quid pro quo, was not tax deductible. Prior to sentencing, the defendant, which had pleaded nolo contendere without a plea agreement, made a multimillion-dollar contribution to an environmental fund that benefitted the state. It argued that the payment should be deductible because the payment was voluntary and was made primarily to compensate the state rather than to punish the defendant. The Tax Court rejected those arguments, holding that the payment was involuntarily made as a quid pro quo for a lower fine, and that its primary purpose was punishment.[557]

As a result of these decisions, a company seeking to resolve environmental criminal charges in part through restitutionary

545. *Id.* §9.406-3.

546. *Id.* §9.406-4(c).

547. *Id.* §9.406-4(c)(3).

548. 26 U.S.C. §162(a), (f); Treas. Reg. §1.162-21(b)(1)(i). A nondeductible "fine or similar penalty" includes an amount paid as a civil penalty or in settlement of actual or potential liability for a fine or penalty. Treas. Reg. §1.162-21(b)(1)(ii), (iii). *See* True v. United States, 894 F.2d 1197 (10th Cir. 1990) (FWPCA civil penalties nondeductible); Colt Indus. Inc. v. United States, 11 Cl. Ct. 140 (1986) (FWPCA civil penalties nondeductible), *aff'd*, 880 F.2d 1311 (Fed. Cir. 1989).

549. Treas. Reg. §1.162-21(b)(2). If such fines are paid under a plea of nolo contendere, however, they are not deductible. Thus, a nolo plea is useful only for collateral estoppel, and not for tax purposes.

550. *See* Waldman v. Commissioner, 88 T.C. 1384 (1987), *aff'd*, 850 F.2d 611 (9th Cir. 1988). The court employed a "primary purpose" test to determine whether a restitutionary payment was a nondeductible penalty or a deductible compensatory payment. The court found that even though the payment was made to a private party, it was still subject to the same treatment as if it were paid to the government, because the payment was a judicially controlled diversion of money. This decision is thus relevant to structuring any environmental restitution with private parties as part of settling an environmental criminal claim.

551. The *Exxon Valdez* plea agreement, for example, was consciously designed to take advantage of the tax deductibility of compensatory payments. There, the restitution was expressly stated to be "exclusively remedial, compensatory, and non-punitive, and . . . separate and distinct from the fines . . . ." United States v. Exxon Corp., Plea Agreement No. A90-015 (Sept. 26, 1991), at 9.

552. 905 F.2d 667 (2d Cir. 1990).

553. *Id.* at 673.

554. 991 F.2d 292 (6th Cir. 1993).

555. *Id.* at 298-99.

556. 63 T.C.M. (CCH) 2672 (1992), *aff'd*, 54 F.3d 767 (3d Cir. 1995).

557. *Id.* at 2681-83.

payments can increase the likelihood—though not the certainty—that they will be characterized as tax-deductible compensatory payments by eliminating any indication, in the plea agreement or elsewhere, that the payments are involuntary. The settlement agreement should also state explicitly that restitution is intended to compensate the receiving entity, and not to punish or deter the defendant.[558]

SEC Disclosure Obligations

The SEC is increasingly concerned with proper disclosure of environmental violations by publicly held companies.[559] There are two main sources of these companies' duty to disclose their environmental liabilities: periodic disclosure requirements and general antifraud provisions.

The SEC's reporting system is centered around Regulation S-K, which lists periodic reporting requirements for registrants.[560] The provisions of Regulation S-K most relevant to environmental matters are: (a) Item 101, which requires a description of the business; (b) Item 103, which requires disclosure of material legal proceedings; and (c) Item 303, which is management's discussion and analysis (MD&A) of financial condition and results of operations.

Under Item 101, the registrant must provide a general description of its business and disclose material effects that compliance with federal, state, and local environmental laws may have on its capital expenditures, earnings, and competitive position.[561]

Under Item 103, disclosure is required if the registrant, its subsidiary, or its property is subject to a proceeding that:

- is material to the registrant's business or financial condition;
- is primarily a claim for damages, or concerns potential monetary sanctions, capital expenditures, deferred charges or charges to income and the amount involved, exclusive of interest and costs, exceeds 10 percent of the current assets of the registrant and its subsidiaries on a consolidated basis; or
- involves a governmental authority as a party and involves potential monetary sanctions, unless the registrant reasonably believes that the proceeding will result in no monetary sanctions or sanctions which, exclusive of interest and costs, are less than $100,000.[562]

A registrant must disclose to its shareholders information about its material environmental liabilities, including pending administrative or judicial proceedings, as well as proceedings that are known to be contemplated by the government.[563] A company considering entering a plea to an environmental crime should discuss with its securities counsel whether, based on its knowledge of contemplated proceedings by the government, the company is required to make public disclosure pursuant to the instructions to Item 103.

Under Item 303, the MD&A narrative discussion of the registrant's financial condition should include those "material events and uncertainties known to management that would cause reported financial information not to be necessarily indicative of future operating results or future financial condition."[564] The MD&A Interpretive Release expands the disclosure requirement to include disclosure of known uncertainties unless management can determine in an objectively reasonable assessment that a material effect is not reasonably likely to occur.[565]

Beyond specific periodic disclosures, general antifraud provisions prohibit the inaccurate representation of a registrant's environmental record. In *United Paper Workers International Union v. International Paper Co.*,[566] a shareholder suit, the court found that the company committed a proxy rule violation by materially misrepresenting its environmental record.

State "Bad Actor" Provisions

A "bad actor" provision is a statute or regulation that denies a license, permit, or other benefit to a person or company based on poor regulatory compliance history. A company facing an environmental criminal charge should carefully review whether its operations are covered by federal or state licensing or regulatory statutes that impose sanctions if the regulated entity, its owners, its key employees, or its affiliates are convicted of a crime.

Virtually all adverse "bad actor" consequences are imposed at the state level.[567] A majority of states has enacted statutes under which a history of poor environmental compliance, particularly an environmental criminal conviction, can jeopardize a person's right to hold operating permits, especially if the permit holder or applicant does not make a substantial effort to correct the condition that led to the violation.[568] These provisions arise primarily in the hazardous waste area as a result of initiatives to address the penetration of organized crime into solid waste disposal. To enforce these restrictions, several states, including Indiana, New Jersey, and Ohio, require affirmative disclosure of compliance history by the hazardous waste license applicant.[569] Failure to disclose compliance history properly can

558. The availability of insurance payments under standard corporate comprehensive general liability policies may also be affected by a guilty plea or conviction, on grounds similar to those concerning tax deductibility. Most policies exclude reimbursement for fines or penalties, which are not considered "damages." The critical questions are (1) what defines a restitutionary payment, as opposed to a penalty, under the insurance contract, and (2) whether the answer is different when the loss is caused by an action for which the insured has been held criminally liable.

559. *See* Richard Y. Roberts & Kurt R. Hohl, *Environmental Liability Disclosure and Staff Accounting Bulletin No. 92*, 50 BUS. LAW. 1, 2 (Nov. 1994).

560. 17 C.F.R. §§229.10 to 229.915.

561. *Id.* §229.101.

562. *See id.* §229.103, Instruction 5.

563. *See* Roberts & Hohl, *supra* note 559, at 2 n.6.

564. 17 C.F.R. §229.303, Instruction 3.

565. *See* Release Nos. 33-6835, 34-26831 (May 18, 1989), 54 Fed. Reg. 22427 (May 24, 1989).

566. 985 F.2d 1190 (2d Cir. 1993).

567. There is a narrow bad actor provision under TSCA. Under §6(e)(1), poor environmental compliance of the applicant, its principals, and its key employees may lead to the denial of an application to store PCBs for disposal. 15 U.S.C. §2605(e)(1), ELR STAT. TSCA §6(e)(1); *see also* 40 C.F.R. §761.65(d), as amended by 58 Fed. Reg. 59372 (Nov. 9, 1993).

568. *See, e.g.*, N.J. STAT. ANN. §13:1E-133.1(a); TEX. ADMIN. CODE tit. 31, §305.66(g).

569. *See* IND. CODE ANN. §13-7-10.2-3(b); N.J. STAT. ANN. §13:1E-127(e); OHIO REV. CODE ANN. §3734.41(D).

provide independent grounds in some states for denial or revocation of hazardous waste permits.

Denial of a crucial permit under a "bad actor" provision could effectively put a party out of business. Therefore, the target has significant incentives to structure any plea in a manner that minimizes the adverse effects on the target's qualifications to do business prospectively. Because disqualification is generally discretionary, permit holders are well advised to discuss the likely consequences with civil regulators well in advance of agreeing to any criminal plea.

Conclusion

The federal government has taken a series of spontaneous, incremental steps to deter commission of environmental crimes. Congress has increased the probability that violations will be detected by augmenting EPA and Justice appropriations for enforcement, converting the CAA to a permit program, and expanding the range of sanctions and the severity of potential sentences. The Sentencing Commission has increased both the likelihood that terms of imprisonment will be imposed on individual offenders and the expected length of such terms. In addition, courts have interpreted environmental laws to require proof only of a minimal showing of awareness, substantially easing the prosecutor's burden at trial. In a complementary measure, civil enforcement efforts have tailored the damages sought to offset any economic benefits the polluter derived from illegal discharges. Each of those steps has increased the deterrent effect of the laws.[570]

At the same time, there has been little apparent effort by any branch of government to think through what the appropriate level of deterrence should be. Nor has there been any systematic effort by Congress or the agencies to analyze whether the current level of enforcement is producing excessive societal costs through, for example, creating incentives for inefficient investment in redundant pollution control equipment, over-deterrence of productive activity, or creation of unnecessary obstacles to environmental auditing. These assessments are commonplace in other regulated fields, such as securities and antitrust law, but have not been undertaken in the environmental area.

Although the environmental crimes program is now almost two decades old, the policy question of its proper role has not yet been answered. The enforcement agencies concentrate on prosecuting individual cases and rarely discuss the systemic effects of their actions. Through 1994, Congress followed the sentiment, once articulated by Mae West, that "too much of a good thing is wonderful." Courts, reasoning by analogy, have concluded that Congress must have intended environmental crimes to be public welfare offenses and have deferred to Congress on the policy implications of that interpretation. As the environmental crimes program enters its adolescence, seasoned observers are beginning to question whether the ambiguity of its policy principles remains appropriate.[571]

At an administrative level, the structure Congress has adopted virtually assures future controversy about how many and what kinds of environmental criminal cases should be brought. Congress has enacted statutes that, as construed by the courts, take a popular principle near to its limit by making virtually every environmental violation subject to criminal prosecution. As commonly happens, Congress has quietly cut back on the realization of the ideal by appropriating enough money to pursue only a fraction of the potential criminal cases. The disparity between the potential reach of the criminal provisions and the expected actual degree of implementation will inevitably generate friction. In prior years, the conflict could be minimized by increased annual appropriations for enforcement, but this solution is problematic in an era of tight-fisted fiscal policy. Unless clearly articulated principles are put in place, this disparity will leave policy officials vulnerable to internal and external criticism that they are not bringing enough prosecutions, as Justice learned in 1993-1994. In addition, the open-ended nature of internal agency standards for authorizing prosecutions—which is so useful to policy officials on a day-to-day basis—facilitates second-guessing of their charging decisions in close cases.

EPA and Justice have announced some preliminary steps toward articulating a comprehensive enforcement policy. In recent speeches, senior officials have declared that criminal efforts will be directed toward particular industries; will focus on pollution affecting minorities and low-income populations; will follow a multimedia approach, rather than a medium-specific basis; and will take an ecosystem (geographic) approach where appropriate.[572]

These steps are minor implementation details adapted from civil permit programs. They do not begin to substitute for an answer to the core question: "What independent role should criminal enforcement play in the administration of the environmental protection laws?" The consequences of continuing to rely on a seat-of-the-pants approach are starkly displayed in the environmental auditing area. There, the absence of a policy framework has precipitated a sterile, legalistic debate that bears little relationship to the actual issue of how the environment can best be protected.

When this long overdue policy analysis is finally conducted, prominent aspects of the current approach will be shown to be clearly correct. These include the primary focus on prosecuting entities operating outside the permit system, ensuring the low-cost detection of regulatory violations by vigorously policing the integrity of the reporting system, and imposing on violators substantial fines and remedial obligations keyed to the economic benefits of a violation. Difficult policy problems will arise, however, concerning whether prosecutions should be filed against companies operating within the permit system when violations are not covered up, but are disclosed by internal audits or periodic reports. The policy rationale for criminal prosecution in these cases will be problematic because (1) the risk of detection is already high, thereby creating incentives for

570. *See* Gary S. Becker, *Crime and Punishment: An Economic Approach*, 76 J. POL. ECON. 169 (1966).

571. *See, e.g.*, Adam Babich, *DOE's Promising First Step*, NAT'L ENVTL. ENFOR. J. 1, 7 (July 1995).

572. *See, e.g.*, Remarks by Assistant Attorney General Lois Schiffer, A.L.I.-A.B.A. Conference on Criminal Enforcement of Environmental Laws, Washington, D.C. (Oct. 20-21, 1994); Memorandum from Steven A. Herman, Assistant Administrator, Office of Enforcement and Compliance Assurance, to Regional Administrators, FY 1995 Guidance Document for Enforcement and Compliance Assurance 7-9 (Sept. 20, 1994) (excerpts reproduced in Appendix A of this book). For standards that will apply in fiscal years 1996-1997, see Memorandum from Steven A. Herman, Assistant Administrator, to Regional Administrators, Final FY 96/97 OECA Memorandum of Agreement Guidance (June 22, 1995) (excerpts reproduced in Appendix A of this book).

prompt remediation by the source; and (2) absent a requirement for proof of intent to violate the law, there is a substantial risk of overdeterrence, which may drive companies and municipalities to make inefficient spending choices to minimize the risk of individual criminal prosecution for operational-level personnel.[573]

These considerations suggest that for entities within the permit system, Justice and EPA should focus carefully on systematic evasion or departure from the permit and evidence of concealment, misrepresentation, or obstruction in the data-gathering and reporting process. The same considerations also mean that companies and municipalities must pay special attention to the integrity of their regulatory compliance programs and to early, accurate disclosure of any violations that are detected. The most important role environmental counsel can play is to assist regulated entities in establishing effective environmental compliance and auditing programs to prevent or minimize problems at the front end.

573. *See* Robert Cooter, *Prices and Sanctions*, 84 COL. L. REV. 1523, 1524-25 (1984); Stephen M. Bundy & Einer Elhauge, *Knowledge About Legal Sanctions*, 92 MICH. L. REV. 261, 269-74 (1993).

Finally, to the extent that EPA and Justice have discretionary enforcement resources, they should take advantage of the flexibility to target criminal prosecutions on the most important pollution problems facing society. On the civil side, EPA and the states are denied this basic authority; they must instead respond to priorities established by Congress in law or by environmental groups in litigation. As internal and external EPA groups concluded in the early 1990s, the resulting system dedicates extensive resources to risks that scientists rank as rather low (such as local groundwater pollution by hazardous waste) and few resources to the most significant environmental risks (such as breakdown of the stratospheric ozone layer). EPA and Justice should determine how their criminal programs could directly support efforts to attack the largest environmental risks, even at the cost of a lower statistical "body count" of criminal convictions. They should defer prosecution of local risks to energized state enforcement programs. Effective use of this freedom might be an important object lesson for Congress of the benefits to be gained by trusting the EPA to determine environmental priorities, rather than codifying the targets in legislation.

Glossary of Acronyms

AWG	Advisory Working Group (of the U.S. Sentencing Commission)
CAA	Clean Air Act
Cal/EPA	California Environmental Protection Agency
CEO	chief executive officer
CERCLA	Comprehensive Environmental Response, Compensation, and Liability Act
ECS	Environmental Crimes Section (of the U.S. Department of Justice)
EPA	U.S. Environmental Protection Agency
FAR	federal acquisition regulation
FBI	Federal Bureau of Investigation
FFDCA	Federal Food, Drug, and Cosmetic Act
FIFRA	Federal Insecticide, Fungicide, and Rodenticide Act
FWPCA	Federal Water Pollution Control Act
HSWA	Hazardous and Solid Waste Amendments
MD&A	management's discussion and analysis
OMB	Office of Management and Budget
OSH Act	Occupational Safety and Health Act
PCBs	polychlorinated biphenyls
RCRA	Resource Conservation and Recovery Act
SEC	Securities and Exchange Commission
TSCA	Toxic Substances Control Act

Statutory Provisions

Statutory Provisions

Table of Contents

Clean Air Act §113
42 U.S.C. §7413

§ 7413. [CAA §113]

Federal enforcement

(a) In general

(1) Order to comply with SIP

Whenever, on the basis of any information available to the Administrator, the Administrator finds that any person has violated or is in violation of any requirement or prohibition of an applicable implementation plan or permit, the Administrator shall notify the person and the State in which the plan applies of such finding. At any time after the expiration of 30 days following the date on which such notice of a violation is issued, the Administrator may, without regard to the period of violation (subject to section 2462 of title 28)—

(A) issue an order requiring such person to comply with the requirements or prohibitions of such plan or permit,

(B) issue an administrative penalty order in accordance with subsection (d) of this section, or

(C) bring a civil action in accordance with subsection (b) of this section.

(2) State failure to enforce SIP or permit program

Whenever, on the basis of information available to the Administrator, the Administrator finds that violations of an applicable implementation plan or an approved permit program under subchapter V of this chapter are so widespread that such violations appear to result from a failure of the State in which the plan or permit program applies to enforce the plan or permit program effectively, the Administrator shall so notify the State. In the case of a permit program, the notice shall be made in accordance with subchapter V of this chapter. If the Administrator finds such failure extends beyond the 30th day after such notice (90 days in the case of such permit program), the Administrator shall give public notice of such finding. During the period beginning with such public notice and ending when such State satisfies the Administrator that it will enforce such plan or permit program (hereafter referred to in this section as "period of federally assumed enforcement"), the Administrator may enforce any requirement or prohibition of such plan or permit program with respect to any person by—

(A) issuing an order requiring such person to comply with such requirement or prohibition,

(B) issuing an administrative penalty order in accordance with subsection (d) of this section, or

(C) bringing a civil action in accordance with subsection (b) of this section.

(3) EPA enforcement of other requirements

Except for a requirement or prohibition enforceable under the preceding provisions of this subsection, whenever, on the basis of any information available to the Administrator, the Administrator finds that any person has violated, or is in violation of, any other requirement or prohibition of this subchapter, section 7603 of this title, subchapter IV-A, subchapter V, or subchapter VI of this chapter, including, but not limited to, a requirement or prohibition of any rule, plan, order, waiver, or permit promulgated, issued, or approved under those provisions or subchapters, or for the payment of any fee owed to the United States under this chapter (other than subchapter II of this chapter), the Administrator may—

(A) issue an administrative penalty order in accordance with subsection (d) of this section,

(B) issue an order requiring such person to comply with such requirement or prohibition,

(C) bring a civil action in accordance with subsection (b) of this section or section 7605 of this title, or

(D) request the Attorney General to commence a criminal action in accordance with subsection (c) of this section.

(4) Requirements for orders

An order issued under this subsection (other than an order relating to a violation of section 7412 of this title) shall not take effect until the person to whom it is issued has had an opportunity to confer with the Administrator concerning the alleged violation. A copy of any order issued under this subsection shall be sent to the State air pollution control agency of any State in which the violation occurs. Any order issued under this subsection shall state with reasonable specificity the nature of the violation and specify a time for compliance which the Administrator determines is reasonable, taking into account the seriousness of the violation and any good faith efforts to comply with applicable requirements. In any case in which an order under this subsection (or notice to a violator under paragraph (1)) is issued to a corporation, a copy of such order (or notice) shall be issued to appropriate corporate officers. An order issued under this subsection shall require the person to whom it was issued to comply with the requirement as expeditiously as practicable, but in no event longer than one year after the date the order was issued, and shall be nonrenewable. No order issued under this subsection shall prevent the State or the Administrator from assessing any penalties nor otherwise affect or limit the State's or the United States authority to enforce under other provisions of this chapter, nor affect any person's obligations to comply with any section of this chapter or with a term or condition of any permit or applicable implementation plan promulgated or approved under this chapter.

(5) Failure to comply with new source requirements

Whenever, on the basis of any available information, the Administrator finds that a State is not acting in compliance with any requirement or prohibition of the chapter relating to the construction of new sources or the modification of existing sources, the Administrator may—

(A) issue an order prohibiting the construction or modification of any major stationary source in any area to which such requirement applies;[1]

(B) issue an administrative penalty order in accordance with subsection (d) of this section, or

(C) bring a civil action under subsection (b) of this section.

Nothing in this subsection shall preclude the United States from commencing a criminal action under subsection (c) of this section at any time for any such violation.

(b) Civil judicial enforcement

The Administrator shall, as appropriate, in the case of any person that is the owner or operator of an affected source, a major emitting facility, or a major stationary source, and may, in the case of any other person, commence a civil action for a permanent or temporary injunction, or to assess and recover a civil penalty of not more than $25,000 per day for each violation, or both, in any of the following instances:

(1) Whenever such person has violated, or is in violation of, any requirement or prohibition of an applicable implementation plan or permit. Such an action shall be commenced (A) during any period of federally assumed enforcement, or (B) more than 30 days following the date of the Administrator's notification under subsection (a)(1) of this section that such person has violated, or is in violation of, such requirement or prohibition.

(2) Whenever such person has violated, or is in violation of, any other requirement or prohibition of this subchapter, section 7603 of this title, subchapter IV-A, subchapter V, or subchapter VI of this chapter, including, but not limited to, a requirement or prohibition of any rule, order, waiver or permit promulgated, issued, or approved under this chapter, or for the payment of any fee owed the United States under this chapter (other than subchapter II of this chapter).

(3) Whenever such person attempts to construct or modify a major stationary source in any area with respect to which a finding under subsection (a)(5) of this section has been made. Any action under this subsection may be brought in the district court of the United States for the district in which the violation is alleged to have occurred, or is occurring, or in which the defendant resides, or where the defendant's principal place of business is located, and

1. So in original. The semicolon probably should be a comma.

such court shall have jurisdiction to restrain such violation, to require compliance, to assess such civil penalty, to collect any fees owed the United States under this chapter (other than subchapter II of this chapter) and any noncompliance assessment and nonpayment penalty owed under section 7420 of this title, and to award any other appropriate relief. Notice of the commencement of such action shall be given to the appropriate State air pollution control agency. In the case of any action brought by the Administrator under this subsection, the court may award costs of litigation (including reasonable attorney and expert witness fees) to the party or parties against whom such action was brought if the court finds that such action was unreasonable.

(c) Criminal penalties

(1) Any person who knowingly violates any requirement or prohibition of an applicable implementation plan (during any period of federally assumed enforcement or more than 30 days after having been notified under subsection (a)(1) of this section by the Administrator that such person is violating such requirement or prohibition), any order under subsection (a) of this section, requirement or prohibition of section 7411(e) of this title (relating to new source performance standards), section 7412 of this title, section 7414 of this title (relating to inspections, etc.), section 7429 of this title (relating to solid waste combustion), section 7475(a) of this title (relating to preconstruction requirements), an order under section 7477 of this title (relating to preconstruction requirements), an order under section 7603 of this title (relating to emergency orders), section 7661a(a) or 7661b(c) of this title (relating to permits), or any requirement or prohibition of subchapter IV-A of this chapter (relating to acid deposition control), or subchapter VI of this chapter (relating to stratospheric ozone control), including a requirement of any rule, order, waiver, or permit promulgated or approved under such sections or subchapters, and including any requirement for the payment of any fee owed the United States under this chapter (other than subchapter II of this chapter) shall, upon conviction, be punished by a fine pursuant to title 18 or by imprisonment for not to exceed 5 years, or both. If a conviction of any person under this paragraph is for a violation committed after a first conviction of such person under this paragraph, the maximum punishment shall be doubled with respect to both the fine and imprisonment.

(2) Any person who knowingly—

(A) makes any false material statement, representation, or certification in, or omits material information from, or knowingly alters, conceals, or fails to file or maintain any notice, application, record, report, plan, or other document required pursuant to this chapter to be either filed or maintained (whether with respect to the requirements imposed by the Administrator or by a State);

(B) fails to notify or report as required under this chapter; or

(C) falsifies, tampers with, renders inaccurate, or fails to install any monitoring device or method required to be maintained or followed under this chapter[2]

shall, upon conviction, be punished by a fine pursuant to title 18 or by imprisonment for not more than 2 years, or both. If a conviction of any person under this paragraph is for a violation committed after a first conviction of such person under this paragraph, the maximum punishment shall be doubled with respect to both the fine and imprisonment.

(3) Any person who knowingly fails to pay any fee owed the United States under this subchapter, subchapter III, IV-A, V, or VI of this chapter shall, upon conviction, be punished by a fine pursuant to title 18 or by imprisonment for not more than 1 year, or both. If a conviction of any person under this paragraph is for a violation committed after a first conviction of such person under this paragraph, the maximum punishment shall be doubled with respect to both the fine and imprisonment.

(4) Any person who negligently releases into the ambient air any hazardous air pollutant listed pursuant to section 7412 of this title or any extremely hazardous substance listed pursuant to section 11002(a)(2) of this title that is not listed in section 7412 of this title, and who at the time negligently places another person in imminent danger of death or serious bodily injury shall, upon conviction, be punished by a fine under title 18 or by imprisonment for not more than 1 year, or both. If a conviction of any person under this paragraph is for a violation committed after a first conviction of such person under this paragraph, the maximum punishment shall be doubled with respect to both the fine and imprisonment.

(5)(A) Any person who knowingly releases into the ambient air any hazardous air pollutant listed pursuant to section 7412 of this title or any extremely hazardous substance listed pursuant to section 11002(a)(2) of this title that is not listed in section 7412 of this title, and who knows at the time that he thereby places another person in imminent danger of death or serious bodily injury shall, upon conviction, be punished by a fine under title 18 or by imprisonment of not more than 15 years, or both. Any person committing such violation which is an organization shall, upon conviction under this paragraph, be subject to a fine of not more than $1,000,000 for each violation. If a conviction of any person under this paragraph is for a violation committed after a first conviction of such person under this paragraph, the maximum punishment shall be doubled with respect to both the fine and imprisonment. For any air pollutant for which the Administrator has set an emissions standard or for any source for which a permit has been issued under subchapter V of this chapter, a release of such pollutant in accordance with that standard or permit shall not constitute a violation of this paragraph or paragraph (4).

(B) In determining whether a defendant who is an individual knew that the violation placed another person in imminent danger of death or serious bodily injury—

(i) the defendant is responsible only for actual awareness or actual belief possessed; and

(ii) knowledge possessed by a person other than the defendant, but not by the defendant, may not be attributed to the defendant;

except that in proving a defendant's possession of actual knowledge, circumstantial evidence may be used, including evidence that the defendant took affirmative steps to be shielded from relevant information.

(C) It is an affirmative defense to a prosecution that the conduct charged was freely consented to by the person endangered and that the danger and conduct charged were reasonably foreseeable hazards of—

(i) an occupation, a business, or a profession; or

(ii) medical treatment or medical or scientific experimentation conducted by professionally approved methods and such other person had been made aware of the risks involved prior to giving consent.

The defendant may establish an affirmative defense under this subparagraph by a preponderance of the evidence.

(D) All general defenses, affirmative defenses, and bars to prosecution that may apply with respect to other Federal criminal offenses may apply under subparagraph (A) of this paragraph and shall be determined by the courts of the United States according to the principles of common law as they may be interpreted in the light of reason and experience. Concepts of justification and excuse applicable under this section may be developed in the light of reason and experience.

(E) The term "organization" means a legal entity, other than a government, established or organized for any purpose, and such term includes a corporation, company, association, firm, partnership, joint stock company, foundation, institution, trust, society, union, or any other association of persons.

(F) The term "serious bodily injury" means bodily injury which involves a substantial risk of death, unconsciousness, extreme physical pain, protracted and obvious disfigurement or protracted loss or impairment of the function of a bodily member, organ, or mental faculty.

(6) For the purpose of this subsection, the term "person" includes, in addition to the entities referred to in section 7602(e) of this title, any responsible corporate officer.

(d) Administrative assessment of civil penalties

(1) The Administrator may issue an administrative order against any person assessing a civil administrative penalty of up to $25,000,

2. So in original. Probably should be followed by a comma.

per day of violation, whenever, on the basis of any available information, the Administrator finds that such person—

(A) has violated or is violating any requirement or prohibition of an applicable implementation plan (such order shall be issued (i) during any period of federally assumed enforcement, or (ii) more than thirty days following the date of the Administrator's notification under subsection (a)(1) of this section of a finding that such person has violated or is violating such requirement or prohibition); or

(B) has violated or is violating any other requirement or prohibition of this subchapter or subchapter III, IV-A, V, or VI of this chapter, including, but not limited to, a requirement or prohibition of any rule, order, waiver, permit, or plan promulgated, issued, or approved under this chapter, or for the payment of any fee owed the United States under this chapter (other than subchapter II of this chapter); or

(C) attempts to construct or modify a major stationary source in any area with respect to which a finding under subsection (a)(5) of this section has been made.

The Administrator's authority under this paragraph shall be limited to matters where the total penalty sought does not exceed $200,000 and the first alleged date of violation occurred no more than 12 months prior to the initiation of the administrative action, except where the Administrator and the Attorney General jointly determine that a matter involving a larger penalty amount or longer period of violation is appropriate for administrative penalty action. Any such determination by the Administrator and the Attorney General shall not be subject to judicial review.

(2)(A) An administrative penalty assessed under paragraph (1) shall be assessed by the Administrator by an order made after opportunity for a hearing on the record in accordance with sections 554 and 556 of title 5. The Administrator shall issue reasonable rules for discovery and other procedures for hearings under this paragraph. Before issuing such an order, the Administrator shall give written notice to the person to be assessed an administrative penalty of the Administrator's proposal to issue such order and provide such person an opportunity to request such a hearing on the order, within 30 days of the date the notice is received by such person.

(B) The Administrator may compromise, modify, or remit, with or without conditions, any administrative penalty which may be imposed under this subsection.

(3) The Administrator may implement, after consultation with the Attorney General and the States, a field citation program through regulations establishing appropriate minor violations for which field citations assessing civil penalties not to exceed $5,000 per day of violation may be issued by officers or employees designated by the Administrator. Any person to whom a field citation is assessed may, within a reasonable time as prescribed by the Administrator through regulation, elect to pay the penalty assessment or to request a hearing on the field citation. If a request for a hearing is not made within the time specified in the regulation, the penalty assessment in the field citation shall be final. Such hearing shall not be subject to section 554 or 556 of title 5, but shall provide a reasonable opportunity to be heard and to present evidence. Payment of a civil penalty required by a field citation shall not be a defense to further enforcement by the United States or a State to correct a violation, or to assess the statutory maximum penalty pursuant to other authorities in the chapter, if the violation continues.

(4) Any person against whom a civil penalty is assessed under paragraph (3) of this subsection or to whom an administrative penalty order is issued under paragraph (1) of this subsection may seek review of such assessment in the United States District Court for the District of Columbia or for the district in which the violation is alleged to have occurred, in which such person resides, or where such person's principal place of business is located, by filing in such court within 30 days following the date the administrative penalty order becomes final under paragraph (2), the assessment becomes final under paragraph (3), or a final decision following a hearing under paragraph (3) is rendered, and by simultaneously sending a copy of the filing by certified mail to the Administrator and the Attorney General. Within 30 days thereafter, the Administrator shall file in such court a certified copy, or certified index, as appropriate, of the record on which the administrative penalty order or assessment was issued. Such court shall not set aside or remand such order or assessment unless there is not substantial evidence in the record, taken as a whole, to support the finding of a violation or unless the order or penalty assessment constitutes an abuse of discretion. Such order or penalty assessment shall not be subject to review by any court except as provided in this paragraph. In any such proceedings, the United States may seek to recover civil penalties ordered or assessed under this section.

(5) If any person fails to pay an assessment of a civil penalty or fails to comply with an administrative penalty order—

(A) after the order or assessment has become final, or

(B) after a court in an action brought under paragraph (4) has entered a final judgment in favor of the Administrator,

the Administrator shall request the Attorney General to bring a civil action in an appropriate district court to enforce the order or to recover the amount ordered or assessed (plus interest at rates established pursuant to section 6621(a)(2) of title 26 from the date of the final order or decision or the date of the final judgment, as the case may be). In such an action, the validity, amount, and appropriateness of such order or assessment shall not be subject to review. Any person who fails to pay on a timely basis a civil penalty ordered or assessed under this section shall be required to pay, in addition to such penalty and interest, the United States enforcement expenses, including but not limited to attorneys fees and costs incurred by the United States for collection proceedings and a quarterly nonpayment penalty for each quarter during which such failure to pay persists. Such nonpayment penalty shall be 10 percent of the aggregate amount of such person's outstanding penalties and nonpayment penalties accrued as of the beginning of such quarter.

(e) Penalty assessment criteria

(1) In determining the amount of any penalty to be assessed under this section or section 7604(a) of this title, the Administrator or the court, as appropriate, shall take into consideration (in addition to such other factors as justice may require) the size of the business, the economic impact of the penalty on the business, the violator's full compliance history and good faith efforts to comply, the duration of the violation as established by any credible evidence (including evidence other than the applicable test method), payment by the violator of penalties previously assessed for the same violation, the economic benefit of noncompliance, and the seriousness of the violation. The court shall not assess penalties for noncompliance with administrative subpoenas under section 7607(a) of this title, or actions under section 7414 of this title, where the violator had sufficient cause to violate or fail or refuse to comply with such subpoena or action.

(2) A penalty may be assessed for each day of violation. For purposes of determining the number of days of violation for which a penalty may be assessed under subsection (b) or (d)(1) of this section, or section 7604(a) of this title, or an assessment may be made under section 7420 of this title, where the Administrator or an air pollution control agency has notified the source of the violation, and the plaintiff makes a prima facie showing that the conduct or events giving rise to the violation are likely to have continued or recurred past the date of notice, the days of violation shall be presumed to include the date of such notice and each and every day thereafter until the violator establishes that continuous compliance has been achieved, except to the extent that the violator can prove by a preponderance of the evidence that there were intervening days during which no violation occurred or that the violation was not continuing in nature.

(f) Awards

The Administrator may pay an award, not to exceed $10,000, to any person who furnishes information or services which lead to a criminal conviction or a judicial or administrative civil penalty for any violation of this subchapter or subchapter III, IV-A, V, or VI of this chapter enforced under this section. Such payment is subject to available appropriations for such purposes as provided in annual appropriation Acts. Any officer, or employee of the United States or any State or local government who furnishes information or renders service in the performance of an official duty is ineligible for payment under this subsection. The Administrator may, by regulation, prescribe additional criteria for eligibility for such an award.

(g) Settlements; public participation

At least 30 days before a consent order or settlement agreement of any kind under this chapter to which the United States is a party (other than enforcement actions under this section, section 7420 of this title, or subchapter II of this chapter, whether or not involving civil or criminal penalties, or judgments subject to Department of Justice policy on public participation) is final or filed with a court, the Administrator shall provide a reasonable opportunity by notice in the Federal Register to persons who are not named as parties or intervenors to the action or matter to comment in writing. The Administrator or the Attorney General, as appropriate, shall promptly consider any such written comments and may withdraw or withhold his consent to the proposed order or agreement if the comments disclose facts or considerations which indicate that such consent is inappropriate, improper, inadequate, or inconsistent with the requirements of this chapter. Nothing in this subsection shall apply to civil or criminal penalties under this chapter.

(h) Operator

For purposes of the provisions of this section and section 7420 of this title, the term "operator", as used in such provisions, shall include any person who is senior management personnel or a corporate officer. Except in the case of knowing and willful violations, such term shall not include any person who is a stationary engineer or technician responsible for the operation, maintenance, repair, or monitoring of equipment and facilities and who often has supervisory and training duties but who is not senior management personnel or a corporate officer. Except in the case of knowing and willful violations, for purposes of subsection (c)(4) of this section, the term "a person" shall not include an employee who is carrying out his normal activities and who is not a part of senior management personnel or a corporate officer. Except in the case of knowing and willful violations, for purposes of paragraphs (1), (2), (3), and (5) of subsection (c) of this section the term "a person" shall not include an employee who is carrying out his normal activities and who is acting under orders from the employer.

(July 14, 1955, ch. 360, title I, §113, as added Dec. 31, 1970, Pub. L. 91-604, §4(a), 84 Stat. 1686, and amended Nov. 18, 1971, Pub. L. 92-157, title III, §302(b), (c), 85 Stat. 464; June 22, 1974, Pub. L. 93-319, §6(a)(1)-(3), 88 Stat. 259; Aug. 7, 1977, Pub. L. 95-95, title I, §111, 112(a), 91 Stat. 704, 705; Nov. 16, 1977, Pub. L. 95-190, §14(a)(10)-(21), (b)(1), 91 Stat. 1400, 1404; July 17, 1981, Pub. L. 97-23, §2, 95 Stat. 139; Nov. 15, 1990, Pub. L. 101-549, title VII, §701, 104 Stat. 2672.)

Codification

Section was formerly classified to section 1857c-8 of this title.

Effective Date Of 1977 Amendment

Amendment by Pub. L. 95-95 effective Aug. 7, 1977, except as otherwise expressly provided, see section 406(d) of Pub. L. 95-95, set out as a note under section 7401 of this title.

Pending Actions And Proceedings

Suits, actions, and other proceedings lawfully commenced by or against the Administrator or any other officer or employee of the United States in his official capacity or in relation to the discharge of his official duties under act July 14, 1955, the Clean Air Act, as in effect immediately prior to the enactment of Pub. L. 95-95 (Aug. 7, 1977), not to abate by reason of the taking effect of Pub. L. 95-95, see section 406(a) of Pub. L. 95-95, set out as an Effective Date of 1977 Amendment note under section 7401 of this title.

Modification Or Rescission Of Rules, Regulations, Orders, Determinations, Contracts, Certifications, Authorizations, Delegations, And Other Actions

All rules, regulations, orders, determinations, contracts, certifications, authorizations, delegations, or other actions duly issued, made, or taken by or pursuant to act July 14, 1955, the Clean Air Act, as in effect immediately prior to the date of enactment of Pub. L. 95-95 (Aug. 7, 1977) to continue in full force and effect until modified or rescinded in accordance with act July 14, 1955, as amended by Pub. L. 95-95 (this chapter), see section 406(b) of Pub. L. 95-95, set out as an Effective Date of 1977 Amendment note under section 7401 of this title.

Clean Water Act §309
33 U.S.C. §1319

§ 1319. [FWPCA §309]

Enforcement

(a) State enforcement; compliance orders

(1) Whenever, on the basis of any information available to him, the Administrator finds that any person is in violation of any condition or limitation which implements section 1311, 1312, 1316, 1317, 1318, 1328, or 1345 of this title in a permit issued by a State under an approved permit program under section 1342 or 1344 of this title he shall proceed under his authority in paragraph (3) of this subsection or he shall notify the person in alleged violation and such State of such finding. If beyond the thirtieth day after the Administrator's notification the State has not commenced appropriate enforcement action, the Administrator shall issue an order requiring such person to comply with such condition or limitation or shall bring a civil action in accordance with subsection (b) of this section.

(2) Whenever, on the basis of information available to him, the Administrator finds that violations of permit conditions or limitations as set forth in paragraph (1) of this subsection are so widespread that such violations appear to result from a failure of the State to enforce such permit conditions or limitations effectively, he shall so notify the State. If the Administrator finds such failure extends beyond the thirtieth day after such notice, he shall give public notice of such finding. During the period beginning with such public notice and ending when such State satisfies the Administrator that it will enforce such conditions and limitations (hereafter referred to in this section as the period of "federally assumed enforcement"), except where an extension has been granted under paragraph (5)(B) of this subsection, the Administrator shall enforce any permit condition or limitation with respect to any person—

(A) by issuing an order to comply with such condition or limitation, or

(B) by bringing a civil action under subsection (b) of this section.

(3) Whenever on the basis of any information available to him the Administrator finds that any person is in violation of section 1311, 1312, 1316, 1317, 1318, 1328, or 1345 of this title, or is in violation of any permit condition or limitation implementing any of such sections in a permit issued under section 1342 of this title by him or by a State or in a permit issued under section 1344 of this title by a State, he shall issue an order requiring such person to comply with such section or requirement, or he shall bring a civil action in accordance with subsection (b) of this section.

(4) A copy of any order issued under this subsection shall be sent immediately by the Administrator to the State in which the violation occurs and other affected States. In any case in which an order under this subsection (or notice to a violator under paragraph (1) of this subsection) is issued to a corporation, a copy of such order (or notice) shall be served on any appropriate corporate officers. An order issued under this subsection relating to a violation of section 1318 of this title shall not take effect until the person to whom it is issued has had an opportunity to confer with the Administrator concerning the alleged violation.

(5)(A) Any order issued under this subsection shall be by personal service, shall state with reasonable specificity the nature of the violation, and shall specify a time for compliance not to exceed thirty days in the case of a violation of an interim compliance schedule or operation and maintenance requirement and not to exceed a time the Administrator determines to be reasonable in the case of a violation of a final deadline, taking into account the seriousness of the violation and any good faith efforts to comply with applicable requirements.

(B) The Administrator may, if he determines (i) that any person who is a violator of, or any person who is otherwise not in compliance with, the time requirements under this chapter or in any permit issued under this chapter, has acted in good faith, and has made a commitment (in the form of contracts or other securities) of necessary resources to achieve compliance by the earliest possible date after July 1, 1977, but not later than April 1, 1979; (ii) that any extension under this provision will not result in the imposition of any additional controls on any other point or nonpoint source; (iii) that an application for a permit under section 1342 of this title was filed for such person prior to December 31, 1974; and (iv) that the facilities necessary for compliance with such requirements are under construction, grant an extension of the date referred to in section 1311(b)(1)(A) of this title to a date which will achieve compliance at the earliest time possible but not later than April 1, 1979.

(6) Whenever, on the basis of information available to him, the Administrator finds (A) that any person is in violation of section 1311(b)(1)(A) or (C) of this title, (B) that such person cannot meet the requirements for a time extension under section 1311(i)(2) of this title, and (C) that the most expeditious and appropriate means of compliance with this chapter by such person is to discharge into a publicly owned treatment works, then, upon request of such person, the Administrator may issue an order requiring such person to comply with this chapter at the earliest date practicable, but not later than July 1, 1983, by discharging into a publicly owned treatment works if such works concur with such order. Such order shall include a schedule of compliance.

(b) Civil actions

The Administrator is authorized to commence a civil action for appropriate relief, including a permanent or temporary injunction, for any violation for which he is authorized to issue a compliance order under subsection (a) of this section. Any action under this subsection may be brought in the district court of the United States for the district in which the defendant is located or resides or is doing business, and such court shall have jurisdiction to restrain such violation and to require compliance. Notice of the commencement of such action shall be given immediately to the appropriate State.

(c) Criminal penalties

(1) Negligent violations

Any person who—

(A) negligently violates section 1311, 1312, 1316, 1317, 1318, 1321(b)(3), 1328, or 1345 of this title, or any permit condition or limitation implementing any of such sections in a permit issued under section 1342 of this title by the Administrator or by a State, or any requirement imposed in a pretreatment program approved under section 1342(a)(3) or 1342(b)(8) of this title or in a permit issued under section 1344 of this title by the Secretary of the Army or by a State; or

(B) negligently introduces into a sewer system or into a publicly owned treatment works any pollutant or hazardous substance which such person knew or reasonably should have known could cause personal injury or property damage or, other than in compliance with all applicable Federal, State, or local requirements or permits, which causes such treatment works to violate any effluent limitation or condition in any permit issued to the treatment works under section 1342 of this title by the Administrator or a State;

shall be punished by a fine of not less than $2,500 nor more than $25,000 per day of violation, or by imprisonment for not more than 1 year, or by both. If a conviction of a person is for a violation committed after a first conviction of such person under this paragraph, punishment shall be by a fine of not more than $50,000 per day of violation, or by imprisonment of not more than 2 years, or by both.

(2) Knowing violations

Any person who—

(A) knowingly violates section 1311, 1312, 1316, 1317, 1318, 1321(b)(3), 1328, or 1345 of this title, or any permit condition or limitation implementing any of such sections in a permit issued under section 1342 of this title by the Administrator or by a State, or any requirement imposed in a pretreatment program approved under section 1342(a)(3) or 1342(b)(8) of this title or in a permit issued under section 1344 of this title by the Secretary of the Army or by a State; or

(B) knowingly introduces into a sewer system or into a publicly owned treatment works any pollutant or hazardous substance which such person knew or reasonably should have known could cause personal injury or property damage or, other than in compliance with all applicable Federal, State, or local requirements or permits, which causes such treatment works to violate any effluent limitation or condition in a permit issued to the treatment works under section 1342 of this title by the Administrator or a State;

shall be punished by a fine of not less than $5,000 nor more than $50,000 per day of violation, or by imprisonment for not more than 3 years, or by both. If a conviction of a person is for a violation committed after a first conviction of such person under this paragraph, punishment shall be by a fine of not more than $100,000 per day of violation, or by imprisonment of not more than 6 years, or by both.

(3) Knowing endangerment

(A) General rule

Any person who knowingly violates section 1311, 1312, 1313, 1316, 1317, 1318, 1321(b)(3), 1328, or 1345 of this title, or any permit condition or limitation implementing any of such sections in a permit issued under section 1342 of this title by the Administrator or by a State, or in a permit issued under section 1344 of this title by the Secretary of the Army or by a State, and who knows at that time that he thereby places another person in imminent danger of death or serious bodily injury, shall, upon conviction, be subject to a fine of not more than $250,000 or imprisonment of not more than 15 years, or both. A person which is an organization shall, upon conviction of violating this subparagraph, be subject to a fine of not more than $1,000,000. If a conviction of a person is for a violation committed after a first conviction of such person under this paragraph, the maximum punishment shall be doubled with respect to both fine and imprisonment.

(B) Additional provisions

For the purpose of subparagraph (A) of this paragraph—

(i) in determining whether a defendant who is an individual knew that his conduct placed another person in imminent danger of death or serious bodily injury—

(I) the person is responsible only for actual awareness or actual belief that he possessed; and

(II) knowledge possessed by a person other than the defendant but not by the defendant himself may not be attributed to the defendant;

except that in proving the defendant's possession of actual knowledge, circumstantial evidence may be used, including evidence that the defendant took affirmative steps to shield himself from relevant information;

(ii) it is an affirmative defense to prosecution that the conduct charged was consented to by the person endangered and that the danger and conduct charged were reasonably foreseeable hazards of—

(I) an occupation, a business, or a profession; or

(II) medical treatment or medical or scientific experimentation conducted by professionally approved methods and such other person had been made aware of the risks involved prior to giving consent;

and such defense may be established under this subparagraph by a preponderance of the evidence;

(iii) the term "organization" means a legal entity, other than a government, established or organized for any purpose, and such term includes a corporation, company, association, firm, partnership, joint stock company, foundation, institution, trust, society, union, or any other association of persons; and

(iv) the term "serious bodily injury" means bodily injury which involves a substantial risk of death, unconsciousness, extreme physical pain, protracted and obvious disfigurement, or protracted loss or impairment of the function of a bodily member, organ, or mental faculty.

(4) False statements

Any person who knowingly makes any false material statement, representation, or certification in any application, record, report, plan, or other document filed or required to be maintained under this chapter or who knowingly falsifies, tampers with, or renders inaccurate any monitoring device or method required to be maintained under this chapter, shall upon conviction, be punished by a fine of not more than $10,000, or by imprisonment for not more than 2 years, or by both. If a conviction of a person is for a violation committed after a first conviction of such person under this paragraph, punishment shall be by a fine of not more than $20,000 per day of violation, or by imprisonment of not more than 4 years, or by both.

(5) Treatment of single operational upset

For purposes of this subsection, a single operational upset which leads to simultaneous violations of more than one pollutant parameter shall be treated as a single violation.

(6) Responsible corporate officer as "person"

For the purpose of this subsection, the term "person" means, in addition to the definition contained in section 1362(5) of this title, any responsible corporate officer.

(7) Hazardous substance defined

For the purpose of this subsection, the term "hazardous substance" means (A) any substance designated pursuant to section 1321(b)(2)(A) of this title, (B) any element, compound, mixture, solution, or substance designated pursuant to section 9602 of title 42, (C) any hazardous waste having the characteristics identified under or listed pursuant to section 3001 of the Solid Waste Disposal Act [42 U.S.C. 6921] (but not including any waste the regulation of which under the Solid Waste Disposal Act [42 U.S.C. 6901 et seq.] has been suspended by Act of Congress), (D) any toxic pollutant listed under section 1317(a) of this title, and (E) any imminently hazardous chemical substance or mixture with respect to which the Administrator has taken action pursuant to section 2606 of title 15.

(d) Civil penalties; factors considered in determining amount

Any person who violates section 1311, 1312, 1316, 1317, 1318, 1328, or 1345 of this title, or any permit condition or limitation implementing any of such sections in a permit issued under section 1342 of this title by the Administrator, or by a State, or in a permit issued under section 1344 of this title by a State,,[1] or any requirement imposed in a pretreatment program approved under section 1342(a)(3) or 1342(b)(8) of this title, and any person who violates any order issued by the Administrator under subsection (a) of this section, shall be subject to a civil penalty not to exceed $25,000 per day for each violation. In determining the amount of a civil penalty the court shall consider the seriousness of the violation or violations, the economic benefit (if any) resulting from the violation, any history of such violations, any good-faith efforts to comply with the applicable requirements, the economic impact of the penalty on the violator, and such other matters as justice may require. For purposes of this subsection, a single operational upset which leads to simultaneous violations of more than one pollutant parameter shall be treated as a single violation.

(e) State liability for judgments and expenses

Whenever a municipality is a party to a civil action brought by the United States under this section, the State in which such municipality is located shall be joined as a party. Such State shall be liable for payment of any judgment, or any expenses incurred as a result of complying with any judgment, entered against the municipality in such action to the extent that the laws of that State prevent the municipality from raising revenues needed to comply with such judgment.

(f) Wrongful introduction of pollutants into treatment works

Whenever, on the basis of any information available to him, the Administrator finds that an owner or operator of any source is introducing a pollutant into a treatment works in violation of subsection (d) of section 1317 of this title, the Administrator may notify the owner or operator of such treatment works and the State of such violation. If the owner or operator of the treatment works does not commence appropriate enforcement action within 30 days of the date of such notification, the Administrator may commence a civil action for

1. So in original.

appropriate relief, including but not limited to, a permanent or temporary injunction, against the owner or operator of such treatment works. In any such civil action the Administrator shall join the owner or operator of such source as a party to the action. Such action shall be brought in the district court of the United States in the district in which the treatment works is located. Such court shall have jurisdiction to restrain such violation and to require the owner or operator of the treatment works and the owner or operator of the source to take such action as may be necessary to come into compliance with this chapter. Notice of commencement of any such action shall be given to the State. Nothing in this subsection shall be construed to limit or prohibit any other authority the Administrator may have under this chapter.

(g) Administrative penalties

(1) Violations

Whenever on the basis of any information available—

(A) the Administrator finds that any person has violated section 1311, 1312, 1316, 1317, 1318, 1328, or 1345 of this title, or has violated any permit condition or limitation implementing any of such sections in a permit issued under section 1342 of this title by the Administrator or by a State, or in a permit issued under section 1344 of this title by a State, or

(B) the Secretary of the Army (hereinafter in this subsection referred to as the "Secretary") finds that any person has violated any permit condition or limitation in a permit issued under section 1344 of this title by the Secretary,

the Administrator or Secretary, as the case may be, may, after consultation with the State in which the violation occurs, assess a class I civil penalty or a class II civil penalty under this subsection.

(2) Classes of penalties

(A) Class I

The amount of a class I civil penalty under paragraph (1) may not exceed $10,000 per violation, except that the maximum amount of any class I civil penalty under this subparagraph shall not exceed $25,000. Before issuing an order assessing a civil penalty under this subparagraph, the Administrator or the Secretary, as the case may be, shall give to the person to be assessed such penalty written notice of the Administrator's or Secretary's proposal to issue such order and the opportunity to request, within 30 days of the date the notice is received by such person, a hearing on the proposed order. Such hearing shall not be subject to section 554 or 556 of title 5, but shall provide a reasonable opportunity to be heard and to present evidence.

(B) Class II

The amount of a class II civil penalty under paragraph (1) may not exceed $10,000 per day for each day during which the violation continues; except that the maximum amount of any class II civil penalty under this subparagraph shall not exceed $125,000. Except as otherwise provided in this subsection, a class II civil penalty shall be assessed and collected in the same manner, and subject to the same provisions, as in the case of civil penalties assessed and collected after notice and opportunity for a hearing on the record in accordance with section 554 of title 5. The Administrator and the Secretary may issue rules for discovery procedures for hearings under this subparagraph.

(3) Determining amount

In determining the amount of any penalty assessed under this subsection, the Administrator or the Secretary, as the case may be, shall take into account the nature, circumstances, extent and gravity of the violation, or violations, and, with respect to the violator, ability to pay, any prior history of such violations, the degree of culpability, economic benefit or savings (if any) resulting from the violation, and such other matters as justice may require. For purposes of this subsection, a single operational upset which leads to simultaneous violations of more than one pollutant parameter shall be treated as a single violation.

(4) Rights of interested persons

(A) Public notice

Before issuing an order assessing a civil penalty under this subsection the Administrator or Secretary, as the case may be, shall provide public notice of and reasonable opportunity to comment on the proposed issuance of such order.

(B) Presentation of evidence

Any person who comments on a proposed assessment of a penalty under this subsection shall be given notice of any hearing held under this subsection and of the order assessing such penalty. In any hearing held under this subsection, such person shall have a reasonable opportunity to be heard and to present evidence.

(C) Rights of interested persons to a hearing

If no hearing is held under paragraph (2) before issuance of an order assessing a penalty under this subsection, any person who commented on the proposed assessment may petition, within 30 days after the issuance of such order, the Administrator or Secretary, as the case may be, to set aside such order and to provide a hearing on the penalty. If the evidence presented by the petitioner in support of the petition is material and was not considered in the issuance of the order, the Administrator or Secretary shall immediately set aside such order and provide a hearing in accordance with paragraph (2)(A) in the case of a class I civil penalty and paragraph (2)(B) in the case of a class II civil penalty. If the Administrator or Secretary denies a hearing under this subparagraph, the Administrator or Secretary shall provide to the petitioner, and publish in the Federal Register, notice of and the reasons for such denial.

(5) Finality of order

An order issued under this subsection shall become final 30 days after its issuance unless a petition for judicial review is filed under paragraph (8) or a hearing is requested under paragraph (4)(C). If such a hearing is denied, such order shall become final 30 days after such denial.

(6) Effect of order

(A) Limitation on actions under other sections

Action taken by the Administrator or the Secretary, as the case may be, under this subsection shall not affect or limit the Administrator's or Secretary's authority to enforce any provision of this chapter; except that any violation—

(i) with respect to which the Administrator or the Secretary has commenced and is diligently prosecuting an action under this subsection,

(ii) with respect to which a State has commenced and is diligently prosecuting an action under a State law comparable to this subsection, or

(iii) for which the Administrator, the Secretary, or the State has issued a final order not subject to further judicial review and the violator has paid a penalty assessed under this subsection, or such comparable State law, as the case may be,

shall not be the subject of a civil penalty action under subsection (d) of this section or section 1321(b) of this title or section 1365 of this title.

(B) Applicability of limitation with respect to citizen suits

The limitations contained in subparagraph (A) on civil penalty actions under section 1365 of this title shall not apply with respect to any violation for which—

(i) a civil action under section 1365(a)(1) of this title has been filed prior to commencement of an action under this subsection, or

(ii) notice of an alleged violation of section 1365(a)(1) of this title has been given in accordance with section 1365(b)(1)(A) of this title prior to commencement of an action under this subsection and an action under section 1365(a)(1) of this title with respect to such alleged violation is filed before the 120th day after the date on which such notice is given.

(7) Effect of action on compliance

No action by the Administrator or the Secretary under this subsection shall affect any person's obligation to comply with any section of this chapter or with the terms and conditions of any permit issued pursuant to section 1342 or 1344 of this title.

(8) Judicial review

Any person against whom a civil penalty is assessed under this subsection or who commented on the proposed assessment of such penalty in accordance with paragraph (4) may obtain review of such assessment—

(A) in the case of assessment of a class I civil penalty, in the

United States District Court for the District of Columbia or in the district in which the violation is alleged to have occurred, or

(B) in the case of assessment of a class II civil penalty, in United States Court of Appeals for the District of Columbia Circuit or for any other circuit in which such person resides or transacts business,

by filing a notice of appeal in such court within the 30-day period beginning on the date the civil penalty order is issued and by simultaneously sending a copy of such notice by certified mail to the Administrator or the Secretary, as the case may be, and the Attorney General. The Administrator or the Secretary shall promptly file in such court a certified copy of the record on which the order was issued. Such court shall not set aside or remand such order unless there is not substantial evidence in the record, taken as a whole, to support the finding of a violation or unless the Administrator's or Secretary's assessment of the penalty constitutes an abuse of discretion and shall not impose additional civil penalties for the same violation unless the Administrator's or Secretary's assessment of the penalty constitutes an abuse of discretion.

(9) Collection

If any person fails to pay an assessment of a civil penalty—

(A) after the order making the assessment has become final, or

(B) after a court in an action brought under paragraph (8) has entered a final judgment in favor of the Administrator or the Secretary, as the case may be,

the Administrator or the Secretary shall request the Attorney General to bring a civil action in an appropriate district court to recover the amount assessed (plus interest at currently prevailing rates from the date of the final order or the date of the final judgment, as the case may be). In such an action, the validity, amount, and appropriateness of such penalty shall not be subject to review. Any person who fails to pay on a timely basis the amount of an assessment of a civil penalty as described in the first sentence of this paragraph shall be required to pay, in addition to such amount and interest, attorneys fees and costs for collection proceedings and a quarterly nonpayment penalty for each quarter during which such failure to pay persists. Such nonpayment penalty shall be in an amount equal to 20 percent of the aggregate amount of such person's penalties and nonpayment penalties which are unpaid as of the beginning of such quarter.

(10) Subpoenas

The Administrator or Secretary, as the case may be, may issue subpoenas for the attendance and testimony of witnesses and the production of relevant papers, books, or documents in connection with hearings under this subsection. In case of contumacy or refusal to obey a subpoena issued pursuant to this paragraph and served upon any person, the district court of the United States for any district in which such person is found, resides, or transacts business, upon application by the United States and after notice to such person, shall have jurisdiction to issue an order requiring such person to appear and give testimony before the administrative law judge or to appear and produce documents before the administrative law judge, or both, and any failure to obey such order of the court may be punished by such court as a contempt thereof.

(11) Protection of existing procedures

Nothing in this subsection shall change the procedures existing on the day before February 4, 1987, under other subsections of this section for issuance and enforcement of orders by the Administrator.

(June 30, 1948, ch. 758, title III, §309, as added Oct. 18, 1972, Pub. L. 92-500, §2, 86 Stat. 859, and amended Dec. 27, 1977, Pub. L. 95-217, §54(b), 55, 56, 67(c)(2), 91 Stat. 1591, 1592, 1606; Feb. 4, 1987, Pub. L. 100-4, title III, §312, 313(a)(1), (b)(1), (c), 314(a), 101 Stat. 42, 45, 46; Aug. 18, 1990, Pub. L. 101-380, title IV, §4301(c), 104 Stat. 537.)

Effective Date Of 1990 Amendment

Amendment by Pub. L. 101-380 applicable to incidents occurring after Aug. 18, 1990, see section 1020 of Pub. L. 101-380, set out as an Effective Date note under section 2701 of this title.

Savings Provision

Section 313(a)(2) of Pub. L. 100-4 provided that: "No State shall be required before July 1, 1988, to modify a permit program approved or submitted under section 402 of the Federal Water Pollution Control Act [33 U.S.C. 1342] as a result of the amendment made by paragraph (1) (amending this section)."

Deposit Of Certain Penalties Into Oil Spill Liability Trust Fund

Penalties paid pursuant to subsection (c) of this section and sections 1321 and 1501 et seq. of this title to be deposited in the Oil Spill Liability Trust Fund created under section 9509 of Title 26, Internal Revenue Code, see section 4304 of Pub. L. 101-380, set out as a note under section 9509 of Title 26.

Increased Penalties Not Required Under State Programs

Section 313(b)(2) of Pub. L. 100-4 provided that: "The Federal Water Pollution Control Act [33 U.S.C. 1251 et seq.] shall not be construed as requiring a State to have a civil penalty for violations described in section 309(d) of such Act [33 U.S.C. 1319(d)] which has the same monetary amount as the civil penalty established by such section, as amended by paragraph (1) [amending this section]. Nothing in this paragraph shall affect the Administrator's authority to establish or adjust by regulation a minimum acceptable State civil penalty."

Actions By Surgeon General Relating To Interstate Pollution

Act July 9, 1956, ch. 518, Sec. 5, 70 Stat. 507, provided that actions by the Surgeon General with respect to water pollutants under section 2(d) of act June 30, 1948, ch. 758, 62 Stat. 1155, as in effect prior to July 9, 1956, which had been completed prior to such date, would still be subject to the terms of section 2(d) of act June 30, 1948, in effect prior to the July 9, 1956 amendment, but that actions with respect to such pollutants would nevertheless subsequently be possible in accordance with the terms of act June 30, 1948, as amended by act July 9, 1956.

Comprehensive Environmental Response, Compensation, and Liability Act §103
42 U.S.C. §9603

§ 9603. [CERCLA §103]

Notification requirements respecting released substances

(a) Notice to National Response Center upon release from vessel or offshore or onshore facility by person in charge; conveyance of notice by Center

Any person in charge of a vessel or an offshore or an onshore facility shall, as soon as he has knowledge of any release (other than a federally permitted release) of a hazardous substance from such vessel or facility in quantities equal to or greater than those determined pursuant to section 9602 of this title, immediately notify the National Response Center established under the Clean Water Act [33 U.S.C. 1251 et seq.] of such release. The National Response Center shall convey the notification expeditiously to all appropriate Government agencies, including the Governor of any affected State.

(b) Penalties for failure to notify; use of notice or information pursuant to notice in criminal case

Any person—

(1) in charge of a vessel from which a hazardous substance is released, other than a federally permitted release, into or upon the navigable waters of the United States, adjoining shorelines, or into or upon the waters of the contiguous zone, or

(2) in charge of a vessel from which a hazardous substance is released, other than a federally permitted release, which may affect natural resources belonging to, appertaining to, or under the exclusive management authority of the United States (including resources under the Magnuson Fishery Conservation and Management Act [16 U.S.C. 1801 et seq.]), and who is otherwise subject to the jurisdiction of the United States at the time of the release, or

(3) in charge of a facility from which a hazardous substance is released, other than a federally permitted release,

in a quantity equal to or greater than that determined pursuant to section 9602 of this title who fails to notify immediately the appropriate agency of the United States Government as soon as he has knowledge of such release or who submits in such a notification any information which he knows to be false or misleading shall, upon conviction, be fined in accordance with the applicable provisions of title 18 or imprisoned for not more than 3 years (or not more than 5 years in the case of a second or subsequent conviction), or both. Notification received pursuant to this subsection or information obtained by the exploitation of such notification shall not be used against any such person in any criminal case, except a prosecution for perjury or for giving a false statement.

(c) Notice to Administrator of EPA of existence of storage, etc., facility by owner or operator; exception; time, manner, and form of notice; penalties for failure to notify; use of notice or information pursuant to notice in criminal case

Within one hundred and eighty days after December 11, 1980, any person who owns or operates or who at the time of disposal owned or operated, or who accepted hazardous substances for transport and selected, a facility at which hazardous substances (as defined in section 9601(14)(C) of this title) are or have been stored, treated, or disposed of shall, unless such facility has a permit issued under, or has been accorded interim status under, subtitle C of the Solid Waste Disposal Act [42 U.S.C. 6921 et seq.], notify the Administrator of the Environmental Protection Agency of the existence of such facility, specifying the amount and type of any hazardous substance to be found there, and any known, suspected, or likely releases of such substances from such facility. The Administrator may prescribe in greater detail the manner and form of the notice and the information included. The Administrator shall notify the affected State agency, or any department designated by the Governor to receive such notice, of the existence of such facility. Any person who knowingly fails to notify the Administrator of the existence of any such facility shall, upon conviction, be fined not more than $10,000, or imprisoned for not more than one year, or both. In addition, any such person who knowingly fails to provide the notice required by this subsection shall not be entitled to any limitation of liability or to any defenses to liability set out in section 9607 of this title: *Provided, however,* That notification under this subsection is not required for any facility which would be reportable hereunder solely as a result of any stoppage in transit which is temporary, incidental to the transportation movement, or at the ordinary operating convenience of a common or contract carrier, and such stoppage shall be considered as a continuity of movement and not as the storage of a hazardous substance. Notification received pursuant to this subsection or information obtained by the exploitation of such notification shall not be used against any such person in any criminal case, except a prosecution for perjury or for giving a false statement.

(d) Recordkeeping requirements; promulgation of rules and regulations by Administrator of EPA; penalties for violations; waiver of retention requirements

(1) The Administrator of the Environmental Protection Agency is authorized to promulgate rules and regulations specifying, with respect to—

(A) the location, title, or condition of a facility, and

(B) the identity, characteristics, quantity, origin, or condition (including containerization and previous treatment) of any hazardous substances contained or deposited in a facility;

the records which shall be retained by any person required to provide the notification of a facility set out in subsection (c) of this section. Such specification shall be in accordance with the provisions of this subsection.

(2) Beginning with December 11, 1980, for fifty years thereafter or for fifty years after the date of establishment of a record (whichever is later), or at any such earlier time as a waiver if obtained under paragraph (3) of this subsection, it shall be unlawful for any such person knowingly to destroy, mutilate, erase, dispose of, conceal, or otherwise render unavailable or unreadable or falsify any records identified in paragraph (1) of this subsection. Any person who violates this paragraph shall, upon conviction, be fined in accordance with the applicable provisions of title 18 or imprisoned for not more than 3 years (or not more than 5 years in the case of a second or subsequent conviction), or both.

(3) At any time prior to the date which occurs fifty years after December 11, 1980, any person identified under paragraph (1) of this subsection may apply to the Administrator of the Environmental Protection Agency for a waiver of the provisions of the first sentence of paragraph (2) of this subsection. The Administrator is authorized to grant such waiver if, in his discretion, such waiver would not unreasonably interfere with the attainment of the purposes and provisions of this chapter. The Administrator shall promulgate rules and regulations regarding such a waiver so as to inform parties of the proper application procedure and conditions for approval of such a waiver.

(4) Notwithstanding the provisions of this subsection, the Administrator of the Environmental Protection Agency may in his discretion require any such person to retain any record identified pursuant to paragraph (1) of this subsection for such a time period in excess of the period specified in paragraph (2) of this subsection as the Administrator determines to be necessary to protect the public health or welfare.

(e) Applicability to registered pesticide product

This section shall not apply to the application of a pesticide product registered under the Federal Insecticide, Fungicide, and Rodenticide Act [7 U.S.C. 136 et seq.] or to the handling and storage of such a pesticide product by an agricultural producer.

(f) Exemptions from notice and penalty provisions for substances reported under other Federal law or is in continuous release, etc.

No notification shall be required under subsection (a) or (b) of this section for any release of a hazardous substance—

(1) which is required to be reported (or specifically exempted from a requirement for reporting) under subtitle C of the Solid Waste Disposal Act [42 U.S.C. 6921 et seq.] or regulations thereunder and which has been reported to the National Response Center, or

(2) which is a continuous release, stable in quantity and rate, and is—

(A) from a facility for which notification has been given under subsection (c) of this section, or

(B) a release of which notification has been given under subsections (a) and (b) of this section for a period sufficient to establish the continuity, quantity, and regularity of such release:

Provided, That notification in accordance with subsections (a) and (b) of this paragraph shall be given for releases subject to this paragraph annually, or at such time as there is any statistically significant increase in the quantity of any hazardous substance or constituent thereof released, above that previously reported or occurring.

(Pub. L. 96-510, title I, §103, Dec. 11, 1980, 94 Stat. 2772; Pub. L. 96-561, title II, §238(b), Dec. 22, 1980, 94 Stat. 3300; Pub. L. 99-499, title I, §103, 109(a)(1), (2), Oct. 17, 1986, 100 Stat. 1617, 1632, 1633.)

Effective Date Of 1980 Amendment

Amendment by Pub. L. 96-561 effective 15 days after Dec. 22, 1980, see section 238 of Pub. L. 96-561, set out as a Short Title of 1980 Amendment note under section 1801 of Title 16, Conservation.

Refuse Act of 1899 (Sections 13 and 16 of the Rivers and Harbors Appropriation Act of 1899)
33 U.S.C. §§407, 411

§ 407. [RHAA §13]

Deposit of refuse in navigable waters generally

It shall not be lawful to throw, discharge, or deposit, or cause, suffer, or procure to be thrown, discharged, or deposited either from or out of any ship, barge, or other floating craft of any kind, or from the shore, wharf, manufacturing establishment, or mill of any kind, any refuse matter of any kind or description whatever other than that flowing from streets and sewers and passing therefrom in a liquid state, into any navigable water of the United States, or into any tributary of any navigable water from which the same shall float or be washed into such navigable water; and it shall not be lawful to deposit, or cause, suffer, or procure to be deposited material of any kind in any place on the bank of any navigable water, or on the bank of any tributary of any navigable water, where the same shall be liable to be washed into such navigable water, either by ordinary or high tides, or by storms or floods, or otherwise, whereby navigation shall or may be impeded or obstructed: *Provided,* That nothing herein contained shall extend to, apply to, or prohibit the operations in connection with the improvement of navigable waters or construction of public works, considered necessary and proper by the United States officers supervising such improvement or public work: *And provided further,* That the Secretary of the Army, whenever in the judgment of the Chief of Engineers anchorage and navigation will not be injured thereby, may permit the deposit of any material above mentioned in navigable waters, within limits to be defined and under conditions to be prescribed by him, provided application is made to him prior to depositing such material; and whenever any permit is so granted the conditions thereof shall be strictly complied with, and any violation thereof shall be unlawful.

§ 411. [RHAA §16]

Penalty for wrongful deposit of refuse; use of or injury to harbor improvements, and obstruction of navigable waters generally

Every person and every corporation that shall violate, or that shall knowingly aid, abet, authorize, or instigate a violation of the provisions of sections 407, 408, and 409 of this title shall be guilty of a misdemeanor, and on conviction thereof shall be punished by a fine not exceeding $2,500 nor less than $500, or by imprisonment (in the case of a natural person) for not less than thirty days nor more than one year, or by both such fine and imprisonment, in the discretion of the court, one-half of said fine to be paid to the person or persons giving information which shall lead to conviction.

Resource Conservation and Recovery Act
42 U.S.C. §6928

§ 6928. [RCRA §3008]

Federal enforcement

(a) Compliance orders

(1) Except as provided in paragraph (2), whenever on the basis of any information the Administrator determines that any person has violated or is in violation of any requirement of this subchapter, the Administrator may issue an order assessing a civil penalty for any past or current violation, requiring compliance immediately or within a specified time period, or both, or the Administrator may commence a civil action in the United States district court in the district in which the violation occurred for appropriate relief, including a temporary or permanent injunction.

(2) In the case of a violation of any requirement of this subchapter where such violation occurs in a State which is authorized to carry out a hazardous waste program under section 6926 of this title, the Administrator shall give notice to the State in which such violation has occurred prior to issuing an order or commencing a civil action under this section.

(3) Any order issued pursuant to this subsection may include a suspension or revocation of any permit issued by the Administrator or a State under this subchapter and shall state with reasonable specificity the nature of the violation. Any penalty assessed in the order shall not exceed $25,000 per day of noncompliance for each violation of a requirement of this subchapter. In assessing such a penalty, the Administrator shall take into account the seriousness of the violation and any good faith efforts to comply with applicable requirements.

(b) Public hearing

Any order issued under this section shall become final unless, no later than thirty days after the order is served, the person or persons named therein request a public hearing. Upon such request the Administrator shall promptly conduct a public hearing. In connection with any proceeding under this section the Administrator may issue subpenas for the attendance and testimony of witnesses and the production of relevant papers, books, and documents, and may promulgate rules for discovery procedures.

(c) Violation of compliance orders

If a violator fails to take corrective action within the time specified in a compliance order, the Administrator may assess a civil penalty of not more than $25,000 for each day of continued noncompliance with the order and the Administrator may suspend or revoke any permit issued to the violator (whether issued by the Administrator or the State).

(d) Criminal penalties

Any person who—

(1) knowingly transports or causes to be transported any hazardous waste identified or listed under this subchapter to a facility which does not have a permit under this subchapter, or pursuant to title I of the Marine Protection, Research, and Sanctuaries Act (86 Stat. 1052) (33 U.S.C. 1411 et seq.),

(2) knowingly treats, stores, or disposes of any hazardous waste identified or listed under this subchapter—

(A) without a permit under this subchapter or pursuant to title I of the Marine Protection, Research, and Sanctuaries Act (86 Stat. 1052) (33 U.S.C. 1411 et seq.); or

(B) in knowing violation of any material condition or requirement of such permit; or

(C) in knowing violation of any material condition or requirement of any applicable interim status regulations or standards;

(3) knowingly omits material information or makes any false material statement or representation in any application, label, manifest, record, report, permit, or other document filed, maintained, or used for purposes of compliance with regulations promulgated by the Administrator (or by a State in the case of an authorized State program) under this subchapter;

(4) knowingly generates, stores, treats, transports, disposes of, exports, or otherwise handles any hazardous waste or any used oil not identified or listed as a hazardous waste under this subchapter (whether such activity took place before or takes place after November 8, 1984) and who knowingly destroys, alters, conceals, or fails to file any record, application, manifest, report, or other document required to be maintained or filed for purposes of compliance with regulations promulgated by the Administrator (or by a State in the case of an authorized State program) under this subchapter;

(5) knowingly transports without a manifest, or causes to be transported without a manifest, any hazardous waste or any used oil not identified or listed as a hazardous waste under this subchapter required by regulations promulgated under this subchapter (or by a State in the case of a State program authorized under this subchapter) to be accompanied by a manifest;

(6) knowingly exports a hazardous waste identified or listed under this subchapter (A) without the consent of the receiving country or, (B) where there exists an international agreement between the United States and the government of the receiving country establishing notice, export, and enforcement procedures for the transportation, treatment, storage, and disposal of hazardous wastes, in a manner which is not in conformance with such agreement; or

(7) knowingly stores, treats, transports, or causes to be transported, disposes of, or otherwise handles any used oil not identified or listed as a hazardous waste under this subchapter—

(A) in knowing violation of any material condition or requirement of a permit under this subchapter; or

(B) in knowing violation of any material condition or requirement of any applicable regulations or standards under this chapter;

shall, upon conviction, be subject to a fine of not more than $50,000 for each day of violation, or imprisonment not to exceed two years (five years in the case of a violation of paragraph (1) or (2)), or both. If the conviction is for a violation committed after a first conviction of such person under this paragraph, the maximum punishment under the respective paragraph shall be doubled with respect to both fine and imprisonment.

(e) Knowing endangerment

Any person who knowingly transports, treats, stores, disposes of, or exports any hazardous waste identified or listed under this subchapter or used oil not identified or listed as a hazardous waste under this subchapter in violation of paragraph (1), (2), (3), (4), (5), (6), or (7) of subsection (d) of this section who knows at that time that he thereby places another person in imminent danger of death or serious bodily injury, shall, upon conviction, be subject to a fine of not more than $250,000 or imprisonment for not more than fifteen years, or both. A defendant that is an organization shall, upon conviction of violating this subsection, be subject to a fine of not more than $1,000,000.

(f) Special rules

For the purposes of subsection (e) of this section—

(1) A person's state of mind is knowing with respect to—

(A) his conduct, if he is aware of the nature of his conduct;

(B) an existing circumstance, if he is aware or believes that the circumstance exists; or

(C) a result of his conduct, if he is aware or believes that his conduct is substantially certain to cause danger of death or serious bodily injury.

(2) In determining whether a defendant who is a natural person knew that his conduct placed another person in imminent danger of death or serious bodily injury—

(A) the person is responsible only for actual awareness or actual belief that he possessed; and

(B) knowledge possessed by a person other than the defendant but not by the defendant himself may not be attributed to the defendant;

Provided, That in proving the defendant's possession of actual knowledge, circumstantial evidence may be used, including evidence that the defendant took affirmative steps to shield himself from relevant information.

(3) It is an affirmative defense to a prosecution that the conduct charged was consented to by the person endangered and that the danger and conduct charged were reasonably foreseeable hazards of—

(A) an occupation, a business, or a profession; or

(B) medical treatment or medical or scientific experimentation conducted by professionally approved methods and such other person had been made aware of the risks involved prior to giving consent.

The defendant may establish an affirmative defense under this subsection by a preponderance of the evidence.

(4) All general defenses, affirmative defenses, and bars to prosecution that may apply with respect to other Federal criminal offenses may apply under subsection (e) of this section and shall be determined by the courts of the United States according to the principles of common law as they may be interpreted in the light of reason and experience. Concepts of justification and excuse applicable under this section may be developed in the light of reason and experience.

(5) The term "organization" means a legal entity, other than a government, established, or organized for any purpose, and such term includes a corporation, company, association, firm, partnership, joint stock company, foundation, institution, trust, society, union, or any other association of persons.

(6) The term "serious bodily injury" means—

(A) bodily injury which involves a substantial risk of death;

(B) unconsciousness;

(C) extreme physical pain;

(D) protracted and obvious disfigurement; or

(E) protracted loss or impairment of the function of a bodily member, organ, or mental faculty.

(g) Civil penalty

Any person who violates any requirement of this subchapter shall be liable to the United States for a civil penalty in an amount not to exceed $25,000 for each such violation. Each day of such violation shall, for purposes of this subsection, constitute a separate violation.

(h) Interim status corrective action orders

(1) Whenever on the basis of any information the Administrator determines that there is or has been a release of hazardous waste into the environment from a facility authorized to operate under section 6925(e) of this title, the Administrator may issue an order requiring corrective action or such other response measure as he deems necessary to protect human health or the environment or the Administrator may commence a civil action in the United States district court in the district in which the facility is located for appropriate relief, including a temporary or permanent injunction.

(2) Any order issued under this subsection may include a suspension or revocation of authorization to operate under section 6925(e) of this title, shall state with reasonable specificity the nature of the required corrective action or other response measure, and shall specify a time for compliance. If any person named in an order fails to comply with the order, the Administrator may assess, and such person shall be liable to the United States for, a civil penalty in an amount not to exceed $25,000 for each day of noncompliance with the order.

(Pub. L. 89-272, title II, §3008, as added Pub. L. 94-580, §2, Oct. 21, 1976, 90 Stat. 2811, and amended Pub. L. 95-609, §7(k), Nov. 8, 1978, 92 Stat. 3082; Pub. L. 96-482, §13, Oct. 21, 1980, 94 Stat. 2339; Pub. L. 98-616, title II, §§232, 233, 245(c), title IV, §403(d)(1)-(3), Nov. 8, 1984, 98 Stat. 3256, 3257, 3264, 3272; Pub. L. 99-499, title II, §205(i), Oct. 17, 1986, 100 Stat. 1703.)

Appendix A

Appendix A—Policy Documents

Table of Contents

Listed in the order in which they are referenced in the analysis.

Memorandum: Environmental Criminal Statistics FY83 Through FY94

Department of Justice (April 7, 1995)

Memorandum

Subject	Environmental Criminal Statistics FY83 Through FY94	Date	April 7, 1995
To	Ronald A. Sarachan, Chief Environmental Crimes Section	From	Peggy Hutchins Paralegal

From the beginning of FY83 to the present date in FY95, the Department of Justice has recorded environmental criminal indictments against 1481 corporate and individual defendants, and 1074 guilty pleas and convictions have been entered. More than $296.6 million in criminal penalties has been assessed (this number includes federal and state restitutions and known costs for remediation). 561 years of imprisonment have been imposed of which 359 years account for actual confinement.

Of the 1481 defendants indicted, 443 were corporations or organizations, and the remaining 1068 were individuals. Of the 1074 convictions, 334 were against organizations, and the remaining 740 were against individuals.

BREAKDOWN

	INDICTMENTS	PLEAS/CONVICTIONS
FY83	40	40
FY84	43	32
FY85	40	37
FY86	94	67
FY87	127	86
FY88	124	63
FY89	101	107
FY90	134	85
FY91	127	96
FY92	187	104
FY93	186	168
FY94	178	124
FY95	100	66
TOTAL	1481	1074

- 2 -

Penalties Imposed		Prison Terms Imposed	Actual Confinement
FY83	$ 341,100	11 yrs.	5 yrs.
FY84	384,290	5 yrs. 3 mos.	1 yr. 7 mos.
FY85	565,850	5 yrs. 5 mos.	2 yrs. 11 mos.
FY86	1,917,602	124 yrs 2 mos. 2 da.	31 yrs. 4 mos. 12da.
FY87	3,046,060	32 yrs 4 mos. 7 da.	14 yrs. 9 mos. 22da.
FY88	7,091,876	39 yrs. 3 mos. 1 da.	8 yrs. 3 mos. 7da.
FY89	12,750,330	51 yrs.25 mos.	36 yrs. 14 mos.
FY90 *	29,977,508	71 yrs.11 mos. 3 da.	47 yrs. 13 mos. 1da.
FY91	18,508,732	24 yrs. 8 mos.	22 yrs. 8 mos.
FY92 **	169,359,344	37 yrs. 6 mos. 1 da.	34 yrs. 1 mo. 1da.
FY93	18,992,968	62 yrs. 8 mos.	55 yrs. 4 mos. 5da.
FY94	27,714,286	69 yrs. 7 mos. 1 da.	69 yrs. 7 mos. 1da.
FY95	5,932,057	24 yrs. 4 mos.	24 yrs. 4 mos.
	$ 296,582,003	554 yrs.86 mos.16 da.	352 yrs. 85 mos. 49da.
	$296,582,003	**561 yrs. 2 mos.16 da.**	**359 yrs. 1 mos. 19da.**

****FY92** This total includes $125 million in criminal assessments against Exxon Corp. and Exxon Shipping Co. for the Valdez oil spill. $125 million of the original $250 million criminal sentence was remitted (forgiven) for pledges by Exxon to expenditures far exceeding this amount on environmental safety projects, a contribution to a response fund for large-scale oil spills, and committing 25% of its total research expenditure on environmental and safety research.

$44 million in $ penalties was assessed at federal sentences in FY92 besides the $125 million Exxon assessment.

***FY90** This total includes a $22 million forfeiture that was obtained in a RICO/mail fraud case against 3 individuals and 6 related waste disposal and real estate development companies. A major portion of this forfeiture was designated for hazardous waste cleanup upon liquidation of assets. Included in the terms of imprisonment are two 12 year/7 month sentences against two of the individuals in the same case.

Memorandum: Criminal Enforcement Priorities for the Environmental Protection Agency

Environmental Protection Agency (October 12, 1982)

UNITED STATES ENVIRONMENTAL PROTECTION AGENCY
WASHINGTON, DC 20460

OCT 12 1982

OFFICE OF
LEGAL AND ENFORCEMENT COUNSEL

MEMORANDUM

SUBJECT: Criminal Enforcement Priorities for the Environmental Protection Agency

FROM: Robert M. Perry *Robert M. Perry*
Associate Administrator

TO: Regional Counsels, Regions I-X

Criminal case development and referrals will constitute an important component of EPA's overall enforcement effort. The success of the criminal enforcement program will depend on the Agency's ability to act with professionalism, and with one mind, in identifying, investigating and referring cases for criminal prosecution.

To achieve this objective, our Criminal Enforcement Division is currently recruiting a staff of 25 experienced criminal investigators. In addition, the Office of Legal and Enforcement Counsel, working with the assistance and guidance of EPA's media program offices, has developed the attached "Criminal Enforcement Priorities" for the Agency. These guidelines have been drafted so that the objectives and interests of EPA's program offices are reflected in, and furthered by, the Agency's criminal enforcement efforts. In addition, the implementation of these guidelines will guarantee that the legal and investigative resources of the Office of Legal and Enforcement Counsel, and the technical resources of EPA's program offices, are focussed on cases of the most serious environmental misconduct.

The attached Criminal Enforcement Priorities are effective immediately, and replace any existing Agency guidance on this subject. Please ensure that these priorities are circulated with the appropriate Regional program offices. Any questions on these priorities can be directed to Peter Beeson, Director, Criminal Enforcement Division, Office of Legal and Enforcement Counsel (FTS 382-4543).

Attachment

cc: Assistant Administrators
Regional Administrators, Regions I-X

CRIMINAL ENFORCEMENT PRIORITIES

United States Environmental
Protection Agency
Effective Date: OCT 12 1982

TABLE OF CONTENTS

PREFACE

A broad range of potential overlap exists among the criminal, civil and administrative enforcement options provided by most environmental statutes. Theoretically at least, the Agency is free to pursue criminal sanctions in every situation presenting evidence supporting the requisite elements of proof.

As a matter of enforcement policy and resource allocation, such an unrestrained use of criminal sanctions is neither warranted nor practical. The commitment of investigative and technical resources necessary for the successful prosecution of a criminal case is high. More importantly, a criminal referral for investigation or prosecution can entail profound consequences for the subject of the referral, and should reflect a considered, institutional judgment that fundamental interests of society require the application of Federal criminal sanctions to a particular set of facts. Accordingly, criminal referrals will be confined to situations that--when measured by the nature of the conduct, the compliance history of the subject(s) or the gravity of the environmental consequences--reflect the most serious cases of environmental misconduct.

This memorandum provides guidelines for the use of criminal sanctions under all environmental statutes. It is divided into two parts. Part I sets out several general factors that Agency personnel should consider in determining whether a criminal referral is warranted in a specific situation. These factors will apply with equal force to referral decisions under each of the Agency's statutes, thereby ensuring cross-media consistency in the use of this enforcement option. Part I has also been drafted so as to reflect guidelines for the exercise of Federal prosecutorial discretion found in the Justice Department's Principles of Federal Prosecution.

Following this general overview, Part II establishes investigative priorities in each of the Agency's program areas. The purpose of this section is to focus the limited criminal investigative resources of the Office of Legal and Enforcement Counsel on the most serious cases of environmental misconduct. These media-specific priorities will be fluid, and will be modified to reflect additional regulatory programs in the Agency as they develop. In addition, the creation of investigative priorities does not preclude the possibility of a criminal referral for conduct not falling within these priorities. Each case will be considered on an individual basis. Further--to emphasize the obvious--these guidelines relate only to the use of criminal sanctions, and do not reflect administrative or civil enforcement priorities.

-2-

These guidelines, and internal office procedures adopted in accordance with these guidelines, are not intended to, do not, and may not be relied upon to create a right or benefit--substantive or procedural--enforceable at law by a party to litigation with the United States. Any attempt to litigate any aspect of these guidelines should be brought immediately to the attention of the Criminal Enforcement Division, Office of Legal and Enforcement Counsel, EPA Headquarters.

These guidelines are effective immediately, and replace any existing guidance on criminal enforcement priorties within the Agency.

PART I: THE DECISION TO PURSUE CRIMINAL SANCTIONS

This Agency's choice among its varying enforcement options--civil, administrative and criminal--is, and must remain, a discretionary judgment that balances essentially subjective considerations. No litmus paper test exists that will reliably distinguish cases falling into each category. This section discusses the varying factors, or considerations, that should be addressed as EPA reaches an institutional decision on the appropriate enforcement option to employ in addressing a specific violation. In essence, it is a discussion of those factors that will normally distinguish a criminal case from all the others.

A. The Scienter Requirement

An individual who engages in conduct prohibited by statute or regulation can be prosecuted civilly or administratively without regard to the mental state that accompanied the conduct. Criminal sanctions, on the other hand, will ordinarily be limited to cases in which the prohibited conduct is accompanied by evidence of "guilty knowledge" or intent on the part of the prospective defendant(s). Referred to as the scienter requirement, this element of proof exists under virtually every environmental statute enforced by the Agency.1/ For example, falsification of records under the Resource Conservation and Recovery Act must be done "knowingly," (42 U.S.C. §6928(d)(3)); violation of hazardous air pollutant standards under the Clean Air Act must be done "knowingly," (42 U.S.C. §7413(c)(1)(c)); and failure to establish or maintain records required under the Toxic Substances Control Act must occur "knowingly or willfully," 15 U.S.C. §2615(b).

1/ One exception to this general rule is the Refuse Act, 33 U.S.C. §407, which has generally been interpreted as a "strict liability" statute. See, e.g. United States v. White Fuel Corporation, 498 F.2d 619 (1st Cir. 1974). In addition, a prosecution for illegal discharges under the Clean Water Act can be based on negligent or willful conduct, 33 U.S.C. §1319(c)(1). "Negligence" is not, strictly speaking, a form of scienter.

-2-

The requirement to prove a culpable mental state, as well as a prohibited act, is certainly the clearest distinction between criminal and civil enforcement actions. Special care will be taken both in investigations, and in drafting criminal referral packages, to assemble and highlight evidence available to meet the specific statutory scienter requirement.

B. The Nature and Seriousness of the Offense

Resources currently available to EPA for criminal case development are limited. In addition, this Agency is only one of dozens that are making demands on the limited prosecutorial staffs of the Justice Department. As a matter of resource allocation, therefore, as well as enforcement philosophy, EPA will investigate and refer only the most serious forms of environmental misconduct.

Of primary importance to this assessment is the extent of environmental contamination or human health hazard that resulted from, or was threatened by, the prohibited conduct. This determination depends in turn on considerations such as the duration of the conduct; the toxicity of the pollutants involved; the proximity of population centers; the quality of the receiving land, air or water; the amount of Federal, State or local cleanup expenditures; and public sentiment supporting strong enforcement action in response to a specific situation.

Also of significance in assessing the seriousness of the illegal conduct is the impact--real or potential--on EPA's regulatory functions. This factor is of particular importance in cases of the falsification or concealment of records, reports or information. For example, even if a technical falsification case can be made, criminal sanctions may not be appropriate if the distortion of information could not reasonably have been expected to have a significant impact on EPA's regulatory process or decision-making. Where the materiality of the falsification is clear, however, criminal sanctions should be pursued. For example, falsification activity might cause EPA to register a pesticide with demonstrated carcinogenic potential; to omit effluent limitations for toxic pollutants in an NPDES permit; or to postpone necessary regulatory action. In such situations, the need for criminal sanctions should be considered.

-3-

C. The Need for Deterrence

Deterrence of criminal conduct by a specific individual (individual deterrence) or by the community at large (general deterrence) has always been one of the primary goals of the criminal law. Where the offense is deliberate and results in serious environmental contamination or human health hazard, the need to achieve deterrence through the application of strong punitive sanctions will almost always exist.

The goal of deterrence may, on occasion, justify a criminal referral for an offense that appears relatively minor. This would be true, for example, for offenses that--while of limited importance by themselves--would have a substantial cumulative impact if commonly committed. This might also be true when addressing violations by an individual with an extended history of recalcitrance and noncompliance.

D. Compliance History of the Subject(s)

The compliance history of the subject(s) of a potential criminal referral is relevant, and should be considered in determining the appropriateness of criminal sanctions. As a general rule throughout Federal criminal enforcement, first offenders will be treated less severely than recidivists. Stated alternatively, criminal sanctions become more appropriate as the incidents of noncompliance increase. The occurrence of past enforcement actions against a company, or the failure of civil/administrative enforcement, is certainly not a prerequisite to a criminal referral. However, a history of environmental noncompliance will often indicate the need for criminal sanctions to achieve effective individual deterrence.

E. The Need for Simultaneous Civil or Administrative Enforcement Action

Simultaneous civil and criminal enforcement proceedings are legally permissible, United States v. Kordel, 397 U.S. 1, 11 (1970), and on occasion are clearly warranted. However, separate staffs will be appointed with the initiation of a grand jury investigation, if not before. Further, the pursuit of simultaneous proceedings provides fertile grounds for legal challenges to one or both proceedings that, even if unsuccessful, will consume additional time and resources. Thus, parallel proceedings should be avoided except where clearly justified.

In this regard, it should be noted that some of the goals of a criminal prosecution, including a degree

-4-

of deterrence and punishment, can be achieved through a civil action that secures substantial civil penalties in addition to injunctive relief. Moreover, recent experience indicates that while some cases may result in periods of incarceration, criminal sentences will often be limited to monetary fines and a probationary period. In light of this reality, the use of the additional time and resources necessary to pursue a criminal investigation--as well as a civil enforcement action--is often not justified.

PART II: CRIMINAL ENFORCEMENT PRIORITIES

The previous section has discussed the general considerations that will guide this Agency's decisions on the investigation and referral of criminal cases. Part II details the substantive investigative priorities that will be pursued in the Office of Legal and Enforcement Counsel's developing criminal enforcement program. The priorities are listed by statute. The order of listing is random, and is not intended to achieve further ranking either within each statute or on a cross-media basis. Unless otherwise stated below, all listed categories of conduct are considered equally significant and worthy of investigation within the constraints of our limited criminal investigative resources.

The criminal investigative staff of the Office of Legal and Enforcement Counsel, acting in partnership with the legal and technical staffs of the Agency, will focus criminal enforcement efforts in the future primarily on cases falling within the categories listed below. The issuance of these priorities is not, however, intended to preclude the possibility of a criminal referral in other cases.2/ As was indicated previously, each case will be considered on its own merits.

A. Investigative Priorities: Resource Conservation and Recovery Act (RCRA):

1. Knowing Endangerment

Section 3008(e) of RCRA, 42 U.S.C. §6928(e), establishes the crime of "knowing endangerment." The provision carries maximum penalties of up to five years of imprisonment and a $1,000,000.00 fine, and reflects a Congressional mandate to pursue strong criminal sanctions for knowing, life-threatening conduct that violates RCRA statutory prohibitions or interim status standards and regulations. RCRA and its legislative history indicate that the "knowing endangerment" provision is intended to apply only in the most serious instances of environmental misconduct. Where the elements of proof can be met, however, EPA will give a high priority to the investigation, referral and prosecution of "knowing endangerment" cases.

2/ For example, because the enforcement provisions of the Safe Drinking Water Act, 42 U.S.C. §§300f *et. seq.*, contain comparatively mild monetary penalties--and no potential terms of incarceration--the statute is not listed as a criminal enforcement priority. This does *not*, however, preclude the possibility of a criminal referral under the Safe Drinking Water Act to address aggrevated cases of non-compliance.

2. Illegal Transportation and Disposal of Hazardous Waste

Section 3008(d)(1-2) of RCRA, 42 U.S.C. §6928(d)(1-2), carries felony penalties of two years of imprisonment and a $50,000.00 fine for the knowing transportation of hazardous wastes to an unpermitted facility (Section 3008(d)(1)) and the knowing disposal of hazardous wastes without obtaining a permit (Section 3008(d)(2)). Both provisions are potentially applicable to midnight dumping in its various forms, i.e., in abandoned sites, company yards, open fields or waterways, or unpermitted waste disposal facilities. A high investigative priority will be placed on illegal transportation or disposal activities that result in, or threaten, serious environmental contamination or human health hazard.

3. Falsification of RCRA Records

Section 3008(d)(3) of RCRA, 42 U.S.C. §6928(d)(3), carries misdemeanor penalties of one year of imprisonment and a $25,000.00 fine for the knowing falsification of material information in records "maintained or used for purposes of compliance" with RCRA. Emphasis will be placed on falsification activity that has--or could reasonably be expected to have--a significant impact on EPA's regulatory process or decision-making.

4. Destruction, Concealment or Alteration of RCRA Records

Section 3008(d)(4) of RCRA, 42 U.S.C. §6928(d)(4), carries misdemeanor penalties of one year of imprisonment and a $25,000.00 fine for incidents of knowing destruction, concealment or alteration of records maintained under RCRA regulations. As in falsification cases, emphasis will be placed on conduct that has--or could reasonably be expected to have--a significant impact on EPA's regulatory process or decision-making.

B. Investigative Priorities: Comprehensive Environmental Response, Compensation and Liability Act (Superfund):

1. Failure to Notify of the Release of a Hazardous Substance

Section 103(b)(3) of Superfund, 42 U.S.C. §9603(b)(3), carries misdemeanor penalties of one year of imprisonment and a $10,000.00 fine for failure to notify the appropriate Federal agency of a release of a hazardous substance in amounts equal to or greater than those determined pursuant to Section 102 of Superfund. The Agency will place a high investigative priority on cases where the "release" results in, or threatens, significant environmental contamination or human health hazard.

2. Destruction or Falsification of Superfund Records

Section 103(d)(2) of Superfund, 42 U.S.C. §9603(d)(2), carries misdemeanor penalties of one year of imprisonment and a $20,000.00 fine for the knowing destruction or falsification of specified Superfund records. Investigative priority should be placed on conduct that has--or could reasonably be expected to have--a significant impact on EPA's regulatory process or decision-making.

C. Investigative Priorities: Clean Water Act (CWA):

1. Violations of the NPDES Permit Program

Section 309(c)(1) of the CWA, 33 U.S.C. §1319(c)(1), carries misdemeanor penalties of one year of imprisonment and a $25,000.00 fine for the willful violation of conditions or limitations in NPDES permits issued by the Administrator or a State. The NPDES permit program is a mature regulatory scheme and the primary mechanism for monitoring and controlling water pollution under the CWA. The Agency will place a high investigative priority on willful NPDES permit violations that result in, or threaten, significant environmental contamination or human health hazard.

2. Falsification of CWA Records and Monitor Tampering

Section 309(c)(2) of the CWA, 33 U.S.C. §1319(c)(2), establishes misdemeanor penalties of six months of imprisonment and a $10,000.00 fine for knowing falsification of records and for tampering with monitoring devices "required to be maintained" under the CWA. Investigative priority should be placed on cases in which the falsification or tampering has--or could reasonably be expected to have--a significant impact on EPA's regulatory process or decision-making.

3. Unpermitted Discharges

Section 301 and 309(c)(1) of the CWA, 33 U.S.C. §§1311, 1319(c)(1)), establish misdemeanor penalties of one year of imprisonment and a $25,000.00 fine for willful discharges into navigable waters without an NPDES or "dredge and fill" permit.3/ A high investigative priority will be placed on willful, unpermitted discharges that cause, or threaten, significant environmental contamination or human health hazard.

D. Investigative Priorities: The Clean Air Act (CAA):

1. Violations of State Implementation Plans

Section 113(c)(1)(A) of the CAA, 42 U.S.C. §7413 (c)(1)(A), carries misdemeanor penalties of one year of imprisonment and a $25,000.00 fine for knowing violations of State implementation plans. SIPs are the cornerstone of a well-established and mature regulatory program and constitute the CAA's primary mechanism for implementing and enforcing air quality standards for criteria pollutants. A high investigative priority will be placed on cases of knowing violation of SIP limitations that result in, or threaten, significant environmental contamination or human health hazard.

2. Violations of Hazardous Air Pollutant Standards

Section 113(c)(1)(C) of the CAA, 42 U.S.C. §7413 (c)(1)(C), establishes misdemeanor penalties of one year of imprisonment and a $25,000.00 fine for knowing violations of standards for hazardous air pollutants. A high investigative priority will be placed on knowing violations of these standards that result in, or threaten, significant environmental contamination or human health hazard.

3/ Also applicable are the provisions of the Refuse Act, 33 U.S.C. §407, which establish misdemeanor penalties of one year of imprisonment (including a 30-day minimum sentence) and a $2,500.00 fine.

-9-

3. Falsification of CAA Records and Monitor Tampering

Section 113(c)(2) of the CAA, 42 U.S.C. §7413(c)(2), establishes misdemeanor penalties of six months of imprisonment and a $10,000.00 fine for knowing falsification of records and for tampering with monitoring devices "required to be maintained" under the CAA. A high investigative priority will be placed on cases in which the falsification or tampering has--or could reasonably be expected to have--a significant impact on EPA's regulatory process or decision-making.

E. Investigative Priorities: The Toxic Substances Control Act (TSCA):

1. Violations of Section 4 Testing Rules or the Section 5(b) Premanufacture Notification Program

Sections 15(1) and 16(b) of TSCA, 15 U.S.C. §§2614(1) and 2615(b), establish misdemeanor penalties of one year of imprisonment and a $25,000.00 fine for knowing or willful violations of any rule promulgated under Section 4 or any requirement prescribed by Section 5 of TSCA. A high investigative priority will be placed on violations that have a significant impact on the Agency's ability to act under Section 4(f)(1), 15 U.S.C. §2603(f)(1), and on situations of falsified test data submitted pursuant to Section 5(b), 15 U.S.C. §2604(b), and the premanufacture notification program.

2. Failure to Report Substantial Risk Information

Sections 8(e), 15(3)(B) and 16(b) of TSCA, 15 U.S.C. §§2607(e), 2614(3)(B) and 2615(b), establish misdemeanor penalties of one year of imprisonment and $25,000.00 fine for knowing or willful failure to submit information to EPA which reasonably supports the conclusion that a chemical substance or mixture manufactured, processed, or distributed in commerce presents a substantial risk of injury to health or the environment. A high investigative priority will be placed on all violations of this reporting requirement.

3. Violation of PCB or Dioxin Regulations

Sections 15(1)(C) and 16(b) of TSCA, 15 U.S.C. §§2614(1)(C) and 2615(b), establish misdemeanor penalties of one year of imprisonment and a $25,000.00 fine for knowing or willful violations of rules issued under Section 6 of TSCA. The Agency has issued regulations governing polychlorinated biphenyls and the disposal of dioxin-contaminated pesticide wastes. A high investigative priority will be placed on knowing or willful violations of these regulations that result in, or threaten, significant environmental contamination or human health hazard.

F. Criminal Enforcement Priorities: The Federal Insecticide, Fungicide and Rodenticide Act (FIFRA):

1. Failure to Report Information on the Unreasonable Adverse Effects of a Registered Pesticide

Section 14(b) of FIFRA, 7 U.S.C. §1361(b), establishes misdemeanor penalties for the knowing violation of any provision of the Act. Section 12(a)(2)(N) provides that it is unlawful to fail to submit information required by Section 6(a)(2). This section requires a registrant to report to EPA any information regarding unreasonable adverse effects on the environment which the registrant has after the time of registration. A high investigative priority will be placed on knowing violations of this reporting requirement.

2. Falsification of FIFRA Records

Sections 12(a)(2)(M) and 14(b) of FIFRA, 7 U.S.C. §§136j(a)(2)(M) and 1361(b), establish misdemeanor penalties for the knowing falsification of specified records maintained or filed under FIFRA, including registration data. A high investigative priority will be placed on falsification activity that has--or could reasonably be expected to have--a significant impact on EPA's regulatory process or decision-making.

3. Violation of Suspension or Cancellation Orders

Sections 12(a)(2)(J), 12(a)(2)(K) and 14(b) of FIFRA, 7 U.S.C. §§136j(a)(2)(J), 136j(a)(2)(K) and 1361(b), establish misdemeanor penalties for knowing violations of the terms of cancellation and suspension orders issued under Section 6 of FIFRA. A high investigative priority will be placed on knowing violations that result in, or threaten, significant environmental contamination or human health hazard.

4. Violation of Stop Sale Orders

Sections 12(a)(2)(I) and 14(b) of FIFRA, 7 U.S.C. §§136j (a)(2)(I) and 1361(b), establish misdemeanor penalties for knowing violations of the terms of stop sale orders under Section 13(a). A high investigative priority will be placed

-11-

on knowing violations that result in, or threaten, significant environmental contamination or human health hazard.

5. Unlawful Uses of Pesticides

Sections 12(a)(2)(G) and 14(b) of FIFRA, 7 U.S.C. §§136j(a)(2)(G) and 136l(b), establish misdemeanor penalties for the knowing use of a pesticide in a manner inconsistent with its labelling. If referred by a State with primary use enforcement responsibilities, a high investigative priority will be assigned to misuse cases that result in, or threaten, significant environmental contamination or human health hazard.

6. Illegal Distribution of Unregistered Pesticides

Sections 12(a)(1)(A) and 14(b) of FIFRA, 7 U.S.C. §§136j(a)(1)(A) and 136l(b), establish misdemeanor penalties for the knowing distribution, receipt etc. of an unregistered pesticide. The pesticide registration process outlined in Section 3 of FIFRA, 7 U.S.C. Section 136(a), is the cornerstone of EPA's program to monitor and regulate the safety of pesticides. A high investigative priority will be placed on illegal transactions involving unregistered pesticides that result in, or threaten, significant environmental contamination or human health hazard.

G. Investigative Priorities: The Marine Protection, Research, and Sanctuaries Act (MPRSA)

1. Unauthorized Ocean-Dumping

Section 105(b) of the MPRSA, 33 U.S.C. §1415(b), establishes misdemeanor penalties of one year of imprisonment and a $50,000.00 fine for the knowing violation of regulations or permits issued under the ocean-dumping program. The Agency will place a high investigative priority on violations that result in, or threaten, significant environmental contamination or human health hazard.

H. Criminal Enforcement Priorities: Willful Contempt of Environmental Consent Decrees

18 U.S.C. §401(3) establishes criminal sanctions for contempt of court resulting from "disobedience or resistence to (the court's) lawful writ, process, order,

rule, decree, or command." The punishment, which may be by fine or imprisonment, is left to the discretion of the court. Historically, most of the EPA's civil litigation referrals have been settled in judicially-enforceable consent decrees containing requirements for plant modification, upgrading or installation of pollution control equipment, and other forms of injunctive relief. Insuring compliance with the terms of these consent decrees will be a significant element of this Agency's enforcement program. A high investigative priority will, therefore, be placed on incidents of willful or deliberate noncompliance with the terms of environmental consent decrees that result in, or threaten, significant environmental contamination of human health hazard.

Memorandum: Appropriateness of Incarceration in Environmental Criminal Cases

Department of Justice (September 5, 1986)

U.S. Department of Justice

Land and Natural Resources Division

Office of the Assistant Attorney General

Washington, D.C. 20530

September 5, 1986

MEMORANDUM

TO: Arnold I. Burns
Deputy Attorney General

FROM: F. Henry Habicht II
Assistant Attorney General
Land and Natural Resources Division

SUBJECT: Appropriateness of Incarceration in Environmental Criminal Cases

Thank you for providing the opportunity to respond to the issues raised in your memorandum of August 20 regarding incarceration for regulatory offenses. It is most important for us to develop a consistent approach to this issue, both to ensure the public that serious problems are being dealt with severely, and to educate the regulated community such that they understand the norms and will not be "surprised" by a criminal prosecution.

The issue of appropriate sanctions in our enforcement cases must be kept in proper context. We and EPA have a spectrum of responses to violations of pollution requirements, including informal administrative enforcement letters and orders, civil injunctions, civil actions for penalties, and, finally, criminal prosecutions only where lesser sanctions would be inappropriate or ineffective. At any given time, criminal prosecutions constitute a tiny percentage of all pending administrative or judicial enforcement matters. We have been working on ensuring that all aspects of environmental enforcement are integrated effectively to promote voluntary compliance and to ensure that limited enforcement resources and tools are not squandered on less serious cases.

With respect to regulatory crimes generally, it is fair to say that Congress is not always sensitive to the traditional elements of criminality in providing for incarceration in regulatory statutes. Both the proper allocation of criminal justice resources and public respect for the criminal justice system generally require that incarceration be reserved for persons who engage in conduct which is harmful to basic interests of the public and which is undertaken with a culpable state of mind. Our experience with environmental crimes prosecutions in recent years convinces us that there exists a significant class of persons who, in making conscious decisions to avoid high regulatory compliance costs, expose the public to what can be very substantial harm or risk of harm. Incarceration is clearly a necessary and appropriate means of punishing and deterring this sort of harmful behavior. Incarceration generally need not be for extensive periods, and as prosecutors we must take a consistent approach to similarly-situated defendants. As the following brief discussion reflects, fines are adequate in less serious cases, but incarceration is warranted in appropriate instances and can virtually eliminate any perceived incentive to evade pollution control costs.

First, federal environmental crimes prosecuted by the Department clearly fall within traditional notions of "mens rea." Our cases are brought against individuals who are fully knowledgeable of the relevant regulatory requirements. These cases do not involve technical breaches of rules that require a Ph.D. to fathom; rather, they mainly involve blatant failures to obtain any of the required permits for toxic pollutant disposal or deliberate falsification of required discharge-monitoring reports, together with associated Title 18 offenses such as conspiracy, mail/wire fraud, and fraud upon the government. The regulatory requirements charged are not subject to legitimate disputes since they involve either blanket prohibitions on conduct (e.g., disposals without permits) or persistent false reporting.

Second, these crimes are widely condemned by the community-at-large due to the potential for violations to affect severely the public health, safety, and fisc. A simple act of unauthorized discharge or dumping of pollutants can have devastating impacts on thousands of innocent victims, either immediately or through long-term, chronic health effects. Examples in cases we have prosecuted include the poisoning by kepone of the entire James River in Virginia, the deliberate dumping of PCBs along 210 miles of highway in North Carolina, and the Louisville sewer explosions caused by direct dumping of volatile pollutants. Direct economic injury to the public from environmental crimes is also a very serious problem. Incidents of illegal toxic waste dumping can <u>each</u> easily require the expenditures of millions in public funds to cleanup contaminated soils and water sources.

Fortunately, many of the environmental crimes with which we deal have not had far-reaching lethal consequences. However, that fact reflects their early discovery and neutralization of effects, not any lack of serious hazards presented. Indeed, our early detection of these actions is partially a result of the proper functioning of the regulatory process, which is based upon permits and self-reporting. Wilfully evading this system, in and of itself can create serious undisclosed hazards. Thus, environmenta. crimes can be extremely serious and warrant substantial punishment.

- 3 -

Such punishment cannot be effected by fines alone. Particularly when we deal with the two ends of the economic spectrum of individual violators, fines alone are inadequate. At one end are well-paid corporate executives who directly or indirectly (through policy) cause environmental crimes to occur. Those people may be able to absorb a fine with minimum inconvenience, perhaps even being indemnified by their businesses. At the other end are the "midnight dumpers," or individuals who would be or have been involved with criminal enterprises and to whom fines are meaningless because they cannot pay them.

In terms of deterrence, if a high-level corporate decision maker faces a strong prospect of imprisonment, he is less likely to allow policies and practices which may expose him to the public stigma and the hardships of imprisonment. Similarly, branch managers and plant operators are less likely to take actions which may expose them to incarceration, whatever the policies from above may be. Further, the prospect of jail must also impact the "midnight dumper," who has little to lose other than his liberty. Finally, an incarceration sanction aids us in deterring the intrusion of sophisticated criminal enterprises into the hazardous waste hauling business.

Plainly, most businesses which generate wastes have chosen the law-abiding course of environmental compliance. However, it is equally clear that there are those who consciously make the opposite decision knowing the unambiguous requirements of the law. This is the sort of culpable conduct with harmful consequences for which the most serious criminal sanctions should be available. Public sentiment, as reflected in recent Bureau of Justice Statistics surveys and our close work with state and local enforcement officials, strongly bears this out. Therefore, as time passes and the environmental laws become more nationally established and understood, the punishment stakes, if anything, should be raised.

Above all, however, I have made it a priority that we focus our limited resources on the most serious, relatively unambiguous cases, such as the recent conviction of a large Seattle wood-treating company which pumped its creosote and other toxic solvents directly into the Puget Sound to save treatment costs. Prudent selection of these early cases ensures that both the public and regulated community will understand and respect this enforcement effort. There has been no serious dispute that the cases which have thus far led to incarceration warranted that punishment. Fines and restitution are also often appropriate and we are developing increasingly formal policies and coordination with state and local agencies to ensure that our efforts are fair, predictable and understandable. With such an approach, serious and harmful evasion of the pollution control laws, I

- 4 -

think, can be effectively deterred. I look forward to your advice and to working closely with you on these and related enforcement policy issues.

cc: John R. Bolton
Stephen S. Trott
Douglas H. Ginsburg
Roger M. Olsen
Richard K. Willard
Wm. Bradford Reynolds
Stephen J. Markman
Charles J. Cooper

Memorandum: The Exercise of Investigative Discretion
Environmental Protection Agency (January 12, 1994)

UNITED STATES ENVIRONMENTAL PROTECTION AGENCY
WASHINGTON, D.C. 20460

OFFICE OF ENFORCEMENT

January 12, 1994

MEMORANDUM

SUBJECT: The Exercise of Investigative Discretion

FROM: Earl E. Devaney, Director
Office of Criminal Enforcement

TO: All EPA Employees Working in or in Support of the Criminal Enforcement Program

I. Introduction

As EPA's criminal enforcement program enters its second decade and embarks on a period of unprecedented growth, this guidance establishes the principles that will guide the exercise of investigative discretion by EPA Special Agents. This guidance combines articulations of Congressional intent underlying the environmental criminal provisions with the Office of Criminal Enforcement's (OCE) experience operating under EPA's existing criminal case-screening criteria.[1]

In an effort to maximize our limited criminal resources, this guidance sets out the specific factors that distinguish cases meriting criminal investigation from those more appropriately pursued under administrative or civil judicial authorities.[2]

---

[1] This guidance incorporates by reference the policy document entitled Regional Enforcement Management: Enhanced Regional Case Screening (December 3, 1990).

[2] This memorandum is intended only as internal guidance to EPA. It is not intended to, does not, and may not be relied upon to, create a right or benefit, substantive or procedural, enforceable at law by a party to litigation with the United States, nor does this guidance in any way limit the lawful enforcement prerogatives, including administrative or civil enforcement actions, of the Department of Justice and the Environmental Protection Agency.

Indeed, the Office of Criminal Enforcement has an obligation to the American public, to our colleagues throughout EPA, the regulated community, Congress, and the media to instill confidence that EPA's criminal program has the proper mechanisms in place to ensure the discriminate use of the powerful law enforcement authority entrusted to us.

II. Legislative Intent Regarding Case Selection

The criminal provisions of the environmental laws are the most powerful enforcement tools available to EPA. Congressional intent underlying the environmental criminal provisions is unequivocal: criminal enforcement authority should target the most significant and egregious violators.

The Pollution Prosecution Act of 1990 recognized the importance of a strong national environmental criminal enforcement program and mandates additional resources necessary for the criminal program to fulfill its statutory mission. The sponsors of the Act recognized that EPA had long been in the posture of reacting to serious violations only after harm was done, primarily due to limited resources. Senator Joseph I. Lieberman (Conn.), one of the co-sponsors of the Act, explained that as a result of limited resources, "... few cases are the product of reasoned or targeted focus on suspected wrongdoing." He also expressed his hope that with the Act's provision of additional Special Agents, "... EPA would be able to bring cases that would have greater deterrent value than those currently being brought."

Further illustrative of Congressional intent that the most serious of violations should be addressed by criminal enforcement authority is the legislative history concerning the enhanced criminal provisions of RCRA:

> [The criminal provisions were] intended to prevent abuses of the permit system by those who obtain and then knowingly disregard them. It [RCRA sec. 3008(d)] is not aimed at punishing minor or technical variations from permit regulations or conditions if the facility operator is acting responsibly. The Department of Justice has exercised its prosecutorial discretion responsibly under similar provisions in other statutes and the conferees assume that, in light of the upgrading of the penalties from misdemeanor to felony, similar care will be used in deciding when a particular permit violation may warrant criminal prosecution under this Act. H.R. Conf. Rep. No. 1444, 96th Cong., 2d Sess. 37, reprinted in 1980 U.S. Code Cong. & Admin. News 5036.

While EPA has doubled its Special Agent corps since passage of the Pollution Prosecution Act, and has achieved a presence in nearly all federal judicial districts, it is unlikely that OCE will ever be large enough in size to fully defeat the ever-expanding universe of environmental crime. Rather, OCE must maximize its presence and impact through discerning case-selection, and then proceed with investigations that advance EPA's overall goal of regulatory compliance and punishing criminal wrongdoing.

III. Case Selection Process[3]

The case selection process is designed to identify misconduct worthy of criminal investigation. The case selection process is not an effort to establish legal sufficiency for prosecution. Rather, the process by which potential cases are analyzed under the case selection criteria will serve as an affirmative indication that OCE has purposefully directed its investigative resources toward deserving cases.

This is not to suggest that all cases meeting the case selection criteria will proceed to prosecution. Indeed, the exercise of investigative discretion must be clearly distinguished from the exercise of prosecutorial discretion. The employment of OCE's investigative discretion to dedicate its investigative authority is, however, a critical precursor to the prosecutorial discretion later exercised by the Department of Justice.[4]

At the conclusion of the case selection process, OCE should be able to articulate the basis of its decision to pursue a criminal investigation, based on the case selection criteria. Conversely, cases that do not ultimately meet the criteria to proceed criminally, should be systematically referred back to the Agency's civil enforcement office for appropriate administrative or civil judicial action, or to a state or local prosecutor.

IV. Case Selection Criteria

The criminal case selection process will be guided by two general measures - significant environmental harm and culpable conduct.

---

[3] The case selection process must not be confused with the Regional Case Screening Process. The relationship between the Regional Case Screening Process and case selection are discussed further at "VI.", below.

[4] Exercise of this prosecutorial discretion in all criminal cases is governed by the principles set forth in the Department of Justice's Principles of Federal Prosecution.

A. Significant Environmental Harm

The measure of significant environmental harm should be broadly construed to include the presence of actual harm, as well as the threat of significant harm, to the environment or human health. The following factors serve as indicators that a potential case will meet the measure of significant environmental harm.

Factor 1. Actual harm will be demonstrated by an illegal discharge, release or emission that has an identifiable and significant harmful impact on human health or the environment. This measure will generally be self-evident at the time of case selection.[5]

Factor 2. The threat of significant harm to the environment or human health may be demonstrated by an actual or threatened discharge, release or emission. This factor may not be as readily evident, and must be assessed in light of all the facts available at the time of case selection.

Factor 3. Failure to report an actual discharge, release or emission within the context of Factors 1 or 2 will serve as an additional factor favoring criminal investigation. While the failure to report, alone, may be a criminal violation, our investigative resources should generally be targeted toward those cases in which the failure to report is coupled with actual or threatened environmental harm.

Factor 4. When certain illegal conduct appears to represent a trend or common attitude within the regulated community, criminal investigation may provide a significant deterrent effect incommensurate with its singular environmental impact. While the single violation being considered may have a relatively insignificant impact on human health or the environment, such violations, if multiplied by the numbers in a cross-section of the regulated community, would result in significant environmental harm.

B. Culpable Conduct

The measure of culpable conduct is not necessarily an assessment of criminal intent, particularly since criminal intent will not always be readily evident at the time of case selection. Culpable conduct, however, may be indicated at the time of case selection by several factors.

---

[5] When this factor involves a fact situation in which the risk of harm is so great, so immediate and/or irremediable, OCE will always cooperate and coordinate with EPA's civil enforcement authorities to seek appropriate injunctive or remedial action.

Factor 1. History of repeated violations.

While a history of repeated violations is not a prerequisite to a criminal investigation, a potential target's compliance record should always be carefully examined. When repeated enforcement activities or actions, whether by EPA, or other federal, state and local enforcement authorities, have failed to bring a violator into compliance, criminal investigation may be warranted. Clearly, a history of repeated violations will enhance the government's capacity to prove that a violator was aware of environmental regulatory requirements, had actual notice of violations and then acted in deliberate disregard of those requirements.

Factor 2. Deliberate misconduct resulting in violation.

Although the environmental statutes do not require proof of specific intent, evidence, either direct or circumstantial, that a violation was deliberate will be a major factor indicating that criminal investigation is warranted.

Factor 3. Concealment of misconduct or falsification of required records.

In the arena of self-reporting, EPA must be able to rely on data received from the regulated community. If submitted data are false, EPA is prevented from effectively carrying out its mandate. Accordingly, conduct indicating the falsification of data will always serve as the basis for serious consideration to proceed with a criminal investigation.

Factor 4. Tampering with monitoring or control equipment.

The overt act of tampering with monitoring or control equipment leads to the certain production of false data that appears to be otherwise accurate. The consequent submission of false data threatens the basic integrity of EPA's data and, in turn, the scientific validity of EPA's regulatory decisions. Such an assault on the regulatory infrastructure calls for the enforcement leverage of criminal investigation.

Factor 5. Business operation of pollution-related activities without a permit, license, manifest or other required documentation.

Many of the laws and regulations within EPA's jurisdiction focus on inherently dangerous and strictly regulated business operations. EPA's criminal enforcement resources should clearly pursue those violators who choose to ignore environmental regulatory requirements altogether and operate completely outside of EPA's regulatory scheme.

V. Additional Considerations when Investigating Corporations

While the factors under measures IV. A and B, above, apply equally to both individual and corporate targets, several additional considerations should be taken into account when the potential target is a corporation.

In a criminal environmental investigation, OCE should always investigate individual employees and their corporate[6] employers who may be culpable. A corporation is, by law, responsible for the criminal act of its officers and employees who act within the scope of their employment and in furtherance of the purposes of the corporation. Whether the corporate officer or employee personally commits the act, or directs, aids, or counsels other employees to do so is inconsequential to the issue of corporate culpability.

Corporate culpability may also be indicated when a company performs an environmental compliance or management audit, and then knowingly fails to promptly remedy the noncompliance and correct any harm done.[7] On the other hand, EPA policy strongly encourages self-monitoring, self-disclosure, and self-correction.[8] When self-auditing has been conducted (followed up by prompt remediation of the noncompliance and any resulting harm) and full, complete disclosure has occurred, the company's constructive activities should be considered as mitigating factors in EPA's exercise of investigative discretion. Therefore, a violation that is voluntarily revealed and fully and promptly remedied as part of a corporation's systematic and comprehensive self-evaluation program generally will not be a candidate for the expenditure of scarce criminal investigative resources.

VI. Other Case Selection Considerations

EPA has a full range of enforcement tools available - administrative, civil-judicial, and criminal. There is universal consensus that less flagrant violations with lesser environmental consequences should be addressed through administrative or civil monetary penalties and remedial orders, while the most serious environmental violations ought to be investigated criminally. The challenge in practice is to correctly distinguish the latter cases from the former.

---

[6] The term "corporate" or "corporation", as used in this guidance, describes any business entity, whether legally incorporated or not.

[7] In cases of self-auditing and/or voluntary disclosure, the exercise of prosecutorial discretion is addressed in the Department of Justice policy document entitled "Factors in Decisions on Criminal Prosecutions for Environmental Violations in the Context of Significant Voluntary Compliance or Disclosure Efforts by the Violator" (July 1, 1991).

[8] See EPA's policy on environmental audits, published at 51 Fed. Reg. 25004 (July 9, 1986)

The case-selection factors described in this guidance should provide the foundation for the communication process that necessarily follows in the Regional Case Screening Process. This guidance envisions application of the case-selection factors first, to be followed by the recurring scrutiny of cases during the Regional Case Screening process.

The fundamental purpose of Regional Case Screening is to consider criminal enforcement in the greater context of all available EPA enforcement and environmental response options, to do so early (at the time of each case opening) before extensive resources have been expended, and to identify, prioritize, and target the most egregious cases. Regional Case Screening is designed to be an ongoing process in which enforcement cases are periodically reviewed to assess not only the evidentiary developments, but should also evaluate the clarity of the legal and regulatory authorities upon which a given case is being developed.[9]

In order to achieve the objectives of case screening, all cases originating within the OCE must be presented fully and fairly to the appropriate Regional program managers. Thorough analysis of a case using the case-selection factors will prepare OCE for a well-reasoned presentation in the Regional Case Screening process. Faithful adherence to the OCE case-selection process and active participation in the Regional Case Screening Process will serve to eliminate potential disparities between Agency program goals and priorities and OCE's undertaking of criminal investigations.

Full and effective implementation of these processes will achieve two important results: it will ensure that OCE's investigative resources are being directed properly and expended efficiently, and it will foreclose assertions that EPA's criminal program is imposing its powerful sanctions indiscriminately.

VII. Conclusion

The manner in which we govern ourselves in the use of EPA's most powerful enforcement tool is critical to the effective and reliable performance of our responsibilities, and will shape the reputation of this program for years to come. We must conduct ourselves in keeping with these principles which ensure the prudent and proper execution of the powerful law enforcement authorities entrusted to us.

---

[9] The legal structure upon which a criminal case is built - e.g., statutory, regulatory, case law, preamble language and interpretative letters - must also be analyzed in terms of Agency enforcement practice under these authorities. Thorough discussion of this issue is beyond the scope of this document, but generally, when the clarity of the underlying legal authority is in dispute, the more appropriate vehicle for resolution lies, most often, in a civil or administrative setting.

Factors in Decisions on Criminal Prosecutions for Environmental Violations in the Context of Significant Voluntary Compliance or Disclosure Efforts by the Violator

Department of Justice (July 1, 1991)

U.S. Department of Justice

Washington, D.C. 20530

FACTORS IN DECISIONS ON CRIMINAL
PROSECUTIONS FOR ENVIRONMENTAL VIOLATIONS
IN THE CONTEXT OF SIGNIFICANT VOLUNTARY
COMPLIANCE OR DISCLOSURE EFFORTS BY THE VIOLATOR

I. Introduction

It is the policy of the Department of Justice to encourage self-auditing, self-policing and voluntary disclosure of environmental violations by the regulated community by indicating that these activities are viewed as mitigating factors in the Department's exercise of criminal environmental enforcement discretion. This document is intended to describe the factors that the Department of Justice considers in deciding whether to bring a criminal prosecution for a violation of an environmental statute, so that such prosecutions do not create a disincentive to or undermine the goal of encouraging critical self-auditing, self-policing, and voluntary disclosure. It is designed to give federal prosecutors direction concerning the exercise of prosecutorial discretion in environmental criminal cases and to ensure that such discretion is exercised consistently nationwide. It is also intended to give the regulated community a sense of how the federal government exercises its criminal prosecutorial discretion with respect to such factors as the defendant's voluntary disclosure of violations, cooperation with the government in investigating the violations, use of environmental audits and other procedures to ensure compliance with all applicable environmental laws and regulations, and use of measures to remedy expeditiously and completely any violations and the harms caused thereby.

This guidance and the examples contained herein provide a framework for the determination of whether a particular case presents the type of circumstances in which lenience would be appropriate.

II. Factors to be Considered

Where the law and evidence would otherwise be sufficient for prosecution, the attorney for the Department should consider the factors contained herein, to the extent they are applicable, along with any other relevant factors, in determining whether and how to prosecute. It must be emphasized that these are examples of the types of factors which could be relevant. They do not constitute a definitive recipe or checklist of requirements. They merely illustrate some of the types of information which is relevant to our exercise of prosecutorial discretion.

It is unlikely that any one factor will be dispositive in any given case. All relevant factors are considered and given the weight deemed appropriate in the particular case. See Federal Principles of Prosecution (U.S. Dept. of Justice, 1980), Comment to Part A.2; Part B.3.

A. Voluntary Disclosure

The attorney for the Department should consider whether the person[1/] made a voluntary, timely and complete disclosure of the matter under investigation. Consideration should be given to whether the person came forward promptly after discovering the noncompliance, and to the quantity and quality of information provided. Particular consideration should be given to whether the disclosure substantially aided the government's investigatory process, and whether it occurred before a law enforcement or regulatory authority (federal, state or local authority) had already obtained knowledge regarding noncompliance. A disclosure is not considered to be "voluntary" if that disclosure is already specifically required by law, regulation, or permit.[2/]

B. Cooperation

The attorney for the Department should consider the degree and timeliness of cooperation by the person. Full and prompt cooperation is essential, whether in the context of a voluntary disclosure or after the government has independently learned of a violation. Consideration should be given to the violator's

---

1/ As used in this document, the terms "person" and "violator" are intended to refer to business and nonprofit entities as well as individuals.

2/ For example, any person in charge of a vessel or of an on shore facility or an offshore facility is required to notify the appropriate agency of the United States Government of any discharge of oil or a hazardous substance into or upon inter alia the navigable waters of the United States. Section 311(b)(5) of the Clean Water Act, 33 U.S.C. 1321(b)(5), as amended by the Oil Pollution Act of 1990, Pub. L. 101-380, § 4301(a), 104 Stat. 485, 533 (1990).

willingness to make all relevant information (including the complete results of any internal or external investigation and the names of all potential witnesses) available to government investigators and prosecutors. Consideration should also be given to the extent and quality of the violator's assistance to the government's investigation.

C. <u>Preventive Measures and Compliance Programs</u>

The attorney for the Department should consider the existence and scope of any regularized, intensive, and comprehensive environmental compliance program; such a program may include an environmental compliance or management audit. Particular consideration should be given to whether the compliance or audit program includes sufficient measures to identify and prevent future noncompliance, and whether the program was adopted in good faith in a timely manner.

Compliance programs may vary but the following questions should be asked in evaluating any program: Was there a strong institutional policy to comply with all environmental requirements? Had safeguards beyond those required by existing law been developed and implemented to prevent noncompliance from occurring? Were there regular procedures, including internal or external compliance and management audits, to evaluate, detect, prevent and remedy circumstances like those that led to the noncompliance? Were there procedures and safeguards to ensure the integrity of any audit conducted? Did the audit evaluate all sources of pollution (<u>i.e.</u>, all media), including the possibility of cross-media transfers of pollutants? Were the auditor's recommendations implemented in a timely fashion? Were adequate resources committed to the auditing program and to implementing its recommendations? Was environmental compliance a standard by which employee and corporate departmental performance was judged?

D. Additional Factors Which May Relevant

1. Pervasiveness of Noncompliance

Pervasive noncompliance may indicate systemic or repeated participation in or condonation of criminal behavior. It may also indicate the lack of a meaningful compliance program. In evaluating this factor, the attorney for the Department should consider, among other things, the number and level of employees participating in the unlawful activities and the obviousness, seriousness, duration, history, and frequency of noncompliance.

2. Internal Disciplinary Action

Effective internal disciplinary action is crucial to any compliance program. The attorney for the Department should consider whether there was an effective system of discipline for employees who violated company environmental compliance policies. Did the disciplinary system establish an awareness in other employees that unlawful conduct would not be condoned?

3. Subsequent Compliance Efforts

The attorney for the Department should consider the extent of any efforts to remedy any ongoing noncompliance. The promptness and completeness of any action taken to remove the source of the noncompliance and to lessen the environmental harm resulting from the noncompliance should be considered. Considerable weight should be given to prompt, good-faith efforts to reach environmental compliance agreements with federal or state authorities, or both. Full compliance with such agreements should be a factor in any decision whether to prosecute.

III. Application of These Factors to Hypothetical Examples[3]

These examples are intended to assist federal prosecutors in their exercise of discretion in evaluating environmental cases. The situations facing prosecutors, of course, present a wide variety of fact patterns. Therefore, in a given case, some of the criteria may be satisfied while others may not. Moreover, satisfaction of various criteria may be a matter of degree. Consequently, the effect of a given mix of factors also is a matter of degree. In the ideal situation, if a company fully meets all of the criteria, the result may be a decision not to prosecute that company criminally. Even if satisfaction of the criteria is not complete, still the company may benefit in terms of degree of enforcement response by the government. The following hypothetical examples are intended to illustrate the operation of these guidelines.

Example 1:

This is the ideal case in terms of criteria satisfaction and consequent prosecution leniency.

3/ While this policy applies to both individuals and organizational violators, these examples focus particularly upon situations involving organizations.

- 7 -

1. Company A regularly conducts a comprehensive audit of its compliance with environmental requirements.

2. The audit uncovers information about employees' disposing of hazardous wastes by dumping them in an unpermitted location.

3. An internal company investigation confirms the audit information. (Depending upon the nature of the audit, this follow-up investigation may be unnecessary.)

4. Prior to the violations the company had a sound compliance program, which included clear policies, employee training, and a hotline for suspected violations.

5. As soon as the company confirms the violations, it discloses all pertinent information to the appropriate government agency; it undertakes compliance planning with that agency; and it carries out satisfactory remediation measures.

6. The company also undertakes to correct any false information previously submitted to the government in relation to the violations.

7. Internally the company disciplines the employees actually involved in the violations, including any supervisor who was lax in preventing or detecting the activity. Also, the company reviews its compliance program to determine how the violations slipped by and corrects the weaknesses found by that review.

8. The company discloses to the government the names of the employees actually responsible for the violations, and it cooperates with the government by providing documentation necessary to the investigation of those persons.

Under these circumstances Company A would stand a good chance of being favorably considered for prosecutorial leniency, to the extent of not being criminally prosecuted at all. The degree of any leniency, however, may turn upon other relevant factors not specifically dealt with in these guidelines.[4/]

Example 2:

At the opposite end of the scale is Company Z, which meets few of the criteria. The likelihood of prosecutorial leniency, therefore, is remote. Company Z's circumstances may include any of the following:

1. Because an employee has threatened to report a violation to federal authorities, the company is afraid that investigators may begin looking at it. An audit is undertaken, but it focuses only upon the particular violation, ignoring the possibility that the violation may be indicative of widespread activities in the organization.

2. After completing the audit, Company Z reports the violations discovered to the government.

[4/] For example, if the company had a long history of noncompliance, the compliance audit was done only under pressure from regulators, and a timely audit would have ended the violations much sooner, those circumstances would be considered.

3. The company had a compliance program, but it was effectively no more than a collection of paper. No effort is made to disseminate its content, impress upon employees its significance, train employees in its application, or oversee its implementation.

4. Even after "discovery" of the violation the company makes no effort to strengthen its compliance procedures.

5. The company makes no effort to come to terms with regulators regarding its violations. It resists any remedial work and refuses to pay any monetary sanctions.

6. Because of the non-compliance, information submitted to regulators over the years has been materially inaccurate, painting a substantially false picture of the company's true compliance situation. The company fails to take any steps to correct that inaccuracy.

7. The company does not cooperate with prosecutors in identifying those employees (including managers) who actually were involved in the violation, and it resists disclosure of any documents relating either to the violations or to the responsible employees.

In these circumstances leniency is unlikely. The only positive action is the so-called audit, but that was so narrowly focused as to be of questionable value, and it was undertaken only to head off a possible criminal investigation. Otherwise, the company demonstrated no good faith either in terms of compliance efforts or in assisting the government in obtaining a full understanding of the violation and discovering its sources.

Nonetheless, these factors do not assure a criminal prosecution of Company Z. As with Company A, above, other circumstances may be present which affect the balance struck by prosecutors. For example, the effect of the violation (because of substance, duration, or amount) may be such that prosecutors would not consider it to be an appropriate criminal case. Administrative or civil proceedings may be considered a more appropriate response.

Other examples:

Between these extremes there is a range of possibilities. The presence, absence, or degree of any criterion may affect the prosecution's exercise of discretion. Below are some examples of such effects:

1. In a situation otherwise similar to that of Company A, above, Company B performs an audit that is very limited in scope and probably reflects no more than an effort to avoid prosecution. Despite that background, Company B is cooperative in terms of both bringing itself into compliance and providing information regarding the crime and its perpetrators. The result could be any of a number of outcomes, including prosecution of a lesser charge or a decision to prosecute the individuals rather than the company.

2. Again the situation is similar to Company A's, but Company C refuses to reveal any information regarding the individual violators. The likelihood of the government's prosecuting the company are substantially increased.

3. In another situation similar to Company A's, Company D chooses to "sit on" the audit and take corrective action without telling the government. The government learns of the situation months or years after the fact.

A complicating fact here is that environmental regulatory programs are self policing: they include a substantial number of reporting requirements. If reports which in fact presented false information are allowed to stand uncorrected, the reliability of this system is undermined. They also may lead to adverse and unfair impacts upon other members of the regulated community. For example, Company D failed to report discharges of X contaminant into a municipal sewer system, discharges that were terminated as a result of an audit. The sewer authority, though, knowing only that there have been excessive loadings of X, but not knowing that Company D was a source, tightens limitations upon all known sources of X. Thus, all of those sources incur additional treatment expenses, but Company D is unaffected. Had Company D revealed its audit results, the other companies would not have suffered unnecessary expenses.

In some situations, moreover, failure to report is a crime. See, e.g., 33 U.S.C. § 1321(b)(5) and 42 U.S.C. § 9603(b). To illustrate the effect of this factor, consider Company E, which conducts a thorough audit and finds that hazardous wastes have been disposed of by dumping them on the ground. The company cleans up the area and tightens up its compliance program, but does not reveal the situation to regulators. Assuming that a reportable quantity of a hazardous substance was released, the company was under a legal obligation under 42 U.S.C. § 9603(b) to report that release as soon as it had knowledge of it, thereby allowing regulators the opportunity to assure proper clean up. Company E's knowing failure to report the release upon learning of it is itself a felony.

In the cases of both Company D and Company E, consideration would be given by prosecutors for remedial efforts; hence prosecution of fewer or lesser charges might result. However, because Company D's silence adversely affected others who are entitled to fair regulatory treatment and because Company E deprived those legally responsible for evaluating cleanup needs of the ability to carry out their functions, the likelihood of their totally escaping criminal prosecution is significantly reduced.

4. Company F's situation is similar to that of Company B. However, with regard to the various violations shown by the audit, it concentrates upon correcting only the easier, less

expensive, less significant among them. Its lackadaisical approach to correction does not make it a strong candidate for leniency.

5. Company G is similar to Company D in that it performs an audit and finds violations, but does not bring them to the government's attention. Those violations do not involve failures to comply with reporting requirements. The company undertakes a program of gradually correcting its violations. When the government learns of the situation, Company G still has not remedied its most significant violations, but claims that it certainly planned to get to them. Company G could receive some consideration for its efforts, but its failure to disclose and the slowness of its remedial work probably mean that it cannot expect a substantial degree of leniency.

6. Comprehensive audits are considered positive efforts toward good faith compliance. However, such audits are not indispensable to enforcement leniency. Company H's situation is essentially identical to that of Company A, except for the fact that it does not undertake a comprehensive audit. It does not have a formal audit program, but, as a part of its efforts to ensure compliance, does realize that it is committing an environmental violation. It thereafter takes steps otherwise identical to those of Company A in terms of compliance efforts and cooperation. Company H is also a likely candidate for leniency, including possibly no criminal prosecution.

In sum, mitigating efforts made by the regulated community will be recognized and evaluated. The greater the showing of good faith, the more likely it will be met with leniency. Conversely, the less good faith shown, the less likely that prosecutorial discretion will tend toward leniency.

IV. Nature of this Guidance

This guidance explains the current general practice of the Department in making criminal prosecutive and other decisions after giving consideration to the criteria described above, as well as any other criteria that are relevant to the exercise of criminal prosecutorial discretion in a particular case. This discussion is an expression of, and in no way departs from, the long tradition of exercising prosecutorial discretion. The decision to prosecute "generally rests entirely in [the prosecutor's] discretion." Bordenkircher v. Hayes, 434 U.S. 357, 364 (1978).[5/] This discretion is especially firmly held by the criminal prosecutor.[6/] The criteria set forth above are intended only as internal guidance to Department of Justice attorneys. They are not intended to, do not, and may not be relied upon to create a right or benefit, substantive or procedural, enforceable

---

5/ Although some statutes have occasionally been held to require civil enforcement actions, see, e.g., Dunlop v. Bachowski, 421 U.S. 560 (1975), those are unusual cases, and the general rule is that both civil and criminal enforcement is at the enforcement agency's discretion where not prescribed by law. Heckler v. Chaney, 470 U.S. 821, 830-35 (1985); Cutler v. Hayes, 818 F.2d 879, 893 (D.C. Cir. 1987) (decisions not to enforce are not reviewable unless the statute provides an "inflexible mandate").

6/ Newman v. United States, 382 F.2d 479, 480 (D.C. Cir. 1967).

at law by a party to litigation with the United States, nor do they in any way limit the lawful litigative prerogatives, including civil enforcement actions, of the Department of Justice or the Environmental Protection Agency. They are provided to guide the effective use of limited enforcement resources, and do not derive from, find their basis in, nor constitute any legal requirement, whether constitutional, statutory, or otherwise, to forego or modify any enforcement action or the use of any evidentiary material. See Principles of Federal Prosecution (U.S. Dept. of Justice, 1980) p. 4; United States Attorneys' Manual (U.S. Dept. of Justice, 1986) 1-1.000.

Bluesheet Revision to the U.S. Attorneys' Manual on Environmental Crimes

Department of Justice (August 23, 1994)

Office of the Attorney General
Washington, D.C. 20530

August 23, 1994

MEMORANDUM FOR ALL U.S. ATTORNEYS AND
THE ENVIRONMENTAL CRIMES SECTION OF THE
ENVIRONMENT AND NATURAL RESOURCES DIVISION

FROM: THE ATTORNEY GENERAL

SUBJECT: Bluesheet Revision to the U.S. Attorneys' Manual on Environmental Crimes

I have today signed a Bluesheet revision to the U.S. Attorneys' Manual on environmental crimes. A copy of the revision is attached for your information. All holders of the relevant U.S. Attorneys' Manual title will also receive copies through the Executive Office for U.S. Attorneys.

This revision is the joint product of U.S. Attorneys and the Environment and Natural Resources Division. I would like to thank all of you who participated by providing written or informal comments and suggestions to the working group who managed the revision process. I would especially like to thank the working group who, among other things, did an excellent job of considering your comments and of incorporating or responding to many of your suggestions.

I have approved the Bluesheet revision because it seeks to strengthen the partnership between U.S. Attorneys and the Environmental Crimes Section. I expect the Department's attorneys to put behind any concerns that belong to the past and to direct our efforts to the aggressive and fair prosecution of environmental crimes. The Bluesheet revision emphasizes that all U.S. Attorney's Offices and the Environmental Crimes Section have critical roles in these prosecutions. I look forward to the results of your continuing efforts in the prosecution of environmental crimes.

Attachment

Office of the Attorney General
Washington, D.C. 20530

MEMORANDUM

TO: Holders of the United States Attorneys' Manual, Title 5

FROM: Office of the Attorney General

Janet Reno
Attorney General

Subject: Environmental Crimes

Affects: USAM 5-11.000

Purpose: This Bluesheet replaces the entire Chapter 11 of Title 5. These procedures are designed to define and strengthen the partnership between the Environment and Natural Resources Division and U.S. Attorney's Offices in the investigation and prosecution of environmental crimes.

This Bluesheet is a final amendment to Chapter 11 and all Department attorneys should immediately begin to follow the procedures set forth in the amendment.

This chapter describes the partnership between U.S. Attorney's Offices and the Environmental Crimes Section ("ECS") of the Environment and Natural Resources Division ("ENRD"). It is the Department's goal to promote cooperation among the U.S. Attorney's Offices and ECS to utilize the strengths of every office and in each case to apply the Department's resources in the most effective manner.

5-11.101 Statutes Administered

Prosecutions initiated pursuant to the following statutes listed in the attachment to this chapter are deemed to be environmental crimes, and the provisions of this chapter apply to all such cases.

5-11.102 Other Criminal Provisions

Experience has shown that cases involving violations of the federal environmental laws identified in USAM 5-11.101, supra, also may involve violations of certain other federal statutes. Therefore, the Environmental Crimes Section is empowered to investigate and prosecute violations of additional criminal statutes when such violations arise within the context of environmental crimes. Examples of some of the statutes which may be involved in those cases include, but are not limited to, the following:

Statute	Subject Matter
18 U.S.C. § 2	Aiding and abetting
18 U.S.C. § 287	False claims
18 U.S.C. § 371	Conspiracy
18 U.S.C. § 641	Theft or conversion of public property or money
18 U.S.C. § 1001	False statement
18 U.S.C. § 1341	Mail Fraud
18 U.S.C. § 1343	Wire Fraud
18 U.S.C. § 1505	Obstruction of administrative proceedings
18 U.S.C. §§ 1621 to 1623	Perjury

5-11.103 Notice of Case Initiation

The Case Initiation Report formerly described in the U.S. Attorneys' Manual for environmental crimes is abolished. When a U.S. Attorney's Office opens a case file for an environmental case or matter, the Office will inform the Environmental Crimes Section, which it may do by entering the case or matter in the Department's computerized case tracking system and identifying the case type as "environmental." If the case or matter is not identified as "environmental" in the case tracking system (for example, due to data entry limitations), the office will inform the Environmental Crimes Section by telephone or in writing. When ECS opens a case file to initiate a case or matter, the Section Chief will provide notice to the U.S. Attorney for the district in which the crime is alleged to have occurred and will confer with the U.S. Attorney's Office pursuant to USAM 5-11.104 or USAM 5-11.105.

5-11.104 Responsibility for Case Development and Prosecution

Responsibility for the approval, investigation, and prosecution of environmental crimes, except in cases of national interest, normally rests with the U.S. Attorney's Office. With the agreement of the U.S. Attorney's Office, ECS may participate as a partner, as the lead, or otherwise in such cases. Cooperation and consultation between U.S. Attorney's Offices and ECS is encouraged, in order to make the most effective use of the Department's resources. When ECS participates in a case, there should be a clear understanding between the offices concerning the allocation of case responsibility.

5-11.105 Cases of National Interest

A case is of national interest if it is a case that presents a novel issue of law (including the first case under a statute, provision, or regulation), a case with simultaneous investigations in multiple districts (unless the U.S. Attorney's Offices in each such district and the ECS conclude that national interests are not involved), a case with international or foreign policy implications, or an urgent or sensitive case as defined in USAM 1-10.230. In a case of national interest, the U.S. Attorney's Office and ECS will participate jointly as co-counsel from the initiation of the investigation through prosecution, unless otherwise agreed. A case may be identified as one of national interest by the U.S. Attorney's Office or the Assistant Attorney General for the ENRD.

5-11.106 Exchanging Case Information

Among ECS' other responsibilities, it is a clearinghouse for information about environmental prosecutions and a source of expertise about the handling of such cases. U.S. Attorney's Offices are encouraged to communicate with ECS early in environmental investigations and prosecutions to benefit from ECS' information and expertise, and to provide ECS with information about successes, obstacles, and strategies that ECS may share with other prosecutors. As part of this consultation, U.S. Attorney's Offices are encouraged to provide ECS with advance notice of indictments. U.S. Attorney's Offices are encouraged to consult with ECS on indictments and other matters with sufficient lead time to allow ECS to have time to provide meaningful input. In any event, U.S. Attorney's Offices will provide copies of indictments or informations within two days after filing. The Attorney General expects that ECS will participate in implementing the Assistant Attorney General's responsibilities pursuant to 28 C.F.R. § 0.65 and that each U.S. Attorney's Office will provide information to ECS to assist it in this purpose, including responding fully and expeditiously to reasonable requests for information.

5-11.107 Notification of Case Resolutions

When ECS is not participating in a case, the U.S. Attorney's Offices shall provide ECS with notice of case resolutions by providing ECS with copies of disposition documents (including any plea agreements) when judgment is entered, except as provided in USAM 5-11.108 and 5-11.115.

5-11.108 Dismissals

In the case of dismissal of indictments, informations, or complaints in criminal cases involving violations of the statutes identified in USAM 5-11.101, *supra*, except when a superseding indictment has been returned or an information or a complaint has been filed against the same defendant or when the individual defendant has died, notification of the dismissal (or, in the case of a written dismissal, a copy) shall be provided to ECS so that it is received seven days before filing.

5-11.109 Declinations

When a U.S. Attorney's Office or ECS declines a case and writes a substantive memo to the file or to the investigative agency, either office will promptly provide a copy of the declination memo to, respectively, ECS or the U.S. Attorney's Office for the district in which the crime is alleged to have occurred. Nothing in USAM 5-11.104 is intended to limit ECS' authority to prosecute a case declined by a U.S. Attorney's Office after consultation with that office, nor shall these provisions limit the authority of a U.S. Attorney's Office to prosecute a case that ECS has declined for reasons that ECS advises do not involve policy considerations.

5-11.110 Staffing

The appointment of Special Assistant U.S. Attorneys shall be approved by the U.S. Attorney of the relevant district and the Assistant Attorney General for the ENRD. In their approval process, the U.S. Attorney and the Assistant Attorney General should seek to ensure sensible and efficient use of government resources.

5-11.111 Policy-Making, Support, and Other Functions of the ENRD

In addition to its litigation activities, ECS helps the ENRD fulfill its other responsibilities:

a) setting policy nationally for the prosecution of environmental crimes;

b) providing training to U.S. Attorney's Offices, federal investigative agencies, and others;

c) providing expertise, information, and support concerning environmental prosecutions nationally, including providing a clearinghouse of prosecution-related documents; and

d) to use environmental criminal enforcement to address environmental and compliance problems, consistent with the standards of federal prosecution.

U.S. Attorney's Offices are encouraged to provide ECS with copies of important pleadings, briefs, search warrant applications, grand jury subpoenas, and similar case documents so that such documents can be made available to other prosecutors.

5-11.112 Parallel Proceedings

Because many of the environmental statutes specifically provide for criminal, civil, and administrative sanctions (see, e.g., 33 U.S.C. § 1319(a), (b), (c), and (d)), this is an area of the law especially susceptible to parallel proceedings. Such proceedings may be appropriate, for example, when in the course of the civil case the government receives evidence of deliberate violations of the law meriting criminal prosecution or when a criminal investigation uncovers evidence of an on-going violation causing environmental contamination which should be stopped quickly through an injunctive action.

Although they may be appropriate in particular circumstances, parallel proceedings must be handled carefully in order to avoid allegations of improper release of grand jury material or abuse of civil process. Therefore, in any case under any of the statutes identified in USAM 5-11.101, supra, in which parallel proceedings arise, the U.S. Attorney's office shall contact the Environmental Crimes Section for the purpose of coordinating the parallel proceedings.

5-11.113 Coordination with State Programs

Most states have environmental enforcement programs which overlap, in whole or in part, with federal programs. U.S. Attorneys should familiarize themselves with state environmental enforcement laws and state enforcement officials. Particular attention should be directed toward the following aspects of state-federal relations in the environmental enforcement field:

A. State environmental enforcement agencies may be a valuable source of information on suspected violations of federal environmental statutes. U.S. Attorneys may be in a position to assist in apprising state officials of the nature of the local federal enforcement program and in developing methods for exchanging information on suspected violations;

B. State authorities often possess evidentiary materials which are relevant to pending federal court proceedings. U.S. Attorneys should be aware of the nature and extent of the states' investigatory resources and should make provision in appropriate circumstances for the exchange of information on pending cases with state authorities;

C. Frequently a particular activity constitutes a violation of both federal and state law. When state officials are proceeding with an environmental enforcement case which may include violations of federal law, the U.S. Attorney in the affected district should monitor that state activity. If it appears that all federal interests in the case will be vindicated in the state court action, action in federal court may be an unnecessary duplication of effort. On the other hand, if federal interests will not be protected completely in state court, federal proceedings may be warranted. See also, USAM 9-2.142 and 9-27.240.

5-11.114 Individual and Corporate Defendants

A. Congress has demonstrated its intent that individuals, as well as corporations, should be criminally prosecuted for violations of federal environmental laws, see, e.g., 33 U.S.C. §§ 1319(c)(5) and 1362(5), thereby recognizing the fact the unlawful acts or omissions of corporations actually can be traced to individual officers or employees. That Congressional intent should be given serious consideration in the development of prosecutions for violations of the statutes identified under USAM 5-11.101, supra.

B. In any case against both a corporation and any of its individual employees the willingness of the offending corporation to enter a guilty plea is not a basis for dismissal as against the individual.

5-11.115 <u>Plea Negotiations and Agreements; Global Settlements"; Alternative Sentencing</u>

A. Without the express approval of the Assistant Attorney General, Environment and Natural Resources Division, in any criminal case arising under the statutes identified in USAM 5-11.101 no plea agreement will be negotiated which compromises the right of the United States to any civil or administrative remedies under those statutes. Efforts by defendants to effect such results may arise in the context of so-called "global settlement" offers.

B. The Assistant Attorney General for the Environment and Natural Resources Division will consider a policy for plea agreements that include "alternative sentencing," meaning a sentence other than fine, imprisonment, or restitution to specific entities for out-of-pocket expenses.

5-11.116 <u>Handling of Appeals</u>

All appeals in criminal cases arising under the statutes identified in USAM 5-11.101, <u>supra</u>, shall be handled as provided for in USAM 5-8.310 and Title 2. When a U.S. Attorney's Office makes a request to handle an appeal, such a request will be resolved by agreement between the U.S. Attorney's Office and the Chief of the Appellate Section of the Environment and Natural Resources Division. In jointly resolving such a request, the following factors among any others should be considered on a case-by-case basis and, if necessary, discussed:

- the relative advantages in this case of staffing the appeal with an Assistant U.S. Attorney who tried the case or with an appellate lawyer who was not involved in the trial;
- the relative advantages in this appeal of the U.S. Attorney's local perspective or the Environment and Natural Resources Division's national perspective;
- whether there are issues in this appeal on which components of the government may have differing viewpoints; and
- the available resources of each office, especially relative to the briefing and argument schedule of the appeal.

Copies of any draft briefs prepared by a U.S. Attorney's Office on behalf of the government shall be forwarded to the Appellate Section in sufficient time to allow review, comment, and approval by the Section and the Assistant Attorney General. Copies of any draft brief prepared by the Appellate Section shall be forwarded to the U.S. Attorney's Office in sufficient time to allow review, comment, and approval by that office. In any appeal, copies of all other briefs by other parties shall be promptly forwarded by the U.S. Attorney's Office to the Appellate Section.

5-11.117 Notice of Appeals

USAM 2.200 describes the manner in which U.S. Attorney's Offices forward notices of appeal or requests to take an appeal to the Environment and Natural Resources Division. For environmental crimes, the Division designates ECS as the unit to which such notices and requests should be sent. ECS will forward the notices and requests to the Division's Appellate Section.

5-11.118 Record on Appeal

Whenever an appeal is taken in a case arising under any statute identified in USAM 5-11.101, supra, for which the U.S. Attorney has taken primary trial level responsibility, and that appeal is to be handled by the Environment and Natural Resources Division, the U.S. Attorney is responsible for assembling and transmitting to the Environment and Natural Resources Division those items which constitute the record of the case of the trial court level.

ATTACHMENT TO CHAPTER 5, TITLE 11 OF THE U.S. ATTORNEYS' MANUAL

Prosecutions initiated pursuant to the following statutes are deemed to be environmental crimes:

FEDERAL INSECTICIDE, FUNGICIDE & RODENTICIDE ACT (FIFRA)
7 USC §§ 136-136y
7 USC § 136l(b) (criminal provision)

ENERGY SUPPLY AND ENVIRONMENTAL COORDINATION ACT
15 USC §§ 791-798
15 USC § 797 (enforcement provision)

TOXIC SUBSTANCES CONTROL ACT (TSCA)
15 USC §§ 2601-2671
15 USC § 2615(b) (criminal provision)
15 USC § 2614 (cross referenced)

PROTECTION OF NAVIGABLE WATERS AND OF HARBOR AND RIVER IMPROVEMENTS GENERALLY
33 USC §§ 401-467
33 USC §§ 406 & 411 RIVERS AND HARBORS ACT (criminal provision)
33 USC §§ 403 & 407 (cross referenced prohibited acts)
33 USC § 421 ACT OF JUNE 23, 1910 (criminal provision)
33 USC § 441 ACT OF JUNE 29, 1888 (criminal provision)

FEDERAL WATER POLLUTION CONTROL ACT (also known as the CLEAN WATER ACT)
33 USC §§ 1251-1387
33 USC § 1319(c) (criminal provision)
33 USC §§ 1311, 1312, 1316, 1317, 1318, 1321, 1328, 1342, 1344, 1345 (cross referenced in criminal provision)

MARINE PROTECTION RESEARCH AND SANCTUARIES ACT (also known as the OCEAN DUMPING ACT)
33 USC §§ 1401-1445
33 USC 1415(b) (criminal provision)
33 USC 1411 (prohibited acts)

DEEPWATER PORT ACT
33 USC §§ 1501-1524
33 USC § 1514(a) (criminal provision)

ACT TO PREVENT POLLUTION FROM SHIPS
33 USC §§ 1901-1912
33 USC § 1908(a) (criminal provision)

SAFE DRINKING WATER ACT
42 USC §§ 300f - 300j-26
42 USC §§ 300h-2, 300h-3, 300i-1 & 300j (criminal provisions)

ATOMIC ENERGY ACT
42 USC §§ 2011-2296
42 USC §§ 2272 & 2273 (enforcement provisions)

NOISE CONTROL ACT
42 USC §§ 4901-4918
42 USC § 4910 (criminal provision)

RESOURCE CONSERVATION AND RECOVERY ACT (RCRA)
42 USC §§ 6901- 6992
42 USC § 6928(d) (criminal provision)

CLEAN AIR ACT (CAA)
42 USC §§ 7401-7671
42 USC § 7413(c) (criminal provision)

COMPREHENSIVE ENVIRONMENTAL RESPONSE, COMPENSATION & LIABILITY ACT (CERCLA)
42 USC § 9601-9675
42 USC § 9603(b) (criminal provision)

EMERGENCY PLANNING AND COMMUNITY RIGHT TO KNOW ACT (EPCRKA)
42 USC §§ 11001-11050
42 USC § 11045(b)(4) (criminal provision)

OUTER CONTINENTAL SHELF LANDS ACT
43 USC §§ 1331-1356
43 USC § 1350(c) & (d) (criminal provisions)

HAZARDOUS MATERIAL TRANSPORTATION ACT (HMTA)
49 USC §§ 1801-1819 and 49 App. §§ 1801-1819
49 USC § 1809(b) and 49 App. § 1809(b) (criminal provisions)

Voluntary Environmental Self-Policing and Self-Disclosure Interim Policy Statement

Environmental Protection Agency (April 3, 1995)

Federal Register / Vol. 60, No. 63 / Monday, April 3, 1995 / Notices 16875

..RL-5184-4]

Voluntary Environmental Self-Policing and Self-Disclosure Interim Policy Statement

AGENCY: Environmental Protection Agency (EPA).

ACTION: Interim policy statement and request for comment.

SUMMARY: The Environmental Protection Agency (EPA) announces and requests comment on an interim policy to provide incentives for regulated entities that conduct voluntary compliance evaluations and also disclose and correct violations. These incentives include eliminating or substantially reducing the gravity component of civil penalties and not referring cases for criminal prosecution where specified conditions are met. The policy also states that EPA will not request voluntary audit reports to trigger enforcement investigations. This interim policy was developed in close consultation with EPA's regional offices and the Department of Justice, and will be applied uniformly by the Agency's enforcement programs.

DATES: This interim policy statement is effective as interim guidance 15 days after publication, in order to give the Agency time to coordinate implementation of the policy throughout EPA Headquarters and the Regions. EPA urges interested parties to comment on this interim policy in writing. Comments must be received by EPA at the address below by June 2, 1995.

ADDRESSES: Submit three copies of comments to the U.S. EPA Air Docket, Mail Code 6102, 401 M Street, SW, Washington, D.C. 20460, attention: Docket #C–94–01.

FOR FURTHER INFORMATION CONTACT: Additional documentation relating to the development of this interim policy is contained in the environmental auditing public docket. Documents from the docket may be requested by calling (202) 260–7548, requesting an index to docket #C–94–01, and faxing document requests to (202) 260–4400. Hours of operation are 8 a.m. to 5:30 p.m., Monday through Friday, except legal holidays. Additional contacts are Geoff Garver or Brian Riedel, at (202) 564–4187.

SUPPLEMENTARY INFORMATION:

I. Background

A. Introduction

One of the Environmental Protection Agency's most important responsibilities is obtaining compliance with federal laws that protect public health and safeguard the environment. That goal can be achieved only with the voluntary cooperation of thousands of businesses and other regulated entities subject to these requirements. Today, EPA is announcing incentives for those who take responsibility for voluntarily evaluating, disclosing and correcting violations. These incentives, developed after nine months of public meetings and empirical analysis, are set forth in detail below and take effect in 15 days. At the same time, EPA expects to continue a dialogue with stakeholders and consider further refinements to this interim policy. The incentives that EPA is offering fall into three distinct categories.

First, the Agency will completely eliminate gravity-based (or "punitive") penalties for companies or public agencies that voluntarily identify, disclose and correct violations according to the conditions outlined in this policy. EPA will also reduce punitive penalties by up to 75% for companies that meet most, but not all, of these conditions. Second, EPA will not recommend to the Department of Justice that criminal charges be brought against a company acting in good faith to identify, disclose, and correct violations, so long as no serious actual harm has occurred. Finally, the Agency will not request voluntary environmental audits to trigger enforcement investigations.

The incentives offered in this policy have been structured above all to protect human health and the environment. For example, even where the conditions for mitigated enforcement are met, EPA will reserve the right to collect full civil penalties for criminal conduct, violations that present an imminent and substantial endangerment or result in serious actual harm, or repeat violations. Sources will not be allowed to gain an economic advantage over their competitors by delaying their investment in compliance. Nor will EPA hesitate to bring a criminal action against individuals responsible for criminal conduct.

EPA is considering additional incentives for voluntary compliance beyond the benefits offered in the policy today. On April 7, 1995, the Agency will announce 12 Environmental Leadership Program (ELP) pilot projects with companies and public agencies to test criteria for auditing and certification of voluntary compliance programs. If successful, standards developed through Environmental Leadership could lead to reduced inspections and public recognition for companies or agencies with state-of-the-art compliance programs. In keeping with the President's announcement on March 16, 1995, EPA also will shortly be announcing additional compliance incentives for small businesses.

The Agency is especially interested in comments relating to whether this interim policy appropriately defines the criteria for determining whether a self-audit, self-evaluation or disclosure is voluntary; whether the interim policy adequately preserves the Agency's authority to assess a gravity penalty component in appropriate cases; and whether, and according to what criteria, the Agency should consider giving credit against the economic benefit component of a penalty for state-of-the-art environmental management systems.

B. Public Process

In May 1994, the Administrator asked the Office of Enforcement and Compliance Assurance to determine whether additional incentives are needed to encourage voluntary disclosure and correction of violations uncovered during environmental audits and self-evaluations.

In developing this interim policy, the Agency held a major two-day public meeting in July 1994 announced in the **Federal Register** on June 20, 1994 (59 FR 31914); published a Restatement of Policies Related to Environmental Auditing in the **Federal Register** on July 28, 1994 (59 FR 38455); considered over 80 written comments submitted to the environmental auditing policy docket; held a focus group meeting in San Francisco on January 19, 1995 with key stakeholders from industry, trade groups, State environmental commissions, State attorneys general offices, district attorneys' offices, environmental and public interest groups, and professional environmental auditing groups; and held a public comment session in San Francisco on January 20, 1995.

In addition to considering opinion from stakeholders, EPA conducted its own analysis of relevant facts. For example, the Agency considered EPA and other Federal policies relating to environmental auditing, self-disclosure, and correction, as well as incentives suggested by State and local policies and legislation, and by applications submitted for the ELP pilot program. The Agency also considered relevant surveys on auditing practices and incentives.

C. Purpose

This interim policy is intended to promote environmental compliance by providing greater certainty as to EPA's enforcement response to voluntary self-evaluations, and voluntary disclosure and prompt correction of violations. The policy further provides guidance for States and local authorities in encouraging this behavior among regulated entities.

Federal laws and regulations set minimum standards for protecting human health and achieving environmental protection goals such as clean air and clean water. EPA will continue to uphold these laws through vigorous enforcement actions that appropriately penalize violators. Penalties help ensure a level playing field by ensuring that violators do not obtain an unfair economic advantage over their competitors who made the necessary investment in compliance. Penalties also promote protection of the environment and public health by encouraging adoption of pollution prevention and recycling practices that limit exposure to liability for pollutant discharges and deterring future violations by the violator and others.

At the same time, the Agency recognizes that we cannot achieve maximum compliance without the cooperation of a regulated community willing to act responsibly by detecting, disclosing, and correcting violations. Already, regulated entities have many compelling incentives to implement environmental management/auditing systems, as noted in EPA's 1986 auditing policy. Indeed, recent surveys show that the vast majority of large companies engage in environmental auditing and/or have environmental management systems in place. Nonetheless, EPA has concluded that the additional incentives in this interim policy will further promote the regulated community's commitment to adopting systems for maximizing compliance.

D. Principles for Voluntary Compliance

The interim policy that EPA is announcing today is based on seven principles:

1. Self-policing by regulated entities can play a crucial role in finding, fixing and preventing violations.
2. Violations discovered through self-policing should be disclosed and promptly corrected.
3. Regulated entities that self-police and that voluntarily disclose and self-correct violations in accordance with this policy should be assessed penalties that are consistently and predictably lower than penalties for those who do not.
4. Regulated entities that self-police and voluntarily disclose and self-correct violations in accordance with this policy should also not be recommended for criminal prosecution.
5. Providing predictable incentives for voluntary disclosure and correction of violations identified through self-policing offers a positive alternative to across-the-board privileges and immunities that could be used to shield criminal misconduct, drive up litigation costs and create an atmosphere of distrust between regulators, industry and local communities.
6. EPA should not seek voluntary environmental audit information to trigger an investigation of a civil or criminal violation of environmental laws.
7. To preserve a level playing field, EPA should recover any economic benefit realized from violations of environmental law.

E. Relationship to Emerging Standards

EPA also recognizes the development of and growing reliance on international voluntary environmental management standards in the U.S. and other countries. These standards, if properly crafted and implemented, can provide a powerful tool for organizations to improve their overall compliance with environmental requirements and move beyond compliance through innovative approaches to pollution prevention. In addition to issuing this interim policy, EPA will continue to pursue a dialogue with interested parties and to pilot policy approaches through programs such as the ELP to determine how EPA can make use of and encourage these standards.

II. Interim Policy

A. Definitions

For purposes of this interim policy, the following definitions apply:

"Environmental auditing" has the definition given to it in EPA's 1986 policy on environmental auditing, i.e. "a systematic, documented, periodic and objective review by regulated entities of facility operations and practices related to meeting environmental requirements."

"Environmental audit report" means all documentation of information relating to an environmental audit, but not including the factual information underlying or testimonial evidence relating to such information.

"Regulated entity" means any entity, including a federal, state, and municipal facility, regulated under the federal environmental laws that EPA administers.

"Self-evaluation" means an assessment, not necessarily meeting all the criteria of a full environmental audit, by a regulated entity of its compliance with one or more environmental requirements.

"Voluntary" means not required by statute, regulation, permit, order, or agreement.

B. Conditions

The conditions for reducing civil penalties and not making criminal referrals in accordance with Sections II.C. and II.D. of this interim policy are as follows:

1. *Voluntary self-policing.* The regulated entity discovers a violation through a voluntary environmental audit or voluntary self-evaluation appropriate to the size and nature of the regulated entity; and

2. *Voluntary disclosure.* The regulated entity fully and voluntarily discloses the violation in writing to all appropriate federal, state and local agencies as soon as it is discovered (including a reasonable time to determine that a violation exists), and prior to (1) the commencement of a federal, state or local agency inspection, investigation or information request; (2) notice of a citizen suit; (3) legal complaint by a third party; or (4) the regulated entity's knowledge that the discovery of the violation by a regulatory agency or third party was imminent; and

3. *Prompt correction.* The regulated entity corrects the violation either within 60 days of discovering the violation or, if more time is needed, as expeditiously as practicable; and

4. *Remediation of imminent and substantial endangerment.* The regulated entity expeditiously remedies any condition that has created or may create an imminent and substantial endangerment to human health or the environment; and

5. *Remediation of harm and prevention of repeat violations.* The regulated entity implements appropriate measures to remedy any environmental harm due to the violation and to prevent a recurrence of the violation; and

6. *No lack of appropriate preventive measures.* The violation does not indicate that the regulated entity has failed to take appropriate steps to avoid repeat or recurring violations; and

7. *Cooperation*: The regulated entity cooperates as required by EPA and provides such information as is reasonably necessary and required by EPA to determine applicability of this policy. Cooperation may include providing all requested documents and access to employees and assistance in any further investigations into the violation.

Where appropriate, EPA may require that to satisfy any of these conditions, a regulated entity must enter into a written agreement, administrative consent order or judicial consent decree, particularly where compliance or remedial measures are complex or a lengthy schedule for attaining and maintaining compliance or remediating harm is required.

C. Reduce Civil Penalties for Voluntarily Disclosed and Promptly Corrected Violations

1. Incentive

Regulated entities will be eligible for the following reductions in civil penalties:

a. EPA will eliminate all of the gravity component of the penalty for violations by regulated entities that meet conditions 1 through 7 outlined in Section II.B., except for violations involving (i) criminal conduct by the regulated entity or any of its employees, or (ii) an imminent and substantial endangerment, or serious actual harm, to human health or the environment.

b. EPA may mitigate up to 75% of the unadjusted gravity component of the penalty, taking into account any of conditions 1–7 in Section II.B. that are met, in the following cases:

(i) cases in which most but not all of the conditions in Section II.B. are met; or

(ii) cases involving an imminent and substantial endangerment, but not serious actual harm, in which all the conditions in Section II.B. are met; or

(iii) cases involving the disclosure of criminal conduct in which all the conditions in Section II.B. are met.

c. EPA will retain its full discretion to recover any economic benefit gained as a result of noncompliance to preserve a "level playing field" in which violators do not gain a competitive advantage through noncompliance. However, EPA may forgive the entire penalty for violations which meet conditions 1 through 7 outlined in Section II.B. and, in EPA's discretion, do not merit any penalty due to the insignificant amount of any economic benefit.

2. Discussion

a. Providing a clear and significant reduction in civil penalties for companies that assume responsibility for finding, disclosing and correcting violations will create a strong incentive for regulated entities to prevent or fix violations before EPA expends enforcement resources. The policy states clearly the conditions under which EPA will forgive all or part of the gravity component of a penalty for voluntary disclosure and correction;

b. The policy appropriately preserves the concept of recovering economic benefit, except where it is insignificant, as recommended by a broad spectrum of commenters, including industry commenters;

c. Retaining EPA's discretion to collect the gravity component of the penalty in appropriate cases, such as where a violation involves criminal conduct, or imminent and substantial endangerment, will help to deter the most egregious environmental violations. At the same time, by preserving flexibility to reduce the gravity element by up to 75% for good faith efforts to disclose and promptly comply even in those cases, the policy will retain an appropriate compliance incentive.

D. Limit Criminal Referrals for Voluntary Disclosure and Correction of Violations

1. Incentive

EPA will not recommend to the Department of Justice that criminal charges be brought against a regulated entity where EPA determines that conditions 1–7 in Section II.B. above for reduction of civil penalties are met, and the violation does not demonstrate or involve (1) a prevalent corporate management philosophy or practice that concealed or condoned environmental violations; (2) high-level corporate officials' or managers' conscious involvement in or willful blindness to the violation; or (3) serious actual harm to human health or the environment. This policy does not apply to criminal acts of individual managers or employees. Where EPA determines pursuant to this Section that a criminal referral to the Department of Justice is unwarranted, EPA may nonetheless proceed with civil enforcement in accordance with Section II.C. of this policy or other applicable enforcement response and penalty policies.

2. Discussion

The policy will promote candid and thorough self-policing by providing greater certainty as to how EPA will exercise its criminal investigative discretion to encourage voluntary disclosure and prompt correction by regulated entities.

E. Eliminate Routine Requests for Audit Reports in Pre-Enforcement Proceedings

1. Incentive

EPA will not request a voluntary environmental audit report to trigger a civil or criminal investigation. For example, EPA will not request an audit in routine inspections. Once the Agency has reason to believe a violation has been committed, EPA may seek through an investigation or enforcement action any information relevant to identifying violations or determining liability or extent of harm.

2. Discussion

a. This policy makes clear that EPA will not routinely request audit reports. At the same time, the policy in no way limits the right of regulated entities to claim common law privileges (e.g., attorney-client and work product) as appropriate. EPA believes that this clarification, along with the other incentives in this interim policy, should greatly reduce any perception that environmental audits may be used unfairly in environmental enforcement.

b. With respect to federal facilities, although federal facility environmental audit reports may be accessible to the public under the Freedom of Information Act (FOIA) in certain circumstances, EPA cannot utilize FOIA to request information from other federal agencies. Thus, EPA will apply this policy on requests for audit reports to federal (and state and municipal) facilities the same as it does for other regulated entities.

F. Applicability

This interim policy applies to violations under all of the federal environmental statutes that EPA administers and supersedes (unless otherwise noted) any conflicting or inconsistent provisions in the media-specific penalty or enforcement response policies and EPA's 1986 Environmental Auditing Policy Statement. Existing enforcement policies will continue to apply in conjunction with this interim policy, except where inconsistent with this policy. In addition, where appropriate, EPA's Supplemental Environmental Project Policy may at EPA's discretion be applied in conjunction with this policy.

III. Favor These Incentives Over Broad Privileges and Immunities

This interim policy offers a positive alternative to across-the-board privileges and immunities that could be used to shield criminal misconduct, drive up litigation costs and create an atmosphere of distrust between regulators, industry and local communities.

A. Discussion

1. Penalty immunity provisions for voluntary disclosures of violations can give lawbreakers an economic advantage over their law-abiding competitors. It makes sense to give substantial penalty reductions for those who come forward with their violations and promptly correct them, but to maintain a level playing field, the federal and state governments must be able to recoup the economic benefit of violations.

2. A principal rationale for environmental audit privileges and penalty immunities for voluntary disclosures is to reduce the exposure of regulated entities that conduct self-evaluations *and act on the findings by immediately correcting violations.* EPA has addressed this concern with the incentives for disclosure and correction outlined above.

3. Privilege runs counter to efforts to open up environmental decisionmaking and encourage public participation in matters that affect people's homes, workplaces and communities.

4. An environmental audit privilege could be misused to shield bad actors or to frustrate access to crucial factual information.

5. Environmental audit privileges and penalty immunities could encourage increased litigation as opposing lawyers battle over what is privileged or immune from penalties and what is not. Litigation over the scope of the privileges and immunities could burden our already taxed judicial system, drain government and private resources, and in some cases prevent quick action to address environmental emergencies.

6. The Supreme Court has noted, "privileges are not lightly created nor expansively construed for they are in derogation of the search for the truth." *United States* v. *Nixon*, 418 U.S. 683, 710 (1974). Moreover, the self-evaluation privilege has regularly and uniformly been rejected by the courts in cases where documents were sought by a governmental agency.

IV. Consequences for States

EPA recognizes that states are important partners in federal enforcement, and that it is desirable to create a climate in which states can be innovative. At the same time, EPA is required to establish a certain minimum consistency in federal enforcement, so that the sanctions a business faces for violating federal law do not depend on where the business is located.

Accordingly, to maintain national consistency:

A. EPA will scrutinize enforcement more closely in states with audit privilege and/or penalty immunity laws and may find it necessary to increase federal enforcement where environmental self-evaluation privileges or penalty immunities prevent a state from obtaining:

1. information needed to establish criminal liability;

2. facts needed to establish the nature and extent of a violation;

3. appropriate penalties for imminent and substantial endangerment or serious harm to human health or the environment, or from recovering economic benefit;

4. appropriate sanctions or penalties for criminal conduct and repeat violations; or

5. prompt correction of violations, and expeditious remediation of those that involve imminent and substantial endangerment to human health or the environment.

B. EPA will bring to the state's attention any provisions of state audit privilege and/or penalty immunity statutes that raise any of the concerns outlined above, and will work with the state to address those concerns and ensure that federal requirements are satisfied.

V. Limitations on Applicability of This Policy

This interim policy sets forth internal guidelines which amend EPA's penalty policies in situations involving voluntary self-policing, disclosure and correction. In conjunction with the applicable penalty policy, these guidelines will aid EPA personnel in proposing appropriate penalties or negotiating settlements in administrative and judicial enforcement actions. The interim policy also serves to structure the Agency's enforcement authority and states the Agency's view as to the proper allocation of its enforcement resources. Deviations from these guidelines, where merited, are authorized so long as the reasons for the deviations are documented.

This interim policy is not final agency action, but is intended solely as guidance. It is not intended, nor can it be relied upon, to create any rights enforceable by any party in litigation with the United States. EPA officials may decide to follow the guidance provided in this interim policy or to act at variance with the guidance based on analysis of case-specific facts and circumstances. Application of this policy to the facts of any individual case is at the sole discretion of EPA and is not subject to review by any court. In addition, the policy has no effect on the calculation of any cleanup costs, remedial costs, natural resources damages or emergency response costs associated with a violation. EPA reserves the right to change this interim policy at any time without public notice.

Dated: March 30, 1995.

Steven A. Herman,

Assistant Administrator for Enforcement and Compliance Assurance.

[FR Doc. 95–8218 Filed 3–31–95; 8:45 am]

BILLING CODE 6560–50–P

Memorandum: Environmental Criminal Conduct Coming to the Attention of Agency Officials and Employees

Environmental Protection Agency (September 21, 1987)

UNITED STATES ENVIRONMENTAL PROTECTION AGENCY
WASHINGTON, D.C. 20460

SEP 21 1987

OFFICE OF ENFORCEMENT AND COMPLIANCE MONITORING

MEMORANDUM

SUBJECT: Environmental Criminal Conduct Coming To The Attention Of Agency Officials And Employees

FROM: Thomas L. Adams, Jr.
Assistant Administrator

TO: Assistant Administrators
Regional Administrators
Deputy Regional Administrators
Associate Enforcement Counsels
Program Enforcement Directors
Regional Counsels I-X

It is important that all acts of the regulated community exhibiting actual or suspected environmental criminal conduct which come to the attention of any employee of the Agency be referred to the Office of Criminal Investigations for review and possible investigation. I urge each of you to communicate this policy regularly to all of the employees under your supervision. It should also be included in any new employee orientation or training that you conduct.

It is not expected or desired that your staff attempt an in depth legal analysis of whether environmental criminal conduct occurred. The highly trained Special Agents in the Office of Criminal Investigations will do that with the help of attorneys in the Office of Criminal Enforcement Counsel, the Office of Regional Counsel and the Environmental Crimes Section of the Department of Justice. However, in order for employees to recognize possible environmental criminal conduct generally and whether the case is meritorious, the factors listed below should assist their efforts. In addition, my office will help provide training to your staff in this essential area of enforcement.

FACTORS TO CONSIDER IN DETERMINING WHETHER
A MATTER SHOULD BE REFERRED FOR CRIMINAL INVESTIGATION

1. Knowing or Willful Behavior. All federal environmental statutes require some degree of intent or voluntariness (usually expressed in the statute as "knowingly" or "willfully") before a criminal case can be proved. Prosecutions under the Clean Water Act can be prosecuted also for simple negligent acts (carelessness) without demonstrating intent, although such situations are generally of lower prosecutorial priority than are knowing

violations. Almost every federal environmental statute expresses the type of mental state required to be shown for an act to be criminally punishable.

When statutes, such as the environmental laws, are enacted for the purpose of protecting public health and welfare, and especially in subject areas where there is a strong likelihood of protective governmental regulation, the government generally only has to prove that a person knew what he was doing and he did it voluntarily, not accidentally, in order to establish the state of mind required for a conviction. It is not necessary to show that he actually knew what the law required or that he acted with the specific purpose of violating that law. Also, the knowledge necessary for a criminal conviction may be proven circumstantially; it need not always be shown directly. For example, while there may be no direct evidence (such as a statement by the defendant) that he knew a particular material was a hazardous waste, a document found in his file describing it as such would be good circumstantial evidence of knowledge. Thus employees should be alert to indirect indicators of knowledge and other elements of the offense.

2. <u>Elements of the Offense</u>. In addition to the required degree of intent, each statutory offense consists of a number of other elements, each one of which must be proved. For example, the crime of disposal of hazardous wastes without a permit in violation of RCRA § 3008 (d) requires the government to prove beyond a reasonable doubt that (1) a person (2) knowingly (3) disposed of (4) any hazardous waste listed or identified by characteristic (5) without a permit. Similarly, every environmental offense must be analyzed in terms of its component elements.

Determining whether the required degree of intent and each of the elements of the offense exists and can be proven sometimes entails a complex legal analysis which should be left to the investigators and their attorneys. When faced with a possible criminal case where the intent may be marginal, it is best to advise employees to err on the side of caution and refer the matter for the investigators and attorneys to analyze.

3. <u>Impact on Government's Regulatory Function</u>. Many of EPA's regulatory systems rely heavily on complete and accurate voluntary reporting from the regulated community. When information or documents required to be filed are falsified, concealed or intentionally destroyed, the integrity of the system is in danger. The degree to which an act may have threatened or damaged the system is another factor that can be weighed in the decision to prosecute, but is not a requirement.

4. <u>Harm</u>. The extent of harm or threat of harm to human health or the environment is another factor that is reviewed to determine whether a case should be prosecuted. Prosecutors may look at the duration of the harm or threat, the toxicity of the

pollutants involved, and the proximity to population centers, among others. Proof of harm is not a prerequisite to prosecution, but is a factor considered in exercising prosecutorial discretion.

5. Patterns or Practices. It is useful to review a subject's historical record of noncompliance before prosecution. The past practices of a company, whether good or bad, can weigh heavily in sentencing, thereby effecting its deterrent value and prosecutorial merit.

6. Deterrence. A major value of criminal prosecution in an environmental enforcement context is its ability to deter others from doing the same type of act for fear of being prosecuted themselves. For the deterrence to be effective, others similarly situated must become aware of the prosecution. In some areas, one criminal conviction with appropriate penalties can motivate much of the regulated industry to be in compliance. Although this factor is considered, it is not a prerequisite for prosecution.

OTHER CONSIDERATIONS

The factors discussed above are not exclusive and are not in any particular order of importance. Many of the factors overlap. How to weigh the various factors in any given case will depend on the circumstances involved.

It is possible that an event involving environmental criminal activity will not be investigated further or prosecuted. There are innumerable reasons for this including, for example, lack of prosecutorial merit, inadequate proof, the matter would be better handled civilly or administratively, the state is prosecuting the matter, the matter is not commensurate with Agency priorities, and lack of resources. However, if the Office of Criminal Investigations determines that criminal activity occurred after formally opening a case investigation, only the United States Attorney (or his representative) in the District or the Department of Justice can decline to criminally prosecute the case.

If a potential environmental criminal matter comes to the attention of an employee, consultation with the Office of Criminal Investigation should be sought at the earliest opportunity. When in doubt, it is far better to consult with the Office of Criminal Investigations on matters that may be questionable than to risk the possibility of overlooking or failing to recognize serious environmental criminal conduct.

Memorandum: Regional Enforcement Management: Enhanced Regional Case Screening

Environmental Protection Agency (December 3, 1990)

UNITED STATES ENVIRONMENTAL PROTECTION AGENCY
WASHINGTON, D.C. 20460

DEC 3 1990

OFFICE OF ENFORCEMENT

MEMORANDUM

SUBJECT: Regional Enforcement Management: Enhanced Regional Case Screening

FROM: James M. Strock
Assistant Administrator

TO: Regional Administrators
Assistant Administrators

The Enforcement Four Year Strategic Plan and the Enforcement in the 1990's project identify several shifts in direction and emphasis that are essential to meeting demands on enforcement over the next several years. This memorandum implements regional case screening for innovative and balanced use of the full range of enforcement authorities called for in the Strategic Plan to be fully operational by Fiscal Year 1991.

Regional case screening and the use of screening committees or other processes to accomplish its objectives are not unfamiliar subjects within EPA. Most Regions already have in place systems for communication and coordination among program enforcement staff, Regional Counsel, Environmental Service Divisions and the criminal investigators on enforcement case selection, development, and follow through. Regions will nonetheless need to be prepared to adjust existing management systems to include those aspects of case screening which are not presently being adequately addressed. At the same time as this office strongly recommends the use of formal enforcement screening committees, we also encourage the Regions to continue to review and revise their overall management systems and organizations to meet Administrator Reilly's high expectations for enforcement. We will share successful management approaches across Regions and use the occasion of program reviews and our OE Regional Counsel audits to assess how various approaches are working.

This memorandum describes: 1) the objectives of case screening; 2) requirements for a regional case screening capability, including the use of case development worksheets to aid the screening process for selected cases; 3) the recommended use of regional case screening committees; 4) the relationship between enforcement case screening and regional strategic planning; and 5) oversight of the screening process.

I. The Objectives of the Regional Enforcement Case Screening Process

Enforcement case screening is a process to link the characteristics of the violator or violations in a particular case with the right response from among alternative courses of action. The concept is not a one-time "screening in" or "screening out" but a continuing process with elements of both. It identifies where decisions must be made, where there may be good candidates for a particular enforcement approach, and where the course of action is or is not clear. It is not intended to preclude or substitute for early and ongoing consultation within Regions, with Headquarters, or with the Department of Justice where appropriate.

Enhanced case screening may operate within existing program guidance on appropriate enforcement response. It need not alter accountability for enforcement, nor who should develop enforcement actions. It should, however, bring to bear, on individual case decisions, a broader perspective on the goals and objectives of enforcement. The premise is that enforcement decisions must not be made unilaterally; the decision-making process must take into account the full panoply of alternatives. This guidance introduces a systematic means of introducing these other factors into the normal case decision process. Civil enforcement issues would be raised to the appropriate program Division Director and Regional Counsel in their traditional line management roles, with conflicts to be resolved at the DRA/RA level. Criminal enforcement issues would be resolved in accordance with the March 28, 1989 memorandum from Edward E. Reich entitled "Planning and Priority-Setting in the Criminal Enforcement Program".

Regional enforcement case screening objectives include, and cases should be systematically screened for, the following:

1. <u>the strategic value of undertaking federal enforcement</u>;

whether the case furthers specific national, Regional or state environmental goals articulated in strategic plans and operating guidance; whether the case reflects appropriate state/federal roles; and the extent to which the case reduces public health risk, protects the environment, prevents pollution or enhances deterrence.

2. <u>the appropriate enforcement response</u>;

whether administrative, civil judicial or criminal enforcement is most appropriate (See attachment 1 for criteria when judicial enforcement may be favored; bullet below for essential discussion of criminal enforcement screening).

3. <u>the appropriate, considered use of innovative settlement conditions or tools</u>;

whether to seek environmental auditing, pollution prevention, contractor listing, suspension and debarment, and whether to leverage broader compliance with outreach, publicity, training, and/or other requirements in enforcement settlements. (See attachment 2 for criteria where innovative settlement terms and tools may be favored);

4. <u>potential multi-media and cross-statutory action</u>; (which may alter the course any single program might otherwise pursue); and

examining multi-media violation status, multi-media compliance history, alternative statutory authorities which might better address a problem, multi-media impacts of proposed settlements and the need for triggering a multi-media team inspection in support of a possible and desirable multi-media enforcement case. (See attachment 3 for further discussion of these factors); and

5. <u>effective integration of criminal and civil enforcement</u>;

reviewing violations for criminal enforcement potential, criminal enforcement leads for priority, the criminal case/investigatory docket for the need for parallel or solely civil proceedings, and criminal cases for innovative use of sentencing and/or probation requirements. (See attachment 4 for further discussion of these factors).

The case screening management structure established to implement enhanced case screening also may have benefits in facilitating the commitment and allocation of resources in support of enforcement cases and in prioritizing cases in circumstances of competing resource demands.

<u>Violations subject to case screening</u> are those potentially suitable for federal enforcement, including those state-lead cases for which the targets for timely and appropriate enforcement response have been exceeded, violations of AOs and/or Consent Decrees, referrals by the State, or other federal-lead violations arising from self-reporting and inspections. (<u>Violations handled</u>

by field citations issued in the field are not subject to this process). These violations should be screened as early as possible following identification so that undue delays are not encountered or opportunities foreclosed. Further, screening can be a sequential or tiered process. For example, screening for appropriate enforcement response, innovative approaches, or multi-media perspective would, in the vast majority of cases, follow a decision that a federal enforcement response is warranted.

II. Structure for Enforcement Case Screening

OE has a strong preference for the use of face-to-face case screening committees. We believe, following consultation with the Regions and review of their experiences to date, that it is the most effective means to meet the screening goals outlined above. However, Regions may choose variant processes that will work best in their own particular circumstances, provided they meet the criteria noted below.

A. Criteria for on Acceptable Case Screening Process

In implementing the enforcement case screening capability, several criteria must be achieved:

1. Decisions on case screening should not be unilateral[1].

2. There should be an effective cross-media capability for coordinating multi-media enforcement initiatives, information on compliance status and histories, making timely decisions on case consolidation, and/or devising settlement conditions involving more than one media.

3. There should be an effective civil/criminal coordination capability to address not only potential criminal enforcement actions and priorities but also the need for parallel or alternative civil enforcement proceedings to address environmental harm. The capability should ensure timely and ongoing access to information which allows independent judgment and direct involvement of appropriate staff with expertise in the review of those cases:

(a) all violations should be reviewed by media program enforcement personnel for criminal enforcement potential;

(b) violations which cross the threshold (see Attachment 4) for criminal enforcement potential are screened both:

---

[1] For a discussion of the meaning of this criterion with regard to criminal enforcement, see Attachment 4, paragraph 2.

(1) by those with criminal enforcement responsibility; and

(2) by media program enforcement personnel.

The method chosen is a matter of Regional discretion, but must reflect the sensitivity of access to criminal enforcement information.

4. Internal policies and procedures should be in place to reinforce screening factors noted here. The use of case screening worksheets described below is an indispensable part of this process.

B. <u>Case Screening Worksheet</u>

The attached worksheet, or revised worksheet(s) tailored to a particular Regions's use, is part of the internal policies and procedures required for an effective regional screening capability. These worksheets are a complement to -- not a substitute for -- the very important face-to- face interactions among key players at appropriate points in the screening process. We envision that they would be used early in the case screening process to help assess what further screening and consultations might be necessary and to help identify early how an enforcement case will be developed. Who completes the worksheet is up to each Region to decide.

Elements may be added or the format of presentation adjusted to facilitate use, but the questions on the attached worksheet and substance must be retained. However, the assessment of criminal enforcement potential may not be altered without consultation with the Office of Criminal Enforcement Counsel, since it is carefully presented to avoid compromising a criminal case during discovery. We caution the Regions to exercise discretion in possibly generating discoverable material during the course of screening committee sessions. The case screening worksheet has been designed with this in mind.

The worksheets provide a systematic means of ensuring that staff explicitly consider the potential for innovative enforcement settlement conditions and tools, a multi-media perspective, and criminal enforcement potential in conjunction with other factors traditionally considered in determining the appropriate enforcement response. It introduces background information on compliance history within the same program and in other programs as well as information on the toxics release inventory for the facility. The worksheets build on the pilot system implemented in Region I.

While the issues raised by the worksheets may have to be revisited at various stages in a case, most factors should be initially considered as early as possible in the process. The worksheets are to be retained as a formal part of case files to facilitate periodic assessments of how the process is working and to help improve our process over the coming years.

C. Focusing and Phasing Case screening

While all cases are "screened" to the extent that strategic value is considered at some point in the process and the appropriate enforcement response defined and reassessed, as necessary, over the course of case development, there are ways in which the Regions can phase in and focus, the enhanced case screening envisioned here:

1. Although we are encouraging Regions to examine multi-media compliance history, it will not be required until the OE data integration project is completed because of the amount of work involved in obtaining violation histories from all media. The OE data integration project should be completed by January 1, 1991.

2. The Toxics Release Inventory (TRI) is an important means of identifying high risk circumstances and the potential for pollution prevention to reduce significant risk at a facility which may be agreed upon through an enforcement settlement negotiation. Since use of the TRI is new to most regional office staff, Regions may establish their own criteria for cases for which TRI data will be sought. However, we would expect movement toward increasing integration of this data.

3. Cases can be packaged and reviewed in summary fashion where the cases present similar violations and violator characteristics. This may be particularly helpful for handling a group of cases involved in an enforcement initiative. Single and multi-media compliance status should still be assessed at individual facilities covered by such an initiative since such information may affect settlement terms with the facility. However, this information may be assessed after such cases are initiated where the Region decides that a packaged and timely single-media initiative is the preferred enforcement response for those violations.

4. Regions may further focus their case screening efforts by defining categories of violations and violators and specific objectives which they do not believe would benefit from the review and accompanying worksheets proposed here. These exclusions from analysis should not be unilateral, in keeping with the spirit of the screening process itself. The screening committee itself is best suited to identify such exclusions. Only those violator/violation categories for which there is no significant, identifiable benefit from the objectives listed should be considered for exclusion. Thus,

no enforcement case should be excluded from screening for current cross-media violations and multi-media impacts of any resulting remedy. Further, cut-offs based solely upon penalty amounts or type of enforcement action (i.e. administrative or judicial enforcement) are not appropriate.

5. Regions with particularly large caseloads in which case screening would represent a substantial initial investment by regional staff, may phase-in screening through the first half of the fiscal year. In any event, by the end of the second quarter of FY 1991 all violations subject to case screening defined in Section I above, must be part of the process.

OE recognizes that one outcome of case screening may be a regional decision not to pursue federal enforcement or to defer action based upon strategic value considerations. OE requests Headquarters programs to review current reporting and tracking systems to assess whether new or revised procedures may be desirable or needed to explicitly address such violations.

D. **Initiation of Criminal Investigations in Cases of Ongoing Releases or Discharges**

Prior to the initiation of a criminal investigation [2] where there is an apparent violation involving the release, discharge, or emission of a contaminant or pollutant which may continue during the course of the investigation [3] an extra degree of coordination and inter-program review is needed. Furthermore, where there is an apparent or potential violation involving the release, discharge, or emission of a contaminant or pollutant which may continue during the course of the criminal investigation, the SAC after consultation with the RCEC, before opening criminal investigation, must inform the Regional program personnel of his intention to open a criminal investigation, providing sufficient information to enable them to assess the facts. The SAC should simultaneously provide, on a continuing

---

[2] This policy is also intended to include cases where there may be no ongoing exposure but the risk or threat of harm is plain. Examples of such cases include improper storage of ignitable or reactive waste, an eroding lagoon, and falsification of drinking water data.

[3] Consistent with Attachment 4, paragraph 2, some initial investigatory actions may commence without such prior coordination if necessary to further characterize the situation.

basis, non-Grand Jury [4] evidence of an ongoing release or discharge which violates EPA requirements.

Regional program technical staff must be consulted regarding whether an ongoing release or discharge in fact does or may present an unacceptable level or risk of harm before the conclusion of the criminal case. Their evaluation of the probable risk is crucial.[5]

The RCEC's role is as a catalyst and counsellor to encourage coordinated Regional decision making regarding criminal enforcement, and, where a consensus is reached to advise on the best legal procedures to obtain the desired results. The RCEC will also help by assuring that the Regional case screening process works well and that any dispute is elevated and resolved.

III. Recommended Case Screening Approach

OE has developed a recommended approach to enforcement case screening. We recommend that Regions establish formal screening committees to coordinate enforcement activities and screen enforcement cases. See Charts 1 (a-c) for the proposed regional screening structure and Chart 2 for existing regional mechanisms.

---

[4] Furthermore, should the criminal investigation result in Grand Jury evidence which demonstrates that an ongoing release or discharge of a pollutant or contaminant in fact does or may present an unacceptable level or risk or harm before the conclusion of the criminal case, OCI shall forthwith discuss with the Government attorneys assigned to prosecute the case whether to seek judicial approval to disclose this evidence to the civil authority. Note that some such information derived from non-Grand Jury proceedings may also require special handling and similar restrictions to those posed by Grand Jury proceedings, for example, if from a confidential source or from an undercover operation.

[5] Sworn law enforcement officers have a duty to report to DOJ apparent criminal violations by an identifiable person. While Headquarters or Regional managers cannot veto a criminal investigation, they can participate in the setting of appropriate priorities among various leads, and their opinion can differ regarding the advisability of a criminal investigation. Should there be a difference of opinion within EPA regarding the relative priority of a criminal investigation or its advisability, before seeking from DOJ a prosecutive determination the parties shall follow the dispute resolution procedure referenced above.

9

It should be noted that most of the Regions are considering revisions to their current systems in keeping with the Strategic Plan requirement for case screening.

1. **Continued reliance on initial screening on a single media basis, supported by case worksheets to promote awareness and consideration of broader strategic concerns:**

In all Regions, there are regular meetings between Regional Counsel and program enforcement staff. Screening takes place on a single media program basis in meetings comprised principally of the Enforcement Branch or Section Chiefs of the Program Divisions and Regional Counsel. We believe that for reasons of efficiency and respect for the level of knowledge of the case at issue, this level of screening must remain the fundamental point at which most of the screening takes place. If not already adopted, we propose that these meetings be formalized as enforcement case screening committees which meet at least monthly. They would continue to review violations in detail for appropriate enforcement response, including identification of any judicial, criminal or multi-media concerns, and the strategic value of any proposed action.

Particular attention must be paid by these groups to determining whether judicial enforcement is appropriate, whether there are criminal and multi-media enforcement issues, and whether the facility's compliance history (viewed from a multi-media perspective) and the nature of the violation merit the use of innovative techniques. To do this, case screening worksheets will help to turn policy to daily practice by translating criteria for case screening into something that will be considered on an ongoing basis within the Region. The worksheets will ensure that those cases most deserving of multimedia considerations will be adequately reviewed for referral to a multi-media process.

2. **Multi-media Screening Committee:**

It is also proposed that the Deputy Regional Administrator, as the primary enforcement contact within the Region, convene monthly a multi-media screening committee comprised of all key Regional managers on enforcement matters. This group would likely include the Regional Counsel, possibly with Regional Counsel Branch Chiefs, Enforcement Branch Chiefs and/or Program Division Directors, the Associate Regional Administrator, as appropriate, and Environmental Service Division Director. This group would review, in detail, cases identified as having a multi-media concern. Regional Counsels' offices can provide a useful bridge between the single and multi-media screening committees by helping to prepare agendas based upon those cases identified during single media screening as having multi-media enforcement potential. Review of cases by the multi-media screening group should not unduly delay processing of single-media cases. As a group, the multi-media committee also could review proposed judicial enforcement actions for a pattern of strategic value, or areas missing a judicial presence.

Several Regions currently have this type of multi-media screening committee structure in place devoted to case screening. Other Regions have multi-media meetings with a broader agenda but at which these multi-media coordination issues may be discussed if they arise; still other regions are actively considering multi-media screening meetings. It is possible that the Regional Counsel could fulfill this function if there is sufficient capability to identify multi-media concerns, assisted with the proposed case worksheets. Nevertheless, the multi-media committee is recommended here to provide region-wide leadership that will facilitate a cross-media approach to facility non-compliance -- we believe it will best serve to meet the Administrator's goal of 25% multi-media cases. It also provides an opportunity for groups such as the ESDs and programs with broad authorities to offer new perspectives on how the agency might better address certain types of violations.

3. Criminal/Civil Integration Screening:

To assure proper integration of civil and criminal enforcement, we offer several approaches. Each includes timely and ongoing access to information for staff with criminal enforcement expertise in the review of cases with any criminal enforcement potential.

Ideally, the Special Agent-in-Charge (SAC)[6] their designees and/or the Regional Criminal Enforcement Counsel (RCEC) would be a part of the deliberations in the single media screening committees (see Chart 1b). However, in most Regions this would prove impractical given the number of programs meeting each month and the sizable number of violations being screened with no criminal enforcement potential. The Regions also could use the current routine meetings with the SAC or RAC and RCEC as a third level of case screening committee (see Chart 1a). The scope of review in most of these meetings has not been as broad as that proposed here. Specifically, this guidance envisions review of the full range of violations which have been identified through the civil enforcement process for criminal enforcement potential (in detail for those above a threshold with periodic reviews of the basis for threshold determinations) (see Attachment 4), review of criminal leads and investigations for priority and review of the need for parallel or alternative civil enforcement. Another approach could provide a documented process of case-by-case consultation on any

---

[6] As used in this guidance, "SAC" also includes Resident Agents-in-Charge, "RAC".

cases with criminal enforcement potential with either the SAC or RCEC (see Chart 1c). This would be supplemented with the use of the current routine reviews of the criminal enforcement docket. All three versions are presented in the Charts.

If a Region attempts to institute screening without face-to-face meetings, it will become even more important for the SAC and RCEC to be kept apprised of the status of regional enforcement cases to provide the necessary judgments on the agency's course of action in particular cases.

The challenge presented by criminal case screening is that it cannot be a one-time event. At any time during the development of a "civil" case, information gathering, discovery, etc., may disclose evidence of criminal conduct requiring the SAC or RCEC to coordinate with and seek a prosecutorial judgment by DOJ. Similarly, during the development of a "criminal" case OCI may develop evidence of sufficient environmental harm that would necessitate commencement of a civil action seeking injunctive relief, requiring consultation and coordination with regional technical program staff and ORC civil attorneys. The regional process should reflect this need for ongoing criminal/civil enforcement integration and appropriately caveat any determinations as to the preferred agency response based upon the stage of review and availability of evidence.

IV. Relationship Between Strategic Planning and Case screening

The more effectively we carry out the strategic planning function, the easier case screening will become. Through strategic planning, the Region can target, in advance, repeat violators for innovative settlement conditions or use of contractor listing, facilities deserving of multi-media inspections and follow up enforcement, geographic areas, pollutants, industries or facilities of concern. Further, a significant violation in one program may lead to a decision to investigate further for its multi-media case potential given the nature of the source and the violation. The least disruptive approach would stress early identification of such opportunities.

Regions also should make use of Headquarters targeting information and early identification of where judicial legal or program precedents are needed in a program area.

V. Oversight of the Screening Process

The Regions are asked to report on their approach to case screening in the FY 1991 Regional Enforcement Strategic Plan submission to OE at the end of the first quarter FY 1991. As the regional systems evolve over the year, we request that OE be kept apprised of any changes. The regional systems should be fully operational by the end of the second quarter FY 1991.

In addition, our Regional Counsel audits, along with those we conduct in cooperation with the Headquarters program offices of regional program operations, will review implementation of this guidance, including use of case screening worksheets, and how effective different approaches are in meeting our screening objectives.

****

In closing, enhanced enforcement case screening by the Regions, in conjunction with strategic planning, is central to meeting the challenges and achieving the new directions we have set for our enforcement program. The Administrator's goals for criminal enforcement and multi-media cases, outlined in his September 25, 1990 Address to the Senior Executive Service, make institution of effective screening all the more urgent. I look forward to continuing to work with the Regions in finding the most effective and efficient ways to see these activities implemented.

Attachments

cc: Deputy Assistant Administrators
Headquarters Compliance Directors
F. Henry Habicht II
Nancy Firestone
Daniel C. Esty

bcc: OE Managers

Attachment 1

Choosing between administrative or judicial enforcement

For reasons of efficiency, administrative enforcement will continue to be the norm in programs with adequate administrative enforcement penalty authority. Screening must provide the necessary impetus to evaluate whether cases which would otherwise be handled administratively, are deserving of judicial action. Factors to be included in a determination of whether judicial enforcement is appropriate include:

- the degree to which the case merits a strong signal of the agency's resolve in dealing with violations posing significant environmental harm or risk given the nature, magnitude, duration of the violation;

- the size of the proposed penalty, particularly in relation to any statutory caps;

- compliance history both within the program and in other programs with particular view toward the need for increased penalty assessment or judicial response to violations of Administrative Order and Consent Decree conditions;

- the need for the greater deterrent value of. judicial as compared to administrative enforcement in sending a message to the source or to the regulated community, particularly from the publicity surrounding judicial action, and including consideration of the expectation that the facility will or will not comply with an administrative order.

- whether the firm or source category is targeted by Headquarters or the Regions for coordinated enforcement initiatives.

- whether legal or program precedents are needed;

- whether the judiciary may be needed to oversee a particular remedy or to impose injunctive relief;

- where there is a repeat violator within or among media programs.

- whether consolidating multi-media violations require a judicial forum to join enforcement procedures.

- whether there is criminal enforcement potential (see attachment 4).

- need for extensive discovery which may be more available in judicial cases.

14

Attachment 2

Identifying candidates for innovative settlement terms or enforcement tools.

Each of the following innovative settlement conditions or enforcement tools should be explicitly considered and used in either administrative or judicial cases where the benefits could justify potential delays in case resolution or additional regional resources.

- **potential for waste minimisation or pollution prevention:** pollution prevention conditions in enforcement settlements are particularly encouraged where 1) elimination or substitution of chemicals offers the best chance to end recurring violations; 2) there would be no negative crossmedia impacts; there are known technological and economically feasible options for pollution prevention.

- **potential for leveraging the single enforcement action to reach the broader regulated community** through source outreach, communications and/or training opportunities. This is particularly encouraged where the category of source or type of violation is one which has a particular compliance or environmental problem or one which is difficult for the agency to detect;

- **need for correction of underlying management problems through the use of an environmental audit provision or use of contractor listing**, or of suspension and debarment warranted by the type of violation and compliance history;

- **potential value of contractor listing to correct a recurring or ongoing violation in air or water or suspension and debarment to address repeat violators in any program.**

Attachment 3

Ensuring a multi-media case screening perspective

1. **Multiple violations at a single facility:** The Regions should have a system in place for identifying violations in more than one program and for making explicit decisions as to the merits of consolidating cases or adjusting proposed settlement terms (e.g. penalty calculations and audit provisions) before commitments are made to pursue administrative or judicial enforcement in any one program.

2. **Multi-media impacts of proposed settlement conditions:** Violations may involve only one media program, but the remedies or the impacts may involve other programs, requiring permits or other approvals for implementation. The Region should have a system in place to identify such cases and to initiate the necessary coordination and support across divisional lines.

3. **Multi-media compliance history:** Regions should screen selected cases for facility compliance history in other programs as well as the program attempting to address a particular violation. Violators with a history of multi-media violations are candidates for increased penalty assessments and special settlement conditions such as environmental auditing to address underlying problems leading to a poor performance record. Also, because compliance monitoring is not always conducted at a frequency to allow detection of violations, multi-media violation history may be an indication of more significant media specific problems than those identified. Screening for multi-media facility violation history will be facilitated by the completion of OE's data integration project. Specific firms with a poor compliance record nationally may be identified by OE Headquarters targeting information and should be taken into account as well.

4. **Selection of best statutory approach:** Some environmental problems are best addressed by using other statutory provisions than those available within the program in which the violation was identified. The Region should establish procedures for identifying when these other statutory authorities should be considered and how such decisions are to be made. Problems posed by groundwater contamination, and toxic chemicals are prime examples.

5. **Coordinated inspection planning/enforcement initiatives:** Regional systems should provide a mechanism for deciding whether to initiate multi-media team inspections when investigating a violation in a single program. Such inspections would be initiated for prime candidates for possible multi-media case development. Systems should also provide for coordination of case screening considerations for multi-media enforcement initiatives.

Attachment 4

Integrating civil and criminal enforcement activities:

All violations ripe for possible federal enforcement with criminal enforcement potential should be reviewed for possible criminal violations; proposed criminal cases should likewise be reviewed for needed injunctive relief. Criminal enforcement cases with multi-media aspects should be identified with systems in place to coordinate case development, sentencing and probation terms.

1. **Reviewing proposed violations for criminal enforcement potential.**

There should be some opportunity for the SAC and/or RCEC to review all violations beyond a certain threshold for possible criminal enforcement. The threshold for review by personnel with criminal enforcement responsibility is as follows:

The presence of both (a) misconduct which threatens accomplishment of a specific nationwide or regional EPA program goal or priority (determined by reading EPA's Operating Year Guidance, as supplemented by the stated priorities of the EPA Regions), and (b) any one or more factors indicating aggravated environmental misconduct, specifically, one or more of the following:

(1) history of repeated violations;

(2) potentially deliberate, knowing or willful misconduct;

(3) concealment of misconduct or falsification of required records, including failure to report where another aggravating factor is present;

(4) tampering with monitoring or control equipment;

(5) business operations of pollution-related activities without a required permit, license, manifest, or other authorizing documentation; or

(6) actual illegal discharge, release, or emission, or other facts demonstrating the presence or potential for harm to the environment or human health.

The larger the number of EPA priorities threatened, or number of aggravating factors present, the less serious any single priority or factor must be.

Regional program staff and attorneys should be encouraged to discuss any potential criminal enforcement cases with the RCEC and/or SAC. In general, the planning process for identifying program priorities for criminal enforcement is described in a memorandum from Edward E. Reich, March 28, 1989, entitled, "Planning and Priority-Setting in the Criminal Enforcement Program."

2. **Reviewing criminal enforcement leads/investigations for program priority.**

With the growth of the criminal enforcement program, it is essential that communications between the criminal and civil enforcement program provide an understanding of how criminal enforcement can most effectively further a program' s environmental and compliance goals. However, Special Agents must bring to the attention of DOJ any substantial evidence of a crime by an identifiable suspect, and DOJ exercises independent prosecutorial judgment with regard to all evidence of criminality which comes to their attention. Despite the caveat that only DOJ may terminate a formal criminal investigation matter, the regional program and Regional Criminal Enforcement Counsel must be asked by the SAC to screen and comment on the potential benefits of all cases deriving from leads and leads received by the Special Agents. Such consultation is not intended to preclude initiation of investigatory activities needed to characterize the situation, for screening purposes.

If the Regional program or legal personnel involved in screening believe that a different case is a greater investigative priority or that a particular case is not appropriate for prosecution, while at the same time DOJ is requesting OCI's investigative assistance on that particular case that it views as appropriate for prosecution (or the SAC disagrees with the EPA screening committee or already has evidence of criminality), the SAC is not free to act unilaterally. Instead, the SAC shall activate the internal EPA dispute resolution procedure before referring the case to DOJ or seeking from DOJ a prosecutive determination. The outcome of the EPA dispute resolution procedure determines whether EPA will not invest further resources in a criminal investigation, which DOJ then may decide to pursue independently.

3. **Reviewing the criminal case docket for the need for parallel civil proceedings.**

If there is the possibility of: 1) an imminent and substantial endangerment, and/or 2) apparent violation involving an ongoing discharge or release that may cause harm during the processing of a criminal enforcement action, it is essential that the Regional program office and ORC civil personnel be informed by criminal enforcement personnel in a timely manner. The program should have an opportunity to request either that a parallel civil enforcement action be pursued, that criminal action not be pursued in favor of civil action, or that the program be closely involved in the progress of the criminal enforcement action, including the design of terms of probation and recommended sentencing and contractor listing or suspension and debarment considerations.

4. Reviewing criminal enforcement cases for sentencing provisions and potential probation requirements

The screening process for integrating criminal and civil enforcement needs to include a review of the criminal docket by the program and regional counsel staff of affected offices to assist in developing and recommending terms for sentencing and probation that properly reflect the source's compliance history and environmental concerns.

Chart 1a
RECOMMENDED REGIONAL ENFORCEMENT CASE SCREENING COMMITTEES

11/90	single media civil case screening	multi-media case screening	civil/criminal integration
who	Program Enforcement Branch / Section Chief Regional Counsel Branch Chief	Deputy Regional Administrator Regional Counsel Environmental Service Division Regional Division Directors or program enf. Branch or Section Chiefs: RC and Program	RC Criminal Enforcement SAIC/RAIC Regional Division Directors or Enforcement Branch/Section Chiefs
what	Violations potentially suitable for Federal Enforcement: e.g. AO and CD violations; State referrals; state-lead violations exceeding timely and appropriate response targets; repeat violators Application of Regional Thresholds and HQ Guidance	Cases w/multi-media violations Cases w/ multi-media impacts Cases w/ multi-media violation history Cases targeted for multi-media inspections	Criminal Leads Criminal Docket Potential criminal cases (civil docket in summary)
how often	monthly	monthly	monthly/as cases with criminal potential are identified
why	No Action/Admin/Judicial Enf. Potential criminal enforcement Application of innovative tools or settlement conditions Multi-media implications	Potential Consolidation of Multi-media cases Coordination of cases with multi-media impacts/settlements Review judicial case profile in general for strategic value Coordination of multi-media enforcement initiatives	Criminal leads for priority Criminal docket for civil enforcement requirement Selected individual cases for criminal case potential

Chart 1b

RECOMMENDED REGIONAL ENFORCEMENT CASE SCREENING COMMITTEES

11/90

	single media civil case screening	multi-media case screening
who	Program Enforcement Branch / Section Chief Regional Counsel Branch Chief RC Criminal Enforcement or SAIC/RAIC	Deputy Regional Administrator Regional Counsel Environmental Service Division Regional Division Directors or Program Enf. Branch or Section Chiefs: RC and Program RC Criminal Enforcement or SAIC/RAIC
what	Violations potentially suitable for Federal Enforcement: e.g. AO and CD violations; State referrals; state-lead violations exceeding timely and appropriate response targets; repeat violators Application of Regional Thresholds and HQ screening guidance	Cases w/multi-media violations Cases w/ multi-media impacts Cases w/ multi-media violation history Cases targeted for multi-media inspections
how often	monthly	monthly
why	No Action/Admin/Judicial Enf. Application of innovative tools or settlement conditions Multi-media implications Potential criminal enforcement Criminal leads for priority Criminal Docket for civil enforcement requirement	Potential Consolidation of Multi-media cases Coordination of cases with multi-media impacts/settlements Review judicial case profile in general for strategic value Coordination of multi-media enforcement initiatives

civil/criminal integration

Chart 1c

RECOMMENDED REGIONAL ENFORCEMENT CASE SCREENING COMMITTEES

11/90

	single media civil case screening	multi-media case screening
who	Program Enforcement Branch / Section Chief Regional Counsel Branch Chief	Deputy Regional Administrator Regional Counsel Environmental Service Division Regional Division Directors or Program Enf. Branch or Section Chiefs: RC and Program
what	Violations potentially suitable for Federal Enforcement: e.g. AO and CD violations; State referrals; state-lead violations exceeding timely and appropriate response targets; repeat violators Application of Regional Thresholds and HQ screening guidance	Cases w/multi-media violations Cases w/ multi-media impacts Cases w/ multi-media violation history Cases targeted for multi-media inspections
how often	monthly	monthly
why	No Action/Admin/Judicial Enf. Application of innovative tools or settlement conditions Multi-media implications Potential criminal enforcement	Potential Consolidation of Multi-media cases Coordination of cases with multi-media impacts/settlements Review judicial case profile in general for strategic value Coordination of multi-media enforcement initiatives

civil/criminal integration

- o Document consultation with criminal enforcement personnel on threshold cases with criminal enforcement potential
- o Use of routine meetings for review of criminal docket and leads

8/14

CHART 2: CURRENT REGIONAL SCREENING STRUCTURES

Regions	I	II	III	IV	V	VI	VII	VIII	IX	X
I. Single media meetings/ committees										
A. Who meets:										
Program Division Director								4	x	x
Program Branch/Section Chief for Enforcement	x	x	x	x	x	x	x	x	x	x
Regional Counsel Branch Chief	x	x	x	x	x	x	x	x	x	x
ESD	4			4			x	x		x
Criminal SAIC/RAIC/OCI				x						
DRA/RA			x				x	4		x
RC/DRC			x			x	x	4	x	x
B. How often:	mo	mo	mo	mo	mo	mo	mo	mo	mo	mo
C. Issues Addressed:	1									
Admin/Judicial Civil	x	x	x	x	x	x	x	x	x	x
Innovative tools/settlements	x						x	x		x
Criminal Enforcement potential	x		x		x		x	x	x	x
Multi-media potential/issues	x		x		x		x	x	x	x
II. Multi-media\ meetings/Committee (Civil)										
A. Who meets:										
DRA			x			3	3	x	3	x
RC	x	x	x			3	3	x	3	x
Division Directors						3	3	x	3	x
Program Branch/Section Chief for Enforcement		x	x		x			x		x
Regional Counsel Branch Chiefs	x	x	x		x			x		
ESD		4				3	3	x		x
Criminal SAIC/RAIC		x						x	3	
B. How often:	2mo	2mo	mo		2mo	mo	wk	Q	Q	mo
C. Issues Addressed:										
Admin/Jud Civil	x	x	2		x			x	3	
Innovative tools/settlements	x							x	3	x
Criminal Enforcement potential							3	x	3	x
Multi-media potential/issues	x	x			x		3	x	3	x
Data Integration/Information		x	x		x		x		3	x
III. Criminal/Civil Enforcement Relationship Meetings/ Committee										
A. Multi-media?	N	Y	N	N	N	Y	Y	Y	N	
B. Who meets:										
DRA		x	x		x	x	x	x		
RC/criminal attorney	x	x	x		x	x	x	x	x	
Division Director/Deputy Division Director	x	x			5	x	x			
Program Branch/Section Chief for Enforcement	x		x	x	5	x			x	
Regional Counsel Branch Chief				x			x		x	
ESD						x	x			
Criminal SAIC/RAIC	x	x	x	x	x	x	x	x	x	
C. How often:	mo	2mo	mo	mo	mo	mo	Q	mo	mo	
D. Issues Addressed:										
Civil Docket for Criminal				x	x	x	x	x	x	
Criminal Docket for Civil		x		x	x	x	x	x		
Priority of Leads		x	x	x	x			x		

Footnotes:
1) Worksheets foster consideration of these factors in all cases.
2) Only proposed judicial referrals are discussed.
3) Meeting is opportunity for screening but it is not sole purpose.
4) May attend as observer.
5) Meeting is expanded every other month to include specific program participation.

Initial Enforcement Case Screening Worksheet[1]

Based on information as of (date) revised revised
Name of Violator
Address

Violation

Type of Business/Manufacturing Process: (SIC?)
(Including indication of whether violator is a federal contractor/owner/operator or American Indian tribal gov't

Repeat Violator in same program? Identify violations:

Recurring Violation ?
Continuing Violation ?

Violations under other statutes or programs?
statute: Violation: (known or suspected) current enforcement?

Multi-media impacts of violation or remedy?

Toxics Release Inventory:
media: total: chemical substances:

Pollution Prevention Potential:
a. Toxics Release Inventory reduction potential? _____
b. Recurring violation amenable to pp? _____
c. Known feasible pp option? _____
d. Program guidance/other? _____

Environmental Auditing Conditions Potential:
a. Underlying management problems likely? _____
b. Likely pattern of violation at other facilities? _____

Contractor Listing Potential:
a. Recurring/continuing viol. of CAA/CWA _____
b. Prior or existing enforcement Action _____
c. Multiple viol. facilities by same owner _____

Suspension and Debarment:
a. Poor Performance _____
b. Misconduct/Lack of Integrity _____
c. Repeat Violators _____

Civil Judicial Enforcement Potential:
a. legal or program precedent _____
b. need to show resolve: signif. harm/risk _____
c. repeat or multi-media violator _____
d. need deterrence message of judicial action _____
e. judiciary needed:oversee remedy/impose relief _____
f. desire to consolidate multi-media case _____
g. substantial penalty _____

Multi-media Potential:
a. Current Violations _____
b. Multi-media impacts _____
c. Multi-media History of non compliance _____
d. Use of other authorities _____

Innovative Settlement Approaches:
a. ADR potential _____
b. Field Citation potential (notice with settlement) _____

Leveraging broad Deterrence:
a. Industrial sector w/ compliance problems? _____
b. Likelihood that training, _____
publicity, _____
technical assistance _____
would enhance compliance?
c. Critical Habitat/geographic area? _____

Criminal Enforcement Potential:[2]
a. potential document falsification
b. unauthorized discharge/emission/shipment or release
c. monitoring or control equipment tampering
d. potentially deliberate/intentional/knowing
e. repeated violations
f. priority violation for criminal enforcement

1 This is a pre-decisional document protected by the deliberative process and attorney work product privileges (and may also be a privileged attorney-client communication). Conclusions or recommendations are intended solely as preliminary information for government personnel. This worksheet contains tentative conclusions and staff-level recommendations and does not create any rights, substantive or procedural, or defenses, as they are not binding on the Agency or DOJ.

2 See also civil judicial enforcement potential criteria which may favor either a civil or a criminal enforcement response the choice between those options being a matter of degree. Evidence of any of these factors, whenever identified, will be screened by the appropriate representatives of the Office of Criminal investigations and regional criminal enforcement attorney.

Memorandum: Initiation of Criminal Investigations in Cases Presenting an Issue of First Impression

Environmental Protection Agency (October 22, 1990)

UNITED STATES ENVIRONMENTAL PROTECTION AGENCY
WASHINGTON, D.C. 20460

OCT 22 1990

OFFICE OF ENFORCEMENT

MEMORANDUM

SUBJECT: Initiation of Criminal Investigations in Cases Presenting an Issue of First Impression

FROM: James M. Strock
Assistant Administrator

TO: Director, National Enforcement Investigations Center
Assistant Director for Criminal Investigations
Special Agents-in-Charge and Resident Agents-in-Charge
Acting Director, Office of Criminal Enforcement
Regional Counsels
Regional Criminal Enforcement Counsels and Contacts

This protocol sets forth additional procedures to be followed prior to the initiation of a criminal investigation where an issue (either factual or legal) of first impression is evident.[1] Experience has shown that the resolutions of such issues may have national and cross-Regional significance. Where there is no past experience to build on, and given the extra burdens of prevailing on such issues in criminal cases (where legal requirements must be clear and unambiguous and where facts must be proved beyond a reasonable doubt), such issues deserve extra consideration at the Headquarters level.

An "issue of first impression" is one which has not previously arisen in a federal environmental case where the

---

[1]When opening a criminal investigation in a case where there was apparent environmental misconduct by a federal employee or government contractor, or otherwise involving a federal facility, the Special Agent-in-Charge in the originating Region shall inform NEIC's Assistant Director for Criminal Investigations and the Director of OCE. Even though such a case may not be within the definition of a case of first impression, it is important that OE management receive an early alert in such a case. The Assistant Administrator must be fully informed before inquiries are received from interested persons, including officials of the federal agency involved.

enforceable requirement is new (contained in a statute or regulation that is newly amended or enacted by Congress or promulgated by EPA; "new" means effective on or after January 2, 1990). This case opening procedure will apply as well to the first case proposed for each new provision of a statute or regulation that becomes effective after the issuance of this policy. Further, an issue of first impression could arise in the context of the application of any statute or regulation, including one which has been used in the past, to new or unfamiliar circumstances. However, since this last category by definition depends upon judgment, I will not seek to further define it here, instead relying upon the regular communications between our agents and our attorneys.

Whenever a criminal investigation is opened in any case, the Special Agent-in-Charge[2] first shall consult with the Regional Criminal Enforcement Counsel or Contact (RCEC). Furthermore, before opening a criminal investigation in a case of first impression, the SAC in the originating Region shall request the analysis and recommendations of the RCEC, and the SAC shall request concurrence in the case opening by NEIC's Assistant Director for Criminal Investigations. The Assistant Director will then inform OCE's Director of the issue and consult with him regarding it.

To assure confidentiality, the RCEC's legal analysis and recommendations shall be in a separate document from the RCEC to the Director of OCE, with a copy to the Region's SAC. Completion of OCE's case review will be expedited by the early request and prompt submission of the RCEC's memorandum. The Director of OCE may consult with others in the Region, EPA Headquarters, and the Department of Justice. OCE will endeavor to complete the case review within two weeks; in every situation, the review shall be completed as expeditiously as possible.

During OCE's case review period, the Regional case screening process should continue, and any dispute should be elevated and resolved as set forth in the memorandum from the then-Acting Assistant Administrator entitled "Planning and Priority-Setting in the Criminal Enforcement Program" (March 28, 1989).[3] A

---

[2]"Special Agent-in-Charge" (SAC) includes Resident Agent-in-Charge (RAC).

[3]Sworn law enforcement officers have a duty to report to DOJ apparent criminal violations by an identifiable person. While Headquarters or Regional managers shall not veto a criminal investigation, they can participate in the setting of appropriate priorities among various leads, and their opinion can differ regarding the advisability of a criminal investigation. Should there be a difference of opinion within EPA regarding the relative

preliminary inquiry may continue without being affected by this protocol and the time for opening an investigation case file will be deferred. In the event of exigent circumstances OCI may take whatever action (such as open an investigation case file and execute a search warrant or make an arrest) as it deems necessary.

cc: Deputy Administrator
Regional Administrators
Deputy Regional Administrators

---

priority of a criminal investigation or its advisability, before seeking from DOJ a prosecutive determination the parties shall follow the dispute resolution procedure.

Memorandum: Policy Statement on Scope of Discharge Authorization and Shield Associated With NPDES Permits

Environmental Protection Agency (July 1, 1994)

UNITED STATES ENVIRONMENTAL PROTECTION AGENCY
WASHINGTON, D.C. 20460

JUL - 1 1994

MEMORANDUM

SUBJECT: Policy Statement on Scope of Discharge Authorization and Shield Associated with NPDES Permits

FROM: Robert Perciasepe
Assistant Administrator for Water

Steven A. Herman
Assistant Administrator for Enforcement

Jean C. Nelson
General Counsel

TO: Regional Administrators
Regional Counsels

Recently, questions have been raised regarding EPA's interpretation of the scope of the "shield" associated with National Pollutant Discharge Elimination System (NPDES) permits under the Clean Water Act (CWA). Section 402(k) of the CWA -- the "shield" provision -- provides that compliance with an NPDES permit shall be deemed compliance, for purposes of section 309 and 505 enforcement, with sections 301, 302, 306, 307 and 403 of the CWA (except for any standard imposed under section 307 for toxic pollutants injurious to human health). This policy statement describes EPA's position on the scope of the authorization to discharge under an NPDES permit, and the shield thus associated with the permit authorization.

Individual NPDES Permits

As part of an application for an individual NPDES permit, EPA requires that an applicant provide information on its facility. In the case of industrial permit applications, this includes specific information about the presence and quantity of a number of specific pollutants in the facility's effluent, as well as on all waste streams and operations contributing to the facility's effluent and the treatment the wastewater receives. Applications for municipal discharges focus primarily on the operation and treatment processes at the municipal treatment works. See 40 C.F.R. § 122.21.

Historically, EPA has viewed the permit, together with material submitted during the application process and information in the public record accompanying the permit, as important bases for an authorization to discharge under section 402 of the CWA. The availability of the section 402(k) shield is predicated upon the issuance of an NPDES permit and a permittee's full compliance with all applicable application requirements, any additional information requests made by the permit authority and any applicable notification requirements. See 40 C.F.R. §§122.41(l) and 122.42 Also see, 45 Fed. Reg. 33311-12, 33522-23 (May 19, 1980).

A permit provides authorization and therefore a shield for the following pollutants resulting from facility processes, waste streams and operations that have been clearly identified in the permit application process when discharged from specified outfalls:

1) Pollutants specifically limited in the permit or pollutants which the permit, fact sheet, or administrative record explicitly identify as controlled through indicator parameters;[1]

2) Pollutants for which the permit authority has not established limits or other permit conditions, but which are specifically identified as present in facility discharges during the permit application process; and

3) Pollutants not identified as present but which are constituents of wastestreams, operations or processes that were clearly identified during the permit application process.[2]

With respect to subparts 2 and 3 of the permit authorization described above, EPA recognizes that a discharger may make changes to its permitted facility (which contribute pollutants to the effluent at a permitted outfall) during the effective period of the NPDES permit. Pollutants associated with these changes (provided they are within the scope of the operations identified in the permit application) are also authorized provided the discharger has complied in a timely manner with all applicable notification requirements (see 40 C.F.R. §§ 122.41(l) and 122.42(a) & (b)) and the permit does not otherwise limit or prohibit such discharges.

---

[1] Of course, authorization is only provided to discharge such pollutants within the limits and subject to the conditions set forth in the permit.

[2] The permit, of course, may explicitly prohibit or limit the scope of such discharges.

- 3 -

Notwithstanding any pollutants that may be authorized pursuant to subparts 1 and 2 above, an NPDES permit does not authorize the discharge of any pollutants associated with wastestreams, operations, or processes which existed at the time of the permit application and which were not clearly identified during the application process.

General NPDES Permits

Section 402(k) also shields discharges of pollutants authorized under a general permit. EPA's position is that general permits authorize the discharge of all pollutants within the specified scope of a particular general permit, subject to all pollutant limits, notification requirements and other conditions within a particular general permit so long as the permittee complies with all EPA application requirements for the general permit.

EPA regulations provide the circumstances for which discharges may be authorized under a general permit. See 40 C.F.R. §122.28. To obtain authorization to discharge under a general permit (and consequently, the protection of the shield), in most cases, the prospective permittee must submit either a written notice of intent to be subject to the general permit or a permit application as appropriate. General permittees are also subject to the notification provisions of 40 C.F.R. §§ 122.41 and 122.42.

Spills

While NPDES permits may authorize the discharge of pollutants associated with intermittent flows, permits do not generally authorize the discharge of pollutants associated with spills. There may be limited circumstances where anticipated spills are fully disclosed to EPA and considered during the permitting process as documented in the public record consistent with applicable NPDES regulations. In such circumstances, the discharge of pollutants from such spills would be authorized so long as the permit does not otherwise limit or prohibit such discharges and such a spill does not violate any statutory or regulatory provision.

CERCLA

Finally, there also has been some question regarding the relationship of the NPDES permit shield and the "federally permitted release" exemption under the Comprehensive Environmental Response, Compensation, and Liability Act (CERCLA).

EPA's position is that the scope of federally permitted releases under CERCLA section 101(10)(A), (B) and (C) is currently defined by the regulations at 40 C.F.R. § 117.12, which implement language in section 311 of the CWA that is very similar to the federally permitted release definitions. Thus, the Agency takes the position that the NPDES permit shield outlined above in no way expands the scope of the federally permitted releases under CERCLA.

Next Steps

The Office of Water has established two regulatory workgroups which are working on revisions to the NPDES permit application regulations for municipal and industrial dischargers. We want the regulations to ensure the applicant has the responsibility to more fully characterize the nature of its effluent, and the contributions of the effluent to the receiving water. In addressing this issue, we will review EPA's position on the scope of the shield provided by §402(k). In addition, we will consider changes to related NPDES permit regulations, including whether to revise the requirements for: facilities to notify EPA (or the State) of modifications to its operations or processes; facilities to notify EPA (or the State) of changes in the discharge; notification to the public of the nature of the discharge limitations a permittee is held responsible for; and the use of indicator pollutants.

We encourage the Regions to actively participate in the development of these updated regulations. The current schedule calls for proposal of the changes to the municipal application requirements in 1994 and promulgation of the revised regulations in 1996. Our new schedule for changes to the industrial application requirements, for which there is more interest in permit shield issues, is proposal of the regulation changes in FY 1995.

If you have any questions on these issues, please contact us or have your staff contact, Cynthia Dougherty in the Office of Water at 202 260-9545, David Hindin in the Office of Enforcement at 202 501-6004, or Richard Witt in OGC at 202 260-7715.

cc: Elliott P. Laws
Regional Water Management Division Directors
ORC Water Branch Chiefs
Lois Schiffer, DOJ
Joel Gross, DOJ

Memorandum: Determining Whether State Hazardous Waste Management Requirements Are Broader in Scope or More Stringent Than the Federal RCRA Program

Environmental Protection Agency (May 21, 1984)

UNITED STATES ENVIRONMENTAL PROTECTION AGENCY
WASHINGTON D C 20460

9541.1984 (4)

MAY 21 1984

OFFICE OF
SOLID WASTE AND EMERGENCY RESPONSE
PIG-84-1

MEMORANDUM

SUBJECT: Determining Whether State Hazardous Waste Management Requirements are Broader in Scope or More Stringent than the Federal RCRA Program

FROM: Lee M. Thomas
Assistant Administrator for
Solid Waste and Emergency Response (WH-562-A)

TO: PIGs Addresses

Issue

How does EPA determine whether a requirement of an authorized State hazardous waste program is broader in scope or more stringent than the Federal RCRA program?

Discussion

The March 15, 1982 Program Implementation Guidance memorandum from William Sullivan entitled "EPA Enforcement of RCRA-Authorized State Hazardous Waste Laws and Regulations" (PIG-82-3) outlined EPA policy on enforcement of Federal and State hazardous waste management requirements in States with cooperative arrangements or authorized RCRA programs.

The Guidance concluded that State-imposed requirements which are beyond the scope of coverage of the Federal program are not part of the Federally approved program (40 CFR 271.1(i) and 271.121(1)). Consequently, such requirements are not enforceable by EPA. PIG 82-3 also concluded that "provisions in State programs which are more stringent than their federal counterparts are, nevertheless, a part of the approved State program and are enforceable by EPA." [Emphasis added.]

Attempts to distinguish between those State requirements that are broader in scope and those that are more stringent than the Federal RCRA program have led to some confusion. The confusion is partly a result of conflicting information in past PIG's on this issue. PIG 81-4, discussing delisting of wastes, indicates that State regulation of more wastes than are regulated by the Federal program would be viewed as a more stringent aspect of the

- 2 -

authorized State program. Similarly, page 7 of PIG 82-3 indicates that "a lesser amount of waste exempted [by the State] from regulation under the small quantity generator exemption" is an example of a more stringent State program requirement. In contrast, page 6 of PIG 82-3 states that the listing by a State of wastes which are not included in the Federal universe is an example of a provision that is broader in scope.

Decision

To determine whether a particular requirement or provision of a State program is "broader in scope" (and therefore not a part of the authorized program) or more stringent (and therefore a part of the authorized program) the questions discussed below should be answered sequentially.

(1) Does imposition of the State requirement increase the size of the regulated community beyond that of the Federal program?

A State requirement that does increase the size of the regulated community is more "extensive", not more stringent, and is an aspect of the State program which goes beyond the scope of the Federally-approved program. Examples of requirements that are broader in scope include:

- a lesser amount of waste exempted from regulation under the small quantity generation exemption;

- listing of wastes which are not in the Federal universe of wastes.

Thus, the examples discussed in PIG 81-4 and on page 7 of PIG 82-3 should have been interpreted as requirements that were broader in scope and not more stringent. (While this guidance corrects these two examples, it does not change the policies and other examples of PIGs 81-4 and 82-3).

If the requirement does not increase the size of the regulated community, the following question should be asked.

(2) Does the requirement in question have a direct counterpart in the Federal regulatory program?

- 3 -

If the State requirement does not have a direct Federal counterpart, the requirement is also beyond the scope of the Federal regulatory program. Examples of such State requirements are:

- controls on traffic outside of a hazardous waste facility or specification of transport routes to the facility;
- requirements for the preparation of an environmental impact statement or the approval of a siting board as part of the permit issuance process;
- licensing of transporters.

However, if the requirement of the authorized State program does have a direct Federal counterpart, the State requirement is either equivalent to or more stringent than the corresponding Federal regulation. Examples of more stringent State requirements are:

- limited financial assurance options for facility closure;
- submittal of an annual rather than a biennial report for generators;
- expiration of permits after five years instead of ten.

This guidance supports those enforcement policies outlined in PIG 82-3, and should resolve many of the questions concerning the scope of the Federal and RCRA authorized State regulatory programs. We also anticipate that this guidance will be useful in focusing the scope of EPA oversight of State programs. As PIG 82-3 states, EPA enforces the more stringent provisions of RCRA authorized programs; therefore, EPA has a corresponding responsibility to overview implementation of those aspects of State programs which are more stringent.

Guidelines for Civil and Criminal Parallel Proceedings
Department of Justice (October 13, 1987)

U.S. Department of Justice

Land and Natural Resources Division

Office of the Assistant Attorney General

Washington, D.C. 20530

OCT 13 1987

LAND AND NATURAL RESOURCES DIVISION

DIRECTIVE NO. 5-87

GUIDELINES FOR CIVIL AND CRIMINAL PARALLEL PROCEEDINGS

Most statutes administered by Environmental Enforcement, Environmental Crimes and Environmental Defense Section attorneys authorize the federal government to secure both civil and criminal sanctions for the same illegal conduct. These statutes*/ often provide as well for federally-approved state programs which are enforceable by both state and federal authorities. However, the prospect of a single incident giving rise to both civil and criminal enforcement actions carries potential risks to fair and effective enforcement unless a systematic approach is followed. Therefore, we are establishing guidelines to be used by Division attorneys in handling cases under the statutes administered by the Environmental Enforcement, Crimes and Defense Sections.

---

*/ The Resource Conservation and Recovery Act (RCRA), 42 U.S.C. 6901, et seq.; Comprehensive Environmental Response, Compensation and Liability Act (CERCLA), 42 U.S.C. 9601, et seq.; Clean Water Act, 33 U.S.C. 1251, et seq.; Toxic Substances Control Act (TSCA), 15 U.S.C. 2601, et seq.; Federal Insecticide, Fungicide and Rodenticide Act (FIFRA), 7 U.S.C. 136, et seq.; Clean Air Act, 42 U.S.C. 7401, et seq.; Marine Protection, Research, and Sanctuaries Act, 33 U.S.C. 1401, et seq.; and Rivers and Harbors Act, 33 U.S.C. 401, et seq.

2

I. WHEN BOTH CIVIL AND CRIMINAL ACTIONS ARE POSSIBLE FOR A SINGLE STATUTE, A CRIMINAL PROCEEDING SHOULD GENERALLY BE BROUGHT AND RESOLVED BEFORE A CIVIL ACTION.

The federal courts have routinely approved simultaneous civil and criminal enforcement actions by the government. Whether they are warranted in a particular case depends on the circumstances. For example, the development of a civil case may produce information that non-compliance was intentional, thus justifying a criminal action. Or, a criminal investigation may reveal ongoing regulatory violations warranting interlocutory or accelerated permanent remedial relief. It is imperative that civil and criminal attorneys be alert to potential parallel proceedings as early as possible in the enforcement process. (If, as should be the rare circumstance, criminal violations are only detected after a civil complaint has been filed, a parallel criminal proceeding may be initiated, with due allowance for the limited ability of the government to control the civil court's docket).

When a criminal proceeding is brought, it should generally precede civil actions because of Speedy Trial Act considerations, the more substantial deterrent and punitive effects of criminal sanctions, because courts may reduce criminal sentences after civil penalties have already been imposed, and because conviction in a criminal case can be used as collateral estoppel in favor of the government in a subsequent civil case on the same issues. In the face of a parallel criminal action, the civil case should ordinarily not proceed unless one of the following factors is present:

1. The civil violations are ongoing and of such concern to the public health or to the environment as to call for preliminary or accelerated permanent injunctive or cost recovery relief.

2. The assets of the defendant are in danger of dissipation. <u>See</u> Attorney General Memorandum on Coordination of Criminal and Civil Fraud, Waste and Abuse Proceedings (July 16, 1986).

3. There is only a marginal relationship between the civil violations and the illegal conduct that is the subject of the criminal proceeding.

4. There is an imminent statute of limitations deadline for the filing of a civil action.

II. INFORMATION DEVELOPED BY OR OBTAINED FROM CRIMINAL ENFORCEMENT INVESTIGATORS SHOULD BE SHARED WITH CIVIL ENFORCEMENT ATTORNEYS ONLY IN ACCORDANCE WITH FEDERAL RULE OF CRIMINAL PROCEDURE 6(e).

Criminal investigations are often cooperative efforts. Not only do Environmental Crimes Section attorneys obtain physical and documentary evidence, but the United States Attorney's Office, the FBI and EPA's National Enforcement Investigations Center may also produce information which may be useful to civil attorneys. However, Rule 6(e), which prohibits disclosure of "matters occurring before the grand jury," with narrow exceptions, should always be consulted before any contemplated exchange of information after a grand jury has convened on the matter under investigation. The following factors should guide collection and dissemination of information compiled in criminal investigations:

1. Where possible, evidence should be obtained by methods other than grand jury subpoena, such as searches and interviews. Records from federal, state and local governments should not be requested pursuant to grand jury subpoenas until other avenues have been exhausted. See Attorney General Memorandum on Coordination of Criminal and Civil Fraud, Waste and Abuse Proceedings.

2. Prior to presentation to a grand jury, investigators should ordinarily be asked to summarize or segregate, to the extent possible, the evidence obtained up to that time, including witness interviews. Similarly, prosecutors should keep a record of all evidence obtained independently of the grand jury.

3. When information is not subject to Rule 6(e), either because no grand jury has met or because the information would not disclose "matters occurring before the grand jury" (see Part II, 4), Division criminal prosecutors may share all relevant information with federal or state officials pursuing related civil investigations.

4. When Rule 6(e) does apply, only federal prosecutors or supervising attorneys may share grand jury information. Prosecutors may disclose grand jury information to other personnel, such as Department civil attorneys or EPA agents, provided the disclosure is necessary to assist the prosecutor in enforcing federal criminal law and meets the notification requirements of Rule 6(e)(3)(B). These "Rule 6(e) list" persons may not utilize grand jury information for any other purpose. With the permission of the court, prosecutors may

also disclose violations of state criminal law to state officials in accordance with Rule 6(e)(3)(C)(iv).

5. Any other disclosure of grand jury information may be made only on a showing of "particularized need" and pursuant to a court-ordered disclosure sought under Rule 6(e)(3)(C)(i).

6. The law with respect to what constitutes "matters occurring before the grand jury" is complex and unsettled. Accordingly, whenever a grand jury has convened, attorneys should be alert to the possibility that any subsequent disclosure of information related to the grand jury probe, even if the information was not actually presented to the grand jury, could run afoul of Rule 6(e). Department guidance in this respect is available from the Office of Legal Policy's Guide on Rule 6(e) After Sells and Baggot (1984). See also United States v. John Doe, 107 S. Ct. 1656 (1987).

III. EVIDENCE OBTAINED THROUGH CIVIL OR ADMINISTRATIVE DISCOVERY OR INSPECTIONS MAY BE SHARED WITH FEDERAL AND STATE CRIMINAL PROSECUTORS.

The constraint which Rule 6(e) imposes on the exchange of information by prosecutors is absent when the flow of information is from civil to criminal authorities. No codified rule bars the transfer, and the courts have usually permitted it. Mindful that civil discovery may not be used exclusively to further a criminal proceeding, the following rules should be observed:

1. Evidence obtained through past or ongoing civil or administrative discovery may be shared with federal and state criminal prosecutors as long as there was a good faith civil or administrative basis for conducting the discovery.

2. Evidence obtained through administrative inspections may be shared with federal and state criminal prosecutors, provided the inspection was "objectively reasonable," i.e.,

a) supported by administrative probable cause;

b) limited to its normal administrative scope, and

c) authorized either by voluntary consent, an administrative search warrant, or a scheme of "pervasive regulation."

3. Before sharing evidence obtained by any method listed in Part III, 1-2, with criminal authorities, civil attorneys should first submit a brief, written statement to the Section Chief setting forth how Part III, 1 or 2, whichever is appropriate, has been satisfied.

4. Evidence obtained through civil or administrative inquiries without the use of formal discovery or other compulsory means may be shared with prosecutors regardless of whether there was a "good faith" civil basis for seeking the information, as long as the government did not deceive the defendant about its intentions.

IV. MIRANDA WARNINGS ARE UNNECESSARY DURING CIVIL DISCOVERY.

Miranda warnings are required only when "custodial interrogation" occurs. Civil discovery proceedings, including depositions, do not require such warnings because they are not "custodial" settings within the scope of the Fifth Amendment. Therefore, civil attorneys should respond to questions by witnesses about the potential for criminal liability or about other rights as follows:

1. General Rule: A civil attorney, if asked about the possibility of criminal liability by a witness during a deposition, shall respond that "the United States is free to choose civil, criminal or administrative enforcement and any decision to take one type of action does not preclude another type of action."

2. Where a witness in a deposition or interview raises concerns about the right to counsel, self-incrimination or other rights, the civil attorney shall inform the witness that it is inappropriate for a government attorney to offer advice on such matters and shall advise the witness that he is free to consult his own attorney on these matters.

V. ENFORCEABILITY OF GUIDELINES.

These guidelines provide only internal Department of Justice guidance. They do not create any rights, substantive or procedural, which are enforceable at law by any party. No limitations are hereby placed on otherwise lawful prerogatives of the Department of Justice.

6

VI. EFFECTIVE DATE.

These procedures implementing the Division's policy regarding civil and criminal parallel proceedings are effective immediately.

Roger J. Marzulla
Acting Assistant Attorney General
Land and Natural Resources Division

Memorandum: Parallel Proceedings Policy

Environmental Protection Agency (June 22, 1994)

UNITED STATES ENVIRONMENTAL PROTECTION AGENCY
WASHINGTON, D.C. 20460

JUN 22 1994

OFFICE OF
ENFORCEMENT

MEMORANDUM

SUBJECT: Parallel Proceedings Policy

FROM: Steven A. Herman
Assistant Administrator

TO: All Assistant Administrators
All Regional Administrators
All Regional Counsels
General Counsel

This is the Environmental Protection Agency's revised policy on initiating and maintaining parallel enforcement proceedings.[1]

Most statutes administered by EPA include both criminal and civil enforcement authorities, as well as information gathering and inspection provisions. The United States has multiple duties and goals in carrying out the mandates of federal environmental laws, which often can be achieved most effectively through use of several investigative and enforcement options. Thus, it is in the public interest that EPA retain maximum flexibility in the use of its options, consistent with all legal requirements.

---

[1]The following policies are hereby superseded:

Memo, Revised EPA Guidance for Parallel Proceedings, from Edward E. Reich, Acting Assistant Administrator, June 21, 1989;

Guidelines on Investigative Procedures for Parallel Proceedings (attachment to 6/21/89 Memo), prepared by Paul R. Thomson, Jr., Deputy Assistant Administrator for Criminal Enforcement;

Memo, Procedures for Requesting and Obtaining Approval of Parallel Proceedings, from Edward E. Reich, Acting Assistant Administrator for Enforcement, June 15, 1989; and

Memo, Supplement to Parallel Proceedings Guidance and Procedures for Requesting and Obtaining Approval of Parallel Proceedings, from James M. Strock, Assistant Administrator for Enforcement, July 18, 1990.

This policy applies in conjunction with other Agency guidances, where applicable, such as those on case screening, participation in grand jury investigations, and referrals.

As used in this policy, the term "proceedings" includes enforcement actions (both investigation and litigation stages) as well as use of information gathering and entry authorities. "Parallel" means simultaneous or successive civil, administrative and criminal proceedings, against the same or related parties, dealing with the same or related course of conduct.

Principles

1. It sometimes is necessary, appropriate, and a reasonable use of resources to bring a civil (administrative or judicial) enforcement action at the same time as an existing or potential criminal investigation or prosecution concerning the same or a related matter. When, in the course of considering appropriate enforcement options, EPA determines that injunctive relief is necessary to obtain compliance with the law or to impose remedial measures, the pendency of a criminal proceeding is not necessarily a sufficient reason to fail to seek appropriate relief.[2]

2. The government legitimately may seek civil penalties which are punitive (i.e., effect retribution or deterrence). On the other hand, punitive civil penalties may have implications under the Double Jeopardy Clause if they are assessed prior, or subsequent, to a criminal prosecution of the same person for the same violations. Although case law has established that civil penalties which are significant in amount can be assessed without implicating Double Jeopardy concerns, it is preferable to avoid the assessment of federal civil penalties against persons who are likely to be subject to subsequent federal criminal prosecution for the same violations.

3. When an environmental criminal matter is investigated by a grand jury, and EPA personnel obtain access to grand jury information, EPA personnel must take care not to violate the secrecy obligation imposed by law, or to use grand jury information for improper purposes. Although the issue of grand jury secrecy can arise in any criminal case, extra care should be taken in the parallel proceedings context.

---

[2]In some cases, it may be appropriate to delay initiation of a civil enforcement action, and/or to seek a remedial order as a condition of probation, or as a condition of the plea agreement, in the criminal action. These decisions must be made on a case by case basis, taking into account the complications which inevitably arise in parallel proceedings (such as defense attempts to use civil discovery to gain information about a criminal investigation), as well as other case-specific considerations (such as the need to prevent persons from learning that they are targets of criminal investigation) and weighing them against the need for the civil action.

- 3 -

4. EPA's regulatory inspections (administrative searches) must be objectively reasonable, and properly limited within the scope of the authorizing statute and warrant. As in every situation, the government has a duty to act in good faith, and must ensure that its use of administrative entry authorities is properly within the mandates of the Fourth Amendment.

5. EPA's information-gathering authorities must be used in accordance with the authorizing statutory provisions. There is no general legal bar to using administrative mechanisms for purposes of investigating suspected criminal matters, unless otherwise specified in the authorizing statute. However, the government must not intentionally mislead a person as to the possibility of use in the criminal enforcement context of information provided in response to such requests, in such a way as to violate the Fifth Amendment Due Process Clause or the Self-Incrimination Privilege.

Procedures

1. The Regional Counsel and the Special Agent in Charge of the Criminal Investigation Division must concur in the initiation (or continuance) of a civil enforcement proceeding (administrative or judicial), when a criminal proceeding is pending or contemplated as to the same or a related matter.[3] During the pendency of any such civil action, the Regional Counsel and the SAC should consult on a continuing basis, in order to avoid undue duplication of effort and interference by one action with the other.[4] As with other aspects of the case screening process, the regions (and HQ offices, where applicable) have flexibility in designing specific procedures to implement these requirements, and issues may be brought to the attention of the Assistant Administrator where agreement cannot be reached.

---

[3]If the civil enforcement action contemplated is a judicial (rather than an administrative) one, Agency referral policy continues to require that the request for referral of a parallel proceeding to the Department of Justice be routed through EPA-HQ, for Assistant Administrator approval. In other words, the "direct referral" policy does not apply to parallel proceedings. Note also that DOJ policy affects the Agency's ability to pursue a civil judicial action that is related to a pending criminal investigation.

[4]When an EPA Headquarters office has the lead in an enforcement matter, both the Enforcement Counsel who has the civil case, and the Director of the Office of Criminal Enforcement (or delegate), must concur in the civil action. These persons should consult on a continuing basis.

2. When a parallel civil action is brought, a claim for civil penalties may be filed, as necessary, to avoid claim-splitting or statute-of-limitation problems. Normally, however, a civil penalty claim should be stayed (not assessed or collected) as to a person who is a target of criminal investigation, until the criminal proceeding is concluded as to that person.

3. In the parallel proceedings context, open communication should be maintained between EPA personnel assigned to the civil-enforcement or information-gathering matter and those assigned to the criminal case, in a manner consistent with the legitimate confidentiality and grand jury secrecy needs of the criminal enforcement program.[5] However, information relating to matters occurring before a grand jury should not be revealed without prior consultation with the attorney for the government (usually a Department of Justice attorney).

4. Prior to any use of EPA's statutory information-gathering or entry authorities to gather evidence of suspected criminal activity, the Regional Counsel (or the OCE Assistant Director for Legal Affairs, for HQ cases) should be consulted, to ensure that constitutional requirements are met.

Reservation of Rights

This policy provides internal Environmental Protection Agency guidance. It is not intended to, and does not, create any rights or privileges, substantive or procedural, which are enforceable by any party. No limitations are hereby placed on otherwise lawful prerogatives of the Environmental Protection Agency.

cc: All Office of Enforcement and Compliance Assurance Personnel

---

[5]Note that it is good professional practice for enforcement personnel to carefully document the sources of information received and the persons with whom information is shared, whether there is a parallel proceeding or not.

Memorandum: FY 1995 Guidance Document for Enforcement and Compliance Assurance (excerpts)

Environmental Protection Agency (September 20, 1994)

UNITED STATES ENVIRONMENTAL PROTECTION AGENCY
WASHINGTON, D.C. 20460

SEP 20 1994

OFFICE OF
ENFORCEMENT AND
COMPLIANCE ASSURANCE

MEMORANDUM

SUBJECT: FY 1995 Guidance Document for Enforcement and Compliance Assurance

FROM: for Steven A. Herman, Assistant Administrator
Office of Enforcement and Compliance Assurance

TO: Regional Administrators

A memorandum dated June 14, 1994, from Elaine G. Stanley, Director, Office of Compliance, transmitted the draft FY 1995 Guidance Document for Enforcement and Compliance and requested your comments. We appreciate your comments and have revised the document to reflect these comments as well as those received from Headquarters' offices. The final guidance document for developing your FY 95 Regional/Headquarters Memorandum of Agreement (MOA) is attached. This document sets the stage for developing a landmark comprehensive and unified enforcement and compliance plan.

We believe this final document is more reflective of our intent to provide Regions with solid direction in developing a plan to address OECA's strategic objectives for assuring compliance, while also allowing the Regions flexibility to meet these objectives during FY 1995. While recognizing the necessity of maintaining traditional enforcement outputs for deterrence purposes, we must strive to create the appropriate balance, as envisioned by the Administrator, between traditional enforcement activities and innovative approaches for ensuring compliance. Further, we need to ensure that any changes in enforcement activities are balanced with measurable, non-traditional activities which promote compliance. During the last several months the National Enforcement Investigation Center (NEIC) has solicited Regional needs for support on their enforcement program in FY 95. The agreements reached for this support should be reflected in MOA negotiations.

OECA has attempted to incorporate in its MOA process the relevant and successful features of MOA processes run by the Office of Air and Radiation and the Office of Pollution Prevention, Pesticides and Toxics. However, as the Agency's first MOA which integrates enforcement and compliance assurance activities from all of EPA's media programs, the OECA MOA is more comprehensive in scope than the single media MOAs you have developed. As we proceed through this first year of the annual OECA MOA process, all participants should recognize that we are implementing this process for the first time, and that it will be improved as we gain more experience.

When submitting your Regional MOA proposal, please provide two copies to the Planning Branch, of the Enforcement Planning, Targeting and Data Division within the Office of Compliance by **November 4, 1994**. The Planning Branch will facilitate the coordination effort for finalizing and negotiating the MOAs and consulting with other offices within OECA in the process. We expect negotiation on the MOA will be concluded by January 13, 1995. Final signed MOAs will be transmitted to the Regions.

I appreciate your commitment to making the enforcement program stronger and more effective and look forward to working together to achieve this goal. I also want to thank you and your staff for past and future cooperation which has helped OECA get off the ground quickly and effectively. Please address any questions or concerns to Jack Neylan, Chief, Planning Branch, at 202/260-7825.

cc: Assistant Administrators
Deputy Regional Administrators
Regional Counsels
Regional Multi-media Coordinators
OECA Office Directors

FY 95 GUIDANCE FOR THE ENFORCEMENT AND COMPLIANCE ASSURANCE MEMORANDUM OF AGREEMENT PROCESS

I. INTRODUCTION

The purpose of the Headquarters/Regional Memorandum of Agreement (MOA) is to implement a consolidated enforcement and compliance program to promote and achieve EPA's national goals. The process is further expected to enhance Headquarters/Regional partnerships within the new organizational structure, as we work together to strengthen well-established methods of enforcement and develop new approaches to compliance assurance.

The FY 95 MOA guidance that follows begins the transition for developing a comprehensive plan by unifying the enforcement and compliance planning process through the preparation of a single MOA. The development of the FY 95 guidance was necessarily compressed due to the fact that the Office of Enforcement and Compliance Assurance (OECA) was not officially reorganized until June 8, 1994. The development of FY 96 guidance will feature a timely and collaborative priority-setting process involving media programs, Regions, states, and other partners. Such a process was not possible for FY 95.

Our FY 95 guidance and MOA process focuses on building successful enforcement and compliance assurance programs. This approach requires that this guidance define success in enforcement and compliance assurance, and the next section provides that definition.

II. DEFINING SUCCESS IN ENFORCEMENT AND COMPLIANCE ASSURANCE

A successful enforcement and compliance assistance program is one which reflects the following strategic objectives:

1.) Achieves compliance and environmental improvement by using a broad range of tools such as compliance monitoring, expanded outreach, compliance assistance, and civil and criminal enforcement actions;

2.) Maintains an imposing enforcement presence by keeping total enforcement outputs at current levels, assures that violators do not profit from these violations, and ensures vigorous, timely, and high quality enforcement against violations of environmental statutes;

3.) Uses multi-media, whole-facility, sector-oriented, and/or place-based approaches to target remediation, enforcement and compliance assurance activities. Also incorporates environmental justice and pollution prevention into targeting and planning activities.

4.) Moves toward measuring results and the impact of activities in more sophisticated and meaningful ways.

As we proceed into FY 95, the MOA process will be used as a tool to integrate these four OECA objectives with enforcement and compliance assurance priorities identified by Headquarters media programs, Regions, and states. The MOA guidance encourages the use of the full range of tools to achieve compliance, but also recognizes the importance of maintaining traditional enforcement outputs (e.g., civil/administrative/criminal actions and inspections) at the level of previous years. The MOA process will be used to strike a balance between the need to move toward new approaches and the need to maintain traditional outputs.

Among the purposes for which your Region should use the MOA submission are to: request Regional adjustments to previously identified Headquarters media program enforcement priorities (i.e., if that priority is not appropriate for your Region); propose Region specific enforcement priorities not reflected in media-specific enforcement guidance (i.e., if you have identified a Regional environmental problem which can be addressed through use of enforcement and compliance assurance tools); and to propose trade-offs in the use of various tools and activities (e.g., the use of compliance assistance in place of compliance monitoring inspections for a particular initiative, greater use of multi-media cases and reduced production of certain single-media cases). All enforcement and compliance assurance portions of MOAs developed in accordance with media-specific guidance should be attached to this MOA.

This guidance explains how adjustments and trade-offs can be proposed in your MOA submission so they can be discussed in MOA negotiations with OECA.

III. SPECIFIC FY 95 ACTIVITIES AND COMMITMENTS

The following discussion provides additional details for each of the four objectives along with Headquarters support directed to each objective and a request for Regional activities which support the objective. Regions should use this discussion as they develop their individual MOAs and tailor activities and resources to their highest priorities. The MOAs should also reflect and incorporate the agreements reached between the National Enforcement Investigation Center (NEIC) and the Regions for support of Regional activities in FY 95. Section IV presents a format for the Regions to use in preparing and submitting their MOA to Headquarters.

Objective 1: Using a Broad Range of Tools to Maximize Enforcement and Compliance

Description: EPA has a wide variety of tools to use to bring about compliance with the nation's environmental laws. These tools can be seen as a spectrum -- from compliance assistance designed to prevent violations, compliance monitoring to identify violations, administrative and civil litigation to correct and deter violations, and criminal prosecutions to deter noncompliance and to punish violators.

A successful program utilizes the full range of tools to achieve maximum compliance. The selection and application of these tools should be tailored to the specific environmental or noncompliance problem being addressed. For some problems, one tool is appropriate, for others a mix of tools is the most effective strategy, while still others might require various tools to be used in stages, over time.

Headquarters Support: To facilitate this element of a broad and innovative enforcement and compliance assurance program, the following activities are planned or underway at Headquarters:

Policies:

- o Issue a shutdown policy for repeat offenders. This policy will focus on the universe of combustion facilities. (Resource Conservation and Recovery Act (RCRA) Enforcement Division)

- o Develop a policy for determining National Pollutant Discharge Elimination System (NPDES) compliance for limits below detection levels. (Water Enforcement Division)

- o Issue a policy providing for enhanced public participation during the enforcement process and will, if appropriate, work with the Regions to launch a pilot project under this policy. (RCRA Enforcement Division and Office of Site Remediation Enforcement)

- o Develop a national Sanitary Sewer Overflow (SSO) policy in coordination with Office of Water. (Water Enforcement Division)

Guidance:

- o Worker Protection Standards Interpretive Guidance. (Agriculture and Ecosystem Division)

- o Guidance on alternative compliance approaches for use with small towns. (Chemical, Commercial Services and Municipal Division)

- o Develop a multi-media plain english guidance to regulations for the dry cleaning industry. (Chemical, Commercial Services and Municipal Division)

- o Draft RCRA Waste Analysis Plan (WAP) Guidance for Boiler and Incinerator Furnaces (BIFs). (Chemical, Commercial Services and Municipal Division)

- o Develop Monetary Awards Program Guidance. (Air Enforcement Division)

- o Develop Field Citations Program Guidance. (Air Enforcement Division)

- o Develop Citizens' Suits Guidance. (Air Enforcement Division)

- o Develop the General Duty Clause Guidance under section 112(r). (Air Enforcement Division)

- o Develop applicability and compliance guidance under the New Source Review provisions. (Air Enforcement Division)

- o Develop guidance for acid rain programs. (Air Enforcement Division)

- o Develop guidance and provide assistance to Regions to ensure effective use of Alternative Dispute Resolution (ADR), De Minimis settlements, and mixed funding. (Office of Site Remediation Enforcement)

Training:

- o Organize and operate a facility in Washington, D.C., to train Headquarters, Regional, and state personnel in traditional enforcement and innovative compliance assurance activities. (Enforcement Capacity and Outreach Office)

- o Develop and conduct a Land Disposal Restrictions Update Course covering the Phase I and II Rules. (RCRA Enforcement Division)

- o Develop and conduct a RCRA Enforcement Practitioners Course for regional and state legal and technical personnel, provided that adequate funding can be obtained through the National Enforcement Training Institute (NETI). (RCRA Enforcement Division) o Guidance and training on Executive Order (E.O.) 12856 Federal Facility Pollution Prevention Plans. (Federal Facilities)

o Provide training on pollution prevention for inspectors and other enforcement personnel. (Enforcement Capacity and Outreach Office)

o Develop and conduct a course to "train-the-trainer" on environmental justice. (Enforcement Capacity and Outreach Office)

Others:

o Finalize a Federal Register Notice announcing EPA's intention to develop pilot projects under the Environmental Leadership Program. (Enforcement Planning, Targeting, and Data Division)

o Continuation of work by an Agency-wide workgroup to address environmental auditing issues. (Enforcement Planning, Targeting and Data Division).

o Assistance in complying with new Municipal Waste Combustion Ash requirements. (Chemical, Commercial Services and Municipal Division)

o Additional Federal Facility Compliance Agreement (FFCA) Inspection Reimbursement Interagency Agreements (IAGs) with Department of Energy (DOE), Department of Defense (DOD), and Civilian Federal Agencies. (Federal Facilities)

o Assist in Maximum Available Control Technology (MACT) standard implementation as rules are promulgated. (Manufacturing, Energy and Transportation Division)

o Promulgate Enhanced Monitoring Rule for major air pollution sources and conduct training for Regions and States. (Manufacturing, Energy and Transportation Division)

o Finalize Field Citations Rule. (Air Enforcement Division)

o Chairmanship of FY 95 Worker Protection Initiative Workgroup and support to regions and states on worker protection compliance monitoring and case development. (Toxics and Pesticides Enforcement Division)

o Develop technical documents on major industrial categories (relating to process, pollution sources, and waste streams) for use by regions and states in enforcement programs. (National Enforcement Investigations Center)

o Work with the Office of Solid Waste and Emergency Response (OSWER) to assure timely implementation of 40 CFR subpart S and Hazardous Waste Identification Rule - Contaminated Media Regulations. (Office of Site Remediation Enforcement)

o Revisit Cost Recovery Strategy to determine if changes to cost threshold are needed. (Office of Site Remediation Enforcement)

- Provide guidance to implement Superfund Reform Act (SRA) changes if SRA passes. (Office of Site Remediation Enforcement)

- Review Enforcement Project Management Handbook, and amend if appropriate. (Office of Site Remediation Enforcement)

- Initiate and maintain an electronic bulletin board for OECA to provide information to the Regions, States, and regulated community. (Enforcement Capacity and Outreach Office)

Regional MOA Commitment:

For Objective 1, each media priority (listed in Appendix 1)[1] should be considered a work component, as discussed in section IV, The MOA Process, "Description of OECA Objectives" As described in this section, for each media priority your submission should provide an explanation of activities, the support you will need from Headquarters, and the Regional commitment you are prepared to make. In the event that the Regions feel the media priorities do not provide a complete discussion of their enforcement and compliance programs, Regions should feel free to provide additional information regarding their ongoing program efforts. Section IV provides a format and examples of the level of detail expected. (To avoid duplication, wherever appropriate, reference the enforcement and compliance assurance portion of your Regional media specific MOA, which you should attach to the OECA MOA.)

The Region should also discuss its overall approach to meeting the objective of using appropriate tools to achieve maximum compliance, highlighting in particular the use of compliance assistance in your Region's enforcement and compliance assurance programs. At the end of this section, the Region should provide a specific list of compliance assistance activities they are undertaking in FY 95, for example, workshops with industry groups on implementation of new regulations or training sessions for states.

Objective 2: Maintaining an Enforcement Presence

Description: EPA must maintain and improve its capacity to use a deterrence-based approach for assuring compliance. Enforcement actions are a primary means for assuring compliance because they demonstrate to the regulated community that noncompliance will be detected and punished. Inspections will remain a strong tool for achieving a Federal presence and for assessing compliance. The credibility of the Agency depends on a strong and effective enforcement program. Traditional enforcement activity remains a major motivating force for the regulated community's efforts to comply with requirements and behave in an environmentally-responsible manner.

A successful program maintains an enforcement presence by keeping total enforcement outputs at current levels. For example, we expect that total inspections should remain at a consistent level, but within that total the targets for those inspections, as well as the mix of single media and multi-media inspections, will necessarily shift over time. This also means that total case outputs should also remain at least at current levels, but within that total there may well be shifts in the number of outputs for particular categories of cases from year to year.

---

[1] Appendix 1 includes the following media programs: Water; Federal Facilities; Air; Toxics; Pesticides; RCRA; Remediation; Multi-media; and Criminal.

Headquarters Support: To facilitate this element of a broad and innovative enforcement and compliance assurance program, the following activities are planned or underway at Headquarters:

Enforcement Response Policies/Guidance:

- Provide revised policy concerning the use of Supplemental Environmental Projects (SEP's). (Multi-media Enforcement Division)
- Complete the revisions to the RCRA Enforcement Response Policy. (RCRA Enforcement Division)
- Revise the Clean Air Act penalty policy. (Air Enforcement Division)
- Complete Municipal NPDES Penalty Policy. (Water Enforcement Division)
- Revise the Significant Noncompliance (SNC) guidance for National Pollutant Discharge Elimination System (NPDES) and Pretreatment. (Water Enforcement Division)
- Develop guidance to enhance settlements. (Office of Site Remediation Enforcement)
- Issue a guidance document that will assist the Regions in calculating the estimated economic benefit of non-compliance. (RCRA Enforcement Division)
- Finalize policy guidance on "global settlements." (Office of Criminal Enforcement/Office of Regulatory Enforcement)
- Hazardous organic National Emission Standards for Hazardous Air Pollutants (NESHAP) inspection guidance. (Chemical, Commercial Service and Municipal Division)
- Multi-media Inspection Enforcement Program Guidance and Interim Final Status Report. (Federal Facilities)

Training:

- Conduct an Advanced Penalty Policy Training Course for Regional personnel. (RCRA Enforcement Division)
- Deliver Superfund Enforcement Course and Attorney Orientation Course. (Office of Site Remediation Enforcement)
- Develop and deliver a comprehensive multi-media inspection training course. (Enforcement Capacity and Outreach Office)
- Present a revised version of the Basic Inspector Training Course. (Enforcement Capacity and Outreach Office)
- Present a revised version of the training course in Negotiations. (Enforcement Capacity and Outreach Office)

- o Continue to provide training in the use of BEN/ABEL to support economic analysis of enforcement case penalties. (Enforcement Capacity and Outreach Office)

Other:

- o Issue a plain language guide to the RCRA Civil Penalty Policy to assist the Regions in explaining RCRA complaints and settlements to the general public. (RCRA Enforcement Division)

- o Draft integrated municipal inspection form for water incorporating NPDES, sludge, and pretreatment. (Chemical, Commercial Service and Municipal Division)

- o Provide BEN/ABEL support for economic analysis of enforcement case penalties. (Multi-media Enforcement Division)

- o Complete Non-Administrative Procedures Act (APA) administrative penalty enforcement procedures. (Water Enforcement Division)

- o Continue work on Sentencing Guidelines for environmental offenses. (Office of Criminal Enforcement)

- o Continue support and participation in the Regional Criminal Enforcement Counsel (RCEC) workgroup, as part of Office of Criminal Enforcement's (OCE's) continuing effort to work with the regions and to define the role of RCECs. (Office of Criminal Enforcement)

Regional MOA Commitments:

Under Objective 2, Regions should include all proposed commitments for targeted measures under the former STARS system. Targeted measures are those for which Headquarters and the Regions negotiate up-front commitments for the coming fiscal year. For OECA purposes, these targeted measures are conducting inspections and addressing drinking water fixed base SNC/exceptions. Forms for these commitments have gone out either under media-specific MOA guidance or under separate memo (i.e. water program). Therefore, the only portion of section IV, The MOA Process, which applies to Objective 2 for reporting purposes is the reference to Regional Commitments. Please attach summary charts to this document or reference pages in your attached media-specific MOAs.

Objective 3: Using New Targeting Approaches

Description: A major purpose of the reorganization was to enhance strategic targeting of enforcement and compliance assurance activities. Innovative approaches to targeting -- such as those organized around multi-media, whole facilities, industrial sectors, and geographic areas -- offer at least two advantages. First, enforcement and compliance assurance resources can be oriented toward the full range of environmental requirements which apply to a facility, industry, or geographic area. Second, enforcement and compliance actions can be organized around environmental problems and broad patterns of noncompliance rather than around individual provisions of single statutes.

A successful enforcement and compliance assurance program identifies opportunities to address environmental problems and noncompliance patterns in industry sectors, geographic areas, and whole facilities. These problems and patterns become targets to which the various enforcement and compliance assurance tools are applied.

Headquarters Support: To facilitate this element of a broad and innovative enforcement and compliance assurance program, the following activities are planned or underway at Headquarters:

- Work with Office of Compliance and Program Office(s) on provision of inspection targeting data in support of initiatives as needed by Regions. (Toxics and Pesticides Enforcement Division)

- Provide Superfund Accelerated Cleanup Model (SACM) coordination support to Regions 4 and 9. (Office of Site Remediation and Enforcement)

- Development of a model sector compliance strategy. (OC Sector Divisions)

- Development of an interagency Memorandum of Understanding (MOU), with Customs, the Securities Exchange Commission (SEC), and the Occupational Safety Health Administration (OSHA). (Enforcement, Planning, Targeting and Data Division)

- For industrial categories, develop national and region-specific rankings based on historical non-compliance patterns and Toxic Release Inventory data. These data will be used to review MOAs, Regional targeting, and set the baseline for measuring success. (Enforcement, Planning, Targeting and Data Division)

- Refine the Fortune 500 compliance and enforcement profile data and provide support to the Regions, OC Sector Divisions, and ORE in the interpretation and use of the data for targeting corporate-wide compliance and enforcement activities. Complete work with Dun & Bradstreet to establish reliable corporate data linkages through Integrated Data for Enforcement Analysis System (IDEA). (Enforcement Planning, Targeting and Data Division)

- Develop demographic and ecosystem targeting methods to support Environmental Justice activities and ecosystem-based efforts such as addressing posted stream segments/contaminated sediments. (Enforcement Planning, Targeting and Data Division)

- Deliver software and user guides to facilitate calculation of wastewater pollutant loadings from point sources. (Environmental Planning, Targeting and Data Division)

- Conduct assessment of current locational data in OECA databases to begin to improve our ability to map facilities. (Environmental Planning, Targeting and Data Division)

- Provide compliance profiles on industrial sectors to facilitate targeting. (Enforcement Planning, Targeting and Data Division/ Manufacturing, Energy and Transportation Division)

- Develop and implement a formal system for strengthening the participation of state, local, and tribal authorities in the development of OECA planning, priority setting, and policy development. (Enforcement Capacity and Outreach Office)

- Endangered Species Strategy (draft 30 days after Federal Register Notice). (Agriculture and Ecosystem Division)

- o Pilot training in environmental justice communities designed to provide information on basic statutory requirements. (Enforcement Capacity and Outreach Office)

- o Ecosystem workplan. (Agriculture and Ecosystem Division)

- o Review State Operating Permit program submittals under Part 71 of the Operating Permit Program; provide legal and technical support to regions, states and local offices on volatile organic compounds (VOCs). (Air Enforcement Division)

- o Implementation of the Investigative Discretion Guidance issued in FY 94 and priorities associated with it, including: data integrity, environmental justice. (Office of Criminal Enforcement)

Regional MOA Commitments:

Under Objective 3, Regions should provide a narrative discussion of their targeting methodologies. Innovative approaches to targeting include: multi-media; whole-facility; sector-oriented; place-based; risk-based; environmental justice; and pollution prevention. Regions should specifically discuss which of these innovative approaches they utilize and should provide detail for the strategies identified. Regions should refer to section IV, The MOA Process, for the format for completing this section. We recognize that this objective incorporates many of these new approaches for enforcement and compliance. Therefore, we are particularly interested in Regional involvement, including pilots, in any of these areas. For each identified area, Regions should describe activities they are undertaking to support this area, requests for Headquarters' support and any associated commitments or outputs.

Objective 4: Moving Toward Measuring Results and Impact

Description: EPA's enforcement and compliance assurance program has relied exclusively on counting activities (e.g., cases issued, and dollars collected) as the sole means of measuring success. Over the next two to three years the program should move toward a more balanced approach which uses result-based and impact-oriented measures to supplement more sophisticated and useful methods of counting activities.

A successful enforcement and compliance assurance program is one which contributes to the development of new national measures and aligns data collection and analysis efforts with those measures. Counting the full range of activities (e.g., enforcement actions and compliance assistance efforts), measuring outcomes (e.g., the actual results of these efforts, not just their initiation), and measuring impact (e.g., compliance rates, improvements in environmental conditions) will be crucial to having a successful enforcement and compliance assurance program. Our proposed approach involves four components, as follows:

1. **Emphasize environmental results in enforcement.** OECA recognizes the need to systematically collect data on environmental results (e.g., environmental conditions, loading reductions) and program impacts (e.g., value and nature of supplemental environmental projects (SEPs) and injunctive relief). To accomplish systematic data collection, we have recommended introduction of the judicial and administrative case completion data sheet. Work on the final data sheet is underway with involvement by staff from several Regions. Preparation of the data sheets will be new work for Regional office staff; however, it is the view of the work group that benefits gained from more systematic data collection (in terms of both data quality and a reduced need for most of the ad hoc end of year

information requests) outweigh any increase in workload. We anticipate piloting the case data sheets in two Regions in the first half of FY 1995, revising as needed and expanding to cover all Regions in the second half of FY 1995.

2. **Maintain current reporting on program measures.** Although the Office of Policy, Planning and Evaluation has announced the discontinuation of the STARS reporting system in FY 1995, continued reporting of core enforcement measures is critical to the mission of OECA. Therefore, we expect the Regions to continue to maintain and report this data. Regions should reference the FY 1994 Goals, Objectives, Commitments and Measures Guidance (Office of the Administrator, March 1994) which presents all Agency FY 94 STARS measures, noting that enforcement measures are identified with an "E" in the code. OECA commits to review the FY 1994 media enforcement measures this year for the purpose of determining which measures may be eliminated for FY 1996 reporting.

3. **Measure compliance as well as enforcement activities.** This re-engineering will be largely accomplished using existing data and applying newly-improved data linkages, SIC codes, and facility location information. The modifications that are planned (e.g., developing cross-media compliance profiles by industrial category) will generally be accomplished through new computer data integration and retrieval capabilities and will be carried out by Office of Compliance staff. We do not anticipate that these changes will add to existing Regional or State reporting burdens.

4. **Broaden measures of enforcement output through the implementation of an Enforcement Activity Index.** We are developing more comprehensive activity indicators to provide comparable visibility to criminal enforcement activities, significant administrative actions, and significant activities that address noncompliance at Federal facilities. These activity measures will also focus needed attention on case conclusions, which as activity measures better link to environmental benefits than case initiations. OECA is recommending a set of four indexes -- one each for civil judicial cases, criminal cases, significant administrative actions, and significant activities that address noncompliance at Federal facilities -- which when viewed together would constitute an enforcement "profile." The index is intended as an enforcement communication and management tool, not as a tool for resource allocation. We anticipate piloting the index in the second half of FY 1995 and that all Regions will be involved in FY 1996.

Headquarters Support: To facilitate this element of a broad and innovative enforcement and compliance assurance program, the following activities are planned or underway at Headquarters:

o Pilot test and implement the Case Completion Data Sheet. (Enforcement Planning, Targeting and Data Division)

o Complete the design and definition of the Enforcement Activity Index and develop guidance to assist the Regions in implementing reporting mechanisms. (Enforcement Planning, Targeting, and Data Division)

o Re-engineer reporting using existing data and measures of SNC and compliance status/rates to incorporate multi-media, sector, and environmental justice perspectives. (Enforcement Planning, Targeting and Data Division)

o Docket will be enhanced to incorporate data needed for OECA Measures of Success effort, and other user recommended changes. (Enforcement Planning, Targeting and Data Division)

- o Federal Facilities Tracking System (FFTS) User's Manual and Training. (Federal Facilities)

- o Annual A-106 Regional Review Guidance. (Federal Facilities)

- o Provide guidance on the compliance and enforcement use of enhanced and periodic monitoring data. (Manufacturing Energy and Transportation Division)

- o Permit Compliance System (PCS) enhancements -- ability to switch from a two digit year code to a four digit year code to input a year greater than 2000 and ability to print on-line retrievals. (Enforcement Planning, Targeting and Data Division)

- o The IDEA system will be enhanced to have a Windows interface. Training on IDEA will continue. Regions will also continue to provide assistance to Regions on special projects. (Enforcement Planning, Targeting and Data Division)

- o Air Facility Subsystem (AFS) -- a PC utility will be provided to assist in the calculation of source class from emission and attainment data. (Enforcement Planning, Targeting and Data Division)

- o Training on OECA enforcement and compliance databases will be scheduled for Regions as needed (including Docket, PCS, etc.) (Enforcement Planning, Targeting and Data Division)

- o Develop acid rain allowance tracking system. (Air Enforcement Division)

Regional MOA Commitments:

For Objective 4, Regions should describe the commitment it is prepared to make to: support development of improved or new measures of success; participate in efforts to collect information (e.g., the case completion data sheet) needed for new measures; and participate in pilot projects to actually implement new measures. Regions should follow the format provided in section IV, The MOA Process; however, the activity should cover whatever new measurement effort they have underway--either participating with Headquarters or independent Regional efforts--and then discuss where Headquarters support is needed and identify any commitments or completion dates if available.

The Region should also discuss its overall efforts to improve the quality of enforcement and compliance assurance data.

IV. THE MOA PROCESS

This section describes the schedule and format for submitting, reviewing, and completing the MOAs.

A. SCHEDULE FOR SUBMISSION/NEGOTIATION PROCESS

o **The Regions will have until November 4, 1994 to submit their MOA proposals.** The Regions should follow the outline provided in this guidance and attach enforcement and compliance assurance sections of their FY 95 media specific MOAs. In FY 96 all enforcement and compliance activities will be consolidated within the OECA MOA guidance. Each Region should submit its MOA proposal to the Planning Branch, of the Enforcement

Planning, Targeting and Data Division within the Office of Compliance. The Planning Branch will coordinate this effort, consulting with other offices within OECA.

o The escalation process for addressing issues prior to MOA submittal will proceed as follows: Staff level discussions will occur early in the process to provide for understanding, clarification, and resolution of issues where possible and will frame the discussion of regional priorities and program tradeoffs as necessary. One contact person from the Region will work with a designated contact person within the Planning Branch of OECA. Where agreement is reached, no further action is required.

Those issues which cannot be resolved or require management decisions will be elevated to Branch Chiefs, Division Directors and Office Directors as needed. Most of the negotiation on program priorities and trade-offs will occur at this level. These negotiations should be done quickly, efficiently, and in a collegial manner. Our intent is to complete these discussions wherever possible prior to formal submittal.

Upon submission of the MOA proposals, communication on remaining unresolved MOA policy issues and negotiation of final commitments will be held only between the OECA Office Directors and Regional Division Directors, or a higher level if necessary, for those significant issues where agreement cannot be reached. The Assistant Administrator/Deputy Assistant Administrator in Headquarters will conduct conference calls with each Regional Administrator/Deputy Regional Administrator in the Region for the purpose of resolving issues and finalizing the Agreement for each Region.

o The negotiation process must be completed no later than January 13, 1995. Final signed MOAs will be transmitted immediately to the Regions.

B. REGIONAL DEVELOPMENT OF AN MOA PROPOSAL

I. Outline of Regional/Headquarters MOA

a. **Transmittal and Highlights Memorandum (no more than 2 pages)**

b. **Regional Program (explained in more detail under Part II. of this section)**

i. **Description of OECA Objectives**
In general, the Regional response to each OECA Objective should be described as follows:

Brief narrative describing, strategically, what the region is doing to meet the objective.

Where the Region is conducting a specific activity towards an objective, the following information should be provided.

Activity Description:
HQ Support:
Regional Commitments & Activities:

ii. **Regional Specific Issues - Optional**
iii. **Resource Utilization Summary (Including investments/ disinvestments)**

c. **Attachments**

- **Enforcement and Compliance Assurance components of the annual planning documents (i.e., MOA, RIP) developed through Media Specific Guidances**
- **Optional Supporting Regional Attachments**

II. Detailed Discussion of Regional Program (item b. from above outline)

The main objective within this section is to describe how compliance and enforcement activities will be directed to meet the OECA's strategic objectives for Enforcement and Compliance Assurance in as brief and concise a manner as possible, and to identify milestones and products to capture and monitor progress.

Regions should submit narrative descriptions for their planned activities unless specifically requested otherwise. Regions will be expected to identify the resources (FTEs and grant dollars) and measurable outputs allocated to each activity and program objective. The format below is designed to assist Regions in organizing this section of the report.

i. Description of OECA Objectives

This section should provide a brief narrative describing how the Region intends to meet the OECA objective. In addition, where appropriate, the Region should provide a more detailed description of work components (activities) that will be conducted to meet the objective. Each activity under each objective should be describe as follows:

Activity Description:

[Specific activity or related groups of activities under each objective]

HQ Support:

[As applicable, discuss needed guidance or other Headquarters actions that potentially may impact the achievement of the stated activity]

Regional Commitments & Activities:

[Specifically define the outputs or commitments that the Region agrees to meet and include appropriate timetables associated with the outputs. Where a Region is seeking flexibility to undertake a specific activity, the Region should discuss the rationale, the impact and identify the measurable results produced by this action.]

For Objective 1, each media priority (listed in Appendix 1) should be considered a work component. Where the Region feels that additional information beyond the media priorities is needed to adequately cover their program, Regions should feel free to add details to provide a more complete discussion. [An example write-up for an activity under Objective #1 is provided in Figure 1].

The Region should also discuss its overall approach to meeting the objective using appropriate tools to achieve maximum compliance, highlighting in particular the use of compliance assistance in your Region's enforcement and compliance assurance program. At the end of this section, the Region should provide a specific list of compliance assistance activities they are undertaking in FY 95.

For Objective 2, Regions should include all proposed commitments for targeted measures (as described in section III.) under the former STARS. For reporting purposes, please attach summary charts or reference pages in attached enforcement and compliance assurance sections of the media specific annual planning documents (i.e., MOA, RIP).

For Objective 3, Regions should provide a brief narrative discussion of their targeting methodologies. Regions should specifically discuss which of these innovative approaches they utilize and should provide detail for the strategies identified. For each identified strategy, a more detailed description of work components (activities) that will be conducted to meet the objective should be included. [An example write-up for Objective #3 is provided in Figure 2.]

For Objective 4, Regions should provide a brief narrative discussion of their efforts to move toward measuring results and impacts. The Region should describe its commitment to develop their own measures projects; to support development of improved or new measures of success; to participate in efforts to collect information needed for new measures; and to participate in pilot projects to actually implement new measures. A more detailed description of activities that will be conducted to meet the objective should be included when appropriate.

ii. Regional Specific Issues - Optional

This section, which is optional, allows the Regions an opportunity to present management issues to Headquarters. It should include impediments that affect the ability of the Region to operate effectively in accomplishing its goals.

iii. Resource Utilization Summary — FTE and State Grant (Including investments/disinvestments)

We are requesting that the Regions provide summary information on utilization of enforcement and compliance assurance FTE and state grant funds.

For FTE, we need to know how many FTE, both federal and Senior Environmental Employees (SEEs), are allocated to four broad functional areas (compliance assistance/promotion, compliance monitoring, enforcement action, and program management) for each of the single-media and multi-media programs of the Region. We would like each Region to submit an FTE Utilization summary for each program area. Please designate separately the SEE and federal FTE. An explanation and example of the FTE Utilization Summary appears in Table I.

For each "Change in Level" indicated on the FTE Utilization Summary, we would like you to provide a summary explanation for the investment/disinvestment. An example of this explanation of investments/disinvestment is provided in Figure 3.

For state grant funds, we are requesting a breakout of grant funds by function, and the chart to be completed for each State is provided in Table II. We understand that FY 95 programs are already negotiated, and thus we are trying to capture a "snapshot" of grant fund allocation rather than shift funds at this late date. For each state, we are asking that you use your best professional judgment to allocate the enforcement portion of those state grants across four functional areas and also indicate the amount of the total grant (i.e., enforcement and non-enforcement).

C. REPORTING REQUIREMENTS

Regions are to submit concise reports at mid-year and end-of-year to reflect progress made and issues unresolved. Where an OECA Regional evaluation coincides with the timing of a mid-year or end-of-year report, Headquarters will discuss with the Region the need for any additional information beyond the Regional evaluation report.

A. Mid-Year Report

o The report should highlight their progress in shifting resources between investment/disinvestment areas.

o The report should discuss where media-specific priority commitment levels, initiatives, and MOA goals/objectives are either being significantly exceeded, or Region is experiencing great difficulty in meeting them.

-Reasons for success/impediments should be clearly defined.

o This information should be provided in a narrative form, with separate headings for each commitment, initiative, or goal being addressed.

o Impediments, success stories, and investment/disinvestment updates should be provided in separate sections.

o Mid-year reports (not to exceed 15 pages) should be submitted to the Planning Branch, EPTDD, OC by May 1, 1995.

B. End-of-Year Report

o Detailed reporting guidance will be provided in the near future identifying time frames, format and required elements.

APPENDIX 1

FY 95 MEDIA SPECIFIC PRIORITIES/INITIATIVES

The following section, drawn from media-specific guidances, identifies priorities and initiatives. In many instances, a brief description of the priority is provided. Regions should refer to the specific guidance document referenced to obtain more detailed information, and to ensure that other aspects of media-specific guidance is being followed. In FY 96, enforcement and compliance assurance guidance for all media will be covered in the OECA MOA guidance.

When developing the Regional MOA, Regions should consider the appropriate balance between base program activities and media priorities and initiatives, and discuss the rationale behind their choices. While we expect Regions to participate in these national initiatives, we also recognize that not all Regions will participate in all initiatives (for example, only certain Regions have a vested interest in the Mississippi River Initiative).

A. Water (also refer to Office of Water FY 94 Operating Guidance, dated March 1993)

Priorities

- Regions and states should target compliance and enforcement efforts to support the priority watershed approach, particularly those streams posted as unfit for fishing and swimming.
- Regions and States should pursue alternative approaches, using a mix of compliance assistance and enforcement, when dealing with nontraditional enforcement problems, such as stormwater, sludge, feedlots, combined sewer overflow (including dryweather flows) and small system compliance.
- Regions and states should target inspections, focus on accurate and complete reporting, and take enforcement actions against nonreporters and facilities reporting fraudulent or incorrect data.
- Regions and states should continue to identify noncompliance among pretreatment publicly owned treatment works (POTWs) and industrial users contributing toxic pollutants into public sewers.
- Regions and states should aggressively implement and enforce the Surface Water Treatment Rule to ensure that unfiltered systems are on an enforceable schedule to install filtration, and to ensure that filtered systems meet requirements.
- Regions should work with states to undertake increased underground injection control (UIC) enforcement efforts, particularly for shallow wells, including expediting remedial actions and obtaining higher penalties.
- Regions and states should implement and enforce the Lead and Copper Rule, with particular attention to issuing administrative orders (AOs) to large systems which are not implementing their corrosion control plans, and any systems where monitoring indicates noncompliance.

Initiative

- Development of Wetlands Enforcement Management System

  Development of this system would involve incorporation of a penalty policy, a model litigation referral package, and a method for prioritizing noncompliance and determining the appropriate enforcement response for wetlands violations.

B. **Federal Facilities (refer to OFFE's 1992 10-Point Strategic Plan)**

<u>Priorities</u> - also refer to other media specific priorities/initiatives

- Enforcement Cases: Continued emphasis on enforcement casework and regulatory programs, especially RCRA and its Federal Facility Compliance Act Amendments.

- Enforcement Policy: Continued work on major policy efforts, including the Federal Facility Policy Group, the Federal Facilities Steering Committee, and Clean Water Act. Policy or statutory changes resulting from these efforts may require shifts in activities during the fiscal year.

- Multi-media Enforcement: Continued emphasis on multi-media inspections. During FY 95, results of the FY 93-94 multi-media initiative will be assessed and efforts made to institutionalize a continued federal facility component in multi-media enforcement activities.

- Environmental Stewardship: Continued efforts to assist federal agencies in complying with environmental requirements and becoming environmental justice leaders. For example, FY '95 will see implementation of the Civilian Federal Agency Compliance Program Improvement Strategy, and continued implementation of Executive Order 12856 including the Green Government Environmental Challenge Initiative, continued innovative technology programs, and the Federal Facilities Roundtable.

- Environmental Tracking, Monitoring, and Analysis. Continued implementation of the Federal Facilities Hazardous Waste Compliance Docket, progress in improving the A-106 budget process, and major implementation of the Federal Facilities Tracking System (FFTS).

C. **Air (refer to FY '95 Office of Air and Radiation Program-Specific Guidance, dated August 9, 1994, especially pgs. 67-79)**

Priorities

o Significant Violators (SV)/Timely and Appropriate (T&A) Implementation:

-implement guidance that defines timely and appropriate enforcement responses for significant violators.
-assist states in identifying, resolving, and prioritizing significant violations, using all available enforcement tools.

o Federal Enforcement Activity:

-prepare and track civil referrals and administrative cases.

o Compliance Monitoring Strategy:

-ensure states identify in Air Facility Subsystem (AFS) sources targeted for inspection.
-assist states in developing and implementing state inspection plans consistent with the strategy.

o Data Integrity:

-ensure states input into AFS and NARS inspection, compliance and enforcement information; track regional and state information.

o Pollution Prevention:

-take enforcement actions, provide compliance assistance and training to enhance pollution prevention activities, inclusion of pollution prevention/innovative technology into injunctive relief and SEPs as appropriate.

o Federal Programs:

Acid Rain Implementation

-review opt-in applications and issue permits
-assist states in developing their permit programs, ensure that acid rain requirements are incorporated in states' Title V permits.
-enforce acid rain permits and continuous emissions monitoring (CEM) certification requirements

Stratospheric Ozone Protection

-enforce servicing of motor vehicle air conditioners and the service, repair or disposal of class I substances used in appliances and industrial process refrigeration
-enforce ban on sale of nonessential products containing chlorofluorocarbons
-enforce restrictions on the importations of certain ozone depleting chemicals

o New Rules, Guidance and Review - Assist in the development and implementation of Agency policy on Enhanced Monitoring, Field Citations, Monetary Awards, Citizen Suits, accidental releases under the general duty clause, and enforcement of State Implementation Plans (SIP) and MACT Standards:

C. **Air (refer to FY '95 Office of Air and Radiation Program-Specific Guidance, dated August 9, 1994, especially pps. 67-79), continued**

Enforcement of MACT Standards

-begin to enforce the dry cleaning MACT, the Coke Oven MACT, and the Hazardous Organic NESHAPS MACT.

Operating Permit Approval

-review state and district operating permit program submittals to determine each program's compliance with requirements under Part 70

o Compliance Planning and Oversight Guidance/Enforcement Response Plan (ERP) - ensure states develop ERP'S consistent with guidance.

o Rule Effectiveness:

-submit commitments for studies, study protocols and final reports to Headquarters.
-submit post-study audits within one year of completion.

o Lead Enforcement:

-as part of the Lead National Ambient Air Quality Standards (NAAQS) Attainment Strategy of August 1990, EPA has determined to enforce current emission limitations for all strategy sources.

Initiatives

o National case development of particle board and plywood industries. (carryover from FY 94)

o Industrial/Commercial Boilers Enforcement Initiative

To address serious compliance/enforcement problems with the New Source Performance Standards (NSPS) for boilers constructed after June 19, 1984, that have a heat input greater than 29MW (100mmBtu/hr), and boilers constructed after June 9, 1989, that have a heat input between 2.9MW and 29MW.

D. Toxics (refer to draft FY '95 MOA Guidance for Pesticides and Toxics, dated July 28, 1994)

Priorities

o Cooperative Agreements - emphasis on quality implementation, oversight, and evaluation for toxics.

o Emergency Planning and Community Right to Know Act (EPCRA) section 313 national priorities are data concerns and non-reporters. Other EPCRA non-313 violations should be pursued where appropriate.

o The national Core Toxics Substances Control Act (TSCA) priorities focus on pollution prevention and risk reduction and are as follows:

-parties to 5(e) risk-based orders
-companies which did not participate in the TSCA 8(e) compliance audit program (CAP)
-non-submitters of Pre-manufacture Notices
-parties subject to Significant New Use Rules

o Asbestos abatement and/or asbestos worker protection - highest priority for asbestos inspections.

o Polychlorinated Biphenyls (PCBs): high-risk, low compliance PCBs are of primary concern. Existing PCB compliance monitoring enforcement resources should be directed toward implementation of PCB 2000 strategy.

o PCB compliance monitoring priorities include:

- inspections at disposal and commercial storage facilities.
- participation in the PCB phaseout.

Initiatives

o TSCA section 5(e) worker exposure initiative.

o TSCA section 8(e) CAP Non-participant enforcement initiative.

o Imports/Exports Transboundary initiative - reduction of environmental and health risks created by transboundary shipments of chemicals in violation of TSCA, FIFRA, and international treaties.

E. **Pesticides (refer to draft FY '95 MOA Guidance for Pesticides and Toxics, dated July 28, 1994)**

Priorities

- Cooperative Agreements - emphasis on quality implementation, oversight, and evaluation for pesticides.

- Worker Protection - Regions should continue to emphasize inspector training, compliance assistance and outreach, and enforcement of worker protection standard label requirements and generic worker protection requirements.

- Special Action Chemicals - Regions should continue to provide necessary field support to follow up on specific cancellation/suspension orders which significantly change a product's labeling or use pattern.

- Pesticide Infrastructure - improvement of program implementation and effectiveness through enhancement of data systems, inspector training, and case development training.

- SEP's - incorporation of supplemental environmental projects in settlement of pesticide enforcement cases.

Initiatives

- Worker Protection Compliance Initiative - phase 1 focuses on enforcement of worker protection standard labeling requirements. Phase 2 focuses on use of worker protection products, both compliance assistance efforts and enforcement actions during the latter portion of FY '95 and the beginning of FY '96.

- Imports/Exports Transboundary Initiative - reduction of environmental and health risks created by transboundary shipments of chemicals in violation of FIFRA, TSCA and international treaties.

F. RCRA (refer to FY 94 and FY 95 RCRA Implementation Plans, dated April 2, 1993 and May 19, 1994, respectively)

Priorities

- Combustion - BIFs and Incinerators
- Waste Minimization Activities:

  -inclusion of waste minimization activities as supplemental environmental projects (SEPs) in case settlements, with a focus on environmental justice, where applicable.

- Statutory Compliance Priority Inspections:

  -federal Transport, Storage and Disposal Facilities (TSDFs)
  -Land Disposal Facilities (LDFs) not inspected in FY 94
  -commercial TSDFs

- Other Priority Inspections:

  -CME or O&M at all new or newly regulated LDFs
  -combustion facilities that were classified an high priority violator (HPV) in FY 94
  -combustion facilities that never received an in-depth inspection in FY 94.

- Federal Facilities Compliance Act - Federal Mandates
- Groundwater Monitoring Inspections
- Non-notifiers identified through tips, complaints, or investigations.
- Address facilities that have remained in significant non-compliance for extended periods of time.
- Land disposal facilities

Initiatives:

- RCRA's industry-specific initiative, based on recommendations of the RCRA enforcement targeting committee.
- RCRA's initiative to support the Administrator's waste minimization strategy.

G. **Remediation (Superfund, RCRA Corrective Action, Oil Pollution Act (OPA) & Underground Storage Tanks (UST)/Leaking Underground Storage Tanks (LUST)**

Priorities

- o Cost Recovery Sites Addressed - In order to assure that Superfund dollars are returned to the trust fund, Regions must target all Statute of Limitations (SOL) cases expiring on or before 3/30/96 with costs greater than or equal to $200,000. Flexibility is available for SOL cases between 11/15/95 and 3/21/96 if non-settler or high dollar cases can be brought instead.

- o De Minimis/De Micromis - To reduce third party litigation and reduce private party transition costs, early settlements with small volume contributors will continue to be a high priority.

- o Enforcement First - In order to maximize the number of cleanups and reduce the number of cases requiring costly litigation, Regions are strongly encouraged to maximize Principal responsible party (PRP) participation upfront in both the removal and remedial programs (70% remedial, 30-35 removal). This will be a measure in FY 95. The key areas of emphasis are early initiation of PRP searches and negotiations with PRPs to maximize PRP conducted response actions.

- o Cleanup Pace - In order to assure that the cleanups are conducted timely, negotiation completions will be targeted in FY 95.

- o RCRA Corrective Action (refer to RCRA Implementation Plans cited in previous sections).

- o Collect penalties for unauthorized discharges of oil or certain hazardous substances in violation of Section 311 (b) of the Oil Pollution Act.

- o Remediate sites where there is an actual or threatened release of oil or a hazardous substance that may be an imminent and substantial threat to the public health or welfare.

- o Remediate sites with leaking underground storage tanks (state lead).

- o Negotiate federal facility IAGs pursuant to Comprehensive Environmental Response Compensation and Liability Act (CERCLA) Section 120.

Initiatives

Superfund Reforms:

- each site will be considered for ADR efficiencies
- state and federal mixed funding will continue to be piloted

- o RCRA Corrective Action's Stabilization Initiative which involves focusing resources on interim actions to achieve near term environmental results at facilities with the most serious problems.

- o Environmental Justice and Community Involvement - Citizens living near Superfund sites must receive equal protection under CERCLA. Accordingly, communities must be guaranteed early and effective ways to participate in the Superfund cleanup process.

H. Multi-media

Priorities

- Integrate and strengthen a cross-program/multi-media perspective and capacity into all stages of the compliance assurance and enforcement planning and decision-making process, including targeting, inspections, case-screening and development, and civil and administrative enforcement actions.

- Expand use of multi-media enforcement to address violations in more than one program at single companies with multiple facilities. This includes where facilities are located within a single Region, or working in cooperation with other Regions and headquarters, where the facilities are located in different Regions.

- Expand use of multi-media enforcement approaches to address ecosystem or geographical problems and environmental justice concerns (e.g., multiple and cumulative exposures in minority population and low-income populations).

- Conduct a minimum of 2 multi-media inspections at federal facility establishments, per the Federal Facilities Multi-Media Enforcement/Compliance initiative.

Initiatives

- National multi-media enforcement case initiative against large companies, such as Fortune 500 companies.

New Multi-media Initiatives

- Common Sense Initiative

The Common Sense Initiative represents the Administrator's desire to do business differently, by regulating on a sector basis instead of on a statute-specific basis. The anticipated result is that all EPA regulations affecting a particular sector will be consistent (i.e., no redundant or conflicting requirements) and pollution prevention opportunities may be surfaced.

- Mississippi River Initiative

In FY 1995 and in subsequent years, OECA intends to enlist the Regions in addressing noncompliance exhibited by facilities along or near the Mississippi River, and its tributaries, including the Missouri and Ohio rivers. A number of Assistant U.S. Attorneys in that area have recently expressed their interest in addressing such noncompliance, and the Agency will seek to work with them and with various other agencies and departments to coordinate enforcement efforts.

Through improved coordination and targeting, this effort should yield a large number of enforcement actions filed or issued in the area by the end of FY 1995, with compliance assurance efforts also increasing. In FY 1995, the Agency also hopes to participate in the development of an interagency agreement to improve coordination and communication regarding related enforcement and compliance efforts.

H. Multi-media, continued

- Compliance Assistance Center Initiative

OECA is pursuing funding through the Environmental Technology Initiative for the purpose of establishing National Compliance Assistance Centers to provide "one-stop shopping" for several industries characterized by small businesses facing substantial multi-media regulatory requirements (potential industries include dry cleaning, printing, metal finishing, etc.). These Centers would provide comprehensive assistance to its small business community. The Centers would develop consolidated, multi-media materials on compliance requirements, pollution prevention, etc. while also developing workshops, seminars and self-auditing methodologies.

I. Criminal

- Continue implementation and emphasis on environmental justice activities and issuing cases in environmental justice communities.
- Continue implementation of the Investigative Discretion Guidance issued in FY '94.
- Multimedia criminal enforcement activities.

Memorandum: Final FY 96/97 OECA Memorandum of Agreement Guidance (excerpts)

Environmental Protection Agency (June 22, 1995)

UNITED STATES ENVIRONMENTAL PROTECTION AGENCY
WASHINGTON, D.C. 20460

JUN 22 1995

OFFICE OF
ENFORCEMENT AND
COMPLIANCE ASSURANCE

MEMORANDUM

SUBJECT: Final FY 96/97 OECA Memorandum of Agreement Guidance

FROM: Steven A. Herman
Assistant Administrator

TO: Regional Administrators

This memorandum provides you with the Office of Enforcement and Compliance Assurance (OECA) final FY 96/97 Memorandum of Agreement (MOA) Guidance. This MOA guidance reflects discussions we have had with you and your staffs about the strategic direction of the enforcement and compliance assurance program over the next two years.

In this final document, we have addressed comments and concerns you raised in response to the draft guidance we distributed March 30, 1995. Significant changes from the draft guidance include:

1. a detailed and streamlined package of measures, known as Reporting for Enforcement and Compliance Assurance Priorities (RECAP), which replaces traditional STARS reporting measures and reduces the number of measures and data to be collected;
2. more detailed pesticides and toxics enforcement program grant guidance;
3. a revised and more complete discussion of compliance assistance measures; and
4. removal of RCRA Corrective Action projections, which will no longer be included in the MOA.

We are expecting the submittal of your Regional MOA proposal between **July 14, 1995, and August 18, 1995.** This submittal interval will provide more time for you to develop and select Regional community-based, media, and sector-specific priority strategies. All facility-specific information provided as part of your MOA should be included as a separate attachment, designated "FOIA exempt." FOIA exempt materials include information directly linked with enforcement proceedings, investigations, or prosecutions. Please see specific guidance in the Agency's FOIA manual and at 5 U.S.C. 552(b)(7)(A) and (E).

Additionally, we are developing a Response to Comments document which identifies and addresses issues or questions raised during review of the draft guidance document. This document will be completed shortly and distributed under separate cover.

When submitting your MOA, please provide two copies to Jack Neylan, Chief, Planning Branch, Enforcement Planning, Targeting and Data Division, Office of Compliance, mailcode 2222-A. We expect all negotiations to be concluded and all MOAs to be in place by October 15, 1995.

I appreciate your continued commitment to making the enforcement and compliance program stronger and more effective, as we strive to achieve our strategic goals together. Over the course of the next two years, in particular at the midway point, we will continue to consult with you as Agency directions change, specifically in the areas of oversight and grant programs. Please direct any questions or concerns on the guidance to Elaine Stanley at (202) 564-2280, mailcode 2221-A.

Attachments

cc: Assistant Administrators
Deputy Regional Administrators
OECA Office Directors
Regional Counsels
Regional MOA Coordinators
OECA MOA Workgroup
Headquarters Media Program Contacts

FY 96/97 OECA MEMORANDUM OF AGREEMENT GUIDANCE

I. INTRODUCTION

The purpose of the Office of Enforcement and Compliance Assurance (OECA) Memorandum of Agreement (MOA) is to implement an effective enforcement and compliance assurance program that will contribute to EPA's national goals. This MOA represents a significant change in strategic direction, shifting from our traditional exclusive focus on media-specific formal enforcement activities, to a balanced program of compliance assistance and enforcement which will address community-based, industry sector-based, and media-specific priorities. During FY 96 and FY 97, we continue to stress the importance of environmental justice, pollution prevention, and multi-media approaches as we implement our programs. This MOA guidance initiates an evolving two-year process designed to address significant environmental and noncompliance problems, use a variety of enforcement and compliance tools to address those problems, and measure the impact of our efforts. This document also serves as grant guidance for enforcement and compliance assurance efforts.

II. GOAL: Maximize Compliance and Ensure Environmental Accountability

The goal of EPA's enforcement and compliance program is to promote responsible environmental behavior by ensuring compliance with legal requirements and encouraging practices that go beyond compliance. Our program will foster accountability of regulated entities so they can meet the full range of environmental requirements and obligations. We will accomplish this by using a variety of enforcement and compliance assurance tools (i.e., compliance assistance, compliance monitoring, incentive and recognition programs, and civil and criminal enforcement). These tools will be used individually or in combination to address significant environmental or noncompliance problems of industry sectors, communities and ecosystems, or pollutant media such as air, water, or land.

III. OPERATING PRINCIPLES

<u>Reduce Risks to Environment and Human Health:</u>

To the maximum extent possible, resources of the enforcement and compliance assurance program should be targeted to reduce risks to human health or the environment.

<u>Use Multi-Media Strategies:</u>

Enforcement and compliance assurance strategies and initiatives should be organized around industry sectors, communities and ecosystems, and other entities that reflect the multi-media nature of environmental problems. Wherever appropriate, Regions and States[1] should employ a multi-media perspective in targeting, developing and delivering compliance assistance, conducting inspections and taking enforcement actions.

---

1 *Reference to State(s) in this document also includes Tribal and Local partners.*

Use the Full Range of Enforcement and Compliance Assurance Tools:

As we address significant environmental or noncompliance problems, we should consider the full range of tools available and select the tool or combination of tools most appropriate for the problem. In formulating the appropriate strategies to address these problems, such factors as the nature and extent of risk to human health and the environment, the compliance profile of a particular violator or sector, and the level of community interest should be examined. For example, when the violations present a significant risk to human health or the environment and the violator has a history of noncompliance, enforcement actions would generally be the appropriate approach. On the other hand, where regulations are new or apply to large numbers of small businesses, compliance assistance may be the most appropriate approach. As these strategies are developed, it is of particular importance that they incorporate pollution prevention and environmental justice considerations.

Build Partnerships and Provide Public Access:

An effective environmental enforcement and compliance assurance program depends upon constructive partnerships with State, Tribal and local governments and increased public involvement. The enforcement and compliance assurance program recognizes and supports the oversight reform efforts of EPA and the States and will be heavily involved in implementing these changes as they become more clearly defined. We are working now to increase the involvement of our partners in setting priorities and developing strategies to address environmental and noncompliance problems. The partnership between EPA Headquarters, EPA Regions, States, and local governments must include consensus on a clear assignment of roles and responsibilities. These roles should utilize the inherent strengths that each party brings to the relationship. To be successful, compliance and enforcement strategies should recognize and build from available expertise and assistance capacity at all levels/sources. We will also enlist the public in our efforts to increase compliance by ensuring the public has access to data about environmental conditions, and improved access to data regarding noncompliance patterns of facilities, companies, and industry sectors. By providing outreach materials, we will succeed in educating the public and regulated community about the requirements, as well as environmental and public health concerns of local interest.

Measure Impact:

Our enforcement and compliance assurance program must measure the results and impact of activities, not just count the activities themselves. During FY 96 and FY 97 major emphasis will be given to improving our capacity to measure changes in compliance rates and environmental improvements that result from our enforcement and compliance assistance initiatives and activities. This shift in our approach to measures is vital to the future of our enforcement program and it will require a commitment from all our partners to make it work.

Maintain a Robust Enforcement and Compliance Assurance Program:

While the enforcement and compliance assurance program addresses the priorities described in this guidance, we will need to maintain a strong core program of cross-cutting functions such as compliance monitoring and inspections, complete and accurate data systems, case development and management, State/Tribal capacity building, enforcement actions and compliance assistance. Headquarters and Regional managers and staff will need to work cooperatively to balance and blend national priorities, core program activities, and Regional and State needs. Striking this balance will require flexibility with regard to output levels (refer to section IX for a more complete discussion of output levels), explicit choices about investments and disinvestments clearly identified in each regional MOA, and a willingness to adapt to new directions. These new directions and approaches are complementary to our traditional enforcement program. While we support resource shifts within and between enforcement and compliance efforts, it is imperative that all enforcement and compliance resources remain committed to supporting these activities only, and not be shifted to activities that are not part of the enforcement and compliance assurance program.

IV. PRIORITIES

The FY 96/97 compliance and enforcement priorities are organized around three themes: community-based protection; industry sectors; and media-specific issues. We recognize that these three themes are all essential to an effective and successful enforcement and compliance program. We strongly encourage the Regions to incorporate all three themes into their compliance and enforcement MOAs. Regions should work with their States in developing a Regional MOA document that identifies and supports the following priorities, as well as describes unique activities they are undertaking.

1. Community-Based Protection

A major component of the FY 96/97 MOA Guidance and the Regional FY 96/97 MOA submissions will be development of multi-media enforcement and compliance strategies for those communities, ecosystems, and places chosen as priorities. The Agency has committed to direct at least 20% of Regional resources toward community-based efforts in FY 96. Nomination of high priority communities or places would be done primarily by Regions working with States, or, in cases where a place-based priority crosses Regional lines or national boundaries, after consultation with OECA and the involved Regions.

Community-based priorities will focus on environmental or noncompliance problems associated with a particular community or place, including ecosystems, (e.g. watersheds, airsheds) or other natural resource areas of local or Regional concern. Community-based approaches also provide opportunities to address environmental justice concerns. Definable geographic areas have proven to be effective units of work which facilitate collaborative planning and return a sense of involvement with environmental decision making to the people living in these communities.

Each Regional MOA should provide a list of community or placed-based initiatives that will be their focus for enforcement and compliance assurance work. We understand that the Region/States will use a variety of factors in selecting communities and the enforcement/compliance activities may not be pertinent in all areas, or at all phases of these projects. It is anticipated that the Regions will consider the range of appropriate compliance and enforcement activities for the places identified in the Community Based Environmental Protection (CBEP) planning done by the Regions in response to the Deputy Administrator's request for CBEP action plans. For each initiative, please describe the environmental and/or noncompliance problems which need to be addressed, the role of enforcement and compliance assurance tools in addressing these problems, and the outcomes or results which will be measured to assess the effectiveness of the initiative.

Refer to Attachment I for a list of Headquarters support activities to assist in the development of community-based priorities.

2. Industry Sector Priorities

A second element of the FY 96/97 MOA Guidance and the Regional MOA submissions is the development of compliance and enforcement strategies for specific industry sectors that warrant priority attention. In an effort to balance the need for a comprehensive national focus on key industry sectors with the need for flexibility to accommodate Regional and State specific issues and concerns, we have developed a tiered approach to establishing sector priorities. In general, the selection of which specific sectors to address will primarily be a Regional/State choice to enable each to address their specific situation(s). To assure that attention is focused on resolution of compliance issues in sectors found to be nationally significant, however, we have identified three sectors as "national priority sectors" and ten others as "significant sectors."[2] These specific sectors were selected as priorities based on factors such as high noncompliance rates; high volume TRI releases; significant presence and impact in most Regions; and feedback provided through Headquarters/Regional in-house expertise.

Designation as an OECA priority sector means that these sectors will receive special emphasis, such as in-depth analysis of sector-specific compliance problems and focused application of the appropriate compliance/enforcement tools which would be most effective in increasing sector compliance. Such attention can result in the establishment of sector-specific compliance assistance centers, technical assistance and focused outreach and follow-up efforts, as well as the balanced use of our traditional enforcement tools where appropriate. Our goal is the development of innovative approaches to achieve increased compliance within these sectors, and we are open to new ideas and approaches while assuring that public health and the environment are ultimately protected.

As explained later in this document, each Region must develop compliance/enforcement strategies for the three national priority sectors - or explain why it is inappropriate to consider a particular sector as a priority for your Region. In addition, each Region is expected to choose two of the ten "significant sectors" to focus compliance/enforcement strategies upon as well.

a. <u>National Priority Sectors</u>

Our analysis has identified the following sectors as national priority sectors which should be addressed by the Regions:

--petroleum refining
--dry cleaners
--primary nonferrous metals

[2]The Office of Compliance is developing and expects to finalize Sector Notebooks for many of these identified sectors during the summer of 1995. Sector Notebooks contain valuable background information on specific industries including, for example, ongoing compliance initiatives, compliance and enforcement profiles, and basic process knowledge.

Not only do these three sectors have noncompliance and high TRI releases, but they have a significant trans-Regional impact. (Attachment II provides an explanation of the factors used to select these sectors.) If a Region feels that a national priority sector does not merit high priority in their Region, they should provide an explanation of their rationale in their MOA, and provide a strategy for another sector they propose to substitute. This would then be discussed during MOA negotiations.

b. Significant Sectors

In addition to the national priority sectors outlined above, ten additional sectors have been selected for increased attention during FY 96/97. While these sectors may not present as universal a national impact, in many Regions and States they are very important and demand attention. We recommend that the Regions develop strategies utilizing both enforcement and compliance tools in at least two of these sectors. Regions should identify in their MOA which of the following sectors they are targeting (these are not listed in any priority order):

--pulp mills
--agricultural practices
--industrial organic chemicals
--mining
--iron and basic steel products
--plastic materials and synthetics
--printers
--auto service\repair shops
--municipalities for combined sewer overflows/sanitary sewer overflows
--coal-fired power plants

c. Other Sectors

Regions and States may have information about other sectors which are unique or problematic to their Region and/or State(s). If any of these other sectors will receive attention from the Regional/State enforcement and compliance assurance program during FY 96/97, the MOA submissions should explain why they were selected and what enforcement or compliance activities are underway or planned.

Coordination with Common Sense Initiative

Three Common Sense Initiative (CSI) sectors are included among the thirteen designated priority sectors - printing, iron and steel, and petroleum refining. Their selection was based solely on the factors outlined above; their participation as CSI Sectors had no bearing on their selection as OECA MOA priorities. OECA's "Operating Principles for the Common Sense Initiative", (dated October 31, 1994, included as Attachment III) clearly states that our policy is that "no one will be singled out for enforcement as a result of participation in the CSI, and no one will be immunized from enforcement as a result of participation in CSI."

To emphasize our support for the integrity of the CSI process, OECA has incorporated within its CSI Operating Principles a "No Surprises Policy" to ensure that advance notice is provided to facilities that are clearly affiliated with companies participating in the CSI Council, subcommittees or workgroups before a civil or administrative action to assess penalties is filed. We strongly reaffirm our adherence to these Operating Principles and will be working with each Region to ensure that the principles are followed in the field.

OECA is firmly committed to work very closely with the CSI Sector Subcommittees to address sector wide compliance concerns. EPA CSI Sector Leads are participating on OECA's MOA Review Teams to review sector-specific strategies proposed by the Regions in their draft MOAs. This input promotes greater understanding in the CSI community of compliance/enforcement activities and initiatives - from both a Regional and national perspective. In addition, OECA and the Regions will work closely with specific CSI sector subcommittees that develop alternative approaches and/or innovative techniques to achieve compliance within these sectors.

Development of Sector Strategies

Regions and States should utilize a broad range of compliance and enforcement tools when developing multi-year strategies to address specific sectors. Some sectors may be particularly well-suited to the initiation of compliance assistance activities, while others may require use of more traditional enforcement tools. As each Region develops its specific sector strategies, however, we strongly encourage you to think very broadly about the nature of the compliance problems facing your selected industries and fashion innovative solutions from the full range of compliance/enforcement tools available to you. We also encourage you to consider outyear impacts and actions in selecting the mix of compliance and enforcement tools.

For each of the five industry sector initiatives called for in this guidance (i.e. three national priority sectors and at least two additional priority sectors chosen by each Region) a strategy will need to be described in your MOA submissions. As a first step in developing those strategies, data from industry sector profile notebooks provided by Headquarters, as well as data from Regional or other sources should be reviewed. This review should consider factors such as: the sector's current or potential impact on human health and the environment; previous compliance history of the sector within your Region; geographic concentration and demographic factors such as size of businesses and facilities; environmental justice impacts; and sector's potential for achieving compliance, embracing pollution prevention and moving beyond compliance as well as CSI participation and planned projects.

The strategy for each industry sector should describe the environmental and/or noncompliance problems which need to be addressed, the compliance assurance and enforcement tools (e.g., compliance assistance, compliance monitoring, incentive and recognition programs, civil and criminal enforcement) that you anticipate will be applied to the sector, and the outcomes or results which will be measured to assess the effectiveness of the strategy.

3. Media-Specific Priorities

The third source of potential enforcement and compliance assurance priorities is pollutant/media-specific environmental and noncompliance problems. Selection of media specific priorities for the enforcement and compliance assurance program has been done collaboratively by OECA, the Regions, and Headquarters' media program offices. Every Region should specifically address each of these priorities in their MOA. These media-specific priorities can be addressed in conjunction with community-based and sector-based activities, where appropriate. If a Region believes that a media-specific priority does not merit high priority in their Region, they should provide an explanation of their rationale in their MOA, which can serve as the basis for negotiations during the MOA process.

Water

Watershed Approach:

--As discussed under the community-based approach, the Regions should work with their States to target compliance and enforcement efforts toward priority watersheds for both surface water and drinking water source protection. Regions should pay particular attention to facilities with wet weather flow problems. Regions should use a full range of compliance and enforcement tools, including those under the Clean Water Act, Public Water System Supervision and Underground Injection Control programs in this approach.

Safe Drinking Water Act:

--The drinking water enforcement and compliance priorities will focus on enforcing those regulations which result in the greatest reduction of risk to public health. Enforcement of the Surface Water Treatment Rule (SWTR) and the Total Coliform Rule (TCR) will improve the microbiological quality of the water. Enforcement of the Lead/Copper rule will reduce the lead and copper in drinking water.

Wetlands Protection:

--Wetlands enforcement and compliance efforts support the protection of sensitive ecosystems. Regions will strengthen the wetlands enforcement and compliance program by implementing the enforcement management system and other infrastructure improvements which are being designed in FY 95. These tools will promote greater understanding of and consistency in approaching wetlands compliance and enforcement efforts. These new tools should also ensure that, when EPA enforcement actions are taken, they are done in a manner which maximizes the environmental benefit and protection of wetlands and achieves the most efficient use of federal enforcement resources.

Toxics, Pesticides and EPCRA

Protect Human Health:

--Conduct compliance and enforcement activities to help ensure a safe occupational environment for all workers who become exposed to hazardous chemicals, including compliance with the FIFRA Worker Protection Standard (WPS) and TSCA section 5, particularly New Chemical Exposure Limits (NCELS) orders. Through enforcement, protect public health and the environment from potential high risk situations involving misuse and ineffective or unregistered pesticides (e.g., products with child resistant packaging (CRP) problems, hospital disinfectants, food safety issues, etc.).

-- Reduce public exposure to lead-based paint and asbestos hazards in indoor environments through enforcement of AHERA, as appropriate per Region, based on identified non-compliance and risk, the revised asbestos Model Accreditation Plan (e.g., audits of training courses and case issuance), the current and revised asbestos Worker Protection Rule (expected to become final in FY 97), and continued planning for enforcement and compliance assistance for the lead-based paint hazard abatement program.

EPCRA §§ 302-312 & EPCRA § 313
-- Ensure that communities have accurate and timely emergency preparation and notification information in addition to chemical storage and release information through EPCRA enforcement initiatives; i.e., a combined EPCRA/CERCLA 103 initiative, targeting an area with high non-compliance, and an EPCRA 313 TRI chemical expansion compliance assistance and enforcement initiative.

RCRA

New Regulations:
-- Develop Regional expertise on new RCRA regulations (e.g.,Universal Treatment Standards, Subpart CC, other HSWA requirements) in order to implement these requirements in a manner that focuses on the greatest risks to human health and the environment and to provide support and education to the States until they become authorized to implement the regulations.

Outreach and Assistance:
-- Employ mechanisms to provide information about the hazardous waste requirements which enhance compliance either directly or indirectly by participating in activities such as responding to requests for clarification on requirements by the regulated community, participating in seminars and workshops, or developing manuals for specific industries.

Generators:
-- Increase enforcement and compliance activities at facilities generating hazardous waste but that are not treating, storing, or disposing of waste on site. Because of potentially higher rates of noncompliance, generators may pose greater risks to human health and the environment. Additionally, the Agency can encourage pollution prevention by focusing on those companies that generate hazardous wastes.

Air

Air Toxics:
-- By 1996, target compliance assistance and enforcement activities to address extremely hazardous air pollutants to bring industry into compliance with regulations applicable to such critical industries as chemical manufacturers, steel industry (coke ovens), dry cleaners, and degreasing/halogenated solvent users, among others, as well as accidental releases of air toxics. State and local permitting authorities must be educated regarding the new requirements, Regions must work with affected sources to ensure understanding of such requirements, target for inspections, and take enforcement actions where necessary to

deter noncompliance. Regions must coordinate internally and with HQ to implement the requirements of §112(r)(1) of the CAA.

Operating Permits:

-- In FY 96, the Regions and HQ will have a short period to review, to the extent resources permit, draft Title V permits to ensure they are practically enforceable and include all applicable requirements relevant to the permitted source, and to review the source's compliance plan, if any. The Regions may also help train permitting staff in writing permits that contain practical and enforceable terms and conditions. In addition, beginning in FY 96, and increasing in FY 97, Regions should begin targeting inspections and taking enforcement actions against Title V permitted sources, particularly in nonattainment areas.

Implementing New Enforcement Tools:

-- The Clean Air Act Amendments authorize EPA to initiate, through rulemaking, a field citations program for minor violations. The final rule is expected to be published by June, 1995. By FY 96, most of the Regions will have been trained in the use of field citations and will implement this tool, particularly in nonattainment areas. The Regions will begin to use the Citizen Awards Program. They will also utilize other new tools as available, including compliance data from continuous emissions monitors, with an emphasis on sources located in nonattainment areas. The Regions will develop expertise necessary to oversee the implementation of federally-enforceable market-based incentive programs.

Superfund[3]

Worst Sites First:

--Regions should focus on the "worst sites first" and expand the use of removal authority to mitigate threats to people and the environment.

Enforcement First/Cost Recovery:

--In order to leverage the number of cleanups we can undertake or oversee we must maximize PRP participation. The key areas of emphasis are: early initiation of PRP searches and negotiations to support SACM and to maximize PRP response leads, particularly in addressing cost recovery actions that will expire under the Statute of Limitations in March 1997; using Alternative Dispute Resolution to resolve costs owed and compliance monitoring to ensure violations are documented.

Enforcement Fairness/Reduce Transaction Costs:

--EPA must assure fair treatment of all potentially Responsible Parties, especially small volume contributors and parties with a limited ability to pay, who will be targeted for early and prompt settlements. PRP searches to pursue parties identified by other PRPs will be emphasized, as will Alternative Dispute Resolution. Allocation of response cost will be emphasized through pilots and mixed funding will be used where possible. Steps will be

[3] *Superfund targets and measures will be negotiated through the SCAP process. The Regions do not need to provide the SCAP negotiated information in the MOAs. Regions should discuss in their MOA any Superfund resources/activities which support sector-based, or community-based activities.*

taken to reduce private sector transaction costs associated with the cleanup of contaminated sites.

V. CRIMINAL ENFORCEMENT AND FEDERAL PROGRAMS

In addition to the priorities, overarching Agency programs exist which impact all media areas, namely Criminal Enforcement Activities, Federal Facilities, and Federal Activities, (which includes international activities). Please integrate the program directions of these areas into all appropriate Regional activities.

Criminal Enforcement

The Office of Criminal Enforcement has identified the following focus areas for emphasis in FY 96 and FY 97: a.) targeted investigation/enforcement of environmental violators located in the Mississippi River Basin; b.) continued implementation and emphasis on environmental justice activities and multi-media approaches to criminal enforcement; c.) continued implementation of the January 12, 1994, Investigative Discretion Guidance; and d.) continued targeting for investigation of persons who provide false data to EPA and State regulators. When developing sector or community-based strategies, consider specifically appropriate use of criminal resources in these focus areas.

Federal Facilities Enforcement

Enforcement and compliance activities at Federal facilities have a connection with a number of the operating principles and priorities established for the FY 96/97 MOA process. For example, the Federal facilities enforcement program launched the multi-media enforcement and compliance initiative in FY 92. Due to its success, OECA will continue this initiative into FY 96 and FY 97 on a nationwide basis. We are requesting that each Region perform a minimum of two multi-media inspections at Federal facilities each year. This initiative is important because it utilizes multi-media strategies and allows EPA to leverage RCRA/FFCA authority.

The Federal facilities program emphasizes the use of compliance assistance in addition to enforcement actions. Providing guidance, outreach and training assists Federal agencies in achieving and maintaining environmental compliance, including activities under Executive Order 12856 which emphasizes pollution prevention. Regions should increase emphasis on outreach and assistance to civilian Federal agencies.

Regions also should consider including selected Federal facilities as part of your strategies to address specific MOA priorities, including significant Federal facilities located in place-based priority areas or within other significant sectors. In addition, Federal facilities should be addressed under media priorities, as appropriate, especially EPCRA reporting (a new requirement in FY 95), RCRA generators and air toxics (a new requirement under CAA Title III).

Office of Federal Activities

The Environmental Review and Coordination (ERC) program will support achievement of several of the OECA's goals and ensure environmental accountability through the National Environmental Policy Act (NEPA) and international technical assistance agreements. The ERC program will emphasize partnerships with other Federal agencies to better integrate into their program EPA's pollution prevention and ecological risk assessment efforts; ERC will particularly emphasize ecosystem protection and the development of sound data and methodologies to assess environmental impact and ecological risks. The program will assure that EPA has a solid program of compliance with NEPA and other applicable statutes, and with environmental justice requirements. This effort will include the environmental assessment of: EPA-issued new source National Pollutant Discharge/ Elimination System (NPDES) permits in non-delegated States, off-shore oil and gas sources, EPA laboratories and facilities, and remaining projects under the construction grants program. The program will also manage the Agency's official filing activity for all Federal Environmental Impact ments (EISs) in accordance with a Memorandum of Understanding (MOU) with the Council on Environmental Quality (CEQ).

In the international arena, the ERC program will participate in the development of international environmental assessment (EA) procedures and project reviews, with specific emphasis on the Mexican Border, and will provide training on EA principles and processes.

To meet these commitments in FY96/FY97, OECA and the Regions should consider enforcement and compliance efforts in the appropriate geographic regions and industry sectors including: a.) the U.S./Mexico border area, b.) implementation of the U.S./Canada Great Lakes Water Quality Agreement, and c.) efforts to address sensitive ecosystems or populations which transcend national boundaries. Priorities will also include other sectors identified for international cooperation by the North American Commission for Environmental Cooperation or by agreement with Mexico or Canada.

OECA and the Regions will also focus on efforts to enforce U.S. requirements adopted under the following multilateral environmental agreements: a.) the Montreal Protocol on Substances that Deplete the Ozone Layer; and b.) when adopted, the Basel Convention on Transboundary Movement of Hazardous Wastes and Their Disposal.

VI. CORE PROGRAM

A core compliance and enforcement program supports all our work and is critical to our continued success. This core program, described in Attachment IV, needs to be maintained for the enforcement and compliance assurance program to address significant environmental and noncompliance problems and apply the appropriate tools to these problems. In each Region's MOA submission, we would like an explicit statement which provides a commitment to maintaining the core program. If a Region cannot make this commitment, an explanation should be provided in the MOA submission.

VII. REGIONAL SPECIFIC PROJECTS AND HIGHLIGHTS

The priorities and infrastructure discussions above present the national perspective and approach for the compliance and enforcement program. We believe this direction is reflective of the Agency's direction and mission. We also recognize that the national perspective alone does not represent the entire scope of enforcement and compliance efforts. Regions should address unique or specific projects which they are involved with, along with the rationale and the anticipated results. This discussion should complete the framework of the Regional compliance and enforcement program. Where Regions are exploring innovative approaches, piloting projects or processes, or undertaking analyses for targeting and risk-based decision making, we would like to share this experience and findings with the other Regions.

VIII. MEASURING RESULTS

Attachment V presents the FY 1996/1997 reporting measures for Enforcement and Compliance Assurance. The measures track with the recommendations made by the Office of Enforcement and Compliance Assurance (OECA) Measures of Success Workgroup (the Final Report of the Workgroup was transmitted in a January 24, 1995, memorandum from Elaine Stanley), and they establish a foundation for more effective measurement of environmental and programmatic results of the Agency's redesigned compliance and enforcement program. The new set of measures has been named "Reporting for Enforcement and Compliance Assurance Priorities (RECAP)."

The Enforcement Planning, Targeting, and Data Division in the Office of Compliance committed to review the former STARS measures that conveyed to OECA from the former Office of Enforcement and the media program offices with an eye toward dropping measures determined no longer to be needed. The attached RECAP measures reflect the results of that review. The only measures which will require upfront numerical commitments/projections will be those for media-specific inspections and drinking water SNC. Refer to Attachment VI for these charts.

The former STARS measures which conveyed to OECA have been reduced by 44%, and the associated data points have been reduced by 27% (these are contained in Sections III, IV, and V). Overall, the total number of measures in RECAP (the former STARS measures plus the new measures recommended by the Workgroup) reduce by 30% the total number of measures that conveyed to OECA, and the number of RECAP data points reported reduce by 12% the number that conveyed to OECA.

In addition to the streamlined measures, RECAP measures include:

1. **Re-engineering of existing reporting on noncompliance rates to create multi-media profiles for sectors, community-based activities, pollutant-specific activities, and corporate perspectives.** EPTDD will report on these measures (contained in Section I of the attachment) through use of existing reporting on noncompliance levels, Significant Noncompliance, enforcement actions, inspections, and TRI releases and transfers. EPTDD will develop the profiles using data integration techniques, newly-improved data linkages, SIC codes, facility location data, and demographic information. Programming work on these reports is ongoing and EPTDD will pilot profile data reporting during the third quarter of FY 1995.

2. **Section I of Attachment V also contains measures for compliance assistance that have been developed by an OECA-led workgroup.** For FY 1996/1997 we are asking the Regions to report on their compliance assistance activities using these measures and to work with their States to ask them to voluntarily use these measures. Use of the measures will enable the States to discuss the positive outcomes of their compliance assistance activities. We anticipate that the measures may change after States and Regions have experience using them. (Attachment VII provides a more detailed discussion and background for the compliance assistance measures.)

3. **Systematic reporting of the environmental and programmatic impacts of compliance and enforcement.** OECA is pilot testing these measures, contained in Section II of Attachment V, in all ten Regions using the recently developed judicial and administrative **case conclusion data sheet.** The measures and definitions may be modified based on an analysis of the pilot reporting process during the summer months. Any modifications to the data collected or the definitions suggested by the analysis will be coordinated with the affected offices in Headquarters and the Regions.

4. **A more comprehensive approach to counting enforcement activities through an <u>Enforcement Activity Index</u>.** The Index (contained in Section IV of the attachment) will use existing reporting to track information on the initiation and conclusion of civil judicial cases, criminal enforcement activities, significant administrative actions, and activities that address significant noncompliance at Federal facilities. Environmental justice cases will also be identified beginning in the second half of FY 95 using new fields available in the Enforcement Docket system. This information will be consistent with the case conclusion data sheet and will allow electronic reporting for both concluded and initiated civil and administrative cases. By showcasing conclusions, staff and managers will demonstrate that case resolution to achieve results and not just case initiation to produce new "beans" is the true value of enforcement actions. OECA is conducting a pilot test of reporting under the index with data for the first two quarters of FY 1995. The results of the pilot will be shared with Headquarters and Regional offices to identify definitional or reporting issues.

IX. OUTPUT LEVELS

EPA's enforcement and compliance assurance program has historically measured its yearly successes by counting various activities, e.g., actions filed, cases referred, penalties assessed. Headquarters has traditionally directed the Regions to meet or exceed the previous year's levels of these activities. This approach has serious limitations when used as the primary or exclusive indicator of success: it says little about the impact, effectiveness, and environmental results achieved through our activities; it does not take into account other enforcement and compliance assurance tools that can contribute to increased compliance; and it can lead to taking low priority enforcement actions in order to meet previous output levels.

Our effort to redefine how success is evaluated is timely as a result of several factors: first, our intention to use a wider range of enforcement and compliance tools requires a more sophisticated set of measures; second, the likelihood of resource reductions makes meeting previous levels problematic; and third, our work on developing measures based on results and outcomes (described in the previous section) has progressed to the point that new measures will be available.

Accordingly, we are providing the following guidance as we move toward more sophisticated measures:

--Although we will continue to collect and publicly report information about case referrals, actions filed, etc., we will no longer direct Regions to necessarily produce enforcement activities at previous levels.

--Although case measures will continue to be used as one indication of program performance, we will no longer use them as the primary measure of effectiveness in evaluating the performance of Regional enforcement programs. We will move as expeditiously as possible to emphasize outcomes and result-based measures.

--We need the full cooperation of the Regions in the development and implementation of the case completion data sheet, the enforcement activity index, and compliance assistance measures.

--In developing strategies to address each of the community-based and sector-based priorities in your MOA, Regions should propose outcome-based measures. In negotiating and finalizing MOAs, Headquarters will align these measures so they can be aggregated at the national level.

X. GRANT GUIDANCE

Regions should use the priorities and activities identified in this MOA guidance as they negotiate all State grant work programs, as delineated below. Since OECA has direct responsibility for the pesticides, toxic and lead enforcement grants but is not directly responsible for administering other media grant programs, this approach has also been cooridinated with the Headquarters media program offices to ensure that our priorities are in concert with their program priorities. Regions should negotiate the enforcement and compliance components of grants in line with this OECA MOA Guidance.

Attachment VIII of this MOA guidance contains information to assist Regions as they negotiate State pesticides and toxics enforcement grant work programs. Specifically, Attachment VIII provides a detailed discussion of key activities which we feel the States need to commit to in order to undertake implementation of priorities identified in the toxic and pesticide areas.

Regions should work with their States to develop pesticide and toxic cooperative agreements that reflect the national priorities contained within this MOA guidance, as appropriate for each State, together with Regional, State, and local priorities. Refer to Section IV.3. for the list of national priorities identified for the pesticides and toxics programs. Also consider the community-based and sector priorities identified in Sections IV.1. and IV.2. when negotiating these cooperative agreements.

XI. RESOURCE INFORMATION

We are not at this time requesting any additional resource information beyond what was provided in the FY 95 MOA submissions. In light of the Workforce Survey recently completed by Regional Offices and Headquarters Program Offices, and given that ongoing or planned Regional reorganizations will make resource estimates problematic, we will not request any resource information as part of your initial FY96/97 MOA submission. If necessary, at the mid-point of this two-year MOA and after Regional reorganizations are completed, we may ask that the resource information provided in your FY 95 MOA be updated.

XII. PROCESS FOR DEVELOPING AND NEGOTIATING FY 96/97 MOAS:

A. Format

To assist in the development of the FY 96/97 MOAs, Attachment IX provides a format for MOA development. Headquarters will also provide the Regions with this file electronically through the POSTMAN system. We hope that all Regions use the standard form. By providing the file, Regions may more easily make adjustments where necessary.

Regions should follow the following outline:

1. **Introduction:** 3-5 page summary of Region's strategic directions and program priorities for FY 96/97. Regions should discuss their overall approach, priority areas, and identify any barriers or impediments to successfully implementing their approach, including the need to build capacity.

2. **Priorities:** address each identified priority in the order it appears in the MOA guidance by developing a strategy with the following elements:

Priority: identify from guidance;

Statement of Problem: describe the environmental, human health or noncompliance problem(s) being addressed;

Activities/Tools to Address Problem: describe the enforcement and/or compliance assurance activities or tools which will be used to address the problem;

EJ Component: identify if this activity has any environmental justice aspects;

P2 Component: identify if this activity has any pollution prevention aspects;

Measuring Results: identify which measures (results, outcome-based measures, and/or traditional activity counts) you will use to determine success in meeting/achieving the activity;

Resource Tradeoffs: in support of each priority activity identify any necessary resource tradeoffs the Region is proposing in order to fulfill the priority activity (for example, FTE shifts both between or within enforcement and compliance programs, or shifts away from core activities);

Regional support needs: identify what support from Headquarters is necessary to assist you in completing the activity. Please note that in FY 96 any support requests for NEIC assistance will be negotiated through the MOA. Regions should feel free to discuss their requests with NEIC before submitting their MOA to Headquarters.

3. **Criminal Enforcement and Federal Programs:** Regions should include summaries of Regional activities which address the identified priority areas from the Criminal, Federal Activities, and Federal Facilities programs.

4. **Core Program:** Regions should address their support of the core program, highlighting any trade-offs they are proposing and supplying a rationale for the trade-off, if this is not already clearly done under the priority discussion.

5. **Regional Initiatives:** Regions should provide information on special or unique projects which they are involved with, such as enforcement or compliance initiatives not discussed elsewhere, pilot studies, special EJ initiatives, and P2 projects that are not adequately covered under the national priorities discussion. Headquarters will analyze and share information between Regions on special projects or innovative approaches.

6. **Measuring Results:** In this section Regions should report on:

a. Traditional enforcement measures under RECAP (Attachment V)
b. Targeted measures which require upfront commitments, such as inspections or projections (charts provided in Attachment VI)
c. Alternative measures of success, looking at both traditional enforcement as well as newer compliance assistance efforts, that you are using by either referencing the priorities discussion or identifying others that do not match a specific priority
d. System enhancements, such as EJ flag, which they are supporting

B. Schedule for Developing and Negotiating FY 96/97 MOAs:

--In March publish draft MOA guidance

--In June publish final MOA guidance

--In July, Headquarters will conduct a series of conference calls with each Region (at both the DRA level and staff level) to discuss status, problems, and sector selection.

--Draft Regional MOAs are due to Headquarters between July 14, 1995 and August 18, 1995, with a first in/first reviewed approach.

--Headquarters will review and negotiate MOAs no later than mid-October, 1995.

--We will consult with the Regions in January, 1996 about whether changes or revisions should be made in priorities or guidance for FY 97, the second year of the MOA.

C. Reporting Schedule for FY 96 and FY 97:

-- Mid Year reports due by May 1, 1996 and 1997. This report and subsequent conversations can also serve as the basis for making adjustments agreed to by both Headquarters and the Regions to address emerging needs, new data, amendment of statutory authorities, etc.

-- In August, 1996 Regions will be requested to submit an MOA update which includes:

-FY 97 commitment information;
-changes or adjustments in Regional activities;
-if necessary, resource information about FTEs and grant dollars.

-- End of Year Report due November 15, 1996 and 1997.

D. Review and Negotiation of MOA

-- We will discuss with each Region their preferred approach to discussing MOA issues/areas needing clarification. This could be one conference call per Region to discuss all areas or one per media (as needed). Before these calls we will fax to the Regional MOA contact the areas to be discussed.

-- Superfund priorities and Headquarters support are defined through the OERR/OSRE joint strategic planning process. Superfund targets and measures will be negotiated through the SCAP process. The Regions do not need to provide the SCAP negotiated information in the MOAs. OSRE will be responsible for including it in the MOAs. Regions should, however, discuss in their MOA Superfund activities/resources which support multi-media, sector based or community based activities. The Regions should identify any Superfund priorities that are impacted by these areas and discuss trade-offs within the SCAP negotiations.

-- RCRA Corrective Action (CA) priorities and Headquarters support are defined through the OSWER RCRA Implementation Plan and Beginning of Year Plans (RIP/BYP). RCRA CA measures will be negotiated through the RIP/BYP process. The Regions do not need to provide the RIP/BYP information in the MOAs. Nevertheless, Regions should discuss in their MOA any RCRA CA activities/resources which support multi-media, sector based or community based activities and any trade-offs this involves.

-- Once staff level discussions and clarifications are complete, senior management discussions will take place between the DAAs and the DRAs. These calls will focus on: discussing the Region's enforcement and compliance program from a more strategic perspective, discussing national goals and directions for the program, and leading negotiations on remaining issues.

E. Link to Regional Evaluations

-- Increasingly, as the MOA process matures, the MOA will establish much of the baseline against which the Regions' enforcement and compliance performance is measured during the Regional evaluations.

-- Prior to each Regional evaluation, the Headquarters participants will familiarize themselves with the content of the MOA and will focus their review of the Region's performance pursuant to the MOA as appropriate.

-- As part of the MOA negotiation process, HQ will review the most recent final evaluation report for each Region and will incorporate, as appropriate, the findings, conclusions, proposals, and commitments into the MOA negotiations and the MOA itself.

-- Where either a Regional evaluation or an end of the year MOA report coincide within a month or two, HQ will take the information provided in the MOA report or questionnaire and cross walk with information requested by the Regional evaluation questionnaire, identify gaps, and tailor our request for additional information accordingly; every effort will be made to avoid covering the same material twice.

-- HQ will provide feedback during the Regional evaluation on the status of HQ support requests expressed in the MOA.

Rationale for Selecting National Priority Sectors

Petroleum Refining:

-- on a national level, ranked number 1 for noncompliance
-- in 8 of the 10 Regions petroleum refining in top ten noncomplying industries:

Reg 2--# 2
Reg 3--# 3
Reg 5--# 5
Reg 6--# 2
Reg 7--# 9
Reg 8--# 6
Reg 9--# 6
Reg 10-# 5

--Sixth highest amount of TRI Releases and Transfers
--For TRI releases of known carcinogens, ranked number 7
--NEIC is developing a document that outlines the problems they have found in this industry.The document will help regions deal with refineries when they start inspecting them.
--Within the next few months, we should have a comprehensive relative ranking of all petroleum refineries in the country.This will also help the regions decide where to go for inspections.The ranking will factoring in TRI release with toxicological weights, demographic information, compliance history and productivity of the facility.

Dry Cleaners

--Dry cleaners are dominated by small businesses, which are usually exempt from TRI reporting due to their size, but have a significant aggregate impact.
--Dry cleaners have a lack of awareness of environmental regulations, yet potential to be highly regulated.
--Industry eager to work with us.
--Potential for us to make an impact, pollution prevention opportunities.
--Recognize need to build compliance data through inspections

Primary Non-Ferrous

--Nationally ranked third for noncompliance
--significant problem in 7 out of 10 Regions
--in 5 of the 10 Regions primary non-ferrous metals in top ten noncomplying industries:

Reg 1--#1
Reg 3--#1
Reg 4--#1
Reg 7--#3
Reg 10-#7

--Fifth highest amount of TRI Releases and Transfers
--For TRI releases of known carcinogens, ranked number 13

October 31, 1994

MEMORANDUM

SUBJECT:OECA's Operating Principles for the Common Sense Initiative

FROM: Steven A. Herman
Assistant Administrator

TO: Administrator
Deputy Assistant Administrator
Assistant Administrators
General Counsel
Regional Administrators
Deputy Regional Administrators
Regional Counsel

The purpose of this memorandum is to establish overall operating principles for handling enforcement and compliance issues for the Common Sense Initiative ("CSI"). The CSI is a unique opportunity to work with our CSI stakeholder partners (i.e., the regulated community, state and local governments, environmental justice, labor, and environmental groups) to develop innovative ways to promote compliance-oriented behavior. These general operating principles are intended to foster the spirit of cooperation that underlies the CSI, and at the same time address key enforcement and compliance related concerns at the outset.

These principles provide a general framework for handling enforcement and compliance concerns during the course of CSI. I anticipate that the CSI sector teams, through pilots, demonstration projects and the like, will generate creative ideas on enforcement and compliance policy for the Agency to consider within the general framework of these operating principles. In addition, OECA expects to consult with the CSI sector teams in the course of several policy reviews currently underway.

Under the CSI, enforcement and compliance assurance concerns are likely to arise in two discrete contexts: 1. as part of the Agency's deliberations regarding whether a CSI project is appropriate at a given facility, and 2. in determining an appropriate response to violations by companies involved in CSI that are identified during the course of CSI. This memorandum sets forth an enforcement response framework that I believe is practical and fair. Simply stated, our policy will be that no one will be singled out for enforcement as a result of participation in CSI, and no one will be immunized from enforcement as a result of participation in CSI. It is our belief that these principles are consistent with the Administrator's goals of fostering a new generation of environmental protection while at the same time maintaining the integrity and effectiveness of the enforcement and compliance assurance program.

I. APPROVAL OF PROJECTS

In reviewing proposed CSI demonstration projects, the Agency should be aware of and consider whether a particular facility is currently scheduled for a planned inspection, under investigation. or involved in an enforcement action with the Agency, the State, local government, or citizens. Information about planned or pending EPA enforcement actions will be shared by OECA on a confidential basis within EPA, and with applicable states as appropriate, and must, for obvious reasons, be taken into account in considering whether or not to undertake a particular demonstration project. The terms of a given proposed project and whether or not it is ultimately approved should depend in part on the nature of the project under consideration and the gravity of any compliance problem under review.

II. COMPLIANCE PROBLEMS AT FACILITIES WITH CSI PROJECTS

CSI participation should not insulate sectors or companies from enforcement when, apart from CSI, information comes to light that calls for enforcement. However, as a general rule, the mere fact that a sector (or facility) is participating in CSI, will not by itself subject that sector (or facility) to greater scrutiny from an enforcement perspective.

Our enforcement response policy under CSI should reflect a line of demarcation between those circumstances in which information comes to our attention solely by virtue of a company's participation in the CSI (i.e., but for CSI the violation either would not have occurred[1] or we would not have discovered it[2]) and circumstances in which information is generated as a result of compliance monitoring activities separate and apart from CSI.With this general framework in mind, we offer the following guidelines.

1. "No surprises" policy-- OECA will endeavor to ensure that those within the Agency who are responsible for managing the CSI effort are aware of impending enforcement strategies and actions involving facilities that are clearly affiliated with companies that are participating in the CSI Council, subcommittees or workgroups. Additionally, in keeping with the spirit of

---

[1] *Some facilities that are working with us on a CSI demonstration project, such as the development of a consolidated reporting form or the demonstration of an innovative environmental technology may, simply by undertaking the project, run an anticipated risk of violating existing legal requirements.*

[2] *We can envision a number of scenarios in which noncompliance information that would not have otherwise been discovered by EPA may come to light as a result of CSI. For example, for some sectors-- particularly those comprised of small businesses-- compliance assistance may be an important part of the overall CSI strategy. During the course of administering compliance assistance, whether through "hot lines," where small businesses could call for basic information about compliance requirements and pollution prevention methods, or through site visits, not for purposes of conducting a compliance inspection, but rather for purposes of offering assistance, actionable noncompliance may be revealed. Similarly, noncompliance information may be discovered when EPA visits a facility to explore innovative technology opportunities or improve understanding of regulatory burdens and streamlining opportunities. In addition, the Agency is likely in a variety of contexts to encourage voluntary submissions of information that may contain information on noncompliance.*

openness that CSI is intended to engender, OECA will ensure that advance notice is provided to facilities that are clearly affiliated with companies participating in the CSI Council, subcommittees or workgroups before a civil or administrative action to assess penalties is brought against them.[3]

2. The Agency must be free to respond to circumstances which may present an imminent and substantial endangerment or other threat to human health or the environment or are criminal in nature, even when discovery of such circumstances is through CSI. With respect to civil violations that do not rise to the level of an endangerment, the Agency's enforcement response policy will necessarily depend on the nature of the project and facility at issue. As appropriate, and subject to such conditions as the circumstances require, the Agency may consider giving facilities performing CSI projects a time-limited opportunity to self-correct violations that are discovered as a result of the project (see, e.g., "Enforcement Response Policy for Treatment of Information Obtained Through Clean Air Act Section 507 Small Business Assistance Programs," August 12, 1994).

3. There may be instances where CSI projects (or specific components of them) by their very design (e.g, the testing of undemonstrated innovative technologies) may raise the risk that existing regulations will be violated during implementation of these projects. In these circumstances, if violations do occur, the fact of the respondent's participation in the CSI project will be taken into account in fashioning an appropriate enforcement response. In particular, such participation may serve to mitigate penalties, if such mitigation is deemed appropriate under the circumstances of the particular project. Further, the interests of the CSI participants and the Agency will be best served if the participants prior to engaging in these projects enter into a written agreement which specifies the terms, conditions, and obligations of the project. The agreement should also speak to the enforcement consequences of project success and failure, as well as how unanticipated results or violations will be addressed.

4. Since the CSI effort is not intended to supplant the Agency's existing enforcement activities, planned and regularly scheduled inspections, on-going investigations, and enforcement actions should continue.[4] Similarly, the deployment of enforcement resources based on current Agency priorities and based on information not secured through CSI will continue. However, as part of its participation on the sector teams, OECA will work closely with the teams to determine how to address any sector-wide compliance concerns.

5. If, consistent with the foregoing, a CSI facility becomes subject to an enforcement action, the facility's performance of a particular CSI project may, consistent with Agency policy, be considered an indicator of good faith efforts to comply for penalty assessment purposes, assuming that the CSI project is related in some way to the violation of concern in the enforcement case.

---

[3] *This is consistent with current practice regarding the filing of civil complaints in federal court under the Civil Justice Reform Executive Order (12778)*

[4] *Regulated facilities are subject to inspection by state and federal authorities at regular intervals; indeed, in some instances, inspection frequency is fixed by law (e.g., RCRA). Moreover, a great deal of compliance information is, by law, self-reported to EPA and the states. Thus, CSI participating facilities will be subject to compliance review as a matter of course.*

cc: OECA Office Directors and Division Directors
Regional CSI Enforcement Contacts
CSI Sector Team Leads
Vivian Daub
Steve Harper

OECA CORE PROGRAM ACTIVITIES

Planning/Management Elements

- o Program planning (including development of MOA, strategic plans, etc.)
- o Budget development/monitoring and oversight
- o State/territory program monitoring and oversight (including oversight of grants/cooperative agreements, etc.)
- o State/territory program capacity building, review and evaluation
- o Contract management, training and oversight

Data Management Elements

- o Data management including data input, review, analysis and QA/QC activities in support of all parts of OECA program (compliance, enforcement, site remediation, criminal, federal facilities)

Compliance Program Elements

- o Compliance Monitoring

  - Conducting inspections not addressed by the States
  - Inspection targeting
  - Inspector training and guidance

- o Review permits, exception reports, certifications, monitoring protocols, self-monitoring reports, etc.
- o Laboratory support
- o Compliance assistance outreach/education/training to regulated community
- o Applicability determinations

Enforcement Program Elements

- Take timely and appropriate enforcement actions.
- Issue proposed and final administrative orders
- Case development and support
- Oversee compliance with schedules contained in final orders and consent decrees
- Develop civil and or criminal referrals to DOJ
- Conduct overfiling where requested or appropriate
- Participate in national initiatives
- Oversight and monitoring of SEPs
- Environmental Services Division support
- Expert witnesses for case support
- Assistance provided to Regional criminal enforcement counsels

Site Remediation Elements

- CERCLA Elements

  - Address Cost Recovery Sites
  - Maximize PRP Participation
  - Achieve early settlements with Small Volume Contributors
  - Support Communities with EJ Concerns related to SF

- RCRA Corrective Action Elements

  - Implement Stabilization Initiative
  - Focus resources at high NCAPS facilities
  - Assess Non-notifiers/converters

- Remediate sites with leaking underground storage tanks
- Collect penalties for violations of Section 311(b) of OPA

Federal Facility Elements (not included in above categories)

- o Negotiate/amend and enforce IAGs for federal facility site cleanups
- o Implement E.O. 12856 and assist Federal Facilities to develop required P2 plans and assessments
- o Pursue reimbursement from Federal agencies for EPA and State cost of RCRA TSD facility inspections
- o Coordinate A-106 annual review process.

Appendix B

Appendix B—Sample Forms and Pleadings

Table of Contents

In re the Search of the Rocky Flats Plant, Golden, Colorado: Application and Affidavit for Search Warrant (excerpts)

United States District Court

DISTRICT OF COLORADO

In the Matter of the Search of

(Name, address or brief description of person, property or premises to be searched)

The Rocky Flats Plant
U.S. Department of Energy
Rockwell International Corporation
Highway 93
Golden, Colorado 80402

APPLICATION AND AFFIDAVIT FOR SEARCH WARRANT

CASE NUMBER

I Jon S. Lipsky being duly sworn depose and say:

I am a(n) Special Agent, Federal Bureau of Investigation and have reason to believe
(Official Title)

that ☐ on the person of or ☒ on the property or premises known as (name, description and/or location)

The Rocky Flats Plant, U.S. Department of Energy, Rockwell International Corporation, Highway 93, Golden, Colorado 80402, (as more particularly described in Attachment 1 incorporated here by reference)

in the State and District of Colorado
there is now concealed a certain person or property, namely (describe the person or property to be seized)

the property described on Attachment 2 (incorporated here by reference)
which is

evidence or the means or instrumentalities of, or the fruits or other results of, criminal violations of the Resource Conservation and Recovery Act, 42 U.S.C. § 6928(d), the Federal Water Pollution Control Act, 33 U.S.C. §§ 1311(a) and 1319(c), and 18 U.S.C. §§ 1001 and 2.

The facts to support a finding of Probable Cause are set forth in Attachment C, incorporated here by reference.

Continued on the attached sheet and made a part hereof. ☒ Yes ☐ No

Signature of Affiant Special Agent, FBI

Sworn to before me, and subscribed in my presence

Date at Denver, Colorado
City and State

Name and Title of Judicial Officer

Signature of Judicial Officer

Attachment 1

The Rocky Flats Plant, located on State Highway 93 near the town of Golden, in Jefferson County, Colorado ("Rocky Flats"), is owned by and part of the U.S. Department of Energy ("DOE"), and is operated by Rockwell International Corporation on DOE's behalf. The entire Rocky Flats property comprises approximately 6,550 acres, with its principal industrial plant and operations on approximately 400 acres. The entire property, located in Section 2, Range 70 West, Township 2 South, is bounded by State Highway 128 on the north, Indiana Street on the east, State Highway 72 on the south and State Highway 93 on the west. The plant's principal entrance on Highway 93 is marked by an approximate 10 feet x 5 feet sign, with white lettering on a light-blue background, stating "United States Department of Energy, Operated by North American Space Operations, Rockwell International." The specific property covered by this warrant are the following buildings, sites and locations, and their surrounding curtillage:

Wind Systems Building
Building 111
Building 115
Building 122
Building 123
Building 371
Building 373
Building 374
Building 443
Building 444
Building 460
Building 551
Building 559
Building 563
Building 668
Building 701
Building 705
Building 708
Building 712
Building 750T
Building 770
Building 771
Building 776
Building 779
Building 780
Building 881
Building 885
Building 910
Building 988
Building 991
Building 995 (and Adjacent Spray Field)
Landfill and Adjacent Pond
North Walnut Creek
Pond A-1
Pond A-2
Pond A-3
Pond A-4
South Walnut Creek
Pond B-1
Pond B-2
Pond B-3
Pond B-4
Pond B-5
Woman Creek
Pond C-1
Pond C-2
North Spray Field
South Spray Field
Pond 207A
Ponds 207B (North, Middle and South)
Pond 207C

Attachment 2

The property covered by this warrant consists of various waste (and related) materials and records pertaining to waste handling activities, both as more particularly described below and in the attached affidavit of Jon S. Lipsky (Attachment 3).

I. **Waste Materials**

As used herein, "waste" or "waste materials" means and includes all hazardous wastes, mixed hazardous and radioactive wastes (including mixed low-level radioactive and transuranic wastes), in whatever form (e.g., sludge, ash, pond crete, etc.) and water pollutants (i.e., any solid waste, sewage, garbage, sewage sludge, chemical wastes, biological materials, or industrial waste discharged into or prepared for discharge into waters at the Rocky Flats Plant, including the A, B and C series ponds, North Walnut Creek, South Walnut Creek, Woman Creek and/or other conveyances leading to such waters), including their containers or carriers (e.g., drums, bags, tanks, vats, boxes, filters, etc.) and the media upon which such wastes or pollutants have been discharged or otherwise deposited (e.g., soil or other ground cover, water, groundwater, creek bottoms, etc.).

II. **Records**

As used herein, "records" means and includes all form and manner of records and documents (including agreements, correspondence, memoranda, notes, messages, journals, inventories, etc., as well as computer and other electronic information, disks, data, etc.), and includes:

1. All blueprints, architectural, engineering or other drawings or diagrams; engineering or technical specifications or performance evaluations; and photographs of: hazardous or radioactive mixed waste treatment, storage, disposal or recycling facilities used or located at the Rocky Flats Plant since November 1980, including, but not limited to, containers; tanks; surface impoundments; waste piles; land treatment facilities; landfills; incinerators; nuclear material recovery units for the processing of "mixed wastes;" thermal treatment units; chemical, physical and biological treatment units; waste water and sewage treatment facilities; underground sumps, pipes, lines, containment areas, and other impoundments and conveyances for the handling or movement of hazardous or "mixed" wastes.

2. All records reflecting the time, quantity or manner of the treatment, storage, disposal, recycling (as used herein "recycling" includes "recovery" of materials) or discharge of hazardous or mixed waste or pollutants at the Rocky Flats Plant since November 1980, including but not limited to: incinerator or other treatment unit operating records or logs; test burn records; records reflecting storage accumulation dates and inventories; certificates of disposal or destruction; and waste

water and sewage treatment plant discharge, sampling and analysis records.

3. All records reflecting the transportation into or out of the Rocky Flats Plant since November 1980 of hazardous or mixed wastes, including, but not limited to, hazardous waste manifests, bills of lading, invoices, shipping papers and driver's logs.

4. All records reflecting payment by or to Rockwell International Corporation (Rockwell) or the United States Department of Energy (DOE) for the transportation, treatment, disposal or recycling of hazardous or mixed wastes generated or located at, or brought to the Rocky Flats Plant since November 1980.

5. All records reflecting studies, inspections, investigations, sampling or monitoring by or on behalf of Rockwell or the DOE regarding the treatment, storage, disposal or recycling of hazardous or mixed wastes or the discharge of pollutants at the Rocky Flats Plant since November 1980, including but not limited to: 1) reports prepared pursuant to DOE Orders establishing procedures for hazardous and mixed waste management such as annual hazardous waste management reports, compliance status reports, compliance action plans, waste management system performance assessments, and waste management plans, 2) other such records pertaining to groundwater contamination; groundwater monitoring; incineration of wastes; recycling or recovery of hazardous or mixed wastes; discharge of pollutants into ponds or creeks; or environmental or health impacts onsite (including on workers at the Rocky Flats Plant) or offsite; and 3) other such records concerning waste stream identification and characterization.

6. All records reflecting communication by Rockwell or DOE, including but not limited to internal communications or communications between Rockwell and DOE, regarding the compliance status of the Rocky Flats Plant with federal, state and local environmental requirements.

7. Other records demonstrating knowledge or awareness on the part of Rockwell or DOE or Rockwell employees or contractors of the nature of the hazardous or mixed wastes or pollutants at the Rocky Flats Plant and/or of laws regulating their generation, transportation, treatment, storage, disposal or recycling.

8. All records concerning evaluations by DOE or others of Rockwell's performance of its environmental duties at the Rocky Flats Plant, including but not limited to records relating to bonus payments to Rockwell from DOE.

9. Documents explaining operation of any computer system containing any of the above information.

10. Documents containing the names, addresses, and telephone numbers of all DOE or Rockwell employees who are or have been employed at the Rocky Flats Plant at any time since November 1980 and the job descriptions or other material defining the nature and scope of each employee's responsibilities.

The property covered by this warrant relates to the facilities and bodies of water located outdoors (as listed on Attachment 1) and to individual buildings located at the Rocky Flats Plant as follows:

Wind Systems Building

Records -- All records described in Paragraphs 1-9 above.

Building 111 (Administrative Offices)

Wastes -- "Developer/fixer" waste and all other "waste materials" designated for treatment, storage, disposal or recycling (hereinafter "TSDR") in Buildings 988 or 995.

Records -- All records described in Paragraphs 1-10 above.

Building 115 (DOE Area Office)

Records -- All records described in Paragraphs 1-10 above.

Building 122 (Medical Building)

Records -- All records described in Paragraphs 1-9 above.

Building 123 (Health/Environment Building)

Records -- All records described in Paragraphs 1-9 above.

Building 371 (Plutonium Recovery)

Waste -- All waste stored or designated for storage in Building 371.

Records -- All records pertaining to the storage of waste in Building 371.

Building 373 (Cooling Tower & Pump House)

Waste -- "Evaporator water" waste, "drips and leaks" waste and all other waste designated for TSDR in Building 373, 988 or 995.

Records -- All records pertaining to the generation or TSDR of "evaporator water," "drips and leaks" and other wastes designated for TSDR in Buildings 373, 988 or 995.

Building 374 (Liquid Waste Treatment Facility)

Wastes -- "Evaporator water" waste and all other wastes designated for TSDR in Buildings 373, 443 or 995.

Records -- All records pertaining to the generation or TSDR or "evaporator water" or other wastes designated for TSDR in Buildings 373, 443 or 995.

Building 443 (Steam Plant)

Wastes -- "Evaporator water" waste and all other wastes designated for TSDR within Building 443.

Records -- All records pertaining to the TSDR of "evaporator water" or other wastes designated for TSDR in Building 443.

Building 444 (Production Operations)

Wastes -- "Blowdown waste" and all other wastes designated for TSDR in Buildings 988 or 995.

Records -- All records pertaining to the generation or TSDR of "blowdown waste" or other waste designated for TSDR in Buildings 988 or 995.

Building 460 (Non-Nuclear Manufacturing)

Wastes -- "Used kimwipes," "cooling tower blowdown" and all other wastes designated for TSDR in the landfill or Buildings 988 or 995.

Records -- All records pertaining to the generation or TSDR of "used kimwipes," "cooling tower blowdown" or other wastes designated for TSDR in the landfill or Buildings 988 or 995

Building 551 (General Warehouse)

Wastes -- "Kimwipes/degreasing residues" and all other wastes designated for TSDR in the landfill.

Records -- All records pertaining to the generation or TSDR of "kimwipes/degreasing residues" or other wastes designated for TSDR in the landfill.

Building 559 (Plutonium Analytical Lab)

Wastes -- "Non-line combustibles" and all other wastes designated for TSDR in Building 771.

Records -- All records pertaining to the generation or TSDR of "non-line combustibles" or other wastes designated for TSDR in Building 771.

Building 563 (Cooling Tower)

Wastes -- "Sump sludge" and all other wastes designated for TSDR in the landfill.

Records -- All records pertaining to the generation or TSDR of "sump sludge" or other wastes designated for TSDR in the landfill.

Building 668 (Drum Certification)

Wastes -- "rags with methyl alcohol" and all other wastes designated for TSDR in the landfill.

Records -- All records pertaining to the generation or TSDR of "rags with methyl alcohol" or other wastes designated for TSDR in the landfill.

Building 701 (Process Development)

Waste -- "Liquid waste" and all other wasted designated for TSDR in Buildings 988 or 995.

Records -- All records pertaining to the generation or TSDR or "liquid waste" or other wastes designated for TSDR in Building 988 or 995.

Building 705 (Coating Laboratory)

Wastes -- "Kimwipes" or other wastes designated for TSDR in the landfill.

Records -- All records relating to the generation or TSDR of "kimwipes" or other wastes designated for TSDR in the landfill.

Building 708 (Compressor Building)

Waste -- "Rags with freon/TCE" and all other wastes designated for TSDR in the landfill.

Records -- All records pertaining to the generation or TSDR of "rags with freon/TCE" or other wastes designated for TSDR in the landfill.

Building 712 (Cooling Tower)

Waste -- "Sump sludge," "water blowdown" and all other . wastes designated for TSDR in the landfill or Buildings 988 or 995.

Records -- All records pertaining to the generation or TSDR of "sump sludge," "water blowdown" or other wastes designated for TSDR in the landfill or Buildings 988 or 995.

Building 750T (Trailer Complex)

Waste -- "Soiled kimwipes," "kimwipes" and all other wastes designated for TSDR in the landfill.

Records -- All records pertaining to the generation or TSDR of "soiled kimwipes," "kimwipes" or other waste designated for TSDR in the landfill.

Building 770 (Pipe Fabrication Shop)

Waste -- "Combustibles," "rags" and all other wastes designated for TSDR in the landfill.

Records -- All records pertaining to the generation or TSDR or "combustibles," "rags" or other wastes designated for TSDR in the landfill.

Building 771 (Plutonium Recovery Facility)

Waste -- "Non-line combustibles," "trash," "burnables" and "kimwipes," and all other wastes designated for TSDR within Building 771.

Records -- All records pertaining to the TSDR of "non-line combustibles,""trash," "burnables," and "kimwipes" and other wastes designated for TSDR within Building 771.

Building 776 (Production Support Building)

Waste -- All hazardous and mixed waste related to the fluidized bed incinerators.

Records -- All records described in paragraphs 1-9 above, including but not limited to all records pertaining to the incineration of waste in the fluidized bed incinerators.

Building 779 (Plutonium Development)

Waste -- "Non-line generated burnables," "trash, "burnables," "kimwipes," "water chiller filters" "Kathene system condensate" and all other wastes designated for TSDR in the landfill or Buildings 771, 988 or 995.

Records -- All records pertaining to the generation or TSDR of "trash," "burnables," "kimwipes" or "Kathene system condensate" or any other wastes designated for TSDR in the landfill or Buildings 771, 988 or 995.

Building 780 (Paint Storage Shed)

Waste -- "Rags with TCE" and all other wastes designated for TSDR in the landfill.

Records -- All records pertaining to the generation or TSDR or "rags with TCE" or other wastes designated for TSDR in the landfill.

Building 881 (Manufacturing and General Support)

Waste -- "Waste beryllium samples," "beryllium chips" "air washer blowdown," "cooling tower blowdown" or all other wastes designated for TSDR in Buildings 988, 991 or 995.

Records -- All records pertaining to the generation or TSDR of "waste beryllium samples," "beryllium chips," "air washer blowdown," "cooling tower blowdown" and other wastes designated for TSDR in Buildings 988, 991 or 995.

Building 885 (Paint and Oil Storage)

Waste -- "Rags" and other wastes designated for TSDR in the landfill.

Records -- All records pertaining to the generation or TSDR of "rags" or other wastes designated for TSDR in the landfill.

Building 910 (Reverse Osmosis Plant)

Waste -- All wastes (including water pollutants) designated for TSDR by or discharged from Buildings 910, 988 or 995.

Records -- All records pertaining to the generation or TSDR of wastes by or the discharge of water pollutants from Buildings 910, 998 or 995 or the transfer of such wastes or pollutants to Buildings 988 or 995.

Buildings 988 and 995 (Sewage Treatment Plant)

Waste -- "Drips and leaks," "cooling tower blowdown," "liquid waste," "water blowdown," "air washer blowdown," "Kathene system condensate," "air washer blowdown," "developer/fixer" waste, "blowdown waste," "dumpster" waste and all other wastes (including water pollutants) designated for TSDR within Buildings 988 and 995 or discharge from the landfill or Buildings 988 or 995.

Records -- All records pertaining to the generation or TSDR of "drips and leaks," "cooling tower blowdown," "liquid waste," "water blowdown," "air washer blowdown," "Kathene system condensate," "air washer blowdown," "developer/fixer" waste, "blowdown waste," "dumpster" waste and all other wastes (including water pollutants) designated for TSDR at the landfill or within Buildings 998 or 995 or discharged from Buildings 988 or 995.

Building 991 (Production Control Product Warehouse)

Waste -- "Waste beryllium samples," "beryllium chips" and any other wastes designated for TSDR within Building 991.

Records -- All records pertaining to the TSDR of "waste beryllium samples," "beryllium chips" or other hazardous or mixed wastes designated for TSDR within Building 991.

Pursuant to this warrant, Special Agent Lipsky and other authorized personnel are specifically empowered to:

a. Take samples of hazardous and mixed wastes from buildings facilities, units and areas specified above.

b. Take samples of water or other liquids in, and sediments from any specified ponds, surface impoundments, creeks, discharge ponds, or other bodies of water on Rocky Flats Plant.

c. Take samples of any adjacent dead or stressed vegetation.

d. Take samples of liquids, sludges, or sediments, from any or all sanitary sewers located on the Rocky Flats Plant.

e. Use remote sensing devices to determine the location of hazardous or mixed wastes or pollutants as necessary to carry out this warrant.

f. Search for and seize any records or documents which pertain to the illegal treatment, storage, disposal or other handling of hazardous or mixed wastes or the illegal discharge of pollutants, as more fully described above.

g. Excavate any areas specified within this warrant where hazardous wastes have been disposed of by burial or other means. DOE and/or Rockwell can be directed to provide the necessary equipment and/or qualified personnel, at the discretion of the FBI and/or EPA, to perform tasks necessary for the excavation.

h. Seize and take any other samples, photographs, and/or videotape, which could demonstrate violations of the laws of the United States, and constitute evidence and instrumentalities of such violations, together with the means and instruments and all other property constituting evidence of the crime.

i. Photograph and/or videotape any of the buildings, facilities, units or bodies of water specified on Attachment 1.

j. Inspect waste handling units, including, but not limited to, incinerators, waste water treatments units, sewage treatment facilities and other waste treatment, storage, disposal or recycling facilities.

Rationale for Multiple-Entry Warrant with Provisions for Nighttime Search

This warrant will be served in the daytime. Your affiant requests permission for multiple entries upon the Rocky Flats Plant and continuation of the search into the nighttime due to: 1) the safety precautions associated with the search of a site with numerous radioactive and chemical hazards will delay the search; 2) the extensive environmental sampling contemplated by the warrant; 3) the desirability of completing the execution of the search warrant as expeditiously as possible so as to minimize disruption to the mission of the Rocky Flats Plant; 4) Rocky Flats' sheer size and the numerous locations to be searched; and 5) the need to secure the premises on a 24-hour basis, pending the warrant's completion.

ATTACHMENT 3

1. <u>INTRODUCTION</u>

1.1. Your affiant is a Special Agent with the Federal Bureau of Investigation ("FBI") assigned at Denver, Colorado. I have been an FBI agent since February, 1984. The FBI derives its general investigatory jurisdiction from Titles 18 and 28 of the United States Code. Title 28, U.S.C. § 535 gives the FBI jurisdiction to investigate alleged crimes involving United States Government officers and employees, and 42 U.S.C. § 2271(b) gives the FBI primary jurisdiction concerning the investigation of alleged crimes committed at United States Department of Energy ("DOE") facilities. The FBI has concurrent jurisdiction with the United States Environmental Protection Agency ("EPA") to investigate the alleged violation of federal environmental laws.

1.2. I have attended three different training sessions concerning the investigation and prosecution of environmental crimes, for a total of 13 days of intensive course work, lectures and seminars on the Resource Conservation and Recovery Act ("RCRA"), the Federal Water Pollution Control Act (popularly known as the "Clean Water Act" or "CWA"), and other federal environmental laws. I have been the lead investigator or a substantial participant in at least 13 investigations of environmental crimes. I have been a lecturer or speaker at three FBI training conferences concerning investigation of environmental crimes. I have received five commendations for my work in this area.

1.3. The other lead investigator concerning this matter is William F. Smith. Mr. Smith is a Special Agent with EPA's Office of Criminal Investigations ("OCI") and is also assigned at Denver, Colorado. Agent Smith has been an OCI Special Agent since November 1984, and also has seven years' experience in other federal law enforcement. In addition to his extensive training concerning the investigation of environmental crimes, Agent Smith has been involved in numerous environmental investigations, has taught at five FBI training conferences concerning environmental crimes and has supervised other OCI agents in investigating such cases.

1.4. This Application is based upon the investigation conducted to date by the FBI and the EPA, including Special Agent Smith and EPA's National Enforcement Investigations Center, together with the United States Department of Justice and the United States Attorney's Office for the District of Colorado. The following statements are based upon a review of numerous studies, reports and documents from federal, state and local governments and agencies, including the EPA and the Colorado Department of Health ("CDH"), as well as materials submitted to various agencies by, or otherwise obtained from or concerning DOE and Rockwell International Corporation ("Rockwell"). The following statements are also based upon my own physical observations and those of others, as well as interviews conducted with various people. All legal analysis is based upon the advice and assistance of the Department of Justice and the United States Attorney's Office. All referenced exhibits are incorporated as part of this Application.

The Department of Energy

1.5. DOE is a department and agency of the United States Government. Prior to DOE's formation, the Atomic Energy Act of 1954 ("AEA"), 42 U.S.C. § 2140, established the Atomic Energy Commission ("AEC") and made it responsible for making nuclear material for defense programs, as well as developing atomic energy for peaceful purposes. Under the AEA, the AEC had regulatory control over nuclear defense facilities and the materials generated there. The Energy Reorganization Act of 1974, 42 U.S.C. § 5801, abolished the AEC and established the Energy Research and Development Administration ("ERDA"), which assumed responsibility for producing nuclear material for defense purposes. ERDA's responsibilities were transferred to DOE pursuant to the Department of Energy Organization Act of 1977, 42 U.S.C. § 7101.

1.6. The basic mission of DOE's defense activities is to produce nuclear material for weapons and naval fuel, and to manufacture nuclear weapons components. DOE is also engaged in research, development and testing programs for nuclear weapons and power systems. Most of DOE's defense activities are carried out at approximately 16 facilities across the United States.

The Rocky Flats Plant

1.7. One of DOE's nuclear weapons facilities is the Rocky Flats Plant ("Rocky Flats"), located approximately 16 miles northwest of Denver, Colorado, in northern Jefferson County between Golden and Boulder. (Exhibit 1.) Based on 1980 census data, approximately 1.8 million people live within 50 miles of the plant.

1.8. Rocky Flats is a United States Government-owned, private contractor-operated facility. The plant is owned by, and part of DOE, and is operated by Rockwell on DOE's behalf. Rocky Flats is administered by DOE as part of its Albuquerque Operations Office, based in Albuquerque, New Mexico. DOE's on-site management is known as the Rocky Flats Area Office and has the street address: Rocky Flats Plant, Highway 93, Golden, Colorado 80402. DOE employs approximately 60 people at Rocky Flats.

1.9. Rocky Flats was built in 1951 and began operations in 1952. The total site now covers approximately 6,550 acres and includes more than 100 buildings and facilities. (Exhibit 2.) Dow Chemical Company operated the plant until

June 30, 1975. Rockwell International Corporation has operated the plant from 1975 to the present time.

1.10. In a submission to the EPA on November 19, 1980, DOE Area Manager Don Ofte described Rocky Flats as follows:

> The Rocky Flats Plant is a Government-owned facility with a primary mission of producing plutonium components for nuclear weapons. Production activities involve the fabrication of plutonium, uranium, beryllium and stainless steel parts. Other activities include chemical processing to recover plutonium from scrap material, R&D work in metallurgy, machining, assembly, nondestructive testing, coatings, remote engineering, chemistry and physics. Parts made at the plant are shipped elsewhere for final assembly.

1.11. "The Rocky Flats Plant is the focal point for fabricating nuclear [weapons] components and processing plutonium materials." United States General Accounting Office ("GAO"), Alternatives for Relocating Rocky Flats Plant's Plutonium Operations (April 1987), at 11. Fabrication of nuclear components involves weapons-grade plutonium, which is pure plutonium from nuclear reactors or plutonium that has been processed and purified. Finished plutonium "triggers" - used to detonate nuclear weapons - are shipped to the Pantex Plant in Amarillo, Texas, for final assembly into weapons. Plutonium-containing residues and wastes are collected from the fabrication process at Rocky Flats and reprocessed for further use. Plutonium residues or wastes from other DOE facilities, as well as plutonium components from retired nuclear weapons, are also sent to Rocky Flats from across the United States (including DOE's Savannah River nuclear reactors in Aiken, South Carolina, the Hanford reactor at Richland, Washington, and DOE's facilities at Los Alamos, New Mexico), where the plutonium is extracted and purified.

Rockwell International Corporation

1.12. Rockwell is a Delaware corporation first established in 1928, with its corporate headquarters in El Segundo, California. In a Dun & Bradstreet report obtained on November 10, 1988, Rockwell indicated total sales of approximately $11.9 billion and net income of almost $812 million for the year ending September 30, 1988. Shareholders' equity as of June 30, 1988, was approximately $3.58 billion.

1.13. Rockwell has managed, operated and maintained Rocky Flats for and on behalf of DOE since June 30, 1975, under a contract with DOE dated January 8, 1975. Rockwell currently operates Rocky Flats pursuant to a Supplemental Agreement effective January 1, 1989 (Modification No. M124 to Contract DE-AC04-76DP03533) (the "DOE-Rockwell Agreement"). Rockwell employs approximately 5,300 people at Rocky Flats.

1.14. Under the DOE-Rockwell Agreement, DOE pays Rockwell the costs of operating Rocky Flats, plus an annual fee. The fee is comprised of a guaranteed base payment and a bonus tied to Rockwell's performance, as determined by DOE.

The estimated cost of Rockwell's operation of Rocky Flats from October 1, 1985, to September 30, 1986, was $493 million.

Environmental, Health and Safety Regulations

1.15. DOE's operations are "potentially one of the more dangerous industrial operations in the world." GAO, Environmental Issues at DOE's Nuclear Defense Facilities (September 1986), at 8. DOE's operations, including those at Rocky Flats, involve widespread use of toxic and hazardous materials and dangerous chemical processes, as well as vast amounts of radioactive material, such as plutonium, uranium and tritium. The hazardous chemicals include acids, nitrates, reactive metals, solvents, heavy metals (e.g., mercury), beryllium and high explosives. Id. Plutonium is a heavy, radioactive man-made metallic substance. Plutonium is toxic if inhaled, ingested or absorbed through an open wound. It is a powerful carcinogen and one of the most toxic substances known to man.

1.16. The AEC, ERDA and DOE have generated and handled radioactive and hazardous wastes and other pollutants at nuclear facilities for more than 40 years. Commencing at various times, such activities have become, and are governed by a number of environmental, health and safety statutes and regulations, as well as DOE's (and its predecessor agencies') policies, orders and regulations. As discussed in greater detail in Part 3, radioactive solid wastes and radioactive liquid effluents are primarily regulated under the Atomic Energy Act. Non-radioactive, but hazardous solid wastes are governed by RCRA, 42 U.S.C. § 6901 et seq., and non-radioactive liquid effluents discharged into waters of the United States are regulated under the Clean Water Act, 33 U.S.C. § 1251 et seq. Air emissions, both radioactive and non-radioactive, are governed by the Clean Air Act, 42 U.S.C. § 7401 et seq.

1.17. Health and safety concerns at DOE facilities, including Rocky Flats, are governed by DOE orders and regulations promulgated under the Atomic Energy Act, 42 U.S.C. § 2201(i)(3). While the Occupational Safety and Health Act ("OSHA"), 29 U.S.C. § 651, does not apply of its own force, DOE has largely adopted OSHA's regulations as its own, including Title 29, Code of Federal Regulations, Parts 1910 and 1926.

Buildings, Records and Samples

1.18. As stated in ¶ 1.9, Rocky Flats covers approximately 6,550 acres and includes more than 100 buildings. Buildings are designated by a three-digit number, such as "Building 771" or "Building 995." (Exhibit 2.) Particular operations are identified with particular buildings.

1.19. Your affiant's investigation involves past and ongoing activities at Rocky Flats, of a protracted and continuous nature. The documents and other information covered by the requested warrant are regularly maintained business and regulatory records which can reasonably be expected to be maintained at Rocky Flats, and many regulatory records are required to be maintained. See, e.g., ¶ 3.9. The investigation also involves a course of conduct, or ongoing and repeated instances of alleged criminal violations, rather than an isolated instance.

1.20. Based on your affiant's review of Rockwell and DOE documents, and interviews with two former Rocky Flats employees who were personally familiar with Rocky Flats' operations and with EPA Region 8 regulator Nathaniel J. Miullo,[1/] Rocky Flats' relevant records, documents and information can reasonably be expected to be found at several locations. First, most buildings maintain their own management office where records concerning that building's operations are located and maintained. Records and documents concerning the incinerator operations in Building 771, for

---

[1/] As EPA Region 8's "Rocky Flats Project Coordinator," Mr. Miullo is EPA's lead regulator concerning Rocky Flats' environmental compliance activities. He is a trained environmental engineer and has been an EPA Region 8 regulator since January 1981. He was Region 8's lead RCRA regulator concerning the Rocky Mountain Arsenal in 1985, and has been closely involved with environmental regulation at Rocky Flats since May 1986. He has conducted hundreds of RCRA compliance inspections, technical proposal reviews and enforcement-related tasks, and has toured, inspected or otherwise been at Rocky Flats approximately 30 times. He is personally familiar with the plant's operations and its environmental-related activities.

example, are maintained in that building. Second, a centralized depository of Rocky Flats' records and documents is located in Building 111, which contains Rockwell's principal on-site management and administrative offices. Third, another centralized depository of documents and information is DOE's "Area Office" at Rocky Flats, located in Building 115, and the DOE "Library," located in Building 706. Documents and information particularly relevant to your affiant's investigation are maintained by Rocky Flats' Health, Safety and Environment personnel in Buildings 122 and 123, and also in the Wind Systems Building, and by the Waste Operations Group in Building 776.

1.21. There is also good reason to believe that various physical, chemical and environmental evidence may be found at Rocky Flats. Various waste streams can reasonably be expected to be evidenced by physical and chemical processes and related wastes, residues and other evidence. Further, many chemicals have a protracted life in the environment and can reasonably be expected to be detected even if they were processed, discharged or otherwise deposited several years ago.

1.22. As discussed in greater detail in Parts 3-10, there is probable cause to believe that records, documents and other information (including physical, chemical and environmental evidence) covered by the requested warrant may be located in the various operational buildings, in Buildings 111, 115, 122, 123, 706, 776 and the Wind Systems Building, and at various outside locations at Rocky Flats, including surface impoundments, creeks, landfills, etc.

2. SYNOPSIS OF PROBABLE CAUSE

2.1. While Rockwell and DOE officials during the early and mid-1980s repeatedly stated to the public and certified to government agencies that Rocky Flats was in compliance with federal and state environmental laws, a DOE memorandum stated in July 1986 that Rocky Flats was "in poor condition generally in terms of environmental compliance," that its permit applications were "grossly deficient" and that some of its waste facilities were "patently 'illegal.'" July 1986 DOE Memorandum, at 4. A GAO report similarly concluded in October 1988 that "[e]nvironmental contamination at [Rocky Flats] is a significant problem," and reported that "it will cost $323 million through fiscal year 1995 for corrective actions to reduce sources of and clean up existing environmental contamination." GAO, Summary of Major Problems at DOE's Rocky Flats Plant (October 1988), at 15.

2.2. Your affiant's investigation to date (together with Special Agent Smith and others) confirms that environmental and other crimes have probably occurred at or concerning Rocky Flats, and the following paragraphs summarize the probable cause supporting the warrant, which is discussed in greater detail in Parts 3-10.

Illegal Treatment, Storage and Disposal of Hazardous and Mixed Wastes

2.3. A careful review of voluminous documents submitted by Rockwell and DOE to EPA and CDH since 1986 reveals that Rocky Flats generates at least 35 to 40 hazardous or mixed wastes which are sent for "final disposal" to various on-site facilities which do not have RCRA permits or "interim status." The knowing treatment, storage or disposal of hazardous or mixed wastes without a permit or interim status is a RCRA felony, in violation of 42 U.S.C. § 6928(d)(2).

Illegal Treatment of Hazardous and Mixed Wastes in an Unpermitted Incinerator

2.4. The investigation to date, including an examination of documents obtained from DOE and/or Rockwell, establishes probable cause to believe that Rocky Flats is using an outdated and unpermitted incinerator in Building 771 to illegally "treat" at least nine hazardous or mixed wastes in violation of the Resource Conservation and Recovery Act, 42 U.S.C. § 6928(d)(2).

2.5. While permit applications submitted by DOE and Rockwell over the past several years contemplated the incineration of a large variety and substantial quantity of hazardous and mixed wastes in a different incinerator in

Building 776, that incinerator, according to DOE and Rockwell, has never been operational.

2.6. Based upon the new incinerator's unavailability and mounting problems with Rocky Flats' legal capacity for storing hazardous and mixed wastes, there is probable cause to believe that the Building 771 incinerator has been illegally operated to treat or dispose of hazardous or mixed wastes, without a permit or interim status, in violation of 42 U.S.C. § 6928(d)(2).

Illegal Discharge of Pollutants

2.7. Walnut Creek and Woman Creek are two surface waters which cross the Rocky Flats property. Both are "navigable waters" within the CWA's meaning, and both lead directly to public drinking water supplies at Great Western Reservoir and Standley Lake, respectively. On November 15 and 16, 1988, Rocky Flats discharged various chemicals into Walnut Creek which are not included in, or permitted by its CWA permit.

2.8. DOE's CWA permit also requires prior notification to EPA concerning any process change which will result in the discharge of new or different pollutants, such as the pollutants found in the November discharges, but such notification was not given. Further, FBI surveillance on three days in December 1988 revealed discharges from Rocky Flats' sewage treatment plant into Woman Creek on each day. DOE is not permitted to discharge pollutants from its sewage treatment plant directly into the creek.

2.9. All of the above are apparent violations of the CWA, which provides criminal penalties for the knowing or negligent discharge of pollutants without a permit or in violation of permit conditions. See 33 U.S.C. §§ 1311(a) and 1319(c).

False Statements and Concealment

2.10. Consistent with their efforts to keep the public from knowing "just how really bad the site is," July 1986 DOE Memorandum (emphasis added), there is probable cause to believe that Rockwell and DOE officials have knowingly and falsely stated Rocky Flats' compliance with environmental laws and regulations, and concealed Rocky Flats' "serious contamination." Id.

2.11. While DOE concluded in December 1988 that groundwater contamination at Rocky Flats was the greatest single environmental hazard at all of DOE's nuclear weapons facilities, there is probable cause to believe that Rockwell and DOE officials falsely certified in November 1985 that Rocky Flats was "in compliance with all applicable [RCRA] groundwater monitoring [requirements]." In fact, and contrary to such certification, various Rockwell and DOE officials were aware of serious contamination and were informed that the monitoring system was deficient, did not comply with

RCRA, and produced data of limited (or questionable) validity.

2.12. In or about May 1987, DOE awarded Rockwell a performance bonus of approximately $8.6 million, based on Rockwell's alleged "excellent" management at Rocky Flats. DOE officials rated the health and safety programs at Rocky Flats "very good" and said that the plant's programs to manage radioactive and toxic wastes were "excellent," despite other DOE findings that some of Rocky Flats' waste facilities were "patently 'illegal,'" that Rockwell had significant problems in controlling radioactive contamination at the plant and that Rockwell provided DOE with erroneous and incomplete reports on environmental, health and safety matters. In addition, three separate DOE inspections at Rocky Flats since 1986 have noted serious health and safety problems and severely criticized Rocky Flats' management.

2.13. In December 1988, Rocky Flats officials failed to report two discharges from Rocky Flats in November 1988 into creeks crossing the Rocky Flats property and leading to metropolitan Denver drinking water supplies, which contained chemical pollutants not authorized by Rocky Flats' CWA permit. Rocky Flats also failed to disclose at least three illegal discharges in December 1988 (¶ 2.8) from the plant's sewage treatment facility.

2.14. There is also probable cause to believe that Rocky Flats operated the plant's Building 771 incinerator in December 1988 to treat or dispose of hazardous or mixed wastes, contrary to public statements that Building 771 was shutdown from October 1988 to late January 1989.

2.15. Such false statements and concealment are apparent violations of various environmental statutes, such as 42 U.S.C. § 6928(d)(3), as well as 18 U.S.C. § 1001.

2.16. In sum, there is probable cause to believe that environmental and other crimes have been committed at Rocky Flats and that evidence of such crimes is located there.

3. Expectations of Privacy

3.1. The Fourth Amendment to the United States Constitution requires that all searches and seizures be reasonable. The reasonableness of any particular search is determined by balancing the governmental interest in conducting the search against the reasonable privacy interests of (or concerning) the person or property being searched. See New Jersey v. T.L.O., 469 U.S. 325 (1985); Camara v. Municipal Court, 387 U.S. 523, 536-537 (1967). Important factors in striking this balance are: (a) the greater or lesser expectations of privacy in a given situation, United States v. Chadwick, 433 U.S. 1, 12-13 (1977); (b) the degree to which society is prepared to recognize such expectations as reasonable or legitimate; and (c) the degree to which such privacy is actually invaded. New York v. Class, 475 U.S. 106, 118-119 (1986).

3.2. Here, the legitimate or reasonable privacy interests of DOE, Rockwell and others at Rocky Flats are in many respects nonexistent or at least substantially limited. By seeking this warrant, neither your affiant nor the FBI or EPA recognize any greater privacy interests than in fact and law exist, and reserve their position that many or all aspects of the anticipated investigation at Rocky Flats are not "searches" within the Fourth Amendment's scope or legal meaning.

Rocky Flats is a Government-Owned Facility

3.3. Rocky Flats is not a private residence or even a private business facility. The real property, buildings and improvements at Rocky Flats, and most of the "personal property," equipment and records located there, are United States Government property.

3.4. The DOE-Rockwell Agreement, ¶ 67(b), provides that (emphasis added):

> Except as otherwise provided by [DOE's] Contracting Officer, title to all materials, equipment, supplies and tangible personal property of every kind and description purchased by [Rockwell], for the cost of which [Rockwell] is entitled to be reimbursed . . . shall pass directly from the vendor to the Government. The Government reserves the right to inspect ... any item of such property.

3.5. The DOE-Rockwell Agreement, ¶ 22(a), also provides that "[e]xcept as otherwise agreed upon by the Government and [Rockwell], all records relating to this contract shall be the property of the Government, and shall be delivered to the Government ... as [DOE's] Contracting Officer may from time to time direct . . ." (Emphasis added.) Generally, personnel records and "corporate records" are excluded from government ownership. "Corporate records" are defined as:

> "all documents and correspondence generated and maintained by [Rockwell] for the sole purpose of communicating plans and information between [Rockwell's] management at the Rocky Flats Plant and organizational elements of [Rockwell] located away from Rocky Flats, including . . . the Corporate Offices."

¶ 22(c) (emphasis added).

Commercial Premises Are Less Protected

3.6. To the extent that the activities at Rocky Flats are considered commercial or industrial (as opposed to residential), Rockwell has a reduced expectation of privacy compared to a private residence. See Donovan v. Dewey, 452 U.S. 594 (1981).

Rocky Flats is Pervasively Regulated

3.7. As described throughout this Application, the operations and activities at Rocky Flats are closely and pervasively regulated (or are supposed to be so). See New

York v. Burger, 107 S.Ct. 2636 (1987); Donovan v. Dewey, supra. Rocky Flats must comply with extensive statutes, regulations, orders and rules touching on virtually every facet of its activities, from the protection of the environment to the health and safety of the plant's workers and the general public. Rockwell's operations at Rocky Flats are subject to DOE's continuous, day-to-day regulation by on-site DOE inspectors, as well as periodic inspections by the EPA and CDH. Accordingly, Rockwell's and DOE's legitimate expectations of privacy (to the extent that DOE has any protected Fourth Amendment interests) are greatly reduced at Rocky Flats.

Large Parts of Rocky Flats are Open Fields

3.8. Rocky Flats covers 6,550 acres and much of it is open fields. Examination of such areas, and even physical intrusion on it, is not a Fourth Amendment search. See United States v. Dunn, 107 S.Ct. 1134 (1987); Dow Chemical Co. v. United States, 476 U.S. 227 (1986) (open areas of industrial complex with numerous structures spread over 2,000 acres are "open fields" even though located within fences). To the extent that the anticipated investigation includes a physical, visual and environmental examination of such open fields and areas, including sampling, there is no Fourth Amendment search, or not an unreasonable one. See Air Pollution Variance Board of Colorado v. Western Alfalfa

Corp., 416 U.S. 861 (1974); United States v. Fahey, 769 F.2d 829, 837-38 (1st Cir. 1985).

Regulatory Records Are Not Protected

3.9. Records required to be kept or maintained by regulatory statutes or programs are not private papers protected by the Fourth Amendment. See Shapiro v. United States, 335 U.S. 1, 32-36 (1948); United States v. Snyder, 668 F.2d 686, 690 (2d Cir.), cert. denied, 458 U.S. 1111 (1982). RCRA and the regulations thereunder require hazardous waste facilities to prepare, maintain and preserve numerous reports and records, such as hazardous waste manifests (which are essentially detailed shipping papers concerning the proper transportation of hazardous wastes); operating records (including a description and quantity of each hazardous waste located at the facility); test results, wastes analyses and all other determinations of waste characteristics; contingency plans; monitoring data; biennial reports; and incident reports. See 40 C.F.R. Part 262, Subpart D; Part 264, Subpart E. All such records must be furnished on EPA's request. 40 C.F.R. § 264.74(a). Other statutes and regulations, such as the Clean Air Act and the CWA, require similar records. See, e.g., 40 C.F.R. § 122.41(j) (recordkeeping requirements for CWA permitees). There is no Fourth Amendment or legitimate privacy interest in such records.

Rockwell Has Consented To Inspection of its Activities and Records

3.10. In entering into its contract with DOE, Rockwell consented that "DOE shall have the right to inspect the work and activities of [Rockwell] under this contract at such time [and] in such manner as [DOE] shall deem appropriate." DOE-Rockwell Agreement, ¶ 58(f). The agreement, ¶ 22(e), further provides that "[a]ll records relating to this contract in the possession of [Rockwell] shall be subject to inspection and audit by the DOE at all reasonable times . . ." See also ¶ 58(b). In addition, the United States Comptroller General and authorized representatives of the GAO have access to, and the right to examine, all of Rockwell's "directly pertinent books, documents, papers, or other records involving transactions related to this contract." DOE-Rockwell Agreement, ¶ 51(b). See also 42 U.S.C. § 2014(e).

6. ILLEGAL TREATMENT, STORAGE AND DISPOSAL OF HAZARDOUS AND MIXED WASTES

Based upon a review of EPA and CDH records, other government documents, reports and studies, and materials submitted by or obtained from DOE and/or Rockwell, as well as other sources of information stated herein, your affiant states as follows:

6.1. Rocky Flats does not have a RCRA permit to treat, store or dispose of hazardous or mixed wastes, and Rocky Flats' December 15, 1987 Part B application is still pending. Accordingly, a particular building or other unit at Rocky Flats may legally treat, store or dispose of hazardous or mixed wastes only if that unit has "interim status." *See* ¶ 4.7. The knowing treatment, storage or disposal of hazardous or mixed wastes without a permit or interim status is a felony RCRA violation. 42 U.S.C. § 6928(d)(2).

6.2. Your affiant has determined the interim status of various buildings or units at Rocky Flats by reviewing the Part A permit applications filed by DOE and/or Rockwell with EPA and CDH, as well as an October 9, 1988 letter from CDH's Fred Dowsett to DOE's Albert E. Whiteman, which summarizes the status of various units. Units not listed on any Part A application do not have (and cannot have) interim status.

6.3. Based upon the review described in ¶ 6.2 and also the WSC information described in ¶¶ 5.38-5.40 (unless other-wise specified), the following buildings or other units at

Rocky Flats either: (a) do not have interim status and receive hazardous or mixed wastes for "final disposal"[7] (and are therefore illegal treatment, storage or disposal facilities); or (b) generate hazardous or mixed wastes which illegally go to such units:[8]

Building	Name or Location	Generator	Unpermitted TSD
111	Administrative Offices	YES	
373	Cooling Tower & Pump House	Y	Y
374	Liquid Waste Treatment Facility	Y	Y
443	Steam Plant		Y
444	Production Operations		Y
460	Non-Nuclear Manufacturing Building	Y	
551	General Warehouse	Y	

---

[7] The term "final disposal," as used in the WSC document, appears to mean the final on-site facility at which the waste is handled. According to EPA Region 8 regulator Nathaniel Miullo, hazardous waste to be shipped off-site is collected at Unit 1, Rocky Flats' main hazardous waste storage unit. Mr. Miullo has also informed your affiant that low-level radioactive waste, which may include mixed wastes, are collected in Units 750 and 904 and in Building 64, before being shipped off-site. Thus, if the destination for "final disposal" is other than Units 1, 750 and 904 or Building 664, it may reasonably be presumed that the waste is not being shipped off-site and that the indicated "final disposal" site is the waste's ultimate destination.

[8] Your affiant has reviewed ¶ 6.3 with EPA's Nathaniel Miullo, who is very familiar with Rocky Flats and its RCRA documents, and has been at Rocky Flats on numerous tours and inspections. Mr. Miullo is not aware of any information that contradicts ¶ 6.3 and he has not been informed by either DOE or Rockwell that the particular WSC information referenced in ¶ 6.3 is not accurate.

559	Plutonium Analytical Laboratory	Y	
563	Cooling Tower	Y	
668	Drum Certification	Y	
701	Process Development	Y	
705	Coatings Laboratory	Y	
708	Compressor Building	Y	
712	Cooling Tower	Y	
750T(2)	Trailer Complex	Y	
770	Pipe Fabrication Shop	Y	
771	Plutonium Recovery Facility		Y
779	Pu Development		Y
780	Paint Storage Shed		Y
881	Manufacturing and General Support		Y
885	Paint and Oil Storage		Y
988/995	Sewage Treatment Plant	Y	Y
991	Production Control Product Warehouse		Y
--	Landfill		Y
--	North Spray Field		Y
--	South Spray Field		Y

<u>Building 443</u>

6.4. Building 443 at Rocky Flats is a steam plant. The building houses two processes and is the final on-site disposal location for at least one hazardous waste stream from another Rocky Flats building. Building 443 has neither a RCRA permit nor interim status. Building 374, the liquid waste treatment facility, generates 10 million gallons per year of "evaporator water" (WSC No. 20500) which is designated as hazardous wastes.[9/] The "final disposal" site for such "evaporator water" is designated in the WSC document as "utilities," which includes Building 443.

6.5. On December 27, 1988, DOE's Albert E. Whiteman submitted an NPDES (i.e., Clean Water Act) permit renewal application to EPA. The application indicates that the evaporator water initially goes to the steam plant (Building 443) and also a cooling tower (designated as Building 373), and then to the sewage treatment plant, Building 998/995.

6.6. Buildings 443, 373 and 995 do not have a RCRA permit or interim status. There is therefore probable cause to believe that hazardous wastes have been, and are being illegally treated, stored and/or disposed of in Buildings 443, 373 and 998/995, in apparent violation of 42 U.S.C.

9/ Rocky Flats' May 30, 1985 Part A permit application stated that all mixed wastes at Rocky Flats were treated in Buildings 774 and 374, and Rocky Flats' April 1986 CEARP indicates that Building 374 has now replaced Building 774 as Rocky Flats' primary radioactive liquid process waste treatment facility. CEARP at V-58. The August 2, 1988 revised Part A application confirms that this amount of "evaporator water" is generated and treated. This further continuity between the WSC document and the pending application confirms the factual basis of this allegation.

§ 6928(d)(2), and that evidence of such crimes is likely to be found in Buildings 443, 373 and 998/995, where the alleged violations take place, and in Building 374, where the wastes were, and are generated, and, as explained in ¶¶ 1.18 - 1.22, in Buildings 111, 115, 122, 123, 706 and 776, as well as the Wind Systems Building.

Building 991

6.7. Building 991 is the production control product warehouse, and it handles various materials and liquids which are received and distributed throughout the plant. EPA's Nathaniel Miullo has previously inspected Building 991 and advises that there are connecting tunnels and/or underground vaults that are a portion of Building 991. The building houses approximately five processes and is the final on-site disposal location for five waste streams (including at least one hazardous and one mixed waste) from other Rocky Flats buildings.

6.8. Although it does not have a RCRA permit or interim status, Building 991 receives the following hazardous and mixed wastes for "final disposal":

Building of Generation	Waste Description	WSC Number
881	Waste beryllium samples	(H) 3340[10/]
881	Beryllium chips	(M) 4590

[10/] This waste is listed as "hazardous" in Rocky Flats' August 2, 1988 revised Part A application, although it was listed in the WSC document as "non-hazardous."

6.9. There is probable cause to believe that hazardous and mixed wastes have been, and are being illegally treated, stored and/or disposed of in Building 991, in apparent violation of 42 U.S.C. § 6928(d)(2), and that evidence of such crimes is likely to be found in Building 991, where the alleged violations take place, and in Building 881, where the wastes were, and are generated, and in Buildings 111, 115, 122, 123, 706 and 776, as well as the Wind Systems Building.

Landfill

6.10. The landfill is not described in the WSC document. According to EPA's Nathaniel Miullo, the landfill is where Rocky Flats' main hazardous waste storage was located prior to such storage being moved inside Rocky Flats' production complex. The landfill is located north of Building 771, outside the production complex. Adjacent to the landfill, on the east side, is a pond which drains into the Walnut Creek drainage system.

6.11. According to the WSC document, the landfill is the final disposal location for approximately 190 waste streams (including at least 13 hazardous and three mixed wastes) from various Rocky Flats buildings.

6.12. Although it does not have a RCRA permit or interim status, the landfill receives the following hazardous or mixed wastes for "final disposal:"

Building of Generation	Waste Description	WSC Number
460	used kimwipes	(H) 890
551	kimwipes/degreasing residues	(H) 6300
563	sump sludge	(H) 20580
668	rags with methyl alcohol	(H) 9570
705	kimwipes	(M) 20060
705	kimwipes	(H) 20250
708	rags with freon, TCE	(H) 10690
712	sump sludge	(H) 20590
750T	soiled kimwipes	(H) 6020
750T	kimwipes	(H) 6040
770	combustibles	(H) 22650
770	rags	(H) 22570
779	water chiller filters	(M) 15730
780	rags with TCE	(H) 9590
885	rags	(H) 5110
995	dumpster	(M) 20620

6.13. There is probable cause to believe that hazardous and mixed wastes have been, and are being illegally disposed of at Rocky Flats' landfill, in apparent violation of 42 U.S.C. § 6928(d)(2), and that evidence of such crimes is likely to be located there, and in Buildings 460, 551, 563, 668, 705, 708, 712, 750T, 770, 779, 780, 885 and 995 where the wastes were, and are generated, as well as Buildings 111, 115, 122, 123, 706 and 776, and the Wind Systems Building.

7. **RCRA INCINERATION VIOLATIONS**

Based upon a review of EPA and CDH records, other government documents, reports and studies, and materials submitted by or obtained from DOE and/or Rockwell, as well as other sources of information stated herein, your affiant states as follows:

7.1. The crux of the allegations concerning Rocky Flats' illegal incineration of hazardous and mixed wastes are twofold. First, by the terms of the WSC document, an old incinerator in Building 771 has been incinerating at least a small quantity of hazardous waste and a substantial quantity of mixed waste, without a RCRA permit or interim status. Second, a second incinerator, located in Building 776, has been the subject of a RCRA permit application, which stated that the Building 776 incinerator would incinerate very large quantities of hazardous and mixed wastes. However, pending resolution of its permit application, DOE has maintained that the Building 776 incinerator was not, and is not being used to incinerate wastes. The large amount of waste designated for incineration in the allegedly dormant Building 776 incinerator, coupled with Rocky Flats' established shortage of legal storage space, makes it likely that some or all of this waste has been illegally incinerated in the Building 776 and/or 771 incinerators, or otherwise illegally stored or handled at Rocky Flats. There is also probable cause to believe that the Building 771 incinerator was operated at a time in December 1988 when EPA and the public were told that the building was shutdown.

Illegal Incineration of Wastes in Building 771

7.2. According to Rocky Flats' officials, Building 771 is a "plutonium recovery" facility and consists of laboratories, "plutonium recovery operations" and related support operations. The building houses approximately 48 processes, including what has been designated as a "Special Nuclear Materials Recovery Incinerator." Building 771 is the final on-site disposal location for 58 waste streams (including at least one hazardous and eight mixed wastes) from other Rocky Flats buildings.

7.3. Although the Building 771 incinerator has a Clean Air Act permit from CDH,[11/] the incinerator does not have a RCRA permit or interim status to "treat" (i.e., incinerate) hazardous or mixed wastes.[12/] Your affiant has also been

11/ The Clean Air permit restricts the incinerator to incineration of plutonium-contaminated plastic, paper, rubber, cloth, wood and other refuse.

12/ The term "treatment" is defined in RCRA, 42 U.S.C. § 6903(34) as:

> any method, technique, or process, including neutralization, designed to change the physical, chemical, or biological character or composition of any hazardous waste so as to neutralize such waste or so as to render such waste nonhazardous, safer for transport, amenable for recovery, amenable for storage, or reduced in volume. Such term includes any activity or processing designed to change the physical form or chemical composition of hazardous waste so as to render it non-hazardous.

informed by EPA's Nathaniel Miullo that because the Building 771 incinerator was constructed in the 1950s - prior to RCRA's hazardous waste incineration standards, it is highly unlikely that the incinerator meets EPA's current stringent performance standards for RCRA incinerators, including the 99.99% destruction and removal efficiency standard for hazardous organic compounds. 40 C.F.R. 264.343.[13]

7.4. According to the WSC document, the following hazardous or mixed wastes are sent to Building 771 for "final disposal" by incineration:

Building of Generation	Waste Description	WSC Number
559	non-line combustibles	(M) 16120
559	non-line combustibles	(M) 16170
559	non-line combustibles	(M) 16220
559	non-line combustibles	(M) 16290
559	non-line combustibles	(M) 16320
779	non-line generated burnables	(M) 19510
779	trash	(M) 15610
779	burnables	(M) 19680
779	kimwipes	(H) 15710[14]

[13] A recent GAO study described Building 771 as "an old chemical plant needing continual repair of tanks, piping and utilities. Aspects of the facility do not meet current building and safety codes." GAO, Summary of Major Problems at DOE's Rocky Flats Plant (October 1988), at 19. Building 371 was completed in 1981 for the purpose of replacing Building 771, but, because of severe design and construction problems, it has not been able to do so. See ¶ 8.1. Building 771 therefore continues to operate "with old and deteriorated equipment." GAO, Alternatives for Relocating Rocky Flats Plant's Plutonium Operations (April 1987), at 8, 16-17.

[14] The August 2, 1988 Part A application does not list these wastes. Rockwell, however, has taken the position that the wastes incinerated in the Building 771 incinerator are "recovered" and are therefore not subject to RCRA. EPA has

7.5. There is probable cause to believe that hazardous and mixed wastes have been, and are being illegally treated (i.e., incinerated) in Building 771, in apparent violation of 42 U.S.C. § 6928(d)(2), and that evidence of such crimes is likely to exist in Building 771, where the alleged violations have occurred, and in Buildings 559 and 779, where the wastes were, and are generated, and in Buildings 111, 115, 122, 123, 706 and 776, as well as the Wind Systems Building, where relevant documents are likely to be maintained.[15/]

---

rejected this position.

DOE's and Rockwell's claim that the Building 771 incinerator only recycles plutonium and does not treat or dispose of other hazardous and mixed wastes is also questionable, given Rocky Flats' intentional mixing of separate wastes. See ¶ 5.34. In its September 28, 1987 Notice of Deficiency (¶ 5.42), CDH found that numerous wastes associated with Building 771 were not adequately analyzed and were incorrectly identified. Various wastes were identified only as "radioactive," even though they had not been analyzed for other hazardous constituents.

15/ On February 1, 1989, the Sierra Club filed a citizen enforcement suit under RCRA, 42 U.S.C. § 6972(b), against DOE and Rockwell concerning alleged RCRA violations involving the Building 771 incinerator. Sierra Club v. Rockwell International Corp. (Civ. No. 84-181, D. Colo.). On April 4, 1989, DOE filed its Answer and admitted to incinerating mixed waste in the Building 771 incinerator, but claimed that such incineration constituted a plutonium-recovery operation and that such incineration was not RCRA-regulated. Department of Justice civil attorneys who filed the Answer on DOE's behalf were unaware of the criminal investigation at Rocky Flats, and were therefore unaware of facts known to the criminal investigators which might bear significantly upon the factual and legal validity of the Answer. In view of the uncertain basis for DOE's Answer, your affiant has been informed that DOE will request a stay of the civil proceeding pending further resolution of the criminal investigation.

Illegal Incineration of Wastes Designated for Incinerators in Building 776

7.7. Building 776 is described in the WSC document as housing various waste handling activities, including incinerators and size reduction processes. On November 8, 1985, Rocky Flats submitted Part A and Part B RCRA permit applications to treat hazardous wastes in two incinerators located in Building 776, described as "fluidized bed incinerators." A fluidized bed incinerator is not a conventional open-flame incinerator, but involves a thermal-chemical process. One of the fluid bed incinerators in Building 776 is described as a "pilot" or test-model incinerator.

7.8. On October 22, 1986, DOE's Albert E. Whiteman submitted a draft "trial burn plan" for the Building 776 incinerator to CDH's Director of Waste Management, Kenneth Waesche.[16/] The letter indicated that the Building 776 incinerator would meet RCRA's incineration standards and also stated (emphasis added):

> We are working toward a preferred time for the trial burn of early February 1987. This time frame is needed since we have limited storage tanks for organics within our waste treatment buildings, and our storage tank capacity should be exceeded in March or April 1987, by current best estimates.

16/ A trial burn demonstrating the proper and safe operation of an incinerator is a requirement for receiving a RCRA permit. *See* 40 C.F.R. 270.62.

7.9. By a letter dated April 6, 1987 from DOE's Assistant Secretary for Defense Programs to U.S. Senator William L. Armstrong, DOE stated that a "trial burn" would only be conducted after DOE received approval from EPA and CDH, and that the Building 776 incinerator, absent such approval, would not be operated on a production basis. Neither EPA nor CDH have ever approved a trial burn.

7.10. On learning that the Building 776 incinerators had in fact been operated more than previously disclosed, CDH requested and received a letter dated May 21, 1987 from DOE's Albert E. Whiteman specifying the total hours that the fluidized bed incinerators had been operated.[17/] The letter (and its attachments) indicates that the incinerators were used on a "trial basis" as follows:

Dates	Hours
6/73 - 6/74	1,100
2/75 - 12/76	1,325
10/76 - 10/79	1,691
3/87[sic] - 7/80	unspecified
5/81	4
10/85	154

7.11. Mr. Whiteman's May 21, 1987 letter also stated that Building 776's incinerators were expected to treat, on an annual basis, over 200 tons of Rocky Flats waste from

[17/] Rocky Flats' November 8, 1985 Part A application described the "use" of a fluid bed incinerator, and stated that the capacity of such incinerator, "based on operational experience," was 34 liters an hour. (Emphasis added).

almost 200 separate waste streams, including approximately 50,000 gallons of liquid hazardous or mixed wastes. The letter's attachment also states, at 47 (emphasis added):

> The Rocky Flats Plant has limited storage capacity that is specifically designed for liquid mixed wastes. At present generation rates, these storage facilities will be nearing capacity in approximately 2-3 months, at which time alternative storage methods will be sought. Therefore, it is necessary that the fluidized bed incinerator start processing this waste backlog under interim status.

7.12. On August 2, 1988, Rocky Flats filed a revised Part A permit application which specified that the following wastes, among others, will be incinerated: various solvents and solvent-contaminated solid wastes, chemically contaminated uranium oxides, waste oil, used filters from plant processes, acids and sludges. The Part A application estimates that over 475,000 pounds of "solid" hazardous and mixed wastes (from over 200 waste streams) and over 110,000 gallons of "liquid" hazardous and mixed wastes (from over 150 waste streams) will be incinerated on a yearly basis.

7.13. Since DOE and Rockwell did not apply (and have never applied) for a RCRA permit for any other incinerator, or obtained interim status for another incinerator, it may reasonably be assumed that such wastes are designated for Building 776's incinerator.

7.14. According to DOE's May 21, 1987 letter (¶ 7.10), the Building 776 incinerator has not been used since October 1985.

7.15. During a regulatory inspection at Building 776 on January 11, 1989, Rocky Flats informed EPA and CDH inspectors that, due to the Building 776 incinerator's non-operational status, the wastes designated for incineration were being stored in Building 776 and Building 556. These storage facilities are the following size, according to a October 9, 1988 letter from CDH's Fred Dowsett to DOE's Albert E. Whiteman:

Building	Unit	Capacity
776	12	20,000 gallons
776	27	2,750 gallons
556	10	6,660 gallons
	Total	29,410 gallons

7.16. This 29,410 gallons of legal storage capacity does not provide for the 110,000 gallons of liquid wastes described in Rocky Flats' August 2, 1988 Part A application (¶ 7.12), let alone the 475,000 pounds of solid wastes.[18/]

[18/] On May 2, 1988, DOE's Albert E. Whiteman filed an Annual Hazardous Waste Generation and Management Report with EPA and CDH, concerning waste activities in 1987 ("1987 Annual Report"), as required by 40 C.F.R. 265.75. The Annual Report requires, among other things, a description and amount of each hazardous and mixed waste shipped off-site. In 1987, only 6,504 gallons of liquid hazardous wastes and 38,053 pounds of solid hazardous wastes were listed as shipped off-site. Both amounts are less than 10% of the estimated wastes in ¶ 7.12.

The 1987 Annual Report may conflict in certain respects with the August 2, 1988 Part A application regarding the treatment of certain wastes. For example, certain wastes which are described as evaporated in the Annual Report appear designated for incineration in the permit application. The Annual Report also indicates thaat Rocky Flats has attempted to minimize (or reduce)

7.17. The large volume of hazardous and mixed wastes continually generated at Rocky Flats, much of which has repeatedly been designated for treatment or disposal in the Building 776 incinerator, combined with public statements that the Building 776 incinerator is not being used and Rocky Flats' shortage of legal storage space, establishes probable cause to believe that one or more crimes have occurred, and are occurring at Rocky Flats, involving the illegal incineration of hazardous and mixed wastes in the Building 776 incinerator (despite statements to the contrary), the illegal incineration of such wastes in the Building 771 incinerator, or other illegal treatment, storage or disposal of hazardous and mixed wastes, in violation of 42 U.S.C. § 6928(d)(2).[19/] There is probable cause to believe that

---

the amounts of approximately 10 kinds of hazardous and mixed wastes generated at the plant. It is unclear whether the August 2, 1988 Part A application was adjusted to reflect these waste minimization efforts, even though it was filed after the 1987 Annual Report. Even if one assumes, however, that some wastes designated for Building 776 have instead been shipped off-site and that the quantities of some wastes have been reduced, the point remains that vast amounts of hazardous and mixed wastes have been designated by plant officials to be incinerated in the Building 776 incinerators, and such wastes have apparently not been properly treated, stored or disposed of.

[19/] The continued, and perhaps clandestine use of the Building 771 incinerator at a time when Building 771 was supposed to be shutdown (¶¶ 7.18 - 7.23) is further reason to believe that one or more of these propositions are true.

Additional probable cause for searching Building 776 is also found in a report concerning the EPA-CDH June 13-17, 1988 inspection at Rocky Flats, stating that Building 776 contains a hazardous waste database, and also houses the facility's "Waste evidence of such crimes is located in Buildings 776 and 771, where such crimes have occurred, and in Buildings 111, 115, 122, 123 and 706, as well as the Wind Systems Building, where relevant documents are likely to be maintained.

False Statements Concerning Building 771 Incinerator

7.18. On October 8, 1988, Rockwell's principal on-site Rocky Flats manager, Mr. Dominic Sanchini, publicly stated that Building 771 would be shut down, due to potential radiation exposure problems, until the necessary improvements and clean-up could be accomplished. Subsequent statements by Rocky Flats' DOE and Rockwell officials reiterated that Building 771 was closed, and would remain closed, until safety problems were adequately addressed. On or about January 20, 1989, DOE officials announced that Building 771 was being reopened.[20/]

Operations Group." It may reasonably be expected that documents and records relevant to Rocky Flats' waste management practices are located in Building 776 as part of these activities.

[20/] An October 1988 GAO study summarized the "shutdown" as follows:

> On October 7, 1988, after discussion with DOE's headquarters [Environment, Safety & Health] staff and DOE's defense program officials, DOE's Albuquerque Operations Office ordered the shutdown of activities in Building 771. Shutdown operations began October 8, and DOE expects the entire operation to be shutdown on or before November 4, 1988. DOE is currently developing a restart plan before resuming operations in Building 771.

7.19. Notwithstanding (and contrary to) such statements by various DOE and Rockwell officials, FBI surveillance has established probable cause to believe that the Building 771 incinerator was in fact operated in December 1988, as explained below.

7.20. On December 9, 10 and 15, 1988, an FBI airplane with infra-red observation and photographic equipment conducted surveillance over Rocky Flats. While a daytime flight on December 9, 1988 indicated that the Building 771 incinerator was not thermally active, similar surveillance on the nights of December 9, 10 and 15 indicate that the incinerator was probably being operated on each of those nights. Your affiant was a passenger on the FBI airplane on December 9 and 15, and has reviewed videotapes taken on all three days.

7.21. EPA experts in infra-red photographic interpretation from the Environmental Monitoring Systems Lab in Las Vegas, Nevada, have interpreted the FBI aerial photography and confirm that the Building 771 incinerator stack was thermally active on the nights of December 9, 10 and 15, 1988. The EPA experts specifically considered and rejected the possibility that Building 771's regular heating system could account for the observed thermal activity.

GAO, Summary of Major Problems at DOE's Rocky Flats Plant (October 1988), at 5 (emphasis added).

7.22. A follow-up FBI overflight on February 28, 1989, after Building 771 was back in operation, indicated that the Building 771 incinerator stack was approximately as hot as the same stack was observed in the December nighttime overflights.

7.23. There is probable cause to believe that the Building 771 incinerator was operated on at least December 9, 10 and 15, 1988, contrary to public statements by DOE and Rockwell officials that Building 771 was shut down, and that material false statements were therefore made, or material facts concealed, concerning matters within EPA's jurisdiction, in violation of 42 U.S.C. § 6928(d)(3) and 18 U.S.C. § 1001. There is also probable cause to believe that evidence of such crimes is located at Rocky Flats, in Buildings 111, 115, 122, 123, 706, 771 and 776, as well as the Wind Systems Building.

United States v. MacDonald & Watson Waste Oil Co.: Grand Jury Indictment

IN THE DISTRICT COURT OF THE UNITED STATES

FOR THE DISTRICT OF RHODE ISLAND

CR [illegible] 032

UNITED STATES OF AMERICA, Plaintiff,	)	CR Nos.
v.	)	
MacDONALD & WATSON WASTE OIL COMPANY, NARRAGANSETT IMPROVEMENT COMPANY, EUGENE K. D'ALLESANDRO, VINCENT CINQUEGRANO, FRAN SLADE FAUST RITAROSSI, and MICHAEL O'LAUGHLIN,	)	Violations Title 42, U.S.C. Sections 6928(d)(1), 6928(d)(2)(A), 6928(d)(2)(B), 6928(d)(3) and 9603(b)(3) and Title 18, U.S.C. Sections 1001, 1341, 1962(c) and 2.
Defendants.	)	

INDICTMENT

The Grand Jury Charges:

INTRODUCTION

1. At all times material to this indictment the defendant MacDONALD & WATSON WASTE OIL COMPANY was a Rhode Island corporation engaged in the business of transporting hazardous waste, solid waste, used oils and soil or other earth materials contaminated with petroleum products. MacDONALD & WATSON WASTE OIL COMPANY'S offices are located at Pole 12, Greenhill Road, Johnston, Rhode Island. MacDONALD & WATSON WASTE OIL COMPANY leased property at Pole 2, Spragueville Road, Smithfield, Rhode Island from November 2, 1981 until July 31, 1986, and

leases a tank facility at 223 Allens Avenue, Providence, Rhode Island from Narragansett Improvement Company, Inc.

2. At all times material to this indictment the defendant NARRAGANSETT IMPROVEMENT COMPANY was a Rhode Island corporation engaged in the manufacture and sale of asphalt concrete. Effective August 5, 1985, NARRAGANSETT IMPROVEMENT COMPANY was issued a permit by the State of Rhode Island to operate a hazardous waste treatment and storage facility at 223 Allens Avenue, Providence, Rhode Island. The permit limited the hazardous waste which could be accepted to: waste oils, solvents, still bottoms and machine coolants. The permit did not seek or grant approval for the treatment, storage or disposal of hazardous waste soil.

3. At all times material to this indictment the defendant EUGENE K. D'ALLESANDRO was the president and a director of MacDonald & Watson Waste Oil Company and manager of the tank facility located at 223 Allens Avenue, Providence, Rhode Island.

4. At all times material to this indictment the defendants VINCENT CINQUEGRANO, FRAN SLADE, FAUST RITAROSSI and MICHAEL O'LAUGHLIN were employees of MacDonald & Watson Waste Oil Company.

5. At all times material to this indictment the Resource Conservation and Recovery Act, Title 42, United States Code, Section 6901 et seq., and the regulations promulgated thereunder, regulated the transportation, treatment, storage and disposal of hazardous waste.

- 3 -

COUNT ONE

The Grand Jury further charges:

On or about July 30, 1986, in the District of Rhode Island, MacDONALD & WATSON WASTE OIL COMPANY, NARRAGANSETT IMPROVEMENT COMPANY, EUGENE K. D'ALLESANDRO, FRAN SLADE and FAUST RITAROSSI did knowingly transport and cause to be transported hazardous waste, namely toluene and soil contaminated with toluene, from Master Chemical Company, Boston, Massachusetts to Narragansett Improvement Company, a facility which had neither interim status nor a permit, under Title 42, United States Code, Section 6925 or 6926, to treat, store or dispose of such waste,

in violation of Title 42, United States Code, Section 6928(d)(1) and Title 18, United States Code, Section 2.

COUNT TWO

The Grand Jury further charges:

On or about July 31, 1986, in the District of Rhode Island, MacDONALD & WATSON WASTE OIL COMPANY, NARRAGANSETT IMPROVEMENT COMPANY, EUGENE K. D'ALLESANDRO, FRAN SLADE and FAUST RITAROSSI did knowingly transport and cause to be transported hazardous waste, namely toluene and soil contaminated with toluene, from Master Chemical Company, Boston, Massachusetts to Narragansett Improvement Company, a facility which had neither interim status nor a permit, under Title 42, United States Code, Section 6925 or 6926, to treat, store or dispose of such waste, in violation of Title 42, United States Code, Section 6928(d)(1) and Title 18, United States Code, Section 2.

COUNT THREE

The Grand Jury further charges:

On or about and between July 30, 1986 and August 31, 1986, all dates being approximate and inclusive, in the District of Rhode Island, MacDONALD & WATSON WASTE OIL COMPANY and NARRAGANSETT IMPROVEMENT COMPANY did knowingly treat, store and dispose of hazardous waste, namely toluene and soil contaminated with toluene, from Master Chemical Company, Boston, Massachusetts, without a permit or interim status under Title 42, United States Code, Section 6925 or 6926,

in violation of Title 42, United States Code, Section 6928(d)(2)(A) and Title 18, United States Code, Section 2.

COUNT FOUR

The Grand Jury further charges:

On or about July 30, 1986, in the District of Rhode Island, and elsewhere, MacDONALD & WATSON WASTE OIL COMPANY, NARRAGANSETT IMPROVEMENT COMPANY, EUGENE K. D'ALLESANDO, FRAN SLADE and FAUST RITAROSSI, in a matter within the jurisdiction of the United States Environmental Protection Agency, an agency of the United States of America, did willfully and knowingly make and use and caused to be made and used, a false writing and document containing a materially false statement, knowing the same to contain such statement, in that, in a Uniform Hazardous Waste Manifest, number C090025, made pursuant to the provisions of Title 42, United States Code, Section 6922 and 6923 and regulations promulgated pursuant thereto, the defendants stated and represented and caused to be stated and represented in said Uniform Hazardous Waste Manifest that the material being transported from Master Chemical Company, Boston, Massachusetts to Narragansett Improvement Company, Providence, Rhode Island pursuant to the Manifest was not hazardous waste in Rhode Island whereas, in truth and fact, as the defendants then well knew, said statement was false,

in violation of Title 18, United States Code, Section 1001 and 2.

COUNTS FIVE THROUGH THIRTEEN

The Grand Jury further charges:

On or about the dates enumerated and set forth below in separate counts, in the District of Rhode Island, and elsewhere, MacDONALD & WATSON WASTE OIL COMPANY, NARRAGANSETT IMPROVEMENT COMPANY, EUGUNE K. D'ALLESANDO, FRAN SLADE and FAUST RITAROSSI, in a matter within the jurisdiction of the United States Environmental Protection Agency, an agency of the United States of America, did willfully and knowingly make and use and caused to be made and used, a false writing and document containing a materially false statement, knowing the same to contain such statement, in that, in a Uniform Hazardous Waste Manifest, the numbers of which are enumerated and set forth below in separate counts, made pursuant to the provisions of Title 42, United States Code, Section 6922 and 6923 and regulations promulgated pursuant thereto, the defendants stated and represented and caused to be stated and represented in said Uniform Hazardous Waste Manifests that the material being transported from Master Chemical Company, Boston, Massachusetts to Narragansett Improvement Company, Providence, Rhode Island pursuant to the Manifest was not hazardous waste in Rhode Island whereas, in truth and fact, as the defendants then well knew, said statement was false,

COUNT	DATE	MANIFEST NUMBER
5	July 30, 1986	C090052
6	July 30, 1986	C090053
7	July 30, 1986	C091222
8	July 30, 1986	C091969
9	July 30, 1986	C091974
10	July 31, 1986	C090051
11	July 31, 1986	C090054
12	July 31, 1986	C090055
13	July 31, 1986	C090056

in violation of Title 18, United States Code, Sections 1001 and 2.

COUNTS FOURTEEN THROUGH SEVENTEEN

The Grand Jury further charges:

INTRODUCTION

1. Paragraphs One through Six of the Introduction to count one of the indictment are hereby realleged and incorporated by reference as though fully set forth herein.

2. The Comprehensive Environmental Response, Compensation and Liability Act (CERCLA), Title 42, United States Code, Section 9601 et seq., authorizes the President to plan, to remove or arrange for the removal of and provide for remedial action relating to the release or threatened release into the environment of any hazardous substances. 42 U.S.C. § 9604.

3. CERCLA permits joint and several liability of certain responsible parties, including those who by contract, agreement or otherwise arrange for the disposal or treatment of hazardous substances, for the costs incurred in responding to releases or potential releases of hazardous substances and for injury to natural resources. 42 U.S.C § 9607.

4. Pursuant to CERCLA the disposal of hazardous waste at an unpermitted facility would constitute a release of a hazardous substance. 42 U.S.C. §§ 9601 and 9602.

The Grand Jury further charges:

1. From on or about April 29, 1986 to on or about October 31, 1986, in the District of Rhode Island, MacDONALD & WATSON WASTE OIL COMPANY, NARRAGANSETT IMPROVEMENT COMPANY, EUGENE K. D'ALLESANDRO, FRAN SLADE and FAUST RITAROSSI did knowingly and willfully devise and intend to devise a scheme and artifice to defraud and obtain money by means of false and fraudulent pretenses, representations and promises from the Estate of Moses Weinman, well knowing that these pretenses, representations and promises were false when made, and which scheme and artifice was in substance as follows:

- 8 -

a. It was part of the scheme and artifice to defraud that MacDONALD & WATSON WASTE OIL COMPANY bid on a contract to remove and dispose of soil contaminated with toluene from the former site of Master Chemical Company, 29 Bradston Street, Boston, Massachusetts.

b. It was further part of said scheme and artifice to defraud that MacDONALD & WATSON WASTE OIL COMPANY assured representatives and agents of the Estate of Moses Weinman that soil contaminated with toluene could legally be transported to and disposed of at Narragansett Improvement Company, Providence, Rhode Island.

c. It was further part of said scheme and artifice to defraud that MacDONALD & WATSON WASTE OIL COMPANY executed a contract for the removal of contaminated soil from the Master Chemical Company site at 29 Bradston Street, Boston, Massachusetts which required that MacDONALD & WATSON WASTE OIL COMPANY carry out the contract in accordance with all applicable federal, state and local laws, regulations and requirements.

d. It was further part of said scheme and artifice to defraud that FRAN SLADE and FAUST RITAROSSI authorized acceptance of the soil contaminated with toluene at the NARRAGANSETT IMPROVEMENT COMPANY.

e. It was further part of said scheme and artifice to defraud that MacDONALD & WATSON WASTE OIL COMPANY removed the soil contaminated with toluene from the Master Chemical site.

f. It was further part of said scheme and artifice to defraud that hazardous waste manifests used to transport the soil contaminated with toluene were marked "Non-Hazardous in Rhode Island Accepted for Processing at Asphalt Plant."

g. It was further part of said scheme and artifice to defraud that NARRAGANSETT IMPROVEMENT COMPANY received and accepted the soil contaminated with toluene from MacDONALD & WATSON WASTE OIL COMPANY.

h. It was further part of said scheme and artifice to defraud that MacDONALD & WATSON WASTE OIL COMPANY and NARRAGANSETT IMPROVEMENT COMPANY disposed of the soil contaminated with toluene by either using the material in the NARRAGANSETT IMPROVEMENT COMPANY asphalt processing plant or comingling the contaminated soil with other soil at the Poe Street lot adjacent to NARRAGANSETT IMPROVEMENT COMPANY and disposing of the comingled soil at Pole 12, Greenhill Road, Johnston, Rhode Island or at American Disposal Company, Pole 13, Greenhill, Road, Johnston, Rhode Island.

i. It was further part of said scheme and artifice to defraud that MacDONALD & WATSON WASTE OIL COMPANY received and caused to be received a payment of $36,356.28 via Foley, Hoag & Eliot on behalf of the Estate of Moses Weinman for the transportation and disposal of hazardous waste soil.

j. It was further part of said scheme and artifice to defraud that NARRAGANSETT IMPROVEMENT COMPANY, MacDONALD & WATSON WASTE OIL COMPANY, and American Disposal Company did not have a permit to dispose of hazardous waste soil.

2. On or about the dates specified below, in the District of Rhode Island, and elswhere, MacDONALD & WATSON WASTE OIL COMPANY, NARRAGANSETT IMPROVEMENT COMPANY, EUGENE K. D'ALLESANDRO, FRAN SLADE and FAUST RITAROSSI, aiding and abetting each other, for the purpose of executing the aforesaid scheme and artiface to defraud, and to obtain money from the Estate of Moses Weinman by false and fraudulent pretenses, representations and promises, and attempting to do so, knowingly caused mail matter to be delivered by the United States Postal Service, according to the directions thereon, as specified more particularly below:

COUNT	DATE	ITEM	MAILED
14	April 29, 1986	Quote for disposal	From: Faust Rittarossi To: Goldberg Zoino Associates
15	May 29, 1986	Contract	From: Foley, Hoag & Eliot To: Fran Slade MacDonald & Watson
16	June 6, 1986	Executed contract	From: MacDonald & Watson To: Foley, Hoag & Eliot
17	October 31, 1986	Check	From: Foley, Hoag & Eliot To: Faust Ritarossi MacDonald & Watson

in violation of Title 18, United States Code, Sections 1341 and 2.

COUNT EIGHTEEN

The Grand Jury further charges:

1. On or about and between July 30, 1986 and July 31, 1986, both dates being approximate and inclusive, in the District

of Rhode Island, a quantity equal to or greater than one pound of a hazardous substance, as defined in Title 42, United States Code, Section 9602, namely soil contaminated with toluene, was released from a facility into the environment and the release was not a federally permitted release.

2. On or about and between July 30, 1986 and July 31, 1986, both dates being approximate and inclusive, MacDONALD & WATSON WASTE OIL COMPANY and NARRAGANSETT IMPROVEMENT COMPANY, having knowledge of the release identified in paragraph one, and being a person in charge of the facility from which the release occurred, failed as soon as it had knowledge of the release to notify immediately the appropriate agency of the United States Government of the release,

in violation of Title 42, United States Code, Section 9603(b)(3).

COUNT NINETEEN

The Grand Jury further charges:

On or about April 7, 1986, in the District of Rhode Island, MacDONALD & WATSON WASTE OIL COMPANY, NARRAGANSETT IMPROVEMENT COMPANY, EUGENE K. D'ALLESANDRO, FRAN SLADE and FAUST RITAROSSI did knowingly transport and cause to be transported hazardous waste, namely toluene and soil contaminated with toluene, from Ainslie Corporation, Braintree, Massachusetts to Narragansett Improvement Company, a facility which had neither interim status nor a permit, under Title 42, United States Code, Section 6925 or 6926, to treat, store or dispose of such waste,

- 12 -

in violation of Title 42, United States Code, Section 6928(d)(1) and Title 18, United States Code, Section 2.

COUNT TWENTY

The Grand Jury further charges:

On or about April 8, 1986, in the District of Rhode Island, MacDONALD & WATSON WASTE OIL COMPANY, NARRAGANSETT IMPROVEMENT COMPANY, EUGENE K. D'ALLESANDRO, FRAN SLADE and FAUST RITAROSSI did knowingly transport and cause to be transported hazardous waste, namely toluene and soil contaminated with toluene, from Ainslie Corporation, Braintree, Massachusetts to Narragansett Improvement Company, a facility which had neither interim status nor a permit, under Title 42, United States Code, Section 6925 or 6926, to treat, store or dispose of such waste,

in violation of Title 42, United States Code, Section 6928(d)(1) and Title 18, United States Code, Section 2.

COUNT TWENTY-ONE

The Grand Jury further charges:

On or about April 9, 1986, in the District of Rhode Island, MacDONALD & WATSON WASTE OIL COMPANY, NARRAGANSETT IMPROVEMENT COMPANY, EUGENE K. D'ALLESANDRO, FRAN SLADE and FAUST RITAROSSI did knowingly transport and cause to be transported hazardous waste, namely toluene and soil contaminated with toluene, from Ainslie Corporation, Braintree, Massachusetts to Narragansett Improvement Company, a facility which had neither interim status nor a permit, under Title 42, United States Code, Section 6925 or 6926, to treat, store or dispose of such waste,

in violation of Title 42, United States Code, Section 6928(d)(1) and Title 18, United States Code, Section 2.

COUNT TWENTY-TWO

On or about and between April 7, 1985 and April 30, 1985, both dates being approximate and inclusive, in the District of Rhode Island, MacDONALD & WATSON WASTE OIL COMPANY and NARRAGANSETT IMPROVEMENT COMPANY did knowingly treat, store and dispose of hazardous waste, namely toluene and soil contaminated with toluene from Ainslie Corporation, Braintree, Massachusetts, without a permit or interim status under Title 42, United States Code, Section 6925 or 6926,

in violation of Title 42, United States Code, Section 6928(d)(2)(A) and Title 18, United States Code, Section 2.

COUNT TWENTY-THREE

The Grand Jury further charges:

On or about April 7, 1985, in the District of Rhode Island, and elsewhere, MacDONALD & WATSON WASTE OIL COMPANY, NARRAGANSETT IMPROVEMENT COMPANY, EUGENE K. D'ALLESANDRO, FRAN SLADE and FAUST RITAROSSI, in a matter within the jurisdiction of the United States Environmental Protection Agency, an agency of the United States of America, did willfully and knowingly make and use and caused to be made and used, a false writing and document containing a materially false statement, knowing the same to contain such statement, in that, in a Uniform Hazardous

Waste Manifest, number C091013, made pursuant to the provisions of Title 42, United States Code, Section 6922 and 6923 and regulations promulgated pursuant thereto, the defendants stated and represented and caused to be stated and represented in said Uniform Hazardous Waste Manifest that the material being transported from Ainslie Corporation, Braintree, Massachusetts to Narragansett Improvement Company, Providence, Rhode Island pursuant to the Manifest was not hazardous waste in Rhode Island whereas, in truth and fact, as the defendants then well knew, said statement was false,

in violation of Title 18, United States Code, Sections 1001 and 2.

COUNTS TWENTY-FOUR THROUGH THIRTY

The Grand Jury further charges:

On or about the dates enumerated and set forth below in separate counts, in the District of Rhode Island, and elsewhere, MacDONALD & WATSON WASTE OIL COMPANY, NARRAGANSETT IMPROVEMENT COMPANY, EUGENE K. D'ALLESANDRO, FRAN SLADE and FAUST RITAROSSI, in a matter within the jurisdiction of the United States Environmental Protection Agency, an agency of the United States of America, did willfully and knowingly make and use and caused to be made and used, a false writing and document containing a materially false statement, knowing the same to contain such statement, in that, in a Uniform Hazardous Waste Manifest, the numbers of which are enumerated and set forth below in separate counts, made pursuant to the provisions of Title 42, United States Code, Section 6922 and 6923 and regulations promulgated pursuant thereto, the defendants stated and represented and caused to be stated and represented in said Uniform Hazardous Waste Manifest that the material being transported from Ainslie Corporation, Braintree, Massachusetts to Narragansett Improvement Company, Providence, Rhode Island pursuant to the Manifest was not hazardous waste in Rhode Island whereas, in truth and fact, as the defendants then well knew, said statement was false,

COUNT	DATE	MANIFEST NUMBER
24	April 7, 1986	C091124
25	April 8, 1986	C091025
26	April 8, 1986	C091167
27	April 9, 1986	C091014
28	April 9, 1986	C091015
29	April 9, 1986	C091016
30	April 9, 1986	C091017

in violation of Title 18, United States Code, Sections 1001 and 2.

COUNT THIRTY-ONE

The Grand Jury further charges:

On or about September 5, 1985, in the District of Rhode Island, MacDONALD & WATSON WASTE OIL COMPANY, NARRAGANSETT IMPROVEMENT COMPANY, EUGENE K. D'ALLESANDRO, FRAN SLADE, and MICHAEL O'LAUGHLIN did knowingly transport and cause to be transported hazardous waste, namely creosote and sand contaminated with creosote from Walpole Woodworkers, Harwichport, Massachusetts to Narragansett Improvement Company, a facility which had neither interim status nor a permit, under Title 42, United States Code, Section 6925 or 6926, to treat, store or dispose of such waste,

in violation of Title 42, United States Code, Section 6928(d)(1) and Title 18, United States Code, Section 2.

COUNT THIRTY-TWO

The Grand Jury further charges:

On or about and between September 5, 1985 and September 30, 1985, both dates being approximate and inclusive, in the District of Rhode Island, MacDONALD & WATSON WASTE OIL COMPANY and NARRAGANSETT IMPROVEMENT COMPANY did knowingly treat, store and dispose of hazardous waste, namely creosote and sand contaminated with creosote, from Walpole Woodworkers, Harwichport, Massachusetts, without a permit or interim status under Title 42, United States Code, Section 6925 or 6926,

in violation of Title 42, United States Code, Section 6928(d)(2)(A) and Title 18, United States Code, Section 2.

COUNT THIRTY-THREE

On or about September 5, 1985, in the District of Rhode Island, MacDONALD & WATSON WASTE OIL COMPANY, NARRAGANSETT IMPROVEMENT COMPANY, EUGENE K. D'ALLESANDRO, FRAN SLADE, and MICHAEL O'LAUGHLIN in a matter within the jurisdiction of the United States Environmental Protection Agency, an agency of the United States of

America, did willfully and knowingly make and use and caused to be made and used, a false writing and document containing a materially false statement, knowing the same to contain such statement, in that, in a Uniform Hazardous Waste Manifest, number B120798, made pursuant to the provisions of Title 42, United States Code, Section 6922 and 6923 and regulations promulgated pursuant thereto, the defendants stated and represented and caused to be stated and represented in said Uniform Hazardous Waste Manifest that the material being transported from Walpole Woodworkers, Harwichport, Massachusetts to Narragansett Improvement Company, Providence, Rhode Island pursuant to the Manifest was not hazardous waste in Rhode Island whereas, in truth and fact, as the defendants then well knew, said statement was false,

in violation of Title 18, United States Code, Sections 1001 and 2.

COUNT THIRTY-FOUR

On or about September 5, 1985, in the District of Rhode Island, MacDONALD & WATSON WASTE OIL COMPANY, NARRAGANSETT IMPROVEMENT COMPANY EUGENE K. D'ALLESANDRO, FRAN SLADE, and MICHAEL O'LAUGHLIN in a matter within the jurisdiction of the United States Environmental Protection Agency, an agency of the United States of America, did willfully and knowingly make and use and caused to be made and used, a false writing and document containing a materially false statement, knowing the same to contain such statement, in that, in a Uniform Hazardous Waste Manifest, number B120799, made pursuant to the provisions of Title 42, United States Code, Section 6922 and 6923 and regulations promulgated pursuant thereto, the defendants stated and represented and caused to be stated and represented in said Uniform Hazardous Waste Manifest that the material being transported from Walpole Woodworkers, Harwichport, Massachusetts to Narragansett Improvement Company, Providence, Rhode Island pursuant to the Manifest was not hazardous waste in Rhode Island whereas, in truth and fact, as the defendants then well knew, said statement was false,

in violation of Title 18, United States Code, Sections 1001 and 2.

COUNT THIRTY-FIVE

The Grand Jury further charges:

On or about and between June 1, 1983 and July 31, 1984, both dates being approximate and inclusive, at Pole 2, Spragueville Road, Smithfield, Rhode Island in the District of Rhode Island, MacDONALD & WATSON WASTE OIL COMPANY, EUGENE K. D'ALLESANDRO and VICENT CINQUAGRANO did knowingly dispose of a hazardous waste, namely xylene, without a permit or interim status, under Title 42, United States Code, Section 6925 or 6926,

in violation of Title 42, United States Code, Section 6928(d)(2)(A), and Title 18, United States Code, Section 2.

COUNT THIRTY-SIX

The Grand Jury further charges:

On or about and between January 1, 1984 and June 30, 1985, both dates being approximate and inclusive, in Providence,

Rhode Island in the District of Rhode Island, MacDONALD & WATSON WASTE OIL COMPANY, NARRAGANSETT IMPROVEMENT COMPANY, EUGENE K. D'ALLESANDRO and VINCENT CINQUAGRANO did knowingly dispose of hazardous waste, namely xylene and xylene sludge, without a permit or interim status, under Title 42, United States Code, Section 6925 or 6926, by dumping said hazardous waste into piles of soil located in a lot owned by Narragansett Improvement Company at the intersection of O'Connell Street and Poe Street Providence, Rhode Island,

in violation of Title 42, United States Code, Section 6928(d)(2)(A), and Title 18, United States Code, Section 2.

COUNT THIRTY-SEVEN

The Grand Jury further charges:

On or about and between June 5, 1985 and June 6, 1985, in the District of Rhode Island, and other places, MacDONALD & WATSON WASTE OIL COMPANY and NARRAGANSETT IMPROVEMENT COMPANY did knowingly transport and cause to be transported hazardous waste, namely xylene and xylene sludges from Narragansett Improvement Company, 223 Allens Avenue, Providence Rhode Island to 3R Services, South Portland, Maine, a facility which had neither interim status nor a permit, under Title 42, United States Code, Section 6925 or 6926, to treat, store or dispose of such waste,

in violation of Title 42, United States Code, Section 6928(d)(1) and Title 18, United States Code, Section 2.

COUNT THIRTY-EIGHT

The Grand Jury further charges:

On or about August 21, 1985, in the District of Rhode Island, MacDONALD & WATSON WASTE OIL COMPANY, NARRAGANSETT IMPROVEMENT COMPANY and FRAN SLADE did knowingly treat, store and dispose of hazardous waste, namely trichloroethylene, in knowing violation of a material condition and requirement of a permit issued pursuant to Title 42, United States Code, Section 6901 et seq., in that a shipment of hazardous waste, namely trichloroethylene in 55-gallon drums with a total chlorination of greater than 7.5%, was accepted from Sherman Screw Products Company in violation of Narragansett Improvement Company's permit (Sections 2.22 and 3.33),

in violation of Title 42, United States Code, Section 6928(d)(2)(B).

COUNT THIRTY-NINE

The Grand Jury further charges:

On or about August 21, 1985, in the District of Rhode Island, MacDONALD & WATSON WASTE OIL COMPANY and FRAN SLADE did knowingly omit and cause the omission of material information and made or caused the making of a false material statement or representation in a manifest, number RIA0001907, used for purposes of compliance with regulations promulgated by the State of Rhode Island and Providence Plantations, knowing that said manifest contained such omission in that the defendants failed to state and represent and caused the failure to state and represent and falsely stated and represented in said manifest that the hazardous waste being transported was lube oil whereas, in truth and fact, as the defendants then well knew the hazardous waste was a combination of lube oil and trichloroethylene,

in violation of Title 42, United States Code, Section 6928(d)(3).

COUNTS FORTY THROUGH FORTY-TWO

The Grand Jury further charges:

1. From on or about April 1, 1986 to May 2, 1986, both dates being approximate and inclusive, in the District of Rhode Island, MacDONALD & WATSON WASTE OIL COMPANY and EUGENE K. D'ALLESANDRO did knowingly and willfully devise and intend to devise a scheme and artifice to defraud and obtain money by means of false and fraudulent pretenses, representations and promises from Murdock Webbing Company, Inc., Central Falls, Rhode Island, well knowing that these pretenses, representations and promises were false when made, and which scheme and artifice was in substance as follow:

a. It was part of the scheme and artifice to defraud that MacDONALD & WATSON WASTE OIL COMPANY had a contract with Murdock Webbing Company to clean out, remove and dispose of the contents of underground storage tanks.

b. It was further part of the scheme and artifice to defraud that MacDONALD & WATSON WASTE OIL COMPANY charged Murdock Webbing Company for the clean up, removal and disposal of the contents of the underground storage tanks based on the number of gallons removed from the tank.

c. It was further part of said scheme and artifice to defraud that on or about April 9, 1986, EUGENE K. D'ALLESANDRO ordered employees of MacDONALD & WATSON WASTE OIL COMPANY to collect approximately 1000 gallons of waste oil from Chamberlain Manufacturing Corporation in a vacuum truck.

d. It was further part of said scheme and artifice to defraud that EUGENE K. D'ALLESANDRO directed MacDONALD & WATSON WASTE OIL COMPANY employees to empty the contents of the vacuum truck into the underground storage tanks at Murdock Webbing Company.

e. It was further part of said scheme and artifice to defraud that on or about April 10, 1986 MacDONALD & WATSON WASTE OIL COMPANY pumped 5,460 gallons of material for disposal out of the Murdock Webbing underground storage tanks.

f. It was further part of said scheme and artifice to defraud that on or about and between April 1, 1986 and April 8, 1986, both dates being approximate and inclusive, EUGENE K. D'ALLESANDRO ordered MacDONALD & WATSON employees to clean out sludge collected in tanks located at Narragansett Improvement Company.

g. It was further part of said scheme and artifice to defraud that the sludge from the tanks was transported to Murdock Webbing Company and emptied into the underground storage tanks.

h. It was further part of said scheme and artifice to defraud that MacDONALD & WATSON WASTE OIL COMPANY billed and accepted payment from Murdock Webbing Company for the removal of 5,460 gallons of oil and water on or about April 10, 1986.

2. On or about the dates specified below, in the District of Rhode Island, MacDONALD & WATSON WASTE OIL COMPANY and EUGENE K. D'ALLESANDRO for the purpose of executing the aforesaid scheme and artifice to defraud, and to obtain money from Murdock Webbing Company by false and fraudulent pretenses, representations and promises, and attempting to do so, knowingly caused mail matter to be delivered by the United States Postal Service, according to the directions thereon, as specified more particularly below:

COUNT	DATE	ITEM	MAILED
40	April 11, 1986	Manifest	From: MacDonald & Watson To: Chamberlain Manufacturing
41	April 18, 1986	Invoice	From: MacDonald & Watson To: Murdock Webbing
42	May 2, 1986	Payment	From: Murdock Webbing To: MacDonald & Watson

in violation of Title 18, United States Code, Sections 1341 and 2.

COUNTS FORTY-THREE THROUGHT FORTY-SIX

The Grand Jury further charges:

1. From on or about July 1984 to on or about February 1985, both dates being approximate and inclusive, in the District of Rhode Island, MacDONALD & WATSON WASTE OIL COMPANY and EUGENE

K. D'ALLESANDRO did knowingly and willfully devise and intend to devise a scheme and artifice to defraud and obtain money by means of false and fraudulent pretenses, representations and promises from the City of Warwick, Rhode Island, well knowing that these pretenses, representations and promises were false when made, and which scheme and artifice was in substance as follows:

a. It was part of the scheme and artifice to defraud that MacDONALD & WATSON WASTE OIL COMPANY entered into a contract with the City of Warwick to remove and dispose of sludge from the Warwick Sewage Treatment Facility.

b. It was further part of the scheme and artifice to defraud that MacDONALD & WATSON WASTE OIL COMPANY was required to transport the sludge to the Rhode Island Central landfill for disposal.

c. It was further part of the scheme and artifice to defraud that MacDONALD & WATSON WASTE OIL COMPANY charged the City of Warwick $4.19 for each ton of material delivered to the Rhode Island Central Landfill.

d. It was further part of the scheme and artifice to defraud that the Rhode Island Central Landfill weighed each MacDONALD & WATSON WASTE OIL COMPANY truck as it entered and exited the landfill.

e. It was further part of the scheme and artifice to defraud that the amount to bill the City of Warwick was determined by subtracting the weight of the truck as it left the Landfill from the weight of the truck as it entered the Landfill.

f. It was further part of the scheme and artifice to defraud that MacDONALD & WATSON WASTE OIL COMPANY partially filled its dump trucks with soil from the Poe Street lot adjacent to Narragansett Improvement Company prior to picking up the sludge from the Warwick Sewage Treatment Facility.

g. It was further part of the scheme and artifice to defraud that MacDONALD & WATSON WASTE OIL COMPANY would on occasion load the top of trucks filled with sludge from the Warwick Sewage Treatment Facility with soil from the Poe Street lot adjacent to Narragansett Improvement Company.

h. It was further part of the scheme and artifice to defraud that MacDONALD & WATSON WASTE OIL COMPANY would partially fill its dump trucks with waste aluminum sodium hydrate prior to picking up the sludge from the Warwick Sewage Treatment Facility.

i. It was further part of the scheme and artifice to defraud that the Rhode Island Central Landfill included the weight of the aluminum sodium hydrate or the Poe Street soil in determing the weight of trucks entering the Landfill.

j. It was further part of the scheme and artifice to defraud that MacDONALD & WATSON WASTE OIL COMPANY charged the City of Warwick for the cost of disposing of the Poe Street soil and aluminum sodium hydrate at the Rhode Island Central Landfill.

2. On or about the dates specified below, in the District of Rhode Island, MacDONALD & WATSON WASTE OIL COMPANY and EUGENE K. D'ALLESANDRO, for the purpose of executing the aforesaid scheme and artifice to defraud, and to obtain money from the City of Warwick, Rhode Island by false and fraudulent pretenses, representations and promises, and attempting to do so, knowingly caused mail matter to be delivered by the United States Postal Service, according to the directions thereon, as specified more particularly below:

COUNT	DATE	ITEM	MAILED
43	October 2, 1984	Invoice	From: MacDonald & Watson To: City of Warwick, Purchasing Department
44	October 17, 1984	Check	From: City of Warwick To: MacDonald & Watson
45	November 20, 1984	Invoice	From: MacDonald & Watson To: City of Warwick Purchasing Department
46	February 14, 1985	Check	From: City of Warwick To: MacDonald & Watson

in violation of Title 18, United States Code, Sections 1341 and 2.

COUNTS FORTY-SEVEN THROUGH FIFTY-TWO

The Grand Jury further charges:

INTRODUCTION

1. At all times material to this indictment the 1956 Rhode Island General Laws, Chapter 23-18.9 (1979 Reenactment)

regulated solid waste management facilities and the disposal of solid waste in the State of Rhode Island and Providence Plantations and provided that:

a. A license issued by the State of Rhode Island and Providence Plantations is required to operate any solid waste management facility within the state. A license fee of $100.00 must be paid to the State.

b. A solid waste management facility is any plant, structure, equipment, real and personal property operated for the purpose of processing, treating or disposing of solid waste.

c. A transfer station is a facility where collection vehicles transfer solid waste to haulage vehicles for transportation to final disposal sites or other solid waste management facilities. A transfer station is a solid waste management facility. A permit is required to operate a transfer station.

d. Solid waste includes garbage, refuse and other discarded solid materials generated by residential, institutional, commercial, industrial and agricultural sources.

e. Oil spill cleanup debris is a solid waste, and is defined as waste resulting from the cleanup of debris caused by spilling, depositing or placing of petroleum distillates, including but not limited to crank case oil, lubricants and hydraulic oil, penetrant oils, tramp oils, quenching oils and kerosene onto the land or waters of the state. Oil spill cleanup debris can only be disposed of within special facilities constructed within sanitary landfills.

2. At all times material to this indictment there were no licensed facilities within the State of Rhode Island and Providence Plantations permitted to dispose of oil spill cleanup debris.

The Grand Jury further charges:

1. From on or about June 1, 1983 to on or about December 31, 1986, both dates being approximate and inclusive, in the District of Rhode Island, and other places, MacDONALD & WATSON WASTE OIL COMPANY, NARRAGANSETT IMPROVEMENT COMPANY, EUGENE K. D'ALLESANDRO and VINCENT CINQUEGRANO did knowingly and willfully devise and intended to devise a scheme and artifice

(a) to defraud the State of Rhode Island and Providence Plantations out of its right to collect license fees for a solid waste management facility namely, a landfill, operated at Pole 12, Greenhill Road, Johnston, Rhode Island;

(b) to defraud the State of Rhode Island and Providence Plantations out of its right to collect license fees for a solid waste management facility namely, a transfer station, operated at the intersection of Poe Street and O'Connell Street, Providence, Rhode Island;

(c) to obtain money by means of false and fraudulent pretenses, representations and promises from Continental/Midland well knowing that these pretenses, representations and promises were false when made;

(d) to obtain money by means of false and fraudulent pretenses, representations and promises from Maurice Linhares well knowing that the pretenses, representations and promises were false when made; and

> (e) to obtain money by means of false and fraudulent pretenses, representations and promises from Evergreen Services well knowing that the pretenses, representations and promises were false,

and which scheme and artifice was in substance as follows:

a. It was part of the scheme and artifice to defraud that NARRAGANSETT IMPROVEMENT COMPANY operated an asphalt concrete production facility at 223 Allens Avenue, Providence Rhode Island.

b. It was further part of the scheme and artifice to defraud that NARRAGANSETT IMPROVEMENT COMPANY was allowed to accept oil spill cleanup debris but only for beneficial reuse as an aggregate in the asphalt production process.

c. It was further part of the scheme and artifice to defraud that MacDONALD & WATSON WASTE OIL COMPANY contracted with third parties to transport their oil spill cleanup debris to NARRAGANSETT IMPROVEMENT COMPANY for disposal as aggregate in the asphalt plant.

d. It was further part of the scheme and artifice to defraud that MacDONALD & WATSON WASTE OIL COMPANY transported oil spill cleanup debris to NARRAGANSETT IMPROVEMENT COMPANY. NARRAGANSETT IMPROVEMENT COMPANY accepted the oil spill cleanup debris which was placed in an adjacent lot at the intersection of Poe Street and O'Connell Street, Providence, Rhode Island.

e. It was further part of the scheme and artifice to defraud that transporters other than MacDONALD & WATSON WASTE

OIL COMPANY transported oil spill cleanup debris to NARRAGANSETT IMPROVEMENT COMPANY. NARRAGANSETT IMPROVEMENT COMPANY accepted such oil spill cleanup debris which was placed in an adjacent lot at the intersection of Poe Street and O'Connell Street, Providence, Rhode Island.

f. It was further part of the scheme and artifice to defraud that MacDONALD & WATSON WASTE OIL COMPANY and other transporters transported soils contaminated with chemicals and other discarded materials from institutional, commercial and industrial sources including but not limited to spent solvents, hydrated lime, and filter cake contaminated with hexanol to NARRAGANSETT IMPROVEMENT COMPANY. NARRAGANSETT IMPROVEMENT COMPANY accepted all such materials which were placed in an adjacent lot at the intersection of Poe Street and O'Connell Street, Providence, Rhode Island.

g. It was further part of the scheme and artifice to defraud that employees of MacDONALD & WATSON WASTE OIL COMPANY did dump and dispose of oils, oil sludges, drums of chemical wastes and other solid wastes in the piles of soil in the lot located adjacent to Narragansett Improvement Company at the intersection of Poe Street and O'Connell Street, Providence, Rhode Island.

h. It was further part of the scheme and artifice to defraud that certain of the materials identified in paragraphs (d) through (g) immediately above were not used as aggregate in the production process of NARRAGANSETT IMPROVEMENT COMPANY.

i. It was further part of the scheme and artifice to defraud that certain of the materials identified in paragraphs (d) through (g) immediately above were transported from the lot at Poe Street and O'Connell Street, Providence, Rhode Island and disposed of or used as fill material at MacDONALD & WATSON WASTE OIL COMPANY, Pole 12, Greenhill Road, Johnston, Rhode Island and American Disposal Company, Pole 13, Greenhill Road, Johnston, Rhode Island.

j. It was further part of the scheme and artifice to defraud that neither MacDONALD & WATSON WASTE OIL COMPANY nor NARRAGANSETT IMPROVEMENT COMPANY had a permit to operate a solid waste management facility, that is a transfer station, at the intersection of Poe Street and O'Connell Street, Providence, Rhode Island.

k. It was further part of the scheme and artifice to defraud that MacDONALD & WATSON WASTE OIL COMPANY did not have a permit to operate a solid waste management facility, that is a sanitary landfill and oil spill cleanup debris disposal site, at Pole 12, Greenhill Road, Johnston, Rhode Island.

2. On or about the dates specified below, in the District of Rhode Island, and elsewhere, MacDONALD & WATSON WASTE OIL COMPANY, NARRAGANSETT IMPROVEMENT COMPANY, EUGENE K. D'ALLESANDRO and VINCENT CINQUEGRANO, aiding and abetting each other, for the purpose of executing the aforesaid scheme and artifice to defraud, and attempting to do so, knowingly caused mail matter to be

delivered by the United States Postal Service, according to the directions thereon, as specified more particularly below:

COUNT	DATE	ITEM	MAILED
47	June 14, 1983	Bid to remove soil	From: MacDonald & Watson To: Continental/Midland 25000 South Western Avenue Park Forest, Illinois 60466
48	August 7, 1986	Manifests	From: Applied Environmental Technologies To: State of Massachusetts Department of Environmental Quality Engineering (re: Maurice Linhares)
49	August 12, 1986	Invoice	From: MacDonald & Watson To: Evergreen Services P.O. Box 1701 60 Rockwood Street Boston, Masachusetts
50	September 12, 1986	Check	From: Evergreen Services To: MacDonald & Watson
51	October 31, 1986	Invoice	From: MacDonald & Watson To: Evergreen Services
52	November 30, 1986	Check	From: Evergreen Services To: MacDonald & Watson

in violation of Title 18, United States Code, Sections 1341 and 2.

COUNT FIFTY-THREE

The Grand Jury further charges:

1. Paragraphs one through six of the Introduction to Count One, Counts Fourteen through Seventeen and Counts Forty-Two through Fifty-Two are hereby realleged and incorporated by reference as though fully set forth herein.

2. At all times material to this indictment MacDONALD & WATSON WASTE OIL COMPANY was an enterprise as that term is used in Title 18, United States Code, Section 1961(4). At all times material to this indictment, the enterprise was engaged in the transportation of hazardous wastes, solid wastes, used oils and soil or other earth materials contaminated with petroleum products.

3. From on or about June 1983 to on or about December 1986, both dates being approximate and inclusive, in the District of Rhode Island, and elsewhere, the defendant EUGENE K. D'ALLESANDRO, being a person employed by and associated with the enterprise described in paragraph 2 above, which was engaged in, and the activities of which affected, interstate and foreign commerce, knowingly conducted and participated, directly and indirectly, in the conduct of the affairs of the enterprise through a pattern of racketeering activity as that term is defined in Title 18, United States Code, Section 1961(5), as set forth below:

RACKETEERING ACT I

4. Any one of the following acts involving mail fraud in relation to the Estate of Moses Weinman:

a. Count 14;
b. Count 15;
c. Count 16; or
d. Count 17;

RACKETEERING ACT II

5. Any one of the following acts involving mail fraud in relation to the City of Warwick:

a. Count 43;
b. Count 44;
c. Count 45; or
d. Count 46;

RACKETEERING ACT III

6. Any one of the following acts involving mail fraud in relation to the State of Rhode Island and Providence Plantations, Maurice Linhares, Continental/Midland or Evergreen Services:

a.	Count 47;	(State/Continental/Midland)
b.	Count 48;	(State/Linhares)
c.	Count 49;	(State/Evergreen)
d.	Count 50;	(State/Evergreen)
e.	Count 51; or	(State/Evergreen)
f.	Count 52;	(State/Evergreen)

RACKETEERING ACT IV

7. On or about and between April 22, 1987 and May 1, 1987, both dates being approximate and inclusive, in the District of Rhode Island, the defendant EUGENE K. D'ALLESANDRO committed an act in violation of Title 18, United States Code, Section 1503, in that the defendant EUGENE K. D'ALLESANDRO did knowingly and corruptly influence, obstruct and impede and endeavor to influence, obstruct and impede the due administration of justice in a Federal proceeding in that EUGENE K. D'ALLESANDRO corruptly advised and instructed a witness to testify before a Federal grand jury sitting in Providence, Rhode Island that he, the witness,

forgot what happened and in testifying to leave out portions of what activities occurred at the lot located at the intersection of Poe Street and O'Connell Street, Providence, Rhode Island, knowing full well that such testimony would be false and would corruptly influence, impede or obstruct a Federal grand jury investigation,

all in violation of Title 18, United States Code, Section 1962(C).

FORFEITURE ALLEGATIONS

1. The Grand Jury realleges count fifty-three of this indictment as though fully set forth herein.

2. The Grand Jury further charges that from June 1983 through December 1986 defendant EUGENE K. D'ALLESANDRO did engage in conduct in violation of Title 18, United States Code, Section 1962(c), thereby subjecting to forfeiture to the United States, pursuant to Title 18, United States Code, Section 1963(a), the following interests and property, as of the date they were acquired or maintained in violation of Title 18, United States Code, Section 1962:

(a) All interests defendant EUGENE K. D'ALLESANDRO acquired and maintained in violation of Title 18, United States Code, Section 1962;

(b) All of the defendant EUGENE K. D'ALLESANDRO's interests in, claims against, security of, and property and contractual rights of any kind affording a source of influence over the MacDONALD & WATSON WASTE OIL COMPANY; and

(c) All property constituting or derived from any proceeds which defendant EUGENE K. D'ALLESANDRO obtained, directly or indirectly, from racketeering activity in violation of Title 18, United States Code, Section 1962.

Specifically, this includes, but is not limited to, the following:

i. All monies, including salaries and bonuses, paid to EUGUENE K. D'ALLESANDRO by MacDonald & Watson Waste Oil Company for the period June 1983 through December 1986,

ii. EUGENE K. D'ALLESANDRO's ownership interest in MacDonald & Watson Waste Oil Company, and

iii. All property, including monies, constituting or derived from any proceeds received by EUGENE K. D'ALLESANDRO as a result of the racketeering activity alleged in count fifty-three.

A TRUE BILL

Foreperson

LINCOLN C. ALMOND
United States Attorney
District of Rhode Island

Attest to True Copy
FREDERICK R. DeCESARIS
Clerk
By Deputy Clerk

United States v. Hofele: Criminal Information; Plea Agreement and Stipulation of Facts Relative to Sentencing; Judgment

UNITED STATES DISTRICT COURT
EASTERN DISTRICT OF MISSOURI
EASTERN DIVISION

FILED

U. S. DISTRICT COURT
E. DISTRICT OF MO.

UNITED STATES OF AMERICA, Plaintiff,	)	
v.	)	Case No. 4:94CR0112 JCH
GEORGE HOFELE, Defendant.	)	

INFORMATION

The United States Attorney charges that:

INTRODUCTION

At all times material to this Information:

Defendant George Hofele was the owner and proprietor of a motor vehicle repair shop located at 8216 Watson Road, Marlborough, Missouri. George Hofele performed service or repair on motor vehicle air conditioners.

The production, importation, and use of chlorofluorocarbons (CFCs) and hydrochlorofluorocarbons (HCFCs) are regulated by the Clean Air Act, 42 U.S.C. Sections 7671-7671q and the implementing regulations set forth at 40 C.F.R. Part 82.

Title VI, Section 609 of the Clean Air Act, 42 U.S.C. 767h, prohibits both the improper use of approved refrigerant and recycling equipment and the use of refrigerant recycling equipment which has not been approved by the Administrator of the Environmental Protection Agency.

Title VI, Section 609 of the Clean Air Act, 42 U.S.C. 7671h, prohibits the servicing of motor vehicle air conditioners for consideration as of January 1, 1992 unless the technician is properly trained and certified pursuant to a technician certification program approved by the Administrator.

As of July 3, 1993, in the Eastern District of Missouri, defendant George Hofele did not possess, use or own approved refrigerant recovery or recycling equipment required for the proper servicing or repairing of motor vehicle air conditioners.

COUNT I

On or about July 3, 1993, defendant George Hofele knowingly repaired or serviced a motor vehicle air conditioner, which involved the refrigerant, for consideration, and was not trained or certified to use approved refrigerant recovery or recycling equipment, in violation of the requirements of Section 609 of the Clean Air Act, 42 U.S.C. Section 7671h(c).

All in violation of 42 U.S.C. Section 7413(c)(1) and 18 U.S.C. Section 2.

Respectfully submitted,

EDWARD L. DOWD, JR.
United States Attorney

PATRICK M. FLACHS
Assistant United States Attorney
Chief, Environmental Crimes
Task Force
1114 Market Street, Room 401
St. Louis, Missouri 63101
(314) 539-2200

UNITED STATES DISTRICT COURT
EASTERN DISTRICT OF MISSOURI
EASTERN DIVISION

UNITED STATES OF AMERICA, Plaintiff, v. GEORGE HOFELE, Defendant.	)	Case No.

PLEA AGREEMENT AND STIPULATION OF FACTS RELATIVE TO SENTENCING

Come now the United States of America, by and through Edward L. Dowd, Jr., United States Attorney; Patrick M. Flachs, Assistant United States Attorney; Daniel L. Doyle, Special Assistant United States Attorney; and Assistant Attorney General for the State of Missouri, and Defendant George Hofele, by and through his undersigned counsel, David V. Capes and Richard E. Greenberg, and, pursuant to Section 6B1.4 of the Federal Sentencing Guidelines and Policy Statement and the Administrative Order of this Court dated January 21, 1991, hereby submit and stipulate to the following facts as relevant for the purposes of sentencing in this cause:

I. General Matters

No promises or predictions have been made to the Defendant, except that an Information would be filed pursuant to a Waiver of Indictment.

The Defendant understands that a statutory fine of not more than two hundred fifty thousand dollars ($250,000) could be imposed for a violation of Title 42, United States Code, Section 7413(c), and imprisonment of up to five (5) years, or both. A special assessment pursuant to Title 18, United States Code, Section 3013, in the amount of fifty dollars ($50) must also be assessed.

The total amount in Special Assessments due from Defendant is fifty dollars ($50). This amount will be paid in full on the date the Plea Agreement is entered.

No threats or promises have been made to induce the Defendant to plead guilty to the charges of the Information other than as set forth in this document.

II. <u>Facts and Circumstances of the Offense and Offense Characteristics</u>

Defendant resides at 1234 Luray in Chesterfield, Missouri. He is the owner and president of G & H Tire, Inc. located at 8216 Watson Road in Marlborough (St. Louis County), Missouri.

In 1993, G & H Tire, Inc. provided motor vehicle repair services, including the repair of motor vehicle air-conditioners.

In 1993, the defendant was the President of G & H Tire, Inc. and the manager of its principal place of business located at 8216 Watson Road, Marlborough, Missouri.

Effective January 1, 1992, Section 609 of The Clean Air Act, 42 U.S.C. § 7671h, provides that no person repairing or servicing motor vehicles for consideration may perform any services on a motor vehicle air-conditioner involving the refrigerant for such air-conditioner without properly using approved refrigerant recycling equipment.

Section 609 of the Clean Air Act, 42 U.S.C. § 7671h provides that no person may perform such service unless such person has been properly trained and certified.

In 1993, Defendant was aware of and had knowledge of the general requirement that repair of motor vehicle air-conditioners, for consideration, required that he be certified and that approved refrigerant recycling equipment be utilized.

The parties agree that in 1993 the Defendant:

a. Repaired or serviced motor vehicles; and

b. That he repaired or serviced motor vehicles for consideration; and

c. That he repaired or serviced motor vehicle air conditioners; and

d. That the service he performed on motor vehicle air conditioners involved the refrigerant for such air conditioners, and

e. That the service he performed on motor vehicle air conditioners involving the refrigerant for such air conditioners was performed without properly using approved refrigerant recycling equipment; and

f. That he was not properly trained and certified prior to servicing the motor vehicle air conditioners.

The refrigerant contained Chlorofluorocarbons(CFC's) and hydrochlorofluorocarbons (HCFC's).

Both Chlorofluorocarbons(CFC's) and hydrochlorofluorocarbons (HCFC's) are pollutants but are not defined by EPA regulations as hazardous or toxic substances.

III. Obstruction

The parties stipulate that Defendant did not obstruct the investigation.

IV. Acceptance of Responsibility

The parties also stipulate that Defendant has demonstrated his acceptance and personal responsibility for his criminal conduct. Defendant has cooperated with the investigation in this matter in admitting his underlying conduct and took no action to conceal the underlying conduct.

V. Criminal History

To the parties' knowledge, Defendant has no prior criminal history.

VI. Appropriate Offense Level

Punishment for a plea of guilty to a violation of 15 U.S.C. § 7413(c) involving a pollutant is governed by Section 2Q1.3 of the Sentencing Guidelines issued under the Sentence Reform Act of 1984 (hereinafter referred to as "Guidelines"). This provides a base level of six (6).

The parties agree that the adjustment for the Role In the Offense, § 3B1.1, and whether the offense involved a discharge, release, or an emission of a pollutant, § 2Q1.3(b)(1), under the "Guidelines," shall be determined by the Court after completion of the presentence investigation by the United States Probation Office in this case. The Defendant is entitled to a two-level decrease for acceptance of responsibility as indicated in paragraph 15 above.

The refrigerant removal equipment used by the defendant was not certified by the Administrator of the Environmental Protection Agency and any discharge of refrigerant was not authorized by her. The offense did not involve a discharge without a permit or in violation of a permit.

The parties agree, pursuant to Rule 11(e)(1)(B), to recommend to the Court that the defendant be fined a total of five thousand dollars ($5,000.00), exclusive of restitution which is recommended in the amount of five thousand dollars ($5,000.00). The restitution amount will be paid to the Missouri Highway Patrol to partially reimburse the cost of this investigation.

VII. Binding Plea Agreement

The foregoing statements of applicability of these sections of the "Guidelines" are not binding upon the Court nor the United States Probation Office and the Defendant may not withdraw his plea of guilty herein solely because the Court or United States Probation Office does not agree with either the statements of applicability or the statements of the circumstances. The final decision regarding sentencing of the Defendant is with the Court.

In exchange for Defendant's agreement to cooperate as anticipated in this Agreement, the United States agrees to move for a downward departure pursuant to Chapter 5, Part K of the "Guidelines" and 18 U.S.C. § 3553(e), if the United States, in its sole discretion, determines that Defendant's cooperation is complete, truthful, and of substantial assistance in the prosecution or investigation of another individual(s).

The United States and the State of Missouri agree not to file any additional charges arising out of the facts discovered during the course of this investigation. The United States agrees that, in regard to Defendant's cooperation subsequent to this Agreement, all information concerning the unlawful activities of others which is self-incriminating information as to the Defendant will not be used against him, and that said information shall not be used in determining the applicable "Guidelines" or range as provided in Section B1.8 of the "Guidelines". The Defendant agrees and understands that nothing in this Agreement, pursuant to 1B1.8 of the "Guidelines", bars the United States from instituting a prosecution for perjury or giving a false statement that occurs during the course of the defendant's cooperation.

Defendant and the United States further agree that each reserves all respective rights to inform the probation officer preparing the Presentence Investigation Report of all relevant facts and circumstances, and to address the Court at the time of sentencing, including presentencing testimony and evidence, proffers of testimony, and evidence and recommendations regarding the appropriate sentence to the extent permitted in any case.

The Defendant and the United States further agree that this written Plea Agreement and Stipulation of Facts Relative to Sentencing constitutes all the terms, conditions, promises, inducements and understandings between them, and that there are no other written agreements, promises or understandings, either oral or written, between the parties considering the disposition of this case.

EDWARD L. DOWD, JR.
United States Attorney

PATRICK M. FLACHS
Assistant United States Attorney

1114 Market Street, Room 401
St. Louis, Missouri 63101
(314) 539-2200

DANIEL L. DOYLE
Special Assistant
United States Attorney and
Assistant Attorney General for
the State of Missouri

GEORGE HOFELE
Defendant

ROSENBLUM, GOLDENHERSH,
SILVERSTEIN & ZAFFT, P.C.

DAVID V. CAPES
RICHARD E. GREENBERG
7733 Forsyth Boulevard
Fourth Floor
Clayton, Missouri 63105
(314) 726-8686

Attorneys for Defendant

AO 245S Modified (08/91) Sheet 1 - Judgment in a Criminal Case

United States District Court

EASTERN DISTRICT OF MISSOURI

UNITED STATES OF AMERICA
V.

JUDGMENT IN A CRIMINAL CASE
(For Offenses Committed On or After 11/1/87)

FILED
JUL 29 1994
U. S. DISTRICT COURT
E. DIST. OF MO.
ST. LOUIS

GEORGE HOFELE
(Name of Defendant)

Case Number: 4:94cr112JCH

Richard Greenberg
Defendant's Attorney

THE DEFENDANT:

[X] *Pleaded guilty to count(s)* 1 .
[ ] *Was found guilty on count(s)* ____ *after a plea of not guilty.*

Accordingly, the defendant is adjudged guilty of such count(s), which involve the following offenses:

Title & Section	Nature of Offense	Date Offense Concluded	Count Number(s)
42USC7413(c)(1) and 18USC2	Fraud	7/3/93	1

The defendant is sentenced as provided in pages 2 through 4 *of this Judgment. The sentence is imposed pursuant to the Sentencing Reform Act of 1984.*

[ ] *The defendant has been found not guilty on count(s)* ____, *and is discharged as to such count(s).*
[ ] *Count(s)* ____ *(is)(are) dismissed on the motion of the United States.*
[X] *It is ordered that the defendant shall pay to the United States a special assessment of $* 50.00, *for count(s)* 1 ____, *which shall be due* [X] *immediately* [ ] *as follows:*

It is further ordered that the defendant shall notify the United States Attorney for this district within 30 days of any change of name, residence, or mailing address until all fines, restitution, costs, and special assessments imposed by this Judgment are fully paid.

Defendant's Soc. Sec. No.: 498-44-3202

Defendant's Date of Birth: 3/18/42

7/29/94
Date of Imposition of Sentence

Defendant's mailing address:

1234 Luray Drive
Chesterfield, MO 63017

Signature of Judicial Officer

Jean C. Hamilton
U.S. District Judge
Name and Title of Judicial Officer

Defendant's residence address:

Same as above

7/29/94
Date

A True Copy of the Original
Filed July 29, 1994
Attest:
By: C. Zuppold
Dated: Aug 4, 1994

AO 245S Modified (08/91) Sheet 4 - Probation

Judgment--Page 2 of 4

Defendant: GEORGE HOFELE
Case Number: 4:94cr112JCH

PROBATION

The defendant is hereby placed on probation for a term of:

Two (2) years

While on probation, the defendant shall not commit another Federal, state, or local crime and shall not illegally possess a controlled substance. The defendant also shall comply with the standard conditions that have been adopted by this court (set forth below). If this Judgment imposes a fine or a restitution obligation, it shall be a condition of probation that the defendant pay any such fine or restitution. The defendant shall comply with the following additional conditions:

STANDARD CONDITIONS OF SUPERVISION

While the defendant is on probation or supervised release pursuant to this Judgment, the defendant shall not commit another Federal, state or local crime. In addition:

1) the defendant shall not leave the judicial district without permission of the court or probation officer;
2) the defendant shall report to the probation officer as directed by the court or probation officer and shall submit a truthful and complete written report within the first five days of each month;
3) the defendant shall answer truthfully all inquiries by the probation officer and follow the instructions of the probation officer;
4) the defendant shall support his or her dependents and meet other family responsibilities;
5) the defendant shall work regularly at a lawful occupation unless excused by the probation officer for schooling, training, or other acceptable reasons;
6) the defendant shall notify the probation officer within seventy-two hours of any change in residence or employment;
7) the defendant shall refrain from excessive use of alcohol and shall not purchase, possess, use, distribute, or administer any narcotic or other controlled substance, or any paraphernalia related to such substances, except as prescribed by a physician;
8) the defendant shall not frequent places where controlled substances are illegally sold, used, distributed, or administered;
9) the defendant shall not associate with any persons engaged in criminal activity, and shall not associate with any person convicted of a felony unless granted permission to do so by the probation officer;
10) the defendant shall permit a probation officer to visit him or her at any time at home or elsewhere and shall permit confiscation of any contraband observed in plain view by the probation officer;
11) the defendant shall notify the probation officer within seventy-two hours of being arrested or questioned by a law enforcement officer;
12) the defendant shall not enter into any agreement to act as an informer or a special agent of a law enforcement agency without the permission of the court;
13) as directed by the probation officer, the defendant shall notify third party risks that may be occasioned by the defendant's criminal record or personal history or characteristics, and shall permit the probation officer to make such notification and to confirm the defendant's compliance with such notification requirement;
14) the defendant shall not possess a firearm or destructive device.

AO 245 S Modified (08/91) Sheet 5 - Fine

Defendant: GEORGE HOFELE
Case Number: 4:94cr112JCH

FINE

The defendant shall pay a fine of $ 5000.00 . *The fine includes any costs of incarceration and/or supervision.*

[X] *This amount is the total of the fines imposed on individual counts, as follows:*

Ct. 1 - $5000.00

[ ] *The Court has determined that the defendant does not have the ability to pay interest. It is ordered that:*

[ ] *The interest requirement is waived.*
[ ] *The interest requirement is modified as follows:*

This fine plus any interest required shall be paid:

[X] *in full immediately.*
[ ] *in full not later than* ______________________.
[ ] *in equal monthly installments over a period of* ______ *months. The first payment is due on the date of this judgment. Subsequent payments are due monthly thereafter.*

[ ] *in installments according to the following schedule of payments:*

If the fine is not paid, the court may sentence the defendant to any sentence which might have been originally imposed. See 18 U.S.C. 3614.

AO 245S Modified (08/91 Sheet 7 - Statement of Reasons

Judgment--Page 4 of 4

Defendant: GEORGE HOFELE
Case Number: 4:94cr112JCH

STATEMENT OF REASONS

[X] *The Court adopts the factual findings in the presentence report as to the applicable guideline factors,*

OR

[ ] *The Court adopts the factual findings in the presentence report as to the applicable guideline factors except:*
(See attachments if necessary)

Guideline Range as Determined by the Court:

Total Offense Level: 10
Criminal History Category: I
Imprisonment Range: 6 *to* 12 *months*
Supervised Release Range: 3 *to* ____ *years*
Fine Range: $ 2,000 *to $* 20,000
(plus $ 1,492.00 cost of imprisonment and $115.30 cost of supervision per month) ____________
*$*__________ *Restitution $* 50.00 *Special Assessment*

[ ] *Fine waived or imposed below guideline range because of inability to pay.*

[ ] *Sentence Imposed is within the guideline range, that range does not exceed 24 months, and the court finds no reason to depart from the sentence called for by application of the guidelines.*

[ ] *Because the width of the guideline range exceeds 24 months, the reason for selecting this particular point within the range is:*

[X] *The Court departs from the Guideline (See attachments if necessary)*

[X] *upon motion of the government, as a result of defendant's substantial assistance.*

[ ] *for the following reason(s):*

[ ] *Court orders transcript of Statement of Reasons to be attached.*

United States v. Exxon Corp.: Plea Agreement; Joint Sentencing Memorandum of Exxon Corp. and Exxon Shipping Co.

Lodged
SEP 30 1991

CHARLES A. De MONACO
Assistant Chief
Environmental Crimes Section
Environment and Natural Resources
Division
U.S. Department of Justice
P.O. Box 23985
Washington, D.C. 20026-3985
(202) 272-9879

Attorney for the United States of America

IN THE UNITED STATES DISTRICT COURT
FOR THE DISTRICT OF ALASKA

UNITED STATES OF AMERICA Plaintiff, v. EXXON CORPORATION and EXXON SHIPPING COMPANY, Defendants.	No. A90-015 CR. PLEA AGREEMENT

I. INTRODUCTION

This document contains the complete plea agreement between the United States of America, plaintiff in the above-captioned action, and the defendants, EXXON SHIPPING COMPANY ("EXXON SHIPPING") and EXXON CORPORATION ("EXXON").

A. The defendant, EXXON SHIPPING, is charged in Counts One, Two and Three of an indictment filed in the District of Alaska with violations of the Clean Water Act, Title 33, United States Code, Sections 1311(a) and 1319(c)(1)(A); the Refuse Act, Title 33, United States Code, Sections 407 and 411; and the Migratory Bird Treaty Act, Title 16, United States Code, Sections 703 and 707(a).

B. The defendant, EXXON, is charged in Count Three of an indictment filed in the District of Alaska with a violation of the Migratory Bird Treaty Act, Title 16, United States Code, Sections 703 and 707(a).

C. The defendant, EXXON SHIPPING, agrees to enter a plea of guilty to the Counts in paragraph IA.

D. The defendant EXXON agrees to enter a plea of guilty to the Count in paragraph IB, subject to the factual basis for the plea being that it was oil owned by EXXON, and transported under contract with EXXON SHIPPING, that killed migratory birds, for which EXXON had no permit.

II. <u>DEFENDANTS' AGREEMENT AND UNDERSTANDING</u>

The defendant, EXXON SHIPPING, is represented by James F. Neal, Esq., James F. Sanders, Esq., and Robert C. Bundy, Esq. The defendant EXXON, is represented by Patrick Lynch, Esq., Edward J. Lynch, Esq., and John F. Clough, III, Esq. The defendants acknowledge that their attorneys have explained all of the elements of each offense charged against them.

A. If EXXON SHIPPING pled not guilty, the United States would have to prove beyond a reasonable doubt each and every one of the following charges to the unanimous satisfaction of a jury:

1. That on or about March 24, 1989, in the District of Alaska, and elsewhere, the defendant, EXXON SHIPPING, did

negligently cause the discharge of pollutants, namely more than ten million gallons of crude oil, from a point source, namely the tank vessel "EXXON VALDEZ," into Prince William Sound, a navigable water of the United States, without a permit, all of which is in violation of and contrary to Title 33, United States Code, Sections 1311(a) and 1319(c)(1)(A).

2. That on or about March 24, 1989, in the District of Alaska, and elsewhere, the defendant EXXON SHIPPING unlawfully did throw, discharge and deposit, and did cause, suffer, and procure to be thrown, discharged and deposited, refuse matter, namely more than ten million gallons of crude oil, from a ship, namely the "EXXON VALDEZ," into Prince William Sound, a navigable water of the United States, without a permit, all in violation of and contrary to Title 33, United States Code, Sections 407 and 411.

3. That on or about March 24, 1989, in the District of Alaska, and elsewhere, the defendant, EXXON SHIPPING, without being permitted to do so by regulation as required by law, did kill migratory birds in violation of Title 16, United States Code, Sections 703 and 707(a) and Title 50, Code of Federal Regulations, Section 21.11.

B. If EXXON pled not guilty, the United States would have to prove the following charge to the unanimous satisfaction of a jury beyond a reasonable doubt:

That on or about March 24, 1989, in the District of Alaska, the defendant EXXON, without being permitted to do so by regulation as required by law, did kill migratory birds in violation of Title 16, United States Code, Sections 703 and 707(a) and Title 50, Code of Federal Regulations, Section 21.11.

C. Legal Basis for the Fines

The defendants, EXXON SHIPPING and EXXON, agree, solely for the purpose of this plea agreement and for no other purpose, that there is a legal basis with respect to the offenses charged in the indictment for the Court to impose the fines agreed to in paragraph IIIC.

D. Consequences of the Plea

1. EXXON SHIPPING understands that by pleading guilty to the Counts under paragraph IC, it is admitting the essential elements of the charges in those Counts.

2. EXXON understands that by pleading guilty to the Count under paragraph ID, it is admitting the essential elements of the charge in that Count on the factual basis set forth in paragraph ID.

3. Each defendant understands that by pleading guilty, it gives up the following rights:

a. The right to be tried by jury;

b. The right to challenge and object to the composition or procedures of the grand jury; and

c. The right to confront and cross-examine witnesses.

E. Upon acceptance of the pleas and imposition of sentence by the Court, the United States will immediately move to dismiss Counts 4 and 5 as to EXXON SHIPPING and Counts 1, 2, 4, and 5 as to EXXON.

III. <u>AGREEMENT OF THE PARTIES REGARDING IMPOSITION OF SENTENCE</u>

A. The United States agrees not to seek additional criminal charges or any civil or administrative penalties, except as provided in paragraph IIIB below, against the defendant EXXON, or any of its present or former officers, directors or employees, or any of its wholly-owned subsidiaries, their present or former officers, directors or employees, for any violation of federal law arising out of the grounding of the "EXXON VALDEZ," the resulting oil spill, the containment or cleanup of that spill, or its or their conduct in connection with the preparation or submission of oil spill contingency plans or related documents to the federal or state government.

B. The parties agree that nothing in this plea agreement limits the right of any agency of the United States, other than the Department of Justice, to seek and take civil or administrative action against EXXON SHIPPING, EXXON, or any other EXXON subsidiaries, or their employees, including any such action relating to suspension or debarment or listing, but not including the civil or administrative penalties referred to in paragraph IIIA.

C. The parties agree, following the entry of pleas by EXXON SHIPPING and EXXON, and the acceptance by the Court thereof, that the defendants shall be sentenced in accordance with the provisions of Rule 11(e)(1)(C), Fed. R. Crim. P., and that under that procedure the appropriate disposition at the time of sentence is the imposition of fines which total $150 million, as follows:

1. With respect to EXXON SHIPPING, the fine shall be $125 million.

2. With respect to EXXON, the fine shall be $25 million.

3. With respect to EXXON SHIPPING, $105 million shall be remitted, and with respect to EXXON, $20 million shall be remitted. The remission of these amounts is appropriate in view of the following facts:

(a) The defendants recognized their responsibilities with respect to the grounding of the "EXXON VALDEZ" and the resulting oil spill;

(b) The defendants have expended in excess of $2.1 billion in response to and clean up of the oil spill in Prince William Sound and its environs;

(c) The defendants have paid in excess of $300 million to claimants allegedly injured by the oil spill; and

(d) The defendants cooperated in the federal criminal investigation of the grounding of the "EXXON VALDEZ" and the resulting oil spill.

(e) The defendants had earlier adopted and have updated environmental policies, toxic substances policies and safety policies. These policies are attached as Appendix A;

(f) The defendants support the environmental codes of conduct adopted by the American Petroleum Institute and the Chemical Manufacturing Association. These codes are attached as Appendix B;

(g) The defendants' environmental expenditures averaged more than $1 billion per year during the 1980s, and defendant will spend $1.6 billion in 1991 on capital projects to enhance environmental and safety performance, all apart from the expenditures relating to the oil spill;

(h) The defendants have committed to contribute $50 million to fund, with contributions from other companies, improvement of the oil industry response capability to deal with large-scale oil spills;

(i) The defendant Exxon's division for U.S. oil and gas operations has created a New Environmental and Safety Department to review and coordinate the management of environmental and safety concerns;

(j) The defendant Exxon Shipping has established a New Environmental Affairs Group and hired as Consultants two former Coast Guard captains with oil spill experience;

(k) The defendants have taken action to prevent recurrence of the offense including actions to improve vessel operating safety, personnel training and oil spill response capability. $40 million has been spent on these activities since the oil spill.

(1) The defendant are currently spending $160 million annually on environmental and safety research which is 25 percent of Exxon's total research expenditure.

D. The parties agree that the fines described in paragraph IIIC represent the full extent of the criminal sanctions to be imposed upon the defendants pursuant to this agreement, and are in full satisfaction of the criminal charges referred to in the indictment and all criminal charges or claims for civil or administrative penalties referred to in Paragraph IIIA. The payment of $20 million by EXXON SHIPPING and $5 million by EXXON shall fully discharge the criminal sanctions to be imposed pursuant to this agreement.

E. The parties agree that $7 million of Exxon Shipping's fine and all of Exxon's $5 million fine be imposed for violation of the Migratory Bird Treaty Act. By operations of law, Title 16, United States Code, Section 4406(b), this fine is to be deposited into the North American Wetlands Conservation Fund to be used solely by the U.S. Department of the Interior to carry out approved wetlands conservation projects in the United States, Canada and Mexico.

IV. <u>RESTITUTIONARY PAYMENTS</u>

A. The defendants, EXXON SHIPPING and EXXON, agree to make payments to the State of Alaska and the United States which total $100 million, $50 million of which shall be paid to the State of Alaska and $50 million of which shall be paid to the United States, within 30 days of the acceptance of this plea agreement by the Court. All monies paid by EXXON SHIPPING and EXXON under this paragraph IVA are remedial and compensatory payments. Such monies are to be used by the State of Alaska and the United States exclusively for restoration projects, within the State of Alaska, relating to the "EXXON VALDEZ" oil spill. Restoration includes restoration, replacement and enhancement of affected resources, acquisition of equivalent resources and services, and long-term environmental monitoring and research programs directed to the prevention, containment, cleanup and amelioration of oil spills.

B. The parties agree that the administration of the monies to be paid under paragraph IVA shall be under the control of each recipient and that upon payment, such monies and any interest which accrues thereon shall be available for the purposes described in paragraph IVA without objection, challenge, or judicial or administrative review.

C. The defendants, EXXON SHIPPING and EXXON, agree, solely for the purpose of this plea agreement and for no other purpose, that there is a legal basis for the Court to impose the payments agreed to in paragraph IV as damages recoverable for compensatory and remedial purposes.

D. The parties agree that all payments made under paragraph IVA are exclusively remedial, compensatory, and non-punitive and are separate and distinct from the fines described in paragraph IIIC and from any other criminal, civil, or administrative penalties that could have been imposed upon the defendants.

V. GENERAL PROVISIONS

A. EXXON guarantees payment of the fine imposed on EXXON SHIPPING under this plea agreement. In the event that defendant EXXON SHIPPING fails to make timely payment of the fine, EXXON shall, within thirty (30) days of the date of demand, make payment in EXXON SHIPPING's stead.

B. The defendants, EXXON SHIPPING and EXXON, understand that the Court has discretion to accept or reject this plea agreement, and that if the Court rejects the plea agreement or does not dismiss the charges referred to in paragraph IIE, each defendant will be permitted to withdraw its plea of guilty.

C. The parties agree, subject to the decision of the Court, that there is in the record information sufficient to enable the meaningful exercise of sentencing authority, pursuant to Rule 32(c) F.R. Cr. P., and agree that waiver of a presentence investigation and report would be appropriate.

The above-stated terms and conditions comprise the entire plea agreement between the United States of America, defendant EXXON SHIPPING and defendant EXXON, and there are no other terms or conditions, express or implied.

FOR THE UNITED STATES OF AMERICA:

CHARLES A De MONACO
Assistant Chief
Environmental Crimes Section
Environment and Natural Resources Division
U.S. Department of Justice

MARK B. HARMON
Trial Attorney

ERIC W. NAGLE
Trial Attorney

MARK R. DAVIS
Special Assistant U.S. Attorney

GREGORY F. LINSIN
Trial Attorney

FOR THE DEFENDANTS:

JAMES F. NEAL
Counsel for Exxon Shipping

ROBERT C. BUNDY
Counsel for Exxon Shipping

PATRICK LYNCH
Counsel for Exxon Corporation

EDWARD J. LYNCH
Counsel for Exxon Corporation

JOHN F. CLOUGH, III
Counsel for Exxon Corporation

DATED THIS 26th day of September, 1991

FILED

SEP 30 1991

UNITED STATES DISTRICT COURT
DISTRICT OF ALASKA
By ______________ Deputy

Robert C. Bundy
Douglas J. Serhahely
Bogle & Gates
1031 West 4th Avenue, Suite 600
Anchorage, Alaska 99501
(907) 276-4557
Attorneys for Exxon Shipping Company

John F. Clough, III
Clough & Associates
431 North Franklin Street, Suite 202
Juneau, Alaska 99801
(907) 586-5777
Attorneys for Exxon Corporation

IN THE UNITED STATES DISTRICT COURT
FOR THE DISTRICT OF ALASKA

UNITED STATES OF AMERICA, Plaintiff, v. EXXON CORPORATION and EXXON SHIPPING COMPANY, Defendants.	)	No. A90-015 CR JOINT SENTENCING MEMORANDUM OF EXXON CORPORATION AND EXXON SHIPPING COMPANY

The defendants submit this renewed and expanded Joint Sentencing Memorandum addressing the subjects identified in 18 U.S.C. § 3553(a) and (c) and § 3572(a)(7), including the nature and seriousness of the offense; acceptance of responsibility; discipline of officers and employees responsible; restoration or restitution involved, including the expenditure of more than $2.1 billion in cleanup and restoration costs (in excess of $30 million in such expenditures since the filing of the March, 1991, Plea Agreement), and payment of more than $300 million in claims; and an analysis of the sentences in other cases involving offenses committed by organizations. Defendants believe the facts and circumstances fully justify this Court's acceptance of the Plea Agreement executed and filed on September __, 1991.

Defendants' intentions are to summarize succinctly the relevant information and attach certain documents, should the Court desire to consider additional information. In summary, the negligent discharge of crude oil in Prince William Sound has resulted in unprecedented consequences for the defendants. The Court should consider the following:

1. Immediate recognition of their responsibilities with respect to the grounding of the Exxon Valdez and the resulting oil spill;

2. Total and complete cooperation of the defendants in investigating the offense;

3. Expenditure as of September 1, 1991, of over $2.1 billion in cleanup and restoration costs;

4. Expenditure as of the same date of over $300 million in payment of claims;

5. Acceptance herein of a total fine of $150 million, with $25 million unremitted, and the agreement to pay $100 million in compensation to the State of Alaska and to the United States;

6. Agreement, pursuant to a proposed civil Consent Decree, to pay $900 million in civil damages, including natural resource damages, with a potential additional payment up to $100 million;

7. Extensive efforts to prevent recurrence of such a spill; and

8. Prompt discipline of employees.

Following the spill, the conduct of the defendants in respect to their responsibilities has been exemplary. In fact, based on Exxon-commissioned scientific studies and published government results associated with the cleanup, the ecosystem is clearly robust and healthy, fish abundance is at or near record levels, spill-affected wildlife such as otters and eagles are thriving, and oil remnants present neither a biologic concern nor recreational impediment. See Attachment A. Yet the consequences to the defendants overwhelm any prior punishments meted out for far more egregious offenses by others, even for willful conduct, fraud, and bribery. See Section V, *infra*. In view of all the circumstances, both the United States and the defendants believe the Plea Agreement is clearly appropriate and both urge its acceptance.

I. ACT OR OMISSION CAUSING THE GROUNDING AND RESULTANT OIL SPILL

Defendant Exxon Shipping has pled guilty to the misdemeanor of negligent discharge of pollutants and to the strict liability misdemeanors of violations of the Refuse Act and the Migratory Bird Treaty Act. Exxon has pled guilty to a violation of the Migratory Bird Treaty Act. They have accepted the Government's Factual Basis For The Guilty Pleas of Exxon Shipping as set forth in the document filed with the Court on

March 22, 1991 by the Government, and with the factual basis for the plea of Exxon Corporation as set forth in the Plea Agreement.

Other than the above, however, defendants do not necessarily agree with other factual assertions which may be made in the Government's Sentencing Memorandum.

At 9:12 p.m. on March 23, 1989, the Exxon Valdez left Valdez, Alaska, carrying approximately 1,260,000 barrels of North Slope crude oil. The crude oil was owned by Exxon, and was being transported under contract with Exxon Shipping.

After leaving the Valdez Narrows, Captain Joseph Hazelwood advised the Vessel Traffic Center (VTC) that he was altering course to avoid icebergs and was coming to a course of 200 degrees. Thereafter, the master ordered the vessel to make a course change to 180 degrees, which ultimately took the vessel outside of the traffic lanes.

Captain Hazelwood, contrary to Exxon Shipping's instructions in the Navigation and Bridge Organization Manual, left the bridge at approximately 11:53 p.m., leaving Gregory Cousins, who possessed a second mate's license but was sailing as third mate, as the sole officer on the bridge. Also on the bridge was Robert Kagan, who possessed a certification from the Coast Guard as an able-bodied seaman, but was sailing as a "step-up" able-bodied seaman. Maureen Jones, who held a third mate's license, but was sailing as an able-bodied seaman, was on the starboard wing of the vessel as a lookout. At the time

Captain Hazelwood left the bridge, the Valdez was on automatic pilot and the engine was set to accelerate slowly to a sea speed of approximately 16 knots (at the time of the grounding, the vessel was traveling at approximately 11.5 knots).

Before leaving the bridge, the master directed Cousins to commence his turn back into the traffic lanes when the vessel was abeam Busby Island Light. When the master left the bridge, at approximately 11:53 p.m., the Valdez was approximately three minutes north of Busby Island Light. The vessel did not begin any turn abeam Busby Island Light.

Exxon Shipping, while not denying the existence of a negligent act or omission which contributed to the grounding of the Valdez on a portion of Bligh Reef at approximately 12:09 a.m., March 24, 1989, after extensive investigation, is even now unable to resolve with certainty what happened between 11:53 p.m. and 12:09 a.m. Several things are clear, however. First, the ship's course recorder reflects that the vessel was on a steady course of 180 degrees from well before 11:53 p.m., March 23, 1989, until 12:01:30 a.m., March 24, 1989, when the Valdez began its turn to starboard; second, the turn, when begun, was not pronounced enough to avoid the reef; and third, the master did leave the bridge at approximately 11:53 p.m. and did not return until the vessel was aground on Bligh Reef.

II. COMMITMENT TO SAFETY BEFORE THE GROUNDING

The grounding of the Exxon Valdez and the resultant oil spill in the early morning hours of March 24, 1989, was an accident for which Exxon Shipping took immediate responsibility. Such an event can overshadow years of commitment to, and reputation for, safety.

Exxon Shipping believes it has operated one of the safest tanker fleets in the oil industry. Its reputation was developed by affirmative efforts to stress safety over a period of years. Defendant does not believe it is irrelevant to this Memorandum to mention, very briefly, its commitment to safety before the unfortunate event of March 24, 1989.

In the merchant marine as a whole, safety is measured, in part, by the "Jones F. Devlin Personnel Safety Awards," which are sponsored annually by the American Institute of Merchant Shipping and the Marine Section of the National Safety Council. Exxon Shipping received eighteen of the sixty-two awards conferred in 1988 throughout the American shipping industry (not just oil transporters). Fourteen of these eighteen awards went to vessels with at least five years of operation without a disabling injury. In 1987, Exxon Shipping received twenty of the fifty-two awards given that year. These commendations are an empirical, objective reflection of defendant's commitment to safety.

In addition to its safety record, Exxon Shipping would point to its "Navigation & Bridge Organization Manual" as another strong reflection of the priority given to safety within the Company. The Manual, developed many years ago, serves as a guide to the crews of vessels, and they are expected to follow its guidelines. Deck officers are specifically required to certify in writing their familiarity with the Manual's contents, as periodically amended and revised. The Manual is not mandated by the Coast Guard or any other government entity; its creation was a project that Exxon Shipping took upon itself.

Most significant, for present purposes, is the Manual's statement of its purpose at the very outset: "To assist the Master and deck officers in planning for the safe navigation of their vessel." This statement of purpose is immediately followed by a description of Exxon Shipping's "Navigation Policy," which holds that "the prime objective when navigating company vessels is the safety of personnel, vessel and cargo." The Policy further recognizes the primacy of safety by observing that while "speed and economy" are important, they are "secondary to safety considerations." See Attachment B, Sections 1.1, 1.2.

III. EFFORTS TO PREVENT RECURRENCE OF THE OFFENSE: ACTIONS AND POLICIES

Since the grounding, a number of initiatives have been undertaken to prevent an oil spill and to enhance capabilities to respond to oil spills.

In an overall sense, the need for safe operations has been emphasized again to all personnel. Exxon has established a new senior executive level position of Corporate Vice President, Environment and Safety. Exxon's Division for U. S. Oil and Gas Operations has created a new Environmental and Safety Department to review and coordinate the management of environmental and safety concerns. In the United States an Interfunctional Oil Spill Policy Task Force was formed to conduct broad reviews of ways to prevent oil spills.

Following the grounding, both defendants reviewed their substance abuse policies and revised them to include, among other things, the institution of random and periodic alcohol and drug testing for certain safety-sensitive positions, including masters and other officers of vessels. These measures were put into effect at a time when no such requirements were mandated by law.

A. Exxon Shipping's Specific Conduct Related to Transportation

Before and after the grounding, Exxon Shipping has required staffing on its vessels beyond that required by the Coast Guard. Although we submit that "manning" played no part in the grounding, effective October 20, 1989, Exxon Shipping created the position of Supplemental Chief Mate in the Port of Valdez to supplement the normal vessel crew complement upon arrival of a vessel at the dock. In addition, since the grounding, Exxon Shipping has strengthened its requirements respecting mandatory rest periods and maximum work hours.

Following the grounding, Exxon Shipping extensively reviewed its navigation procedures. One of several revisions that took place was the prescription of only daylight transit when ice of sufficient size and quantity to hinder tanker navigation is reported in or near traffic lanes. The policy further prescribes reduced speed when ice is present, and permits deviation from the traffic lanes only in limited circumstances. In addition, tankers in Prince William Sound are being escorted by tugs.

Exxon Shipping, since the grounding, has instituted a new Bridge Simulator Training Program to incorporate state-of-the-art techniques as a supplement to the simulator training used in the years prior to the grounding to instill principles of navigation safety.

Exxon Shipping also established a new Environmental Affairs Group, which includes among others, two consultants who are former Coast Guard captains with oil spill experience, and established a new Safety, Environmental and Regulatory Department.

B. Overall Exxon Corporation Environmental Policy, Including Divisions and Affiliates

Exxon has expressed its uncompromising commitment to human and environmental welfare by the adoption and maintenance of several policies that guide its corporate conduct. The Corporation adopted a formal Environmental Policy in 1971. That policy has been re-examined and revised to ensure that it reflects up-to-date concerns. In addition, the Corporation has a Toxic Substances Policy and a Safety Policy, which address related, and integrated, issues of human and environmental safety awareness.

The full text of these policies are reprinted in full as collective Attachment C. They enumerate specific approaches that the Corporation employs to further the implementation of these policy goals. In brief, the Environmental Policy pledges that Exxon

> is committed to continuous efforts to improve environmental performance throughout its activities. It will encourage concern and respect for the environment, emphasize every employee's responsibility in environmental performance, and ensure appropriate operating practices and training. The Corporation will communicate with the public on environmental matters and share its experience with others to facilitate improvements in industry performance.

Among the approaches taken to further these goals, the Corporation will, as a matter of policy,

> manage its business with the goal of preventing incidents, and design, operate and maintain facilities to this end, . . .
>
> conduct and support research to improve understanding of the impact of its business on the environment, to improve methods of environmental protection, and to enhance its capability to make operations and products compatible with the environment, [and]
>
> undertake appropriate reviews and evaluations of its operations to measure progress and to ensure compliance with this environmental policy.

The Toxic Substances Policy declares a commitment, <u>inter alia</u>, to

> continuous efforts to identify and manage risks associated with such substances to provide an appropriate margin of safety for people and the environment.
>
> In furtherance thereof, the Corporation will:
>
> maintain toxic effects as a priority consideration in planning and development of products or processes,
>
> not manufacture, use or sell materials where it is not possible to adequately control the risks from toxic substances through proper equipment design, procedures or practices, [and]
>
> conduct and support research to extend knowledge about the toxic effects of materials produced, used or sold by the Corporation, promptly applying significant findings and sharing them with employees, customers, the scientific community, government agencies and the public.

Exxon's Safety Policy similarly expresses a commitment to

> protect[] the safety of employees, others involved in its operations, customers and the public, [to]
>
> strive to prevent all accidents, injuries and occupational illnesses through the active participation of every employee, [and to]
>
> stress to all employees their responsibility and accountability for safety performance.

As a complement to these policies, Exxon has a Business Ethics Policy that mandates compliance with company policies as well as with the law. Business Practice Reviews are conducted periodically with all employees to provide employees with a forum to discuss compliance with the policies and to underscore management's commitment to compliance with company policies as well as the law.

Exxon also has pledged to abide by the environmental codes of conduct adopted by the American Petroleum Institute and The Chemical Manufacturers Association, attached as Collective Exhibit D.[1] In many instances, however, Exxon's own policies contain environmental control responsibilities beyond those found in these two industry codes.

These policies have been translated into action. Wholly apart from the more than $2.4 billion in expenditures already made relating to the Prince William Sound spill, during the 1980's environmental expenditures averaged more than $1 billion per year. For 1991, again excluding Valdez-related expenses, the Corporation will spend $1.6 billion on capital

---

[1] In early 1991, Exxon's Board of Directors opposed and its shareholders overwhelmingly voted against three shareholder proposals related to environmental issues, including one advancing the so-called "Valdez Principles." The rejection of these proposals did not reflect an indifference to environmental concerns, but rather a recognition that the issues dealt with in the specific proposals had already been appropriately addressed by the Corporation. The Board also based its recommendation as to the Valdez Principles on the excessive and ambiguous reporting policies which were a part of the proposal, and on the failure of the proposal to acknowledge the need to balance environmental protection with the need for adequate energy reserves and a stable and healthy economy.

It should be noted that Exxon shareholders are by no means alone in rejecting the "Valdez Principles." So far in 1991, resolutions containing the "Valdez Principles" were contained in the proxy statements of 53 companies. No major corporation has endorsed them.

projects designed to enhance environmental and safety performance. And research on environment and safety problems now account for annual expenditures of $160 million -- fully 25 percent of Exxon's total research expenditures.

All of these policies pledge not only to comply with all applicable laws and regulation, but to apply responsible standards where no laws or regulations exist. For example, since 1987 the Corporation reduced its discharges reported on the EPA Toxic Release Inventory by 25 percent, and has voluntarily committed to reduce by 50 percent by 1995 substances the EPA has identified as high priority.

C. Oil Spill Response Capabilities

Finally, Exxon continues to strengthen its existing and demonstrated capacities to respond to the emergency presented by an oil spill (if one occurs despite best efforts at prevention). In 1990, Exxon joined 19 other oil companies in forming a large industry organization that will spend more than $800 million in the next five years to fund the establishment of an industry response capability of unprecedented scope for dealing with large-scale oil spills, to monitor readiness of spill response forces, and to conduct research and development.

Exxon and Exxon Shipping also are participants in two voluntary regimes that address financial responsibility for spills on a worldwide basis: Exxon Shipping (and other Exxon ship-owning affiliates) in the Tanker Owners Voluntary

Agreement Concerning Liability for Oil Pollution (TOVALOP), which imposes responsibility on tanker owners for reimbursing losses caused by oil spills; and Exxon in the Contract Regarding an Interim Supplement to Tanker Liability for Oil Pollution (CRISTAL), which establishes related obligations for cargo owners.

IV. DISCIPLINE OF THE OFFICER OR EMPLOYEE RESPONSIBLE FOR THE OFFENSE

Under 18 U.S.C. § 3572(a)(7), in imposing a fine on an organization and determining the amount thereof, a sentencing court is required to consider any measure taken by the organization to discipline any officer or employee responsible for the offense.

In the light of this code section and in [illegible] preceding sections of this Memorandum, Exxon Shipping would point out to the Court that it had in place on the Valdez, and effective on the night of the grounding, its Navigation & Bridge Organization Manual. Each master and each mate was required to have read and studied this Manual and to have represented in writing that he or she was aware of the Manual's provisions.

The Navigation & Bridge Organization Manual required that Captain Hazelwood be on the bridge under the circumstances existing immediately before and during the grounding. See Attachment B, Sections 2.1, 8.4 and 8.5. After the grounding,

Exxon Shipping disciplined the Captain for violation of Company policy by terminating his employment.[2]

V. ANALYSIS OF SENTENCES IN OTHER OFFENSES INVOLVING ORGANIZATIONS

In waiving a presentence report, the Court directed the parties to provide information respecting sentences imposed in other cases involving offenses by organizations. Defendants believe that the information summarized below responds to the Court's directive. Attachments E and F are enclosed, however, should the Court desire to consider additional information.

A. Punishment in Other Environmental Cases

In United States v. Ashland Oil Co., Cr. 88-146 (W.D. Pa. 1989), the Court, after accepting a nolo contendere plea, imposed a fine of $2,225,000, based on the negligent discharge of 500,000 gallons of diesel fuel. No restitution was provided as a part of the sentence. Civil litigation was pending before the sentencing judge and that judge left restitutionary relief to that litigation.[3] Defendants believe the Ashland Oil fine to be the largest ever imposed in any prosecution involving

2 Mr. Cousins' license as a mate was suspended by the Coast Guard for nine months. In addition, Exxon Shipping reassigned him to the status of an able-bodied seaman. Mr. Cousins has now resigned from his employment with Exxon Shipping.

3 There is pending in this Court a proposed Consent Decree. The terms offered by the defendants in this Decree is a factor which may be considered by the Court, even though acceptance of this Plea Agreement is not dependent upon approval of the civil settlement.

negligent discharge of pollutants under the Clean Water Act.[4] This fine was imposed even after the Court made a finding that the defendant's conduct involved more than simple negligence. See Transcript of Sentencing Proceedings, pp. 45-47, 99. (Counsel will have this substantial transcript available for the Court at the sentencing proceedings.)

According to the November 15, 1990, Department of Justice press release, approximately $56 million was imposed in criminal fines and restitution in federal environmental cases during fiscal years 1983 through 1990. See Attachment E, page 6. The press release does not contain a breakdown between fines and restitution nor does it indicate whether any of the fines were suspended. In the instant case, the payment of $25 million in fines by these defendants constitutes nearly half of the total amount of fines and restitution imposed during the entire eight (8) year period, ending with fiscal year 1990. And this calculation does not take into account the additional $100 million compensatory payments being made to the United States and the State of Alaska.

According to the OVERVIEW OF EPA FEDERAL PENALTY PRACTICES FY 1989, issued April 1990, criminal fines assessed

---

4 Defendants are not unmindful of the fine imposed on Allied Chemical in the James River kepone pollution case in which a $5 million fine was imposed in addition to a required $8 million contribution to an environmental trust fund. A brief analysis of the facts of that case demonstrates that it is not comparable to the instant situation. See Moore v. Allied Chemical Corp., 480 F. Supp. 364, 367-68 (E.D. Va. 1979); United States v. Allied Chemical Corp., 420 F. Supp. 122 (E.D. Va. 1976).

in fiscal year 1989 totalled $12.5 million, with $10.2 million unsuspended. See Attachment F, page 1.

B. <u>The Fine Proposed in This Case and the Compensatory Payments Are Reasonable When Compared to Those Paid in Other More Serious Cases</u>

The defendants have agreed, in connection with this negligent discharge of crude oil, to fines totalling $150 million and an unremitted fine of $25 million. They have also agreed to make remedial and compensatory payments totalling $100 million. Although that discharge resulted in environmental damage and the death of birds, sea otters, and other animals, it was not caused by "willful" misconduct and it resulted in no loss of human life. In two recent cases, where the government charged violation of regulations regarding worker safety that resulted in the deaths of many persons, much smaller penalties were assessed.

Specifically, in August of this year, Phillips Petroleum agreed to pay the United States $4 million in penalties to settle government charges that its "willful" violation of Occupational Safety and Health Administration (OSHA) regulations had resulted in the deaths of 23 workers at Phillips' chemical plant near Houston, Texas in October, 1989. Stipulation and Settlement Agreement, OSHRC Dkt. No. 90-1549, Aug. 22, 1991; see Wall Street Journal, August 23, 1991, p. B-4. In January of this year, Arco Chemical Company paid less than $3.5 million to settle charges of "serious" OSHA violations arising out of a July 1990 explosion at its plant in

Channelview, Texas that killed 17 workers. Informal Settlement Agreement, OSHA Insp. No. 110318540, Jan. 3, 1991. These penalties, in circumstances involving far more serious conduct than simple negligence and resulting in the loss of many human lives, place into sharp relief the size of the fines, not to mention the $100 million compensatory payments that defendants have agreed to pay in this case.[5]

In another recent case of note as a benchmark against which to measure the reasonableness of the fine here, Sperry and Unisys Corporations, on September 6, 1991, pleaded guilty to eight felony counts -- bribery of government officials, conspiracy to defraud the United States, filing false claims with the United States, presenting false statements, conversion of government property and wire fraud -- and were fined $4 million pursuant to 18 U.S.C. § 3571(c). United States v. Sperry Corporation, Crim. No. 91-355 (E.D. Va. 1991). The government did not seek to invoke 18 U.S.C. § 3571(d) and therefore did not seek a fine based upon the "gross pecuniary loss" caused the United States by virtue of these violations.[6]

---

[5] Similarly instructive is United States v. Collins, 756 F. Supp. 1253 (W.D. Mo. 1991), where a construction company was convicted of a "knowing" violation of a regulation regarding the handling and storage of explosive materials that resulted in the deaths of several firemen. The company was sentenced to pay a fine of $15,000, and the provisions of 18 U.S.C. § 3571(d) were not invoked.

[6] As a further part of their plea agreement, the corporations agreed to pay the United States up to $163 million, principally in restitution, thus documenting the significant losses to the United States caused by the defendants in that case.

C. Recent Actions of the Sentencing Commission Clearly Justify Acceptance of the Plea Agreement

On May 1, 1991, the U. S. Sentencing Commission submitted to Congress its recommended Sentencing Guidelines for organizations for all offenses more serious than a Class B misdemeanor, such as violation of the Migratory Bird Treaty Act. Although these guidelines have not yet become effective, and unless amended, the fine formula provisions would not apply to environmental offenses, the concepts embodied in the proposals clearly argue for the acceptance of the plea agreement submitted in this case.

A fine of the magnitude contemplated by the plea agreement can be sustained only on the basis of 18 U.S.C. § 3571(d). While defendants have accepted, arguendo, the application of § 3571(d) for purposes of this plea agreement, it is appropriate to call to the Court's attention aspects of the Sentencing Commission's recommendations which support defendants' view regarding § 3571(d) and therefore justify this Court's acceptance of the plea agreement.

Thus, § 8C2.4(a)(3) establishes that the "base fine" available under the guidelines is the greater of, inter alia, "the pecuniary loss from the offense caused by the organization, to the extent the loss was caused intentionally, knowingly, or recklessly." While this provision does not apply directly to the offenses alleged here -- see § 8C2.1(a) -- the fact that the Sentencing Commission has derived its definition of "pecuniary loss" from § 3571(d) and has defined that term as relating only to losses that were "intentionally, knowingly, or recklessly caused" strengthens the arguments that defendants have previously made concerning § 3571(d).

Defendants contended that Congress used the term "pecuniary" to limit the scope of the losses under § 3571(d) to those which the defendant intended to impose. The Sentencing Commission's requirement that the loss be "intentionally" or "knowingly" caused represents a similar interpretation of "pecuniary loss." Moreover, a finding of "reckless" behavior, an alternative predicate for applying a pecuniary loss standard in calculating a loss under the guidelines, is tantamount to a finding of "willful" misconduct. See Stewart Transp. Co. v. Allied Towing Corp., 596 F.2d 609, 614 (4th Cir. 1979). Plainly, in pleading to offenses that entail only the proof of simple negligence or strict liability, defendants fall far short of the standard that the Sentencing Commission has set for the use of a pecuniary-loss based fine in the proposed sentencing guidelines.

In another respect, the Sentencing Commission's actions underscore the reasonableness of the plea agreement submitted in this case. Section 8B1.1 directs the court to order restitution under 18 U.S.C. §§ 3663 and 3664 for Title 18 and certain Title 49 offenses or to impose it as a condition of probation as to all other offenses, "if a restitution order would be authorized under 18 U.S.C §§ 3663-3664" (emphasis added). Section 3663(a) does not authorize both a restitution order and a fine for misdemeanors:

> The court, when sentencing a defendant convicted of an offense under this title [18] or under [certain provisions of Title 49] may order, in addition to, or, in the case of a misdemeanor, in lieu of any other penalty authorized by law, that the defendant make restitution to any victim of such offense. (Emphasis added.)

Here, Exxon Shipping has pleaded guilty to three misdemeanors, all arising out of the same conduct, and defendant Exxon Corporation has pleaded guilty to a single Class B misdemeanor. Thus, it would have been reasonable for the parties to have provided only for the significant fine stipulated here. Nevertheless, the Plea Agreement provides for the compensatory payments referred to in Section VI, infra.[7]

In still another respect, the Sentencing Commission's proposals show the reasonableness of the terms of the Plea Agreement proposed in this case. Section 8C4.9, a Policy Statement relating to the court's function in setting a fine within the parameters established by the fine formula, provides as follows:

> If the organization has paid or has agreed to pay remedial costs arising from the offense that greatly exceed the gain that the organization received from the offense, a downward departure [in the formula fine] may be warranted. In such a case, a

7 Section 3663(a)(3) provides that, notwithstanding § 3663(a)(1), "The court may also order restitution in any criminal case to the extent agreed to by the parties in a plea agreement."

> substantial fine may not be necessary in order to achieve adequate punishment and deterrence....

This provision, although not directly applicable to this case even if the Guidelines are allowed to become effective as proposed by the Sentencing Commission, bears importantly upon assessment of the terms of the Plea Agreement proposed in this case. Defendants in this case have pleaded to offenses that involve only negligent conduct or strict liability misdemeanors. Prior to the execution of the Plea Agreement in this case, the defendants have expended more than $2.1 billion in the cleanup of Prince William Sound, and they have paid more than $300 million of claims by fishermen and other persons affected by the oil spill. Although the defendants are agreeing to pay substantial fines, in these circumstances, it is most clearly the case, in the words of the Sentencing Commission, that "a substantial fine may not be necessary in order to achieve adequate punishment and deterrence."

VI. THE PLEA AGREEMENT AND ATTENDANT CIRCUMSTANCES ADDRESS THE MATTER OF RESTITUTION

An organization found guilty of an offense shall be sentenced in accordance with the provisions of 18 U.S.C. § 3553. (18 U.S.C. § 3551(c)). Title 18 U.S.C. § 3553, as well as 18 U.S.C. § 3572, directs a sentencing court to consider restitution as a part of a criminal sentence. Because the offenses to which these defendants have pled guilty are not

Title 18 offenses, however, restitution is not required. (18 U.S.C. § 3663(a)). In United States v. Ashland Oil Co., Cr. 88-146 (W.D. Pa. 1989), a prosecution under the Clean Water Act, the Court concluded that restitution was not a necessary part of the sentence. Moreover, as stated in Part V., supra, the proposed Sentencing Guidelines do not contemplate both fines and restitution for misdemeanor convictions.

Nevertheless, the Plea Agreement provides for compensatory payments to the United States and to the State of Alaska in the amount of $100 million. Moreover, there remains a number of pending civil suits brought by other individuals and entities involving contested issues of law and fact.[8]

In view of all of the above, defendants submit that the Plea Agreement and the attendant circumstances adequately address the matter of restitution.

VII. IMPACT OF THE SPILL ON EXXON CORPORATION, ITS AFFILIATES AND STOCKHOLDERS

In the prior Plea Agreement and Sentencing Memorandum, the defendants failed to apprise the Court of the consequences of the spill on the parties and their stockholders. The impact has been severe.

As of the date of this submission, with a multitude of lawsuits still pending, the defendants have paid and agreed to

---

8 All of this is in addition to the pending proposed Consent Decree. See footnote 3, supra.

pay an amount totalling more than $3.4 billion.[9] This is almost equal to the entire total world-wide net income of Exxon Corporation, including affiliates, for 1989, and approximately 70 percent of their total annual world-wide net income for the years 1988 and 1990.

In its March 1991 Form 10-K Annual Report filed with the U.S. Securities and Exchange Commission, Exxon Corporation described the previous civil Consent Decree and the Plea Agreement in this matter and reported their respective anticipated costs. As to the financial impact of the settlement, Exxon said:

> The settlement will not have a noticeable effect on the registrant's financial results for 1991 because of the book reserves established in prior periods.

This statement, and a similar statement made in an Exxon press release announcing the signing of the agreements, referred only to 1991 earnings. It has been misinterpreted by some as a statement that Exxon Corporation has not been hurt financially by the costs incurred because of the spill. In fact, Exxon and its shareholders have paid a heavy price.

In 1989, the year of the oil spill, Exxon management prudently, in strict compliance with good accounting practice approved by its outside public accountants, estimated the anticipated costs of the accident and made provisions in the

---

[9] This includes more than $2.1 billion in clean-up costs, more than $300 million in payment of claims, and approximately $1 billion in the Plea Agreement and the proposed Civil Consent Decree.

accounts in an amount believed to be sufficient to cover those costs. Consequently, Exxon's before-tax operating earnings for 1989 were reduced by $2,545,000,000, or more than 30 percent of the total. As a result, Exxon Corporation's world-wide earnings for 1989 were the lowest in ten (10) years.

CONCLUSION

In conclusion, defendants and the United States government believe that this matter should be settled and that the terms of the Plea Agreement are clearly appropriate. We believe that the settlement appropriately addresses all of the factors Congress has directed a sentencing court to consider, and further suggest that the terms of the Plea Agreement send a strong message to the public and industry.

Believing that settlement is in the best interest of the parties and the public, defendants are waiving what they believe, and what the Court has acknowledged, are serious legal questions, including the applicability of the Alternative Fines Act, 18 U.S.C. § 3571(d), which, if resolved in favor of the defendants, would allow only a small fraction of the fine agreed to in this case. Consistent with that waiver, therefore, defendants acknowledge that the Court has the power to impose a $150 million fine and has the power to remit the amount identified in the Plea Agreement.

Respectfully submitted,

James F. Neal
James F. Sanders
Edmund L. Carey, Jr.
Neal & Harwell
2000 One Nashville Place
150 Fourth Avenue, North
Nashville, TN 37219
(615) 244-1713

Robert C. Bundy
Douglas J. Serdahely
Bogle & Gates
1031 West 4th Avenue
Suite 600
Anchorage, Alaska 99501
(907) 276-4557

By: ______________________
Counsel for Defendant
Exxon Shipping Company

Warren Christopher
Patrick Lynch
O'Melveny & Myers
400 South Hope Street
Los Angeles, CA 90071
(213) 669-6000

Edward J. Lynch
Associate General Counsel
Exxon Corporation
225 E. John W. Carpenter
Freeway
Irving, TX 75062-2298
(214) 444-1000

John F. Clough III
Clough & Associates
431 North Franklin Street
Suite 202
Juneau, Alaska 99801
(907) 586-5777

By: ______________________
Counsel for Defendant
Exxon Corporation

CERTIFICATE OF SERVICE

I hereby certify that a copy of the foregoing has been served by hand or telefax on Mark R. Davis, Special Assistant United States Attorney, Anchorage, Alaska 99503; and Charles A. De Monaco, Assistant Chief, Environmental Crimes Section, U. S. Department of Justice, 10th & Constitution Avenue, N.W., Washington, D.C. 20530, this the 26th day of September, 1991.

Examples of Approved Jury Instructions

(1) *United States v. Greer*, 850 F.2d 1447, 18 ELR 21387 (11th Cir. 1988)

Illegal disposal of a hazardous waste, in violation of 42 U.S.C. §6928(d)(2)(A):

The government must prove:

(1) that Greer "knowingly disposed of or caused others to dispose of a chemical waste . . . on or about August 12, 1982";

(2) that the material so disposed was a "chemical waste primarily containing 1,1,1-trichloroethane";

(3) that Greer "knew that the chemical waste had the potential to be harmful to others or to the environment, and, in other words, it was not an innocuous substance like water";

(4) that "1,1,1-trichloroethane was listed or identified by the United States [Environmental Protection Agency] as a hazardous waste pursuant to [42 U.S.C. §9601(14) (1982)]"; and

(5) that Greer "had not obtained a permit from [the Environmental Protection Agency] authorizing the disposal under [42 U.S.C. §6925 (1982)]."

Failure to report release of a hazardous waste (42 U.S.C. §9603(b)(3)):

The government must prove:

(1) that Greer "was, in fact, in charge of the facility at which the release occurred";

(2) that "one pound or more of 1,1,1-trichloroethane was released from the facility";

(3) that Greer "knew of such release"; and

(4) that Greer, "after learning of the release[,] . . . failed to immediately notify the National Response Center of the United States Coast Guard."

(2) *United States v. Sellers*, 926 F.2d 410, 21 ELR 20787 (5th Cir. 1991)

In order to establish the offenses of knowing disposal of hazardous waste without a permit, in violation of 42 U.S.C. §6928(d)(2)(A), the government must prove each one of the following elements by proof beyond a reasonable doubt.

First. That the defendant knowingly disposed of, or commanded and caused others to dispose of, wastes as charged in the indictment.

Second. That the defendant knew what the wastes were.

Third. That the wastes were listed or identified or characterized by the United States Environmental Protection Agency, . . . as a hazardous waste pursuant to the Resource Conservation and Recovery Act (RCRA).

And Fourth. That the defendant had not obtained a permit from either the EPA or the State of Mississippi authorizing the disposal under [RCRA].

Although the government must prove that the waste disposed of was listed or identified or characterized by the EPA as a hazardous waste, the government is not required to prove that the defendant knew that the waste was a hazardous waste within the meaning of the regulations. In other words, the government need only prove that the defendant knew what the waste was; that is, paint and paint solvent waste, along with the other essential elements the Court has previously given you.

However, the government is not required to establish that the waste in question actually entered the environment, was emitted into the air, or discharged into water. It is sufficient for the government to prove that the hazardous waste was placed into or on the land in such a manner that it could enter the environment, the air, or water, including groundwater.

The term hazardous waste, as used in the RCRA statute, includes any refuse and other discarded or abandoned material, including solid, liquid, or semi-solid material resulting from industrial or commercial operations and community activities, which because of its quantity, concentration, or physical, chemical, or infectious characteristics may: (A) cause or significantly contribute to an increase in serious, irreversible, or incapacitating reversible illness; or (B) pose a substantial presence or potential hazard to human health or the environment if improperly treated, stored, transported, or disposed of, or otherwise managed, and which has been identified or listed as a hazardous waste by the United States Environmental Protection Agency.

(3) *United States v. Laughlin*, 10 F.3d 961, 24 ELR 20221 (2d Cir. 1993)

In order to prove that the defendant had illegally disposed of hazardous waste, the government must prove beyond a reasonable doubt that:

(1) "the defendant knowingly disposed of or caused others to dispose of creosote sludge on or about the date set forth in the indictment";

(2) "pursuant to [RCRA], the creosote sludge was hazardous";

(3) "the defendant knew creosote sludge had a potential to be harmful to others or the environment or, in other words, it was not a harmless substance like uncontaminated water"; and

(4) "neither [the individual defendant nor the corporation] had obtained a permit or interim status which authorized the disposal of hazardous waste under [RCRA]."

(4) *United States v. Hopkins*, 53 F.3d 533, 25 ELR 21178 (2d Cir. 1995)

In order to prove the knowledge element required for conviction under the Clean Water Act, 33 U.S.C. §1319(c):

> Knowledge may be established by direct or circumstantial evidence. One may not willfully or intentionally remain ignorant of a fact, material or important to his conduct to escape the consequences of criminal law.
>
> If you find beyond a reasonable doubt that the defendant was aware that there was a high probability that employees of [the company] were tampering with a monitoring device or method but he deliberately and consciously avoided confirming this fact so that he could deny knowledge if apprehended, then you may treat this deliberate avoidance of [sic] the equivalent of knowledge, unless you find the defendant actually believed that [the company's] employees were not tampering with a monitoring device or method.
>
> A showing of negligence, mistake, or even foolishness on the part of the defendant is not enough to support an inference of knowledge.
>
> It is not necessary for the government to prove that the defendant intended to violate the law or that the defendant had any specific knowledge of the particular statutory, regulatory, or permit requirements imposed under the Clean Water Act.
>
> The government must prove, beyond a reasonable doubt, however, that the defendant acted voluntarily or intentionally to falsify, tamper with, or render inaccurate a monitoring device or method and that he did not do so by mistake, accident, or other innocent reason.

In order to prove the knowledge element for conviction of conspiracy, in violation of 18 U.S.C. §371:

> [W]hile the government must prove that the defendant entered the conspiracy knowingly and willfully, understanding the purpose of the agreement, it need not establish that the defendant acted with a specific intent to violate or disregard the law.
>
> Thus, if you are convinced beyond a reasonable doubt that the defendant entered the conspiracy with an understanding that the purpose of the conspiracy was to falsify or tamper with a monitoring device or method, and/or to violate the state discharge permit, it is immaterial whether the defendant knew such acts are unlawful.

Documents Available

Miscellaneous Documents Available Through the ELR Document Service

The following documents are available from ELR—The Environmental Law Reporter's *document service for a fee that helps defray costs of handling and postage. To order, please call* ELR's *documents editor at (202) 939-3813 or (800) 433-5120. Documents are arranged in reverse chronological order.*

(For Documents from EPA's General Enforcement Policy Compendium, see *numbers AD-865 through AD-937)*

Enforcement and Compliance Assurance Accomplishments Report FY 1994
(EPA 5/95) (194 pp.) . . . . ELR No. AD-1236

EPA Internal Guidance on Application of Statute of Limitations to Administrative and Judicial Civil Penalty Proceedings
(EPA 7/13/94) (3 pp.) . . . . ELR No. AD-324

Enforcement Accomplishments Report FY 1993
(EPA 4/94) (182 pp.) . . . . ELR No. AD-229

Internal Review of the Department of Justice Environmental Crimes Program: Report to the Associate Attorney General
(DOJ 3/10/94) (354 pp.) . . . . ELR No. AD-164

BEN: A Model to Calculate the Economic Benefits of Noncompliance: User's Manual
(EPA 12/93) (216 pp.) (with August 1994 software) . . . . ELR No. AD-284

Final Report of Advisory Working Group on Environmental Offenses: Proposed Sanctions on Environmental Offenses
(U.S. Sentencing Comm'n Advisory Working Group 11/16/93) (37 pp.) . . . . ELR No. AD-170

Environmental Crime: Issues Related to Justice's Criminal Prosecution of Environmental Offenses
(GAO 11/3/93) (36 pp.) . . . . ELR No. AD-138

Integrated Enforcement Approaches for EPA: Executive Summary of the EPA Enforcement Reorganization Task Force
(EPA 9/1/93) (20 pp.) . . . . ELR No. AD-124

Enforcement Accomplishments Report FY 1992
(EPA 4/93) (220 pp.) . . . . ELR No. AD-93

Working Draft of Recommended Sentencing Guidelines Setting Forth Criminal Penalties for Organizations Convicted of Federal Environmental Crimes
(U.S. Sentencing Comm'n 3/5/93) (34 pp.) . . . . ELR No. AD-73

Change in Methodology for Determining BEN Model's Discount Rate for Settlement Penalty Purposes
(EPA 11/92) (2 pp.) . . . . ELR No. AD-573

Enforcement Accomplishments Report FY 1991
(EPA 4/92) (154 pp.) . . . . ELR No. AD-15

National Penalty Report: Overview of EPA Federal Penalty Practices–Fiscal Year 1991
(EPA 3/92) (17 pp.) . . . . ELR No. AD-25

National Penalty Report: Overview of EPA Federal Penalty Practices, FY 1990
(EPA 4/91) (26 pp.) . . . . ELR No. AD-2

Enforcement Accomplishments Report FY 1990
(EPA 2/91) (119 pp.) . . . . ELR No. AD-1

Draft Regional Enforcement Management: Enhanced Regional Case Screening
(EPA 10/10/90) (23 pp.) . . . . ELR No. AD-1231

Documenting Penalty Calculations and Justifications in EPA Enforcement Actions
(EPA 8/9/90) (6 pp.) . . . . ELR No. AD-1047

Supplement to Parallel Proceedings Guidance and Procedures for Requesting and Obtaining Approval of Parallel Proceedings
(EPA 7/18/90) (4 pp.) . . . . ELR No. AD-1055

Multi-Media Settlements of Enforcement Claims
(EPA 2/6/90) (5 pp.) . . . . ELR No. AD-1046

Agency Judicial Consent Decree Tracking and Follow-up Directive
(EPA 1/11/90) (12 pp.) . . . . ELR No. AD-1048

Guidelines on Sampling, Preservation, and Disposal of Technical Evidence in Criminal Enforcement Matters
(EPA 4/18/84) (10 pp.) . . . . ELR No. AD-1050
Guidelines for Enforcing Federal District Court Orders (GM-27)
(EPA 4/18/84) (8 pp.) . . . . ELR No. AD-890
Races to the Courthouse
(EPA 3/20/84) (4 pp.) . . . . ELR No. AD-1029
Delegation of Authorities to the Deputy Administrator
(EPA 3/19/84) (3 pp.) . . . . ELR No. AD-1028
Guidance Concerning Compliance With the Jencks Act
(EPA 3/8/84) (9 pp.) . . . . ELR No. AD-1051
Headquarters Review and Tracking of Civil Referrals (GM-26)
(EPA 3/08/84) (38 pp.) . . . . ELR No. AD-889
Analysis of Existing Law Enforcement Emergency Authorities
(DOJ 3/6/84) (28 pp.) . . . . ELR No. AD-1049
The Use of Administrative Discovery Devices in the Development of Cases Assigned to the Office of Criminal Investigations (GM-36)
(EPA 2/16/84) (16 pp.) . . . . ELR No. AD-899
Policy and Procedures on Parallel Proceedings at the Environmental Protection Agency (GM-30)
(EPA 1/23/84) (13 pp.) . . . . ELR No. AD-893
Guidance on Evidence Audit of Case Files (GM-20)
(EPA 12/30/83) (12 pp.) . . . . ELR No. AD-883
Consent Decree Tracking Guidance (GM-19)
(EPA 12/16/83) (21 pp.) . . . . ELR No. AD-882
Implementation of Direct Referrals for Civil Cases (GM-18)
(EPA 11/28/83) (11 pp.) . . . . ELR No. AD-881
Working Principles Underlying EPA's National Compliance/Enforcement Programs (GM-24)
(EPA 11/22/83) (15 pp.) . . . . ELR No. AD-887
Guidance Concerning Compliance With the Jencks Act (GM-23)
(EPA 11/21/83) (10 pp.) . . . . ELR No. AD-886
Guidance for Drafting Judicial Consent Decrees (GM-17)
(EPA 10/19/83) (74 pp.) . . . . ELR No. AD-880
Direct Referral
(EPA 9/29/83) (5 pp.) . . . . ELR No. AD-1026
Regional Counsel Reporting Relationship (GM-16)
(EPA 8/03/83) (2 pp.) . . . . ELR No. AD-879
Clearance of Significant Enforcement Pleadings
(EPA 1/25/83) (2 pp.) . . . . ELR No. AD-1015
Headquarters Review of Pleadings
(EPA 12/2/82) (5 pp.) . . . . ELR No. AD-1022
Clearance of Briefs and Significant Pleadings
(EPA 10/27/82) (2 pp.) . . . . ELR No. AD-1021
Procedures for Withholding Filing of Referred Cases
(EPA 9/8/82) (1 p.) . . . . ELR No. AD-1020
Case Referrals for Civil Litigation (GM-13)
(EPA 9/07/82) (5 pp.) . . . . ELR No. AD-876
Request to Department of Justice to Withhold Action in Referred Cases
(EPA 9/3/82) (1 p.) . . . . ELR No. AD-1019
General Operating Procedures for EPA's Civil Enforcement Program (GM-12)
(EPA 7/06/82) (23 pp.) . . . . ELR No. AD-875
Section Directives Concerning 60-Day Report and Processing New Referrals
(EPA 6/22/82) (5 pp.) . . . . ELR No. AD-1018
Reorganization of the Office of Regional Counsel (includes Administrator's Memorandum of September 15, 1981) (GM-10)
(EPA 5/07/82) (77 pp.) . . . . ELR No. AD-874
Agency Guidelines for Participation in Grand Jury Investigations (GM-9)
(EPA 4/30/82) (17 pp.) . . . . ELR No. AD-873
Quantico Guidelines for Enforcement Litigation (GM-8)
(EPA 4/08/82) (9 pp.) . . . . ELR No. AD-872
EPA Enforcement of RCRA-Authorized State Hazardous Waste Laws and Regulations
(EPA 3/15/82) (16 pp.) . . . . ELR No. AD-1203